The Winter We Danced

THE WINTER WE DANCED

Voices From the Past, the Future,
and the Idle No More Movement

Edited by The Kino-nda-niimi Collective

ARP BOOKS · WINNIPEG

Copyright ©2014 The Kino-nda-niimi Collective

ARP BOOKS (Arbeiter Ring Publishing)
201E-121 Osborne Street
Winnipeg, Manitoba
Canada R3L 1Y4
arpbooks.org

Printed in Canada by Marquis
Design by Relish New Brand Experience Inc.

Third printing, March 2015

Cover image: Aboriginal Blockade Mba 20130116: Aboriginal protestors
pray at the end of their blockade of a CN railroad track just west of Portage
La Prairie, Man., on Wednesday, January 16, 2013. They ended their protest
without incident. THE CANADIAN PRESS/John Woods

ARP acknowledges the financial support of the Government of Canada
through the Canada Book Fund for our publishing activities.

ARP acknowledges the support of the Province of Manitoba through the
Book Publishing Tax Credit and of Manitoba Culture, Heritage, and Tourism
through the Book Publisher Marketing Assistance Program.

We acknowledge the support of the Canada Council for our publishing program.

With the generous support of the Manitoba Arts Council.

Printed on paper with 50% PCW.

LIBRARY AND ARCHIVES CANADA CATALOGUING IN PUBLICATION

The winter we danced : voices from the past, the future, and the Idle No
More movement / [edited by] The Kino-nda-niimi Collective.

ISBN 978-1-894037-51-8 (pbk.)

1. Idle No More (Movement). 2. Idle No More (Movement)--Literary
collections. 3. Protest movements--Canada. 4. Protest movements--
Canada--Literary collections. 5. Native peoples--Canada--Government
relations. 6. Native peoples--Canada--Government relations--Literary
collections. I. Kino-nda-niimi Collective, editor of compilation

E92.W56 2014   323.1197'071   C2014-900179-7

For those who danced…
and are still dancing.

Michelle White Hunt, Kristin Beck, and Meredith Schummer light some sage against the machine in Ottawa during the Idle No More World Day of Action, January 28, 2013. (HANNAH YOON)

A HEALING TIME

SkyBlue Mary Morin

We dance
to soften the hard lumps
that have formed
in the heart,
the hurt inside.

We dance, the Stomp
We stomp, stomp along
with stumbling feet
in a snakelike rope
of people.
We join in the singing
of the lead singer
and see laughter
as he goes
with the people.
We see smiles.
To you, I wave
a gesture of warmth
following the actions
of the lead dancers.
Then stomp,
stomp along
with heavy feet
in the twisting
snake of people.
We dance again
to share the hurt
with friends
to share the pain.
We dance
the Friendship Dance.
Take my hand
And hold it tight

gentle if that's
the way with you.
Then dance with me
in this friendship dance
Follow me through
The throng of people.
Sing along
with the leader, too.
I'll sing strong
for this song's for you.
Dance with me
in this friendship dance
I will follow you
through the smiling faces.
Let's dance among
the people's smiles
for, this dance is ours
and so is this song of love.
Again, we dance,
to snag someone,
women, men/men, women
to know each other.
Two by two, men and women
dance to pass under
the bridge of arms.
Women squeal with laughter
When caught in this dance of love.
Then we ask the women
to dance the shuffle
as only they know how,
to honour them
to show respect.
They shuffle, shuffle
the feet
to the drum beat
swinging their hips
to follow the feet.

Indian women
this dance is theirs
to show respect
the men sing for them.
Never lifting the feet
off the trodden ground
for they must stay
close to Mother Earth
for they are one
with her.
They shuffle, shuffle
their feet
to the drum beat
and swing their hips
to follow the feet.

We dance
to soften the hard lumps
that have formed
in the heart,
the hurt inside.

Previous spread: In Victoria, a hopeful end to 2012. December 30.
(BRUCE DEAN)

TABLE OF CONTENTS

IDLE NO MORE:
The Winter We Danced

The Kino-nda-niimi Collective

Indigenous peoples have been protecting homelands; maintaining and revitalizing languages, traditions, and cultures; and attempting to engage Canadians in a fair and just manner for hundreds of years. Unfortunately, these efforts often go unnoticed—even ignored—until flash-point events, culminations, or times of crisis occur. The winter of 2012-2013 was witness to one of these moments. It will be remembered—alongside the maelstrom of treaty-making, political waves like the Red Power Movement and the 1969-1970 mobilization against the White Paper, and resistance movements at Oka, Gustefson's Lake, Ipperwash, Burnt Church, Goose Bay, Kanostaton, and so on—as one of the most important moments in our collective history. "Idle No More," as it came to be known, was a watershed time, an emergence out of past efforts that reverberated into the future. The clear lesson regarding this brief note of context is that most Indigenous peoples have never been idle in their efforts to protect what is meaningful to our communities—nor will we ever be.

This most recent link in this very long chain of resistance was forged in late November 2012, when four women in Saskatchewan held a meeting called to educate Indigenous (and Canadian) communities on the impacts of the Canadian federal government's proposed Bill C-45. The 457 pages of multiple pieces of legislation, an "omnibus" of new laws, introduced drastic changes to the Indian Act, the *Fisheries Act*, the *Canadian Environmental Assessment Act*, and the *Navigable Water Act* (amongst many others). Entitled Idle No More, this "teach-in" organized by Sylvia McAdam, Jess Gordon, Nina Wilson and Sheelah Mclean raised concerns regarding the removal of specific protections for the environment (in particular water and fish habitats), the improper "leasing" of First Nations territories, as well as the lack of consultation with the people most affected even where treaty and Aboriginal rights were threatened. With the help of social media and grassroots Indigenous activists, this meeting inspired a continent-wide movement with hundreds of thousands of people from Indigenous communities and urban centres participating in sharing sessions, protests, blockades and round dances in public spaces and on the land, in our homelands, and in sacred spaces.

From the perspective of our collective and based on the curated articles in this book, the Idle No More movement coalesced around three broad motivations or objectives:

1. The repeal of significant sections of the Canadian federal government's omnibus legislation (Bills C-38 and C-45) and specifically parts relating to the exploitation of the environment, water, and First Nations territories.

2. The stabilization of emergency situations in First Nations communities, such as Attawapiskat, accompanied by an honest, collaborative approach to addressing issues relating to Indigenous communities and self-sustainability, land, education, housing, healthcare, among others.

3. A commitment to a mutually beneficial nation-to-nation relationship between Canada, First Nations (status and non-status), Inuit, and Metis communities based on the spirit and intent of treaties and a recognition of inherent and shared rights and responsibilities as equal and unique partners. A large part of this includes an end to the unilateral legislative and policy process Canadian governments have favoured to amend the Indian Act.

Admittedly, the movement goes beyond even these issues. The creativity and passion of Idle No More necessarily revealed long-standing abusive patterns of successive Canadian governments in their treatment of Indigenous peoples. It brought to light years of dishonesty, racism and outright theft. Moreover, it engaged the oft-slumbering Canadian public as never before. Within four months, Idle No More moved beyond the turtle's continental back and became a global movement with manifold demands.

Idle No More is, in the most rudimentary terms, a culmination of the historical and contemporary legacies emerging from colonization and violence throughout North America and the world. These involve land theft, treaty violations, and many misunderstandings. There is therefore much to talk about, reflect upon, and take action to redress. In this way, Idle No More represents a unique opportunity: a chance to deepen everyone's understanding of the circumstances and choices that have led to this time and place; and a forum for how we can come up with solutions together. This movement represents an important moment for conversations about how to live together meaningfully and peacefully, as nations and as neighbours.

That being said, the nature and enormity of Idle No More meant that it was sometimes bewildering in scope and complexity. As it grew, the movement became broad-based, diverse, and included many voices. There were those focused on the omnibus legislation, others who mobilized to protect land and support the resurgence of Indigenous nations, some who demanded justice for the hundreds of missing and murdered Indigenous women, and still others who worked hard to educate and strengthen relationships with non-Indigenous allies. Many did all of this at once. Idle No More adopted a radically decentralized character, having no single individual or group "leader." Instead, communities would join together for distinct purposes, temporarily or for long-term activism. Events were local, regional, and wide-scale. This often confused and frustrated those (particularly in the media) who looked for the "voice" of the movement or somebody who could—or would—speak on behalf of all participants. Idle No More, however, was inherently different. It defied orthodox politics.

Indigenous women have always been leaders in our communities and many took a similar role in the movement. As they had done for centuries when nurturing and protecting families, communities, and nations, women were on the front lines organizing events, standing up and speaking out. Grandmothers, mothers, aunties, sisters, and daughters sustained us, carried us, and taught through word, song, and story. When Indigenous women were targeted with sexual violence during the movement, many of us organized to support those women and to make our spaces safer. Many also strived to make the movement an inclusive space for all genders and sexual orientations and to recognize the leadership roles and responsibilities of our fellow queer and two-spirited citizens. The movement also didn't escape the heteropatriarchy that comes with several centuries of colonialism. We have more work to do collectively to build movements that are inclusive, respectful, and safe for all genders and sexual orientations.

At almost every event, we collectively embodied our diverse and ancient traditions in the round dance by taking the movement to the streets, malls, and highways across Turtle Island. The powerful events and emotions of the round dance are captured beautifully in SkyBlue Mary Morin's poem "A Healing Time"—which is why we started off the book in this way. It is also worth remembering how the dance started. Cree Elder John Cuthand explains the origin and significance of the dance:

> The story goes there was a woman who loved her mother very much. The daughter never married and refused to leave her mother's side. Many years later the mother now very old passed away. The daughter's grief was unending. One day as she was walking alone on the prairie her thoughts filled with pain. As she walked she saw a figure standing alone upon a hill. She came closer and saw that it was her mother. As she ran toward her she could see her mother's feet did not touch the ground. Her mother spoke and told her she could not touch her. "I cannot find peace in the other world so long as you grieve," she said, "I bring something from the other world to help the people grieve in a good way." She taught her the ceremony and the songs that went with it. "Tell the people that when this circle is made we the ancestors will be dancing with you and we will be as one. The daughter returned and taught the people the round dance ceremony."[1]

In the winter of 2012-2013, our Ancestors danced with us. They were there in intersections, in shopping malls, and in front of Parliament buildings. They marched with us in protests, stood with us at blockades, and spoke through us in teach-ins. Joining us were our relatives, long-tenured and newly arrived Canadians, and sometimes, when we were lucky, the elements of creation that inspired action in the first place.

[1]   See: creeliteracy.org/2012/12/19/elder-john-cuthand-shares-the-story-of-the-round-dance/

Speaking of inspiration, the impact of Chief Theresa Spence's fast on the movement—which many in this book speak about—cannot be understated. We also danced to honour and protect the fasting Ogichidaakwe, who went without food for six weeks on Victoria Island in Omàmìwinini (Algonquin) territory, Ottawa, to draw attention to unfulfilled treaties and the consequences on her community. While originally unrelated to any legislation or to those four Saskatchewan women, her simultaneous protest galvanized the movement. Her commitment provided an urgency that motivated our communities and our leaders to confront the legacy of this colonial relationship. Her sacrifice encouraged so many others to act.

A unique aspect of Idle No More is that the movement often went around mainstream media, emerging in online and independent publications as articles, essays, and interviews. This was the first time we had the capacity and technological tools to represent ourselves and our perspectives on the movement and broadcast those voices throughout Canada and the world—we wrote about the movement while it was taking place. Through social media—but also through good old word of mouth and discussions in lodges and kitchen tables —these words spread quickly and dynamically, trending through venues like Twitter and Facebook. Never before have Indigenous and non-Indigenous writers and artists presented to Canadians such rich art, stories, and expressive forms to others in such personal, intimate, and dynamic ways that provoke and evoke visions of the past, present, and future. During the winter we danced, the vast amount of critical and creative expressions that took place is like the footprints we left in the snow, sand, and earth: incalculable. And, for the most part, it was full of a positive, creative, and joyful energy that continues to spark critical dialogues.

The Winter We Danced is a collection of much of this important work and a hopeful contribution to the new trajectories of Idle No More and the new movements to come. This book reflects what the movement represents in our history and asks critical questions about the state of Indigenous activism today. More importantly, it also gifts us a look into our future. Like a round dance, readers are invited to reflect upon this beautiful and significant moment, to remember, celebrate, think, and contribute to change we all can benefit from. *The*

Winter We Danced hopes to serve as a space for everyone to join in, and maybe even inspire some more movement.

The Winter We Danced brings together the writings of both actors and activists within Idle No More but also Indigenous and non-Indigenous thinkers, organizers, leaders, artists and advocates—all of whom in various ways are embedded in community and their homelands. We begin with "First Beats"—a group of writing that captures the origins of the movement. "Singers and Dancers" builds upon these beginnings with a series of critical perspectives on core issues and events throughout the movement. "Image Warriors" features some of the most influential and powerful visual art emerging during the movement. "Friendships" reflects our relationships with supporters and allies across lines and borders, while "Next Steps" considers where we might collectively go from here. The resulting volume is an ambitious primer on the history of Idle No More and its implications, but also provides a platform for responses to the movement's very existence. This collection has been curated by a group of Anishinaabeg and Neyihaw editors who were part of the movement at various stages and, in some cases, helped shape it. We reached out to colleagues and friends in the north, the west and the east to bring their issues and voices into the book. There are, however, some unfortunate absences in the book as a result of time constraints.

Finally, it should be stated that *The Winter We Danced* is not a complete body of work documenting the movement nor a comprehensive analysis of Idle No More. We have included as many voices as possible from the many who acted and danced and sang and lived in an incredibly diverse movement. At the same time, we have tried to provide a detailed overview of major events over a very complex time. Intended to be read by diverse audiences, this collection is ensconced with distinct politics and perspectives that do not always represent the ideas of all members of the collective. The text will serve as an invitation for those within Indigenous nations, Canada, and elsewhere to learn about Idle No More, reflect on this moment in history, and consider possibilities for the future of Indigenous and non-Indigenous relationships. The spirit and the work of the winter we danced continues, like it always has, into the future.

Acknowledgments

The Kino-nda-niimi Collective would like to thank the following editors and publications for allowing us to republish previously published pieces in *The Winter We Danced*: Eric Ritskes and the *Decolonization, Indigenity & Society* journal and blog; Christi Belcourt and the *Divided No More* blog; *Briarpatch Magazine*; *Intercontinental Cry*; *First Nations Strategic Bulletin*; *MediaIndigena*; *âpihtawikosisân*; *RPM.fm*; Cy Gonick and *Canadian Dimension*; *The Ottawa Citizen*; *Theytus Books*; *Straight.com*; *The Globe and Mail*; *Turtle Island Musings*; *The Winnipeg Free Press*; *Honor the Earth* blog; *Nightwoods Editions*; *Matrix Magazine*; *The Toronto Star*; *Rabble. ca*; Ryan McMahon and the *Redman Laughing Podcast*; *The Tyee*; *Yes Magazine*; *The Dominion*; *The Media Co-op*; *Redwire Magazine*; *kimiwan zine*; *Herald Press*; *Policy Options/Options Politiques*; *Lastrealindians.com*, and *Inanna Publications*.

We would like to thank the many photographers who recorded events and gave permission to include their work throughout the book. It was our intention to illustrate not only a written recording of Idle No More, but also a visual experience of it, and due to your tremendous generosity, readers have it. The Kino-nda-niimi Collective—and in particular curator Wanda Nanibush—also deeply thanks all visual artists for their enthusiasm in supporting this book and allowing their work to appear. Thanks to all of the artists and writers for graciously allowing us to reprint your work in *The Winter We Danced* and for supporting the donation of royalties to the Native Youth Sexual Health Network. The Kino-nda-niimi Collective thanks Skyblue Mary Morin for her permission to reprint "A Healing Time," which originally appeared in *Seventh Generation: Contemporary Native Writing*, ed. Heather Hodgson, Penticton: Theytus Books, 1989.

We would also like to thank Idle No More, Indigenous Nationhood Movement, Defenders of the Land, Academics in Support of Chief Spence, Canadian Artists in Support of Idle No More, Canadian Union of Postal Workers, Indigenous Women of Turtle Island, and the Native Youth Sexual Health Network for allowing us to reprint their materials. There are not enough words to thank Kali Storm and the staff and students at Migizii Agamik (The Aboriginal Student Centre) at the University of Manitoba—who gave this book a home physically and financially. Miigwech to Shirley Williams and Doug Williams for their help and guidance in the use of Anishinaabemowin throughout this text—any mistakes are our own.

There are also many more individuals who helped with the assembling of *The Winter We Danced* and not enough room to thank everyone. First, we thank Leah Gazan for acquiring several key interviews for the collection and spending many hours meeting, networking, and enabling these to be included. We would also like to thank those who helped the book individually and at different stages: Tasha Hubbard, Melody McKiver, Richard Van Camp, Sheelah Maclean, Renate Eigenbrod, Priscilla Settee, Christi Belcourt, Glen Coulthard, Dory Nason, and Ana Collins (and all those involved in *Niigaan: In Conversation*). Assistants who tirelessly and thanklessly worked on the project (transcribing and assisting Niigaan with the hundreds of little things) were Audrey Lafreniere and Brandy Dennis.

Special thanks to John K. Samson, Rick Wood, and all of the kind and supportive folks at ARP Books for believing in this project and helping us in getting the manuscript to print in a very short period of time. John in particular was enormously helpful and supportive of the collective, and his contributions made the book better, miigwech.

Last but not least, chi'miigwech/Tansi/Mahsi Cho/Nai:wen to our parents, grandparents, and our Ancestors who were never idle and worked so very hard to ensure that we survived to carry their legacy of love of our homelands, our languages, and our cultures to the coming generations.

FIRST BEATS

Idle No More round dance at the Eaton Centre in Toronto,
December 30, 2012. (KEVIN KONNYU)

COME MY WAY

Tara Williamson

I've always been fighting, I've tried to be brave
But, while the others are marching, my mind wanders away
I wonder why we're hiding, there's no need to be ashamed
If it weren't for love we wouldn't have to protest anyway

So, come my way, love
Come my way

The women shut the cities down, the men they stopped the trains
A hundred fires, a fasting kwe whose hunger marks our days
A nation waits with baited breath, while another nation breathes
And, if you were here, I wouldn't have to say it you'd just see

You'd just see, love
You'd just see

I've never been idle, I've tried to be brave
But, while the others are marching, my mind wanders away
I wonder why we're hiding, there's no need to be ashamed
If it weren't for love we wouldn't have to protest anyway

So, come my way, love
Come my way

My heart's been on fire a hundred times before
My heart's been on fire a hundred times before
My heart's been on fire a hundred times before
My heart's been on fire
My heart, she's on fire

Forthcoming release on the EP *ndn summer.*

#IDLENOMORE IN HISTORICAL CONTEXT

Glen Coulthard

Much has been said recently in the media about the relationship between the inspiring expression of Indigenous resurgent activity at the core of the #IdleNoMore movement and the heightened decade of Native activism that led Canada to establish the Royal Commission on Aboriginal Peoples (RCAP) in 1991. I offer this short analysis of the historical context that led to RCAP in an effort to get a better sense of the transformative political possibilities in our present moment of struggle.

The federal government was forced to launch RCAP in the wake of two national crises that erupted in the tumultuous "Indian summer" of 1990. The first involved the legislative stonewalling of the Meech Lake Accord by Cree Manitoba MLA Elijah Harper. The Meech Lake Accord was a failed constitutional amendment package negotiated in 1987 by then Prime Minister of Canada, Brian Mulroney, and the ten provincial premiers. The process was the federal government's attempt to bring Quebec "back in" to the constitutional fold in the wake of the province's refusal to accept the constitutional repatriation deal of 1981, which formed the basis of the *The Constitution Act, 1982*. Indigenous opposition to Meech Lake was staunch and vocal, in large part due to the fact that the privileged white men negotiating the agreement once again refused to recognize the political concerns and aspirations of First Nations. In a disruptive act of legislative protest, Elijah Harper initiated a filibuster in the days immediately leading up to the accord's ratification deadline, which ultimately prevented the province from endorsing the package. The agreement subsequently tanked because it failed to gain the required ratification of all ten provinces within three years of reaching a deal.

The second crisis involved a 78-day armed "standoff" beginning on July 11, 1990, between the Mohawk nation of Kanesatake, the Quebec provincial police (SQ), and the Canadian armed forces near the town of Oka, Quebec. On June 30, 1990, the municipality of Oka was granted a court injunction to dismantle a peaceful barricade erected by the people of Kanesatake in an effort to defend their sacred lands from further encroachment by non-Native developers. The territory in question was slotted for development by a local golf course, which planned on extending nine holes onto land the Mohawks had been fighting to have recognized as their own for almost 300 years. Eleven days later, on July 11, one hundred heavily armed members of the SQ stormed the community. The police invasion culminated in a 24-second exchange of gunfire that killed SQ Corporal Marcel Lemay. In a display of solidarity, the neighbouring Mohawk nation of Kahnawake set up their own barricades, including one that blocked the Mercier Bridge leading into the greater Montreal area. Galvanized by the Mohawk resistance, Indigenous peoples from across the continent followed suit, engaging in a diverse array of solidarity actions that ranged from leafleting to the establishment of peace encampments to the erection of blockades on several major Canadian transport corridors, both road and rail. Although polls conducted during the standoff showed some support by non-Native Canadians outside of Quebec for the Mohawk cause, most received their information about the so-called "Oka Crisis" through the corporate media, which overwhelmingly represented the event as a "law and order" issue fundamentally undermined by Indigenous peoples' anger and resentment-fuelled criminality.[2]

For many Indigenous people and their supporters, however, these two national crises were seen as the inevitable culmination of a near decade-long escalation of Native frustration with a colonial state that steadfastly refused to uphold the rights that had been recently "recognized and affirmed" in section 35 (1) of the *The Constitution Act, 1982*. By the late 1980s, this frustration was clearly boiling over, resulting in a marked rise in First Nations' militancy and land-based direct action. The following are some of the more well-documented examples[3] from the time:

1. The Innu occupation and blockade of the Canadian Air Force/ NATO base at Goose Bay, Labrador. The occupation was led largely by Innu women to challenge the further dispossession

2   On the lasting signifance and impact of the Mohawk resistance at Kanesatake, see Leanne Betasamosake Simpson and Kiera Ladner (Eds.), *This is an Honour Song: Twenty Years Since the Blockades* (Winnpeg: Arbeiter Ring Press, 2012).

3   For a useful discussion of these and other examples of First Nations activism of the time, see Boyce Richardson (Ed.), *Drumbeat: Anger and Renewal in Indian Country* (Ottawa: Published by Summerhill Press and The Assembly of First Nations, 1989).

of their territories and the destruction of their land-based way of life by the military industrial complex's encroachment onto the Innu peoples' homeland of *Nitassinan*;

2. The Lubicon Cree struggle against oil and gas development on their traditional territories in present-day Alberta. The Lubicon Cree have been struggling to protect a way of life threatened by intensified capitalist development on their homelands since at least 1939. Over the years, the community has engaged in a number of very public protests to get their message across, including a well-publicized boycott of the 1988 Calgary Winter Olympics and the associated Glenbow Museum exhibit, *The Spirit Sings*;

3. First Nations blockades in British Columbia. Throughout the 1980s, First Nations in B.C. grew extremely frustrated with the painfully slow pace of the federal government's comprehensive land claims process and the province's racist refusal to recognize Aboriginal title within its borders. The result was a decade's worth of very disruptive blockades, which at its height in 1990 were such a common occurrence that Vancouver newspapers felt the need to publish traffic advisories identifying delays caused by First Nation roadblocks in the province's interior. Many of the blockades were able to halt resource extraction on Native land for protracted periods of time;

4. The Algonquins of Barriere Lake. By 1989, the Algonquins of Barrier Lake were embroiled in a struggle to stop clear-cut logging within their traditional territories in present-day Quebec because these practices threatened their land and way of life. Under the leadership of customary chief Jean-Maurice Matchewan, the community used blockades to successfully impede clear-cutting activities affecting their community.

5. The Temagami First Nation blockades of 1988 and 1989 in present-day Ontario. The Temagami blockades were set up to protect their nation's homeland from further encroachment by non-Native development. The blockades of 1988-89 were the most recent assertions of Temagami sovereignty in over a century-long struggle to protect the community's right to land and freedom from colonial settlement and development.

From the vantage point of the colonial state, by the time the 78-day standoff at Kanesatake had begun, things were already out of control in Indian Country. If settler-state stability and authority are required to ensure "certainty" over lands and resources to create a climate friendly for expanded capitalist accumulation, then the barrage of Indigenous practices of disruptive counter-sovereignty that emerged with increased frequency in the 1980s was an embarrassing demonstration that Canada no longer had its shit together with respect to managing the so-called "Indian Problem." On top of this, the material form that these expressions of Indigenous sovereignty took on the ground—*the blockade*, explicitly erected to impede constituted flows of racialized capital and state power from entering Indigenous territories—must have been particularly troubling to the settler-colonial elite. All of this activity was an indication that Indigenous people and communities were no longer willing to wait for Canada (or even their own leaders) to negotiate a just relationship with them in good faith. There was also growing concern that Indigenous youth in particular were no longer willing to play by Canada's rules—especially regarding the potential use of political violence—when it came to advancing their communities' rights and interests. As then National Chief of the Assembly of the First Nations, Georges Erasmus, warned in 1988: "Canada, if you do not deal with this generation of leaders, then we cannot promise that you are going to like the kind of violent political action that we can just about guarantee the next generation is going to bring to you." Consider this "a warning," Erasmus continued, "We want to let you know that you're playing with fire. We may be the last generation of leaders that are prepared to sit down and peacefully negotiate our concerns with you."[4]

In the wake of having to engage in one of the largest military operations since the Korean War, the federal government announced on August 23, 1991 that a royal commission would be established with a sprawling 16-point mandate to investigate the abusive relationship that had clearly developed between Aboriginal peoples and the Canadian state. Published two years behind schedule in November 1996, the $58 million, five-volume, approximately 4,000-page *Report of the Royal Commission on Aboriginal Peoples* (RCAP) includes 440

4   "Act or Face threat of violence, native leader warns Ottawa," *Toronto Star* (June 1, 1988), A1.

recommendations which call for a renewed relationship based on the core principles of "mutual recognition, mutual respect, sharing and mutual responsibility." The material conditions that informed the decade of Indigenous protest that led to the resistance at Kanesatake created the political context that RCAP's call for recognition and reconciliation was supposed to pacify—namely, the righteous anger and resentment of the colonized transformed into an insurgent reclamation of Indigenous difference that threatened to *un-settle* settler-colonialism's sovereign claim over Indigenous people and our lands.

With respect to the emergent #IdleNoMore movement, although many of the conditions that compelled the state to undertake the most expensive public inquiry in Canadian history are still in place, a couple of important ones are not. The first condition that appears to be absent is the perceived threat of political violence that was present in the years leading to the resistance at Kanesatake. #IdleNoMore is an explicitly non-violent movement, which accounts for its relatively wide spectrum of both Native and non-Native support at the moment. However, if the life of Attawapiskat Chief Theresa Spence continues to be recklessly put in jeopardy by a Prime Minister who negligently refuses to capitulate to her reasonable demands, it is my prediction that the spectre of political violence will re-emerge in Indigenous peoples' collective conversations about what to do next. The responsibility for this rests solely on the state. The second condition that differentiates #IdleNoMore from the decade of Indigenous activism that led to RCAP is the absence (so far) of widespread economic disruption unleashed by Indigenous direct action. If history has shown us anything, it is this: if you want those in power to respond swiftly to Indigenous peoples' political efforts, start by placing Native bodies (with a few logs and tires thrown in for good measure) between settlers and their money, which in colonial contexts is generated by the ongoing theft and exploitation of our land and resource base. If this is true, then the long-term efficacy of the #IdleNoMore movement would appear to hinge on its protest actions being distributed more evenly between the malls and front lawns of legislatures on the one hand, and the logging roads, thoroughfares, and railways that are central to the accumulation of colonial capital on the other. For better and for worse, it was our peoples' challenge to these two pillars of colonial sovereignty that led to the recommendations of

RCAP: the Canadian state's claim to hold a legitimate monopoly on use of violence and the conditions required for the ongoing accumulation of capital. In stating this, however, I don't mean to offer an unqualified endorsement of these two challenges, but rather a diagnosis of our present situation based on an ongoing critical conversation about how these differences and similarities ought to inform our current struggle.

Originally appeared on Decolonization: Indigeneity, Education & Society *(decolonization.wordpress.com), December 24, 2012.*

WHY ARE WE IDLE NO MORE?

Pamela Palmater

The Idle No More movement, which has swept the country over the holidays, took most Canadians, including Prime Minister Stephen Harper and his Conservative government, by surprise. That is not to say that Canadians have never seen a native protest before, as most of us recall Oka, Burnt Church, and Ipperwash. But most Canadians are not used to the kind of sustained, coordinated, national effort that we have seen in the last few weeks—at least not since 1969. 1969 was the last time the federal government put forward an assimilation plan for First Nations. It was defeated then by fierce native opposition, and it looks like Harper's aggressive legislative assimilation plan will be met with even fiercer resistance.

In order to understand what this movement is about, it is necessary to understand how our history is connected to the present-day situation of First Nations. While a great many injustices were inflicted upon the indigenous peoples in the name of colonization, indigenous peoples were never "conquered." The creation of Canada was only possible through the negotiation of treaties between the Crown and indigenous nations. While the wording of the treaties varies from the peace and friendship treaties in the east to the numbered treaties in the west, most are based on the core treaty promise that we would all live together peacefully and share the wealth of this land. The problem is that only one treaty partner has seen any prosperity.

The failure of Canada to share the lands and resources as promised in the treaties has placed First Nations at the bottom of all

Steve Teekens at a round dance in Toronto, January 28, 2013.
(IRINA POPOVA)

socio-economic indicators—health, lifespan, education levels and employment opportunities. While indigenous lands and resources are used to subsidize the wealth and prosperity of Canada as a state and the high-quality programs and services enjoyed by Canadians, First Nations have been subjected to purposeful, chronic underfunding of all their basic human services like water, sanitation, housing, and education. This has led to the many First Nations being subjected to multiple, overlapping crises like the housing crisis in Attawapiskat, the water crisis in Kashechewan, and the suicide crisis in Pikangikum.

Part of the problem is that federal "Indian" policy still has, as its main objective, to get rid of the "Indian problem." Instead of working toward the stated mandate of Indian Affairs "to improve the social well-being and economic prosperity of First Nations," Harper is trying, through an aggressive legislative agenda, to do what the White Paper failed to do—get rid of the Indian problem once and for all. The Conservatives don't even deny it—in fact Harper's speech last January at the Crown-First Nation Gathering focused on the unlocking of First Nations lands and the integration of First Nations into Canadian society for the "maximized benefit" of all Canadians. This suite of approximately 14 pieces of legislation was drafted, introduced, and debated without First Nation consent.

Idle No More is a coordinated, strategic movement, not led by any elected politician, national chief or paid executive director. It is a movement originally led by indigenous women and has been joined by grassroots First Nations leaders, Canadians, and now the world. It originally started as a way to oppose Bill C-45, the omnibus legislation impacting water rights and land rights under the Indian Act; it grew to include all the legislation and the corresponding funding cuts to First Nations political organizations meant to silence our advocacy voice.

Our activities include a slow escalation from letters to MPs and ministers, to teach-ins, marches and flash mobs, to rallies, protests, and blockades. The concept was to give Canada every opportunity to come to the table in a meaningful way and address these long-outstanding issues, and escalation would only occur if Canada continued to ignore our voices. Sadly, Prime Minister Harper has decided to ignore the call for dialogue just as he has ignored the hunger-striking Attawapiskat Chief Theresa Spence.

Although Idle No More began before Chief Spence's hunger strike, and will continue after, her strike is symbolic of what is happening to First Nations in Canada. For every day that Spence does not eat, she is slowly dying, and that is exactly what is happening to First Nations, who have lifespans up to 20 years shorter than average Canadians. Idle No More has a similar demand in that there is a need for Canada to negotiate the sharing of our lands and resources, but the government must display good faith first by withdrawing the legislation and restoring the funding to our communities. Something must be done to address the immediate crisis faced by the grassroots in this movement.

I am optimistic about the power of our peoples and know that in the end, we will be successful in getting this treaty relationship back on track. However, I am less confident about the Conservative government's willingness to sit down and work this out peacefully any time soon. Thus, I fully expect that this movement will continue to expand and increase in intensity. Canada has not yet seen everything this movement has to offer. It will continue to grow as we educate Canadians about the facts of our lived reality and the many ways in which we can all live here peacefully and share the wealth.

After all, First Nations, with our constitutionally protected aboriginal and treaty rights, are Canadians' last best hope to protect the lands, waters, plants, and animals from complete destruction—which doesn't just benefit our children, but the children of all Canadians.

Originally appeared in The Ottawa Citizen, *December 28, 2012.*

OCCUPY(ED) CANADA:
The Political Economy of Indigenous Dispossession
Shiri Pasternak

The political economy of Canada rests on claims of ownership to all lands and resources within our national borders. So, what, in concrete terms, does it mean to talk about Occupy(ed) Canada to express the demands of the 99 percent?

Last week, *The Globe and Mail* reported that the Canadian Forces' National Counter-Intelligence Unit has been keeping tabs on the activities of Indigenous organizations. While the Department of National Defence—the unit that released the surveillance documents—is tasked with protecting citizens from espionage, terrorists and saboteurs, the content of these co-intel reports do not contain a single shred of evidence that Canadians' safety is at stake. In fact, what these surveillance reports starkly reveal is that the self-determination, well-being, and territorial heritage of Indigenous peoples are at the heart of Indigenous protest and land reclamation.

Even Indian and Northern Affairs Canada (INAC) confirm this observation. In a 2007 presentation to the RCMP, INAC states that "the vast majority of Hot Spots" of so-called Native unrest are "related to lands and resources," with most conflicts "incited by development activities on traditional territories." It seems, in other words, that "Native unrest" is largely a euphemism for bands that are protecting their lands from ecological damage, or in the case of land claim disputes, from dispossession. More broadly, "Native unrest" has become rhetoric of dismissal for the struggle to exercise inherent Indigenous rights. So why is the Department of National Defence spying on Indigenous communities in Canada?

It is the fear of economic disruption that is driving Canada to spy on Indigenous peoples. Moreover, in recent years, it has become the fear of an exceedingly more dangerous risk to business-as-usual in this country than paranoid phantoms of espionage. It is the fear of Aboriginal Title. Since 1997, Indigenous politics in Canada have unfolded against a changing landscape of economic consequence. In that year, the Supreme Court of Canada recognized in Delgamuukw v. British Columbia that Aboriginal Title is the collective proprietary interest of Aboriginal peoples in their unceded traditional territories. Therefore, wherever treaties had not been signed, Aboriginal proprietary rights underlie provincial, federal, and private property lands. And in addition to unceded or unsurrendered lands, as Arthur Manuel and Nicole Schabus pointed out in an article in Chapman Law Review in 2005, "Many Indigenous Peoples argue that the 'spirit and intent' of the treaties also ensures Indigenous control over their traditional territories."

Unceded and treatied lands cover a massive amount of territory in Canada from coast to coast, translating into significant uncertainty for industry and government. There is no question that the active defence of Indigenous rights and lands has major economic consequences for Canada. In 1990, INAC commissioned a study by Price Waterhouse on the economic value of uncertainty associated with Indigenous claims in B.C., for example. The report concluded that around $1 billion of capital expenditures involving up to 1,500 jobs in the mining and forestry sectors would likely be affected by the land claims process.

This problem is not going away. It is only intensifying with the current global scramble for energy, minerals, oil and gas. Key natural resource projects cannot proceed without Indigenous consent and cooperation. In the last few years alone, Kitchenuhmaykoosib Inninuwug shut down Platinex mining in northern Ontario Ojicree territory, 64 B.C. First Nations threaten the development of the west coast Enbridge pipeline to the Pacific Coast from the Alberta tar sands, and local Tsilhqot'in Nation sank the Prosperity copper and gold mine at Fish Lake in B.C. Moreover, mega-projects like the Canadian Boreal Forest Agreement, Plan Nord in Quebec, and the Ring of Fire in northern Ontario have all been hampered by the failure of ENGOs, government and industry to recognize the land rights of Indigenous peoples.

These developments are hardly new. Indigenous peoples have been on the geographic frontier of capital accumulation for over 500 years of permanent resistance. Indigenous peoples' labour and lands have shaped the political economy of Canada, from the time of the fur trade to bankrolling industrialization with their lands and resources, and today, by confronting neo-liberal policy in the form of continental restructuring and intensified resource grabs.

One example of the economic role of Indigenous lands historically and today can be found in the case of railways, to which Canada maintained a pre-emption right to clear Indigenous lands, and that facilitated the industrial pathways for capitalist development. Over a hundred years later, authorities have become well aware of the risky correlation between Indigenous lands and the steel rails that cross the country from coast to coast. In an RCMP briefing to CSIS on operational responses to Aboriginal occupations and protest, the RCMP warn: "The recent CN strike [referring to the Tyendinaga Mohawk rail blockades in

April 2007] represents the extent in which a national railway blockade could affect the economy of Canada." In addition to these massive expanses of treaty areas and unceded traditional territories, Indigenous lands were historically fragmented into isolated and remote reserves by successive colonial administrations. There are over 2,600 Indian reserves across Canada today.

This forced settlement resulted in a unique spatial phenomenon that unwittingly placed Indian reserves on the frontier of vital national and regional boundaries: frontiers, for example, for natural resource extraction, suburban development, military training grounds, oceans and inland waterways, state borders, and energy generation. Despite their wealth in land and resources, economic racism prevents Indigenous peoples from obtaining financial benefits from their traditional territories. Their proprietary interests have been largely ignored and Aboriginal Title is extinguished through the land claims settlement process. Chronic underfunding of reserves has deepened the gap formed by deprivation from traditional subsistence economies due to land loss and ecological deterioration. The Royal Commission on Aboriginal Peoples (RCAP) commissioner stated in 1996 that "current levels of poverty and underdevelopment are directly linked to the dispossession of Indigenous Peoples from their lands and the delegitimization of their institutions of society and governance."

In addition to systemic impoverishment, and where Indigenous populations join the 99 percent, austerity programs attack the weakest first. Murray Angus, in his slim but critical book "And the Last Shall be First: Native Policy in an Era of Cutbacks," gives three main reasons for why Indigenous people are the first ones out of the social security boat when austerity programs roll around: (1) funding—money for Indigenous people comes from the "social envelope," which is under attack; (2) demographics—Indigenous peoples are the fastest growing population—so even maintaining programs is expensive; (3) and racism—white people will look after their own first.

The government has been doling out austerity programs to Indigenous peoples for decades by downloading their responsibilities onto provincial and territorial governments, as well as through bogus self-government policies. But as bureaucrats cast around for deep cuts that Harper has demanded, austerity measures will trim whatever is left in Aboriginal budgets that cannot be tied down. In 2010, the Aboriginal Healing Foundation lost funding, an organization that financed community-based programs to address abuse suffered at residential schools. That same year, Harper's Conservatives cut funding to the Sister in Spirit research project that brought to light hundreds of cases of missing and murdered Indigenous women. Most recently, Department of Aboriginal Affairs Minister John Duncan announced upcoming budget cuts to his department amounting to a $100 million slash. The wealth of the nation still depends fundamentally on land. Financial investment for resource development projects is funneled through the same banks protested against across the u.s. and Canada, such as RBC Royal Bank that funds tar sands development on Treaty 8 lands. Global structural inequality can only be addressed then by questioning the sources of authority by which resources are bought and sold. If you don't own it, Canada, how can you give it away?

Originally appeared on rabble.ca, *October 20, 2011.*

DECOLONIZING TOGETHER:
Moving Beyond a Politics of Solidarity Toward a Practice of Decolonization

Harsha Walia

Canada's state and corporate wealth is largely based on subsidies gained from the theft of Indigenous lands and resources. Conquest in Canada was designed to ensure forced displacement of Indigenous peoples from their territories, the destruction of autonomy and self-determination in Indigenous self-governance, and the assimilation of Indigenous peoples' cultures and traditions. Given the devastating cultural, spiritual, economic, linguistic, and political impacts of colonialism on Indigenous people in Canada, any serious attempt by non-natives at allying with Indigenous struggles must entail solidarity in the fight against colonization.

Non-natives must be able to position ourselves as active and integral participants in a decolonization movement for political liberation, social transformation, renewed cultural kinships, and the development of an economic system that serves rather than threatens our collective life on this planet. Decolonization is as much a process as a goal. It requires a profound recentering on Indigenous worldviews. Syed Hussan, a Toronto-based activist, states: "Decolonization is a dramatic reimagining of relationships with land, people, and the state. Much of this requires study. It requires conversation. It is a practice; it is an unlearning."

Indigenous Solidarity on its Own Terms

A growing number of social movements are recognizing that Indigenous self-determination must become the foundation for all our broader social justice mobilizing. Indigenous peoples in Canada are the most impacted by the pillage of lands, experience disproportionate poverty and homelessness, are overrepresented in statistics of missing and murdered women, and are the primary targets of repressive policing and prosecutions in the criminal injustice system. Rather than being treated as a single issue within a laundry list of demands, Indigenous self-determination is increasingly understood as intertwined with struggles against racism, poverty, police violence, war and occupation, violence against women and environmental justice.

Incorporating Indigenous self-determination into these movements can, however, subordinate and compartmentalize Indigenous struggle within the machinery of existing leftist narratives. Anarchists point to the antiauthoritarian tendencies within Indigenous communities, environmentalists highlight the connection to land that Indigenous communities have, anti-racists subsume Indigenous people into the broader discourse about systemic oppression in Canada, and women's organizations point to the relentless violence inflicted on Indigenous women in discussions about patriarchy.

We have to be cautious not to replicate the Canadian state's assimilationist model of liberal pluralism, forcing Indigenous identities to fit within our existing groups and narratives. The inherent right to traditional lands and to self-determination is expressed collectively and should not be subsumed within the discourse of individual or human rights. Furthermore, it is imperative to understand that being

Indigenous is not just an identity but a way of life, which is intricately connected to Indigenous peoples' relationship to the land and all its inhabitants. Indigenous struggle cannot simply be accommodated within other struggles; it demands solidarity on its own terms.

The Practice of Solidarity

One of the basic principles of Indigenous solidarity organizing is the notion of taking leadership. According to this principle, non-natives must be accountable and responsive to the experiences, voices, needs and political perspectives of Indigenous people themselves. From an anti-oppression perspective, meaningful support for Indigenous struggles cannot be directed by non-natives. Taking leadership means being humble and honouring frontline voices of resistance as well as offering tangible solidarity as needed and requested. Specifically, this translates to taking initiative for self-education about the specific histories of the lands we reside upon, organizing support with the clear consent and guidance of an Indigenous community or group, building long-term relationships of accountability, and never assuming or taking for granted the personal and political trust that non-natives may earn from Indigenous peoples over time.

In offering support to a specific community in the defence of their land, non-natives should organize with a mandate from the community and an understanding of the parameters of the support being sought. Once these guidelines are established, non-natives should be proactive in offering logistical, fundraising and campaign support. Clear lines of communication must always be maintained, and a commitment should be made for long-term support. This means not just being present for blockades or in moments of crisis, but developing an ongoing commitment to the well-being of Indigenous peoples and communities.

Organizing in accordance with these principles is not always straightforward. Respecting Indigenous leadership is not the same as doing nothing while waiting around to be told what to do. "I am waiting to be told exactly what to do" should not be an excuse for inaction, and seeking guidance must be weighed against the possibility of further burdening Indigenous people with questions. A willingness to decentre oneself and to learn and act from a place of responsibility rather than guilt are helpful in determining the line between being too interventionist and being paralyzed.

Cultivating an ethic of responsibility within the Indigenous solidarity movement begins with non-natives understanding ourselves as beneficiaries of the illegal settlement of Indigenous peoples' land and unjust appropriation of Indigenous peoples' resources and jurisdiction. When faced with this truth, it is common for activists to get stuck in their feelings of guilt, which I would argue is a state of self-absorption that actually upholds privilege. While guilt is often a sign of a much-needed shift in consciousness, in itself it does nothing to motivate the responsibility necessary to actively dismantle entrenched systems of oppression. In a movement-building round table, long-time Montreal activist Jaggi Singh said: "The only way to escape complicity with settlement is active opposition to it. That only happens in the context of on-the-ground, day-to-day organizing, and creating and cultivating the spaces where we can begin dialogues and discussions as natives and non-natives."

Sustained Alliance Building

Sustaining a multiplicity of meaningful and diverse relationships with Indigenous peoples is critical in building a non-native movement for Indigenous self-determination. "Solidarity is not the same as support," says feminist writer bell hooks. "To experience solidarity, we must have a community of interests, shared beliefs and goals around which to unite, to build Sisterhood. Support can be occasional. It can be given and just as easily withdrawn. Solidarity requires sustained, ongoing commitment."

Who exactly one takes direction from while building networks of ongoing solidarity can be complicated. As in any community, a diversity of political opinions often exists within Indigenous communities. How do we determine whose leadership to follow and which alliances to build? I take leadership from and offer tangible support to grassroots Indigenous peoples who are exercising traditional governance and customs in the face of state control and bureaucratization, who are seeking redress and reparations for acts of genocide and assimilation, such as residential schools, who are opposing corporate development

"Idle No More Peguis" at the Manitoba Legislature Winter Solstice Rally, December 21, 2012. (DAWN THOMAS)

on their lands. I support those who are pushing back against the oppressions of hetero-patriarchy imposed by settler society, who are struggling against poverty and systemic marginalization in urban areas, who are criticizing unjust land claims and treaty processes and who are affirming their own languages, customs, traditions, creative expression, and spiritual practices. Alliances with Indigenous communities should be based on shared values, principles, and analysis. For example, during the anti-Olympics campaign in 2010, activists chose not to align with the Four Host First Nations, a pro-corporate body created in conjunction with the Vancouver Olympics organizing committee. Instead, we took leadership from and strengthened alliances with land defenders in the Secwepemc and St'át'imc nations and Indigenous people being directly impacted by homelessness and poverty in the Downtown Eastside. In general, however, differences surrounding strategy within a community should be for community members to discuss and resolve. We should be cautious of a persistent dynamic where solidarity activists start to fixate on the internal politics of an oppressed community. Allies should avoid trying to intrude and interfere in struggles within and between communities, which perpetuates the civilizing ideology of the white man's burden and violates the basic principles of self-determination.

Building intentional alliances should also avoid devolution into tokenization. Non-natives often choose which Indigenous voices to privilege by defaulting to Indigenous activists they determine to be better-known, easier-to-contact or "less hostile." This selectivity distorts the diversity present in Indigenous communities and can exacerbate tensions and colonially imposed divisions between Indigenous peoples. In opposing the colonialism of the state and settler society, non-natives must recognize our own role in perpetuating colonialism within our solidarity efforts. We can actively counter this by theorizing about and discussing the nuanced issues of solidarity, leadership, strategy, and analysis—not in abstraction, but within our real and informed and sustained relationships with Indigenous peoples.

Decolonizing Relationships

While centring and honouring Indigenous voices and leadership, the obligation for decolonization rests on all of us. In "Building a 'Canadian' Decolonization Movement: Fighting the Occupation at 'Home,'" Nora Burke says: "A decolonization movement cannot be comprised solely of solidarity and support for Indigenous peoples' sovereignty and self-determination. If we are in support of self-determination, we too need to be self-determining. It is time to cut the state out of this relationship, and to replace it with a new relationship, one which is mutually negotiated, and premised on a core respect for autonomy and freedom."

Being responsible for decolonization can require us to locate ourselves within the context of colonization in complicated ways, often as simultaneously oppressed and complicit. This is true, for example, for radicalized migrants in Canada. Within the anticolonial migrant justice movement of No One Is Illegal, we go beyond demanding citizenship rights for racialized migrants as that would lend false legitimacy to a settler state. We challenge the official state discourse of multiculturalism that undermines the autonomy of Indigenous communities by granting and mediating rights through the imposed structures of the state, and that seeks to assimilate diversities into a singular Canadian identity. Andrea Smith, Indigenous feminist intellectual, says: "All non-Native peoples are promised the ability to join in the colonial project of settling indigenous lands. In all of these cases, we would check our aspirations against the aspirations of other communities to ensure that our model of liberation does not become the model of oppression for others." In B.C., immigrants and refugees have participated in several delegations to Indigenous blockades, while Indigenous communities have offered protection and refuge for migrants facing deportation.

Decolonization is the process whereby we create the conditions in which we want to live and the social relations we wish to have. We have to commit ourselves to supplanting the colonial logic of the state itself. Almost a hundred years ago, German anarchist Gustav Landauer wrote: "The State is a condition, a certain relationship between human beings, a mode of behaviour; we destroy it by contracting other relationships." Decolonization requires us to exercise our sovereignties differently and to reconfigure our communities based on shared experiences, ideals, and visions. Almost all Indigenous formulations of sovereignty—such as the Two Row Wampum agreement of peace, friendship, and respect between the Haudenosaunee nations and settlers—are premised on revolutionary notions of respectful coexistence and stewardship of the land, which goes far beyond any Western liberal democratic ideal.

I have been encouraged to think of human interconnectedness and kinship in building alliances with Indigenous communities. Black-Cherokee writer Zainab Amadahy uses the term "relationship framework" to describe how our activism should be grounded. "Understanding the world through a Relationship Framework … we don't see ourselves, our communities, or our species as inherently superior to any other, but rather see our roles and responsibilities to each other as inherent to enjoying our life experiences," says Amadahy. From Turtle Island to Palestine, striving toward decolonization and walking together toward transformation requires us to challenge a dehumanizing social organization that perpetuates our isolation from each other and normalizes a lack of responsibility to one another and the Earth.

Originally appeared in Briar Patch Magazine, *January 1, 2012. This is an altered and condensed version of a chapter from the 2012 book* Organize! Building from the Local for Global Justice, *edited by Aziz Choudry, Jill Hanley, and Eric Shragge.*

HARPER LAUNCHES MAJOR FIRST NATIONS TERMINATION PLAN:
As Negotiating Tables Legitimize Canada's Colonialism
Russell Diabo

On September 4, the Harper government clearly signalled its intention to:

1. Focus all its efforts to assimilate First Nations into the existing federal and provincial orders of government of Canada;

2. Terminate the constitutionally protected and internationally recognized Inherent, Aboriginal, and Treaty rights of First Nations.

Termination in this context means the ending of First Nations pre-existing sovereign status through federal coercion of First Nations into Land Claims and Self-Government Final Agreements that convert First Nations into municipalities and their reserves into fee simple lands, and brings about extinguishment of their Inherent, Aboriginal and Treaty Rights. To do this the Harper government announced three new policy measures:

- A *"results-based"* approach to negotiating Modern Treaties and Self-Government Agreements. This is an assessment process of 93 negotiation tables across Canada to determine who will and who won't agree to terminate Inherent, Aboriginal, and Treaty rights under the terms of Canada's Comprehensive Claims and Self-Government policies. For those tables who won't agree, negotiations will end as the federal government withdraws from the table and takes funding with them.

- First Nation regional and national political organizations will have their core funding cut and capped. For regional First Nation political organizations, the core funding will be capped at $500,000 annually. For some regional organizations this will result in a funding cut of $1 million or more annually. This will restrict the ability of Chiefs and Executives of Provincial or Territorial. organizations to organize and/or advocate for First Nations rights and interests.

- First Nation Band and Tribal Council funding for advisory services will be eliminated over the next two years, further crippling the ability of Chiefs and Councils and Tribal Council executives to analyze and assess the impacts of federal and provincial policies and legislation on Inherent, Aboriginal and Treaty rights.

These three new policy measures are on top of the following unilateral federal legislation the Harper government is imposing over First Nations:

- **Bill C-27:** First Nations Financial Transparency Act
- **Bill C-45:** *Jobs and Growth Act, 2012* [an omnibus Bill that includes Indian Act amendments regarding voting on-reserve lands surrenders/designations]

- **Bill S-2**: Family Homes on Reserves and Matrimonial Interests or Rights Act
- **Bill S-6**: *First Nations Elections Act*
- **Bill S-8**: Safe Drinking Water for First Nations
- **Bill C-428**: Indian Act Amendment and Replacement Act [Private Conservative MP's Bill—supported by Harper government]

Then there are the Senate Public Bills:

- **Bill S-207**: An Act to amend the Interpretation Act (non-derogation of aboriginal and treaty rights)
- **Bill S-212**: First Nations Self-Government Recognition Bill

The Harper government's bills listed above are designed to undermine the collective rights of First Nations by focusing on individual rights. This is the *"modern legislative framework"* the Conservatives promised in 2006. The 2006 Conservative Platform promised to:

> *Replace the* Indian Act *(and related legislation) with a modern legislative framework which provides for the devolution of full legal and democratic responsibility to aboriginal Canadians for their own affairs within the Constitution, including the Charter of Rights and Freedoms.*

Of course "modern" in Conservative terms means assimilation of First Nations by termination of their collective rights and off-loading federal responsibilities onto the First Nations themselves and the provinces. One Bill that hasn't been introduced into Parliament yet, but is still expected, is the First Nations' Private Ownership Act (FNPOA). This private property concept for Indian reserves—which has been peddled by the likes of Tom Flanagan and tax proponent and former Kamloops Chief Manny Jules—is also a core plank of the Harper government's 2006 electoral platform.

The 2006 Conservative Aboriginal Platform promised that if elected a Harper government would "support the development of individual property ownership on reserves, to encourage lending for private housing and businesses." The long-term goals set out in the Harper government's policy and legislative initiatives listed above are not new; they are at least as old as the Indian Act and were articulated in the federal 1969 White Paper on Indian Policy, which set out a plan to terminate Indian rights as the time.

Previous Termination Plans: 1969 White Paper and Buffalo Jump of the 1980s

The objectives of the 1969 White Paper on Indian Policy were to

- Assimilate First Nations.
- Remove legislative recognition.
- Neutralize constitutional status.
- Impose taxation.
- Encourage provincial encroachment.
- Eliminate Reserve lands and extinguish Aboriginal Title.
- Economically underdevelop communities.
- Dismantle Treaties.

As First Nations galvanized across Canada to fight the Trudeau Liberal government's proposed 1969 termination policy, the federal government was forced to consider a strategy on how to calm the Indian storm of protest. In a memo dated April 1, 1970, David Munro, an Assistant Deputy Minister of Indian Affairs on Indian Consultation and Negotiations, advised his political masters Jean Chrétien and Pierre Trudeau as follows:

...in our definition of objectives and goals, not only as they appear in formal documents, but also as stated or even implied in informal memoranda, draft planning papers, or casual conversation. We must stop talking about having the objective or goal of phasing out in five years... We can still believe with just as much strength and sincerity that the [White Paper] policies we propose are the right ones... The final [White Paper] proposal, which is for the elimination of special status in legislation, must be relegated far into the future... my conclusion is that we need not change the [White Paper] policy content, but we should put varying degrees of emphasis on its several components and we should try to discuss it in terms of its components rather than as a whole... we should adopt somewhat different tactics in relation to [the White Paper]

policy, but [that] we should not depart from its essential content.
(emphasis added)

In the early 1970's, the Trudeau Liberal government did back down publicly on implementing the 1969 White Paper on Indian Policy, but as we can see from Mr. Munro's advice the federal bureaucracy changed the timeline from five years to a long-term implementation of the 1969 White Paper objectives of assimilation/termination. In the mid-1980s the Mulroney Conservative government resurrected the elements of the 1969 White Paper on Indian Policy, through a Cabinet memo. In 1985, a secret federal Cabinet submission was leaked to the media by a DIAND employee. The report was nicknamed the "Buffalo Jump of the 1980s" by another federal official. The nickname referred to the effect of the recommendations in the secret Cabinet document, which if adopted, would lead Status Indians to a cultural death—hence the metaphor. The Buffalo Jump Report proposed a management approach for First Nations policy and programs, which had the following intent:

- Limiting and eventually terminating the federal trust obligations;
- Reducing federal expenditures for First Nations, underfunding programs, and prohibiting deficit financing;
- Shifting responsibility and costs for First Nations services to provinces and "advanced bands" through co-management, tripartite, and community self-government agreements;
- "Downsizing" of the Department of Indian Affairs and Northern Development (DIAND) through a devolution of program administration to "advanced bands" and transfer of programs to other federal departments;
- Negotiating municipal community self-government agreements with First Nations which would result in the First Nation government giving up their Constitutional status as a sovereign government and becoming a municipality subject to provincial or territorial laws;
- Extinguishing aboriginal title and rights in exchange for fee simple title under provincial or territorial law while giving the province or territory underlying title to First Nations lands.

The Mulroney government's "Buffalo Jump" plan was temporarily derailed due the 1990 "Oka Crisis." Mulroney responded to the "Oka Crisis" with his "Four Pillars" of Native Policy:

- Accelerating the settlement of land claims;
- Improving the economic and social conditions on Reserves;
- Strengthening the relationships between Aboriginal Peoples and governments;
- Examining the concerns of Canada's Aboriginal Peoples in contemporary Canadian life.

In 1991, Prime Minister Brian Mulroney also announced the establishment of a Royal Commission on Aboriginal Peoples, which began its work later that year; the establishment of an Indian Claims Commission to review Specific Claims; the establishment of a B.C. Task Force on Claims, which would form the basis for the B.C. Treaty Commission Process. In 1992, Aboriginal organizations and the federal government agreed, as part of the 1992 Charlottetown Accord, on amendments to the Constitution Act of 1982 that would have included recognition of the inherent right of self-government for Aboriginal people. For the first time, Aboriginal organizations had been full participants in the talks; however, the Accord was rejected in a national referendum.

With the failure of Canadian constitutional reform in 1992, for the last 20 years, the federal government—whether Liberal or Conservative—has continued to develop policies and legislation based upon the White Paper/Buffalo Jump objectives and many First Nations have regrettably agreed to compromise their constitutional/international rights by negotiating under Canada's termination policies.

Canada's Termination Policies Legitimized by Negotiation Tables

It has been 30 years since Aboriginal and Treaty rights have been "*recognized and affirmed*" in section 35 of Canada's constitution. Why hasn't the constitutional protection for First Nations' Inherent, Aboriginal, and Treaty rights been implemented on the ground?

One answer to this question is, following the failure of the First Ministers' Conferences on Aboriginal Matters in the 1980s, many First

Nations agreed to compromise their section 35 Inherent, Aboriginal and Treaty rights by entering into or negotiating Modern Treaties and/ or Self-Government Agreements under Canada's unilateral negotiation terms. These Modern Treaties and Self-Government Agreements not only contribute to emptying out section 35 of Canada's constitution of any significant legal, political, or economic meaning. Final settlement agreements are then used as precedents against other First Nations who are negotiating. Moreover, Canada's Land Claims and Self-Government policies are far below the international standards set out in the Articles of the United Nations Declaration on the Rights of Indigenous Peoples (UNDRIP). Canada publicly endorsed the UNDRIP in November 2010, but obviously Canada's interpretation of the UNDRIP is different from that of most First Nations, considering their unilateral legislation and policy approach.

Canada voted against UNDRIP on September 13, 2007, stating that the UNDRIP was inconsistent with Canada's domestic policies, especially the articles dealing with Indigenous Peoples' Self-Determination, Land Rights, and Free, Prior Informed Consent. Canada's position on UNDRIP now is that they can interpret it as they please, although the principles in UNDRIP form part of international, not domestic, law. The federal strategy is to maintain the Indian Act (with amendments) as the main federal law to control and manage First Nations. The only way out of the Indian Act for First Nations is to negotiate an agreement under Canada's one-sided Land Claims and/or Self-Government policies. These Land Claims/Self-Government Agreements all require the termination of Indigenous rights for some land, cash and delegated jurisdiction under the existing federal and provincial orders of government.

Canada has deemed that it will not recognize the pre-existing sovereignty of First Nations or allow for a distinct First Nations order of government based upon section 35 of Canada's constitution. Through blackmail, bribery, or force, Canada is using the poverty of First Nations to obtain concessions from First Nations who want out of the Indian Act by way of Land Claims/Self-Government Agreements. All of these Agreements conform to Canada's interpretation of section 35 of Canada's constitution, which is to legally, politically and economically convert First Nations into what are essentially ethnic municipalities. The first groups in Canada who have agreed to compromise their section 35 Inherent and Aboriginal rights through Modern Treaties have created an organization called the Land Claims Agreement Coalition. The Coalition Members are

- Council of Yukon First Nations (representing nine land claim organizations in the Yukon)
- Grand Council of the Crees (Eeyou Istchee)
- Gwich'in Tribal Council
- Inuvialuit Regional Corporation
- Kwanlin Dun First Nation
- Maa-nulth First Nations
- Makivik Corporation
- Naskapi Nation of Kawawachikamach
- Nisga'a Nation
- Nunavut Tunngavik Inc.
- Nunatsiavut Government
- Sahtu Secretariat Inc.
- Tlicho Government
- Tsawwassen First Nation
- Vuntut Gwitchin First Nation

The Land Claims Agreement Coalition Members came together because the federal government wasn't properly implementing any of their Modern Treaties. So the Coalition essentially became a lobby group to collectively pressure the federal government to respect their Modern Treaties. According to Members of the Coalition Modern Treaty implementation problems persist today. The fact that Canada has already broken the Modern Treaties shouldn't inspire confidence for those First Nations who are already lined up at Canada's Comprehensive Claims and Self-Government negotiation tables.[5]

Those First Nations who are negotiating at these 93 tables are being used by the federal government (and the provinces and territories)

5   According to the federal Department of Aboriginal Affairs there are 93 Modern Treaty and/or Self-Government negotiation tables across Canada [www.aadn-caandc.gc.ca/eng/1346782327802/1346782485058].

to legitimize its Comprehensive Claims and Self-Government policies, which are based upon extinguishment of Aboriginal Title and termination of Inherent, Aboriginal and Treaty rights. The First Nations who have been refusing to negotiate and are resisting the federal Comprehensive Claims and Self-Government negotiating policies are routinely ignored by the federal government and kept under control and managed through the Indian Act (with amendments). Attempts by non-negotiating First Nations to reform the federal Comprehensive Claims and Self-Government policies aren't taken seriously by the federal government because there are so many First Nations who have already compromised their Inherent, Aboriginal, and Treaty rights by agreeing to negotiate under the terms and funding conditions of these Comprehensive Claims and Self-Government policies.

For example, following the 1997 Supreme Court of Canada Delgamuukw decision, which recognized that Aboriginal Title exists in Canada, the Assembly of First Nations tried to reform the Comprehensive Claims policy to be consistent with the Supreme Court of Canada Delgamuukw decision. However, the then Minister of Indian Affairs Robert Nault on December 22, 2000, wrote a letter addressed to then Chief Arthur Manuel that essentially said why should the federal government change the Comprehensive Claims policy if First Nations are prepared to negotiate under it as it is? A fair question: why do First Nations remain at negotiation tables that ultimately lead to the termination of their peoples' Inherent and Aboriginal rights, especially since it appears that Modern Treaties are routinely broken after they are signed by the federal government?

Many of these negotiations are in British Columbia where despite the past twenty years of negotiations the B.C. Treaty process has produced two small Modern Treaties, Tsawwassan, and Maa'Nulth. The Nisga'a Treaty was concluded in 2000, outside of the B.C. Treaty process. All of these Modern Treaties have resulted in extinguishing Aboriginal Title, converting reserve lands into fee simple, removing tax exemptions, converting bands into municipalities, among other impacts on Inherent and Aboriginal rights.

Prayer flags at the site of Chief Theresa Spence's hunger strike on Victoria Island. A reminder that Idle No More is very much a spiritual movement.
(LEANNE BETASAMOSAKE SIMPSON)

The Harper Government's Termination Plan

Aside from the unilateral legislation being imposed, or the funding cuts and caps to First Nations and their political organizations, the September 4, 2012, announcement of a "results-based" approach to Modern Treaties and Self-Government negotiations amounts to a "take it or leave it" declaration on the part of the Harper government to the negotiating First Nations. Canada's Comprehensive Claims Policy requires First Nations to borrow money from the federal government to negotiate their "land claims." According to the federal government: To date, the total of outstanding loans to Aboriginal groups from Canada to support their participation in negotiations is $711 million. This represents a significant financial liability for the Aboriginal community. In addition, the government of Canada provides $60 million in grants and contributions to Aboriginal groups every year for negotiations.

It is Canada's policies that forced First Nations to borrow money to negotiate their "claims," so the "financial liability" was a policy measure designed by the federal government to pressure First Nations into settling their "claims" faster. As the federal government puts it, the Comprehensive Claims negotiation process has instead "spawned a negotiation industry that has no incentive to reach agreement." This accumulated debt of $711 million along with the annual $60 million in grants and contributions have compromised those negotiating First Nations and their leaders to the point where they are unable or unwilling to seriously confront the Harper government's termination plan.

Over 50 percent of the Comprehensive Claims are located in B.C. and the First Nations Summit represents the negotiating First Nations in B.C., although some negotiating First Nations have now joined the Union of B.C. Indian Chiefs (UBCIC), thus blurring the historic distinctions between the two political organizations. The latter organization previously vigorously opposed the B.C. Treaty process, but now the UBCIC remains largely silent about it. These two main political organizations—the First Nations Summit and the UBCIC—have now joined together into the B.C. First Nations Leadership Council, further blending the rights and interests of their respective member communities together, not taking into account whether they are in or out of the B.C. Treaty process.

This may partially explain why the chiefs who are not in the B.C. Treaty process also remain largely silent about the Harper government's "results-based" approach to Modern Treaties and Self-Government negotiations. First Nations in British Columbia are failing to capitalize on the fact that since the Delgamuukw Decision, the governments have to list unresolved land claims and litigation as a contingent liability. Such liabilities can affect Canada's sovereign credit rating and provincial credit ratings. To counter this outstanding liability, Canada points to the British Columbia Treaty Process as the way they are dealing with this liability, pointing to the fact that First Nations are borrowing substantive amounts to negotiate with the governments.

Another recent example of how disconnected B.C. First Nations and their organizations are on international versus domestic policy and law, is the First Nations' outcry over the recent Canada-China treaty. The B.C. Chiefs and their organizations are publicly denouncing the Canada-China Foreign Investment Promotion and Protection Agreement as adversely impacting on Aboriginal Title and Rights, yet they say or do nothing about Harper's accelerated termination plan. It seems the negotiating First Nations are more worried about the Canada-China Treaty blocking a future land claims deal under the B.C. Treaty process.

The Chiefs and their organizations at the B.C. Treaty process negotiation tables have had 20 years to negotiate the *"recognition and affirmation"* of Aboriginal Title and Rights, but this continues to be impossible under Canada's policies aimed at the extinguishment of collective rights. As a result only two extinguishment Treaties have resulted from the process. Even Sophie Pierre, Chair of the B.C. Treaty Commission has said *"If we can't do it, it's about time we faced the obvious—I guess we don't have it, so shut her down."* By most accounts the 20-year-old B.C. Treaty process has been a failure. It has served the governments' purpose of countering their contingent liabilities regarding Indigenous land rights. Yet it seems the negotiating First Nations are so compromised by their federal loans and dependent on the negotiations funding stream that they are unable or unwilling to withdraw from the tables en masse and make real on the demand that the Harper government reform its Comprehensive Claims and Self-Government policies to be consistent with the Articles of the UNDRIP.

The same can also be said for the negotiating First Nations in the Ontario, Quebec and Atlantic regions. The Chiefs who are not in the B.C., Quebec or Atlantic negotiating processes have not responded much, if at all, to Harper's *"results-based"* approach to Modern Treaties and Self-Government. The non-negotiating Chiefs seem to be more interested in managing programs and services issues than their Aboriginal Title and Rights. As one federal official put it, the Chiefs are involved in the elements of the 1969 White Paper on Indian Policy like economic and social development while ignoring the main White Paper objective—termination of First Nations legal status.

Given their silence over the Harper government's *"results-based," "take it or leave it"* negotiations approach, it seems many of the negotiating First Nations at the Comprehensive Claims and/or Self-Government tables are still contemplating concluding agreements under Canada's termination policies. This can only lead to further division among First Nations across Canada as more First Nations compromise their constitutional and international rights by consenting to final settlement agreements under the terms and conditions of Canada's termination policies, while undermining the political positions of the non-negotiating First Nations. In the meantime, Harper's government will continue pawning off Indigenous lands and resources in the midst of a financial crisis through free trade and foreign investment protection agreements, which will secure foreign corporate access to lands and resources and undermine Indigenous Rights.

Some First Nation leaders and members have criticized AFN National Chief Shawn Atleo for agreeing to a joint approach with the Harper government, including the Crown-First Nations Gathering (CFNG), but to be fair, the Chiefs across Canada did nothing to pressure Prime Minister Harper going into the CFNG. Instead, many Chiefs used the occasion as a photo opportunity with the Prime Minister. The negotiating First Nations who are in joint processes with Canada seem to be collectively heading to the cliff of the *"Buffalo Jump"* as they enter termination agreements with Canada, emptying out section 35 in the process. Much of the criticism of AFN National Chief Atleo has come from the Prairie Treaty Chiefs. Interestingly, if one looks at the federal chart of the 93 negotiation tables <www.aadnc-aandc.gc.ca/eng/1346782327802/1346782485058>, not too many First Nations from historic Treaty areas are involved in the Self-Government tables, except for the Ontario region where the Union of Ontario Indians and Nisnawbe-Aski Nation are negotiating Self-Government agreements. As a result of the September 4, 2012, announcements regarding changes to Modern Treaties and Self-Government negotiations, cuts and caps to funding First Nations political organizations and unilateral legislation initiatives, it is obvious that Prime Minister Harper has tricked the AFN National Chief and First Nations by showing that the CFNG *"outcomes"* were largely meaningless. One commitment that Prime Minister Harper made at the CFNG—which he will probably keep—is making a progress report in January 2013. The Prime Minister will probably announce the progress being made with all of the negotiating tables across Canada, along with his legislative initiatives. It appears First Nations are at the proverbial *"end of the trail"* as the Chiefs seem to be either co-opted or afraid to challenge the Harper government. Most grassroots peoples aren't even fully informed about the dangerous situation facing them and their future generations. The only way to counter the Harper government is to

- have all negotiating First Nations suspend their talks;
- organize coordinated National Days of Action to register First Nations opposition to the Harper government's termination plan;
- demand Canada suspend all First Nations legislation in Parliament and cease introducing new Bills; and
- change Canada's Land Claims and Self-Government Policies to "recognize and affirm" the Inherent, Aboriginal and Treaty Rights of First Nations, including respect and implementation of the Historic Treaties.

If there is no organized protest and resistance to the Harper government's termination plan, First Nations should accept their place at the bottom of all social, cultural, and economic indicators in Canada, just buy into Harper's jobs and economic action plan—and be quiet about their rights.

Originally appeared in First Nations Strategic Bulletin, *November 9, 2012.*

ARMED WITH NOTHING MORE THAN A SONG AND A DRUM:
Idle No More

Sylvia McAdam (Saysewahum)

I woke up during the night and heard the familiar constant rumble of logging trucks rolling down the Stoney Lake road right by my little shelter. I suppose it shouldn't surprise me that they're hauling out the trees from my people's territory as fast as they can like thieves in the night.

Like anything, a journey begins somewhere perhaps even before a person realizes their path. Idle No More resistance began long before in different names, different locations through the generations since the arrival of Europeans. My own personal journey began when I was writing a chapter in my new book about land. I felt disconnected from my collection of fond childhood memories out on the territory of my people. I decided to return after a lengthy absence, so leaving the city behind I headed to my parents' traditional lands and waters.

Returning to the land didn't just mean a physical return; it had to be done through the eyes and words of my people's history and ceremony. Returning meant visiting the graves of my people who were nearly wiped out from disease, starvation, and residential school. I sat by the graves hearing once again that horrible history and much more. It also meant a spiritual and emotional return to lands in the process of being devastated by logging activities and other developments.

I felt such grief for the devastation and development I was witnessing; I began to feel a profound and protective love for the lands in which my people were buried and have hunted since time immemorial. Through the spring and summer, I explored a vast area often camping in various places. I would find old cabins which would trigger sadness and interest for the abandoned hunting equipment and glimpses of a past life immersed in indigenous knowledge as I took pictures of old sweat lodges and wood stoves. Sometimes I would fall asleep and dream at those cabins and lands.

Soon I had many questions that led me to the offices of Saskatchewan Environment which I won't detail here; needless to say the logging of my people's trees will not stop. As it turns out, that was a minor issue compared to what was to come.

Someone tagged me on Facebook about Omnibus Budget Bill C-45 in the fall of 2012 and I was not very interested...at first. Then I went back and took a second look and began reading. Needless to say, I was angry and stunned. Fortunately, the other ladies and I connected; we realized we had the same concerns, so we made a decision not to stay silent. We had to reach people. Sheelah came up with the idea of sharing this information in a form of a teach in. So on November 10 in Saskatoon we had our first teach-in and invited as many people as possible to come and hear what Bill C-45 was about, as well as the other bills.

Shortly after that, I made arrangements to talk to elders; they gave us their support and prayers to try and reach as many people as possible. They also said we must use our own laws; one of our most sacred and peaceful law is "nahtamawasewin." This law is invoked in times of crisis and great threat. "Nahtamawasewin" means to defend for the children, all human children; it's also a duty to defend for the non-human children from the trees, plants, animals, and others. The Elders said, you ladies must invoke this law and let it guide your actions. We must always be prayerful and peaceful.

With this information guiding and directing Idle No More we reached out to people on social media, and fortunately our call for help was answered by grassroots people. We had hoped to reach people but Idle No More seemed to resonate to all people from many different lands.

Through the ensuing months Idle No More became a global grassroots movement. Even with all of our resounding "no consent" protests, rallies, and teach-ins, the Canadian state passed almost all the bills aimed at privatizing Treaty lands, extinguishing Treaty terms and promises as well as Indigenous sovereignty.

However, it has awakened Nations of people to their surroundings; questions and information about the environment, treaties and Indigenous sovereignty are posted and tweeted—constantly something that has long been silent.

Canadian laws are constantly changing; a gun law was recently repealed after millions of dollars was spent. These bills can be repealed; Indigenous Nations have stated they will not recognize Bill C-45 or the other bills.

In the meantime, the extraction of Indigenous resources goes unfettered under the guise of "consultation and consent." For the Indigenous people, the ceremonies and lodges continue to pray for the healing of the lands and waters.

Amazingly, more and more settler people are recognizing and understanding, as a people we cannot continue to devastate the very things needed to sustain humanity—our lands and waters— for the generations to come.

Idle No More has taken me to different lands where I have met other Indigenous peoples. I had an opportunity to speak at the United Nations in Geneva, Switzerland. I declared in my language "We are Nehiyawak, we are still here and we need your support to stop the genocide of Indigenous people." While there, I heard other Indigenous people weep recalling the horror and death they are enduring because of their lands and resources. I made a commitment to myself I would defend for the lands and waters to the best of my ability. I do not want to return to the United Nations weeping for my lands and waters.

I am forever changed by Idle No More. This journey has not ended; it's still unfolding as I write this. My journey takes me back to my people's lands and waters; it is in the lands and waters that Indigenous people's history is written. Our history is still unfolding; it's led by our songs and drums.

"OUR PEOPLE WERE GLOWING":
An Interview with Tanya Kappo
Tanya Kappo with Hayden King

HAYDEN KING (HK): I'm with Tanya Kappo, who is from Sturgeon Lake Cree Nation and a citizen of Treaty 8 in northern Alberta. Tanya is a University of Manitoba law graduate and working towards becoming a lawyer. She is also a mother of three children. Hi, Tanya, I know you were involved early on in the Idle No More movement, even since before it began. [After] meeting Sylvia McAdam at a conference in early 2012, the two of you kept in touch via Facebook, sharing information about impending federal legislation that would negatively affect Aboriginal and Treaty Rights. After McAdam (and others) began organizing events in Saskatchewan to bring awareness to the new laws, I know you were inspired to lead a teach-in at Louis Bull First Nation in Alberta and this specifically involved promoting the event on Facebook and Twitter, using the hashtag #IdleNoMore—a simple act that helped spark the Movement. Over the past four or five years it seems that Native people have become a huge presence on social media. Why do Native people love Facebook and Twitter so much?

TANYA KAPPO (TK): I think it's because our voices have been silenced for such a long time. Not only by society generally but also by our own communities sometimes. So social media has provided a forum for us. It's like this constant community meeting and you can go and hang out there anytime, a regular space to visit. And especially now that our people live in so many different locations, social media has also become the place to share thoughts on anything and everything. Because of the nature of our societies now, it's really an ideal medium for important conversations.

HK: What about in relation to Idle No More? Since the movement emerged, have you seen any tangible, real-world outcomes from the use of social media?

TK: When I started to get involved in this movement, my intentions were about the community—getting them informed about what was going on. In the beginning I didn't even have a political outcome. I was simply interested in getting our community talking about these kinds of things. Social media turned out to provide a really effective tool. And as we were talking it became really clear that our people want to know. They want to hear and read about this. They want to talk and have this conversation. The coming together through Idle No More contributed to a growing sense of community and even a resurgence in starting to think about nationhood, our identity and what happened to us, historically. Suddenly everything that had seemed normal wasn't anymore. People started to say, "Why did I even think that was normal? That's completely wrong." Social media helped continue the conversation and also helped build community.

HK: Were there any drawbacks to the use of social media throughout the movement?

TK: It was mid-January when it started to become clear in my mind that Idle No More was starting to be moving towards an urban phenomenon rather than one based in First Nation, Metis, or even Inuit communities. Social media might have had a lot to do with that. Many people in communities might not have internet access, limited access, or just be not as connected. So that meant a lack of engagement over time. The movement was also volunteer-based and in the middle of winter so social media was convenient. That being said, there was still an interest in communities, but because things were increasingly done primarily through social media, they were sometimes left out.

HK: Given that Idle No More moved away from First Nations, to a degree, do you think that meant less of a focus on challenging our political leaders in communities?

TK: For me, the issue wasn't about our community leaders. I felt that responsibility for raising the awareness belonged primarily to our regional and national organizations. In my mind, a big reason they exist was to be working towards the protection of our rights, which means sounding the alarm when necessary—to let the community leadership know if and when government, industry, and anyone else are doing anything that might affect our aboriginal and treaty rights. So I had a really big hesitation in the beginning, and I still do, at laying any blame at First Nation or Metis community leaders because they deal with life and death situations every day. The enormity of what they, and communities, have to do on a regular basis, the thousands of reports they have to submit, the constant encroachment of industry, is huge.

HK: Looking back, do you think that regional, political and treaty organizations responded to concerns that people in the Movement had regarding leadership?

TK: I can only speak to my experience at home. And within my communities in Treaty 8 territory they've certainly had an appreciation or at least awareness of Idle No More. They've been trying to find out what the movement is and talk about and think about it and figure out how to work together. It goes back to the idea of community. My intention from the beginning was never to come in and take over, but to offer help and take up my own responsibility and not leave it solely to political leadership. So in my area the response from leadership is there and there is actually an opportunity to move forward.

HK: So what do you think about the disunity narrative that emerged from the media regarding Idle No More?

TK: I think that the discourse in the media around division had an effect. I think if the media was ignored, it wouldn't have been an issue. But I think the media really played a role in characterizing disagreement and lending to this idea that First Nations people, Indigenous peoples, should always be united in some way. But why? Who says that? Whose rule is that? That was never the case. That's not even the nature of humanity to always agree. We still buy into these ideas of unity that are actually detrimental to our efforts.

HK: Maybe we should have stuck to social media?

TK: This has been my position all along. In the beginning of the Movement people were saying, "Media isn't paying attention, media isn't paying enough attention." But why do we need them to? We don't need them to. This isn't about them, this isn't about getting anybody's attention but our own and putting our own voice out there in our own way. That's why social media was so critically important. Because we could write and create our own blogs and our own stories, everything was ours and nobody could take it or use it against us. But when the mainstream media took notice, that's exactly what started to happen.

HK: What is it that still resonates with you from Idle No More? Is it social media or something else?

TK: The round dance revolution, the flash mob round dances for sure. They were a really intense and beautiful moment for me because they somehow brought to life what I had personally hoped the Movement would address. Those issues were first, our sense of ourselves and communities, and second, our existence in this country. I remember going to the round dance at the West Edmonton Mall—it was massive—the amount of people who showed up to drum, the people that came to sing and dance or just be there was incredible. The power and energy that was there, it was like we were glowing, our people were glowing. For the first time, I saw a genuine sense of love for each other and for ourselves. Even if it was only momentary it was powerful enough to awaken in them what needed to be woken up—a remembering of who we were, who we are. And as for the second point, the non-Native people at the mall that day, people who were just doing their Christmas shopping, there was nothing they could do. They had no choice but to stop and wonder, and to see us, really see us. And it was amazing.

THE IDLE NO MORE MANIFESTO

Jessica Gordon & The Founders of Idle No More

We contend that: The Treaties are nation-to-nation agreements between The Crown and First Nations who are sovereign nations. The Treaties are agreements that cannot be altered or broken by one side of the two Nations. The spirit and intent of the Treaty agreements meant that First Nations peoples would share the land, but retain their inherent rights to lands and resources. Instead, First Nations have experienced a history of colonization which has resulted in outstanding land claims, lack of resources, and unequal funding for services such as education and housing.

We contend that: The state of Canada has become one of the wealthiest countries in the world by using the land and resources. Canadian mining, logging, oil, and fishing companies are the most powerful in the world due to land and resources. Some of the poorest First Nations communities have mines or other developments on their land but do not get a share of the profit. The taking of resources has left many lands and waters poisoned—the animals and plants are dying in many areas in Canada. We cannot live without the land and water. We have laws older than this colonial government about how to live with the land.

We contend that: Currently, this government is trying to pass many laws so that reserve lands can also be bought and sold by big companies to get profit from resources. They are promising to share this time Why would these promises be different from past promises? We will be left with nothing but poisoned water, land, and air. This is an attempt to take away sovereignty and the inherent right to land and resources from First Nations peoples.

We contend that: There are many examples of other countries moving towards sustainability, and we must demand sustainable development

Sylvia McAdam, Parliament Hill in Ottawa, December 21, 2012.
(NADYA KWANDIBENS)

as well. We believe in healthy, just, equitable, and sustainable communities and have a vision and plan of how to build them.

Please join us in creating this vision.

"OUR PEOPLE ARE FRUSTRATED":
An Interview with Chief Isadore Day
Ryan McMahon and Wab Kinew with Chief Isadore Day

RYAN MCMAHON (RM): It's December 5, 2012, and this is the podcast *Red Man Laughing*. I'm with Wiindawtegowinini or Isadore Day, who is the elected Chief of Serpent River First Nation, located on the North Channel of Lake Huron in Northern Ontario, Canada. Yesterday we witnessed Chiefs from many nations joining together to travel to Parliament and take some long-standing concerns to the federal government. Some might dismiss the work that many of these Chiefs are doing but I think that's too easy. It's important to deconstruct the Indian Act and the work and baggage that comes with it but it's also important to become part of the solution. Chief Isadore Day certainly understands that balance. This is our feature chat with him where we get into that with him, and the way forward, listening to community and including community which he does a great job of in his home community of Serpent River First Nation.

WAB KINEW (WK): I wanted to start by saying you did a pretty amazing thing yesterday along with some of the other leaders. We've been talking about the events of yesterday and some of the implications. Since most of us were not there yesterday, could you talk about what happened yesterday.

ISADORE DAY (ID): Well, I think what happened was an accumulation of frustration by many. Our people have been constantly bombarded by requests to respond to evolution of this legislation and the onslaught of this legislative machine totally disregarding First Nations people. This was a message we carried forward on behalf of our citizens and community members. Chief Wallace Fox asked us to take notice of what was happening in the House of Commons yesterday and take the opportunity to set the record straight and establish a tone of direct action to prompt this government to take notice of our issues and concerns with this wide gamut of legislation that is before the House and that it is being pushed through despite what First Nations are saying are our concerns.

WK: This situation could have easily escalated. There was a shoving match going on. You're a big guy, part of you may have thought you could have done something crazy. Why did cooler heads prevail? Why did you decide to hold your ground and leave it at that?

ID: We knew the potential was there. We rely on the ceremony, we rely on the drum. The Pipe was there. It was very clearly set out what we need to do. We needed to draw that line in the sand. On one side of that line we stand our ground and try to get across to the Harper government that they can no longer impose this legislative machine and deny us having a say with respect to these various pieces of legislation. This was done the way our Anishinaabeg, Haudenosaunee, and Cree brethren do things—through ceremony and protocol. If we didn't have that, possibly things could have gotten out of hand. We had the strength and clarity around why we needed to do what we did.

RM: One of the messages I see going forward is exactly that. You were holding the Wampum belt, the drum was present. All of our sacred things come from the land. When we talk about the land, we are not talking about creating our own resources-based economy or anything like that. To be clear, we are talking about our own version of God, which is found in the land. Being led by ceremony and our ceremonial items, it is important to note that. Seeing it yesterday, it was the right way to be led into that situation. When you were there did you feel there was a chance you would be let into the room [the House of Commons] or did you think you would be met by the guards?

ID: We knew we would be met by the guards. We were more focused on the media that was there. We knew we would be met by resistance in trying to get into the House of Commons. Our main objective was for the Canadian public to really see what was going on. Anyone can go into the House, but if you are going into the House with a message of truth and the truth of what is happening with this legislation, you will be met with resistance. Our goal was for the Canadian public to get a clear vision of what our people are feeling about this, what our key issues and concerns were, and that a clear line was drawing in a sand. We knew what we would be met with.

RM: The tone has been set. Many of the Chiefs we saw on television yesterday and in the sound bites that emerged from the ground and you've heard the internet, you know what the young people in your community want because you are engage. Let's talk about the way forward and what the next steps are. I was watching this chat on Ustream and everyone is talking about the sellout Indian Act Chiefs. I don't appreciate this nor do I think it is helpful. You know the path forward, Chief Day, in your own community and certainly with the Chiefs of Ontario. Can you speak about what the best path forward is, now that we have been locked outside of these talks?

ID: I am really glad this question is coming to the forefront. I think that what our people are saying, even the ones that are skeptical about the way forward and this passing notion of Indian Act leaders. I don't think we are at this place anymore. What is very clear is that we need to get to the root of the issue. The root of the issues is that this legislation, this continued imposition of colonial rule is insidious. It is very discreeet and very sneaky. We have really become accustomed to proactive disengagement. The government operated in such a way and has pulled us in and fed us enough and fed us enough food and water to keep us alive but they have not let us in in any substantive way. We have been open to a new relationship but this government is not key on that anymore. This government is very blunt and crude in how they are going to deal with us. The way forward now is for us to manifest the truth. We need to now interpret what is really going on. We need to now interpret this and we need to get a lot clearer sense at the community level what this legislative machine is doing. What are the dynamics and characteristics of this legislation and what does it mean to our people. Once we have this discussion with our people, they will tell us what to do and give us direction. We are seeing a divide here: on one side, a top-down colonial government that is trying to impose and our grassroots people that are pushing up, and rightly so. Our people are frustrated. They don't want an Indian Act approach to us dialoguing with the government and I agree with that. We have to accept what is going on. We are going to go through a little bit of a tough time at the beginning. But I think that there will be a sense of renewal and reconfiguration as to how we put our issues on the table and we are going to need our community members to get this done.

wk: What is the response you expect from the federal government now that they have seen leaders, and part of the afn (Assembly of First Nations) are not scared to make a stand. One option might be that they cut funding to the pto (Provincial and Treaty Organizations) and some of the other organizations, or they could throw more money at those organizations to buy silence and complicity. What do you think the reaction will be on the federal side?

id: I think they will respond. I don't think for one second that this is a government that will react quickly. I think they are having very concerted and very important discussion on how to respond to us. I think we have to be mindful that this is a government that will do everything they can to maintain power, control, and oppression over our people. We need to recognize that we still need to progress forward as communities and we cannot lose the commitments already made, the apology, advancing First Nations economy and access to resources that are there. We have to recognize that this legislation is continuing stripping away our rights and it is eroding our jurisdiction and that we really are sovereign and we have section 35 rights that set us apart from other Canadians. There is a lot of work that has to be done to look at what the government is going to do to push back and control. I think this is stronger than that. There really is a movement happening and we just need high-level coordination and a collective response.

wk: What's going on today in Ottawa? Obviously there are conversations taking place across Canada and on social media, but what's the afn saying and some of the circles you are involved in, what are they saying?

id: Well, there is a lot of talk that people are relieved that we are finally seeing this type of a movement forward. We are breaking past a new threshold here and opening a new door that will create a new space. People are anticipating that. I think that there is a more clear enthusiasm, a sense of hope, duty and people are going to start to join forces on this. I think the AFN regions in Ottawa will go back and work on collective movement in terms of responding to the legislation. I think we will see direct action and how do we manage that, and what type of direction action will keep people safe, get the issues out there, and move our agenda forward.

RM: When we think about moving forward with direct action, do you see a divide within the AFN between the Chiefs that support that and those that don't? Let me put it another way: Is there still a split amongst Chiefs in terms of accepting or rejecting the Indian Act? Is everyone on board?

ID: Let's face it. If you were to ask the question "Is the Indian Act good for our people, if you had the power and control to do something for our people would you chose the Indian Act?" I am going to say is that no Chief would pick that. What they are going to say is that it is there now and how do we manage the change from the Indian Act if it is removed, altered, repealed, changed. What we are really looking at the complexities this act has had on our peoples since 1876 and how do we ensure our communities still have a sense of semblance and to operate our First Nations governments at the current state. It is a complex issue. If there is any resistance around Indian Act changes it is around what we are going to do to fill that gap. I like to be very mindful that there is a belief amongst all First Nations leaders that the Indian Act is not for us, that it is not ours. What do we do going forward? That is something that we have to take the time over the next several months to build a national collective response to the private member's bill going forward and how we address the legislative objective going forward now.

RM: Going forward, it is a very tricky issue and there is not going to be a simple solution. Imagining a world as a post-Indian Act apocalypse in our communities is the big fear especially with communities that have more ties to corporations and resource-based economies in their local areas. Has there been discussion about what this might potentially look like? No one knows what a post-Indian Act system looks like or feels like. This is one of the big fears on the ground. Do we have a plan?

ID: I go back to the First Nations Crown gathering when the Prime Minister said we are not going to get rid of the Indian Act and look what is happening now. It is something that is in the legislative machine right now for change. We have to go back to our own communities, regions, and nations, the Anishinaabeg nation and have the discussion as to what the post-Indian Act system looks like. We have to rely on our self-government models that we have been working on for quite some time. It is a governance framework discussion. What is our governance? It is also the land and the resources and the economic streams that come from our lands and it is also our people. How do we deal with the social ramifications of a post-Indian Act era. At the heart of the truest issue for the Conservative government is control and financial resources. I think that one of the things we as First Nations people need to push on is that there is a very important discussion in 2014 with respect to the equalization payment program. They have taken resource royalties and excises, nationally and provincially, as part of consolidated pool and there is an agreement on how those will be shared across the country in the provinces so there is a baseline fiscal stability so that these provincial governments and their municipalities can operate. I think now is the time for us to push hard, the AFN and regional governments to tell the provinces and the federal government that we want in on those discussions. We need a new fiscal reality. It really does boil down to an issue of resources and making sure that we have the ability to run our own governments. It is a multi-pronged approach but resources is a big one. How the government is responding to that is opening up our territories to business by unilaterally signing trade deals when there is unfinished business here. The Chiefs are saying no. We want a new fiscal reality. We want more fiscal autonomy in our territories so that we can see a post-Indian Act era.

WK: It is a really good point. It seems like for the past few decades the relationships has been defined largely in the political arena, but for the next decade or two decades the relationship between Aboriginal Peoples and Canada is going to be defined by natural resources and whether or not that relationship occurs in a meaningful way. Yesterday, we saw Chief Fox and yourself, Grand Chief Madabee and Grand Chief Nepinak from here in Manitoba at the forefront, and where was the National Chief in all this? What does this say about the AFN today if you guys are the ones taking the lead?

ID: I am glad the question is coming out. I have to be very mindfully respectful of the process. From the outside looking in, most people would ask that question. What we agreed to is that because there are processes out there the National Chief and the executive are dealing with, we felt we would take the first step forward. We wanted acknowledgement from the National Chief and the executive that this was an important enough issue to close down the assembly. They did with support from the Chiefs. Once we got to Parliament Hill, the National Chief and many of the executive were there. We said that we would go in and bring that message forward. There will be an opportunity in time to coordinate our messaging and figure out where the National Chief and the executive fit in. I want to draw attention to the reality that we need to build bridges and make sure there are no seams in our processes as we advocate and push our issues forward. We have to support one another. The National Chief has indicated his support for this direct action approach and he has said the most important thing is to build a unified approach and if we need your strong leaders at the front that is what will happen. I think we will see more involvement from this National Chief and if not, we will ask him to participate, and if he is not willing to advance some of these issues we will do it anyway for our communities and our children.

Originally appeared on Red Man Laughing *as "The Idle No More Podcast," December 5, 2012 (full podcast is available at soundcloud.com/ rmcomedy/red-man-laughing-idle-no-more).*

GHOSTS OF INDIGENOUS ACTIVISM PAST, PRESENT, FUTURE:
#IdleNoMore's Transformative Potential

Hayden King

Earlier this week, from Goose Bay to Yellowknife, thousands of Nehiyaw, Dene, Metis peoples (joined by Canadians supportive of them) gathered in front of provincial legislatures, and constituency and Aboriginal Affairs offices. They sang honour songs, danced jigs, and waved their flags and homemade protest signs out in the cold and the wind. This hashtag movement known to some as #IdleNoMore (#NativeWinter to others) is challenging manifold issues in the Indigenous-Canadian relationship. Among the more critical:

- the move to strip environmental protections from most of this country's waterways;
- a lack of consultation on amendments to the Indian Act;
- the chronic failure to maintain and uphold treaties;
- the continued refusal to acknowledge the rights of those still without treaties;
- repeated calls for a national inquiry on missing and murdered Aboriginal women.

We've protested before; in fact, we do it often. At the very earliest origins of Canada as a country, Mississauga leaders (concerned by continued European encroachment) diplomatically expressed their frustration this way: "You came as a wind blown across the Great Lake. We received you, we planted you, and we nursed you. We protected you till you became a mighty tree that spread throughout our Hunting Land. With its branches you now lash us." When diplomacy failed, protest gave way to active, physical resistance throughout the late 1800s by Metis and Cree peoples on the Plains, the Tsilhqot'in and others in B.C., and the aforementioned Anishinaabe in Ontario.

With incidents of violence followed by more heavy-handed government suppression, appeals were made directly to individual Canadians. In 1923, Cayuga leader Deskaheh would complain, "We are tired of calling on the governments of pale-faced peoples in America and in Europe. We have tried that and found it was no use. They deal only in fine words—we want something more than that. We want justice from now on." The pan-Indian political organization The League of Indians was formed soon after, sharing some of the same goals as Deskaheh. The Canadian government responded by banning the League: in fact, the time would soon come when all such Indigenous organizing would be prohibited under the Indian Act.

Eventually, returning World War II vets and victims/survivors of residential schools did get organized. They forced changes to both the school system and the Indian Act throughout the 1950s in what was becoming the so-called "Red Power" movement. Their efforts culminated in a powerful response to the White Paper in 1969-70. And yet it wasn't enough to prevent ongoing dispossession. Once again, Indigenous forms of protest evolved into more provocative confrontations, at places like Gustafsen Lake, Oka, Ipperwash, and highways and rail lines during the action. The efficacy of these movements should not be discounted.

They are directly responsible for the fact that our peoples still have some semblance of culture and lands remaining today, as well as legal rights (however limited). Still, those earlier movements also failed in many ways. Ultimately, we've been largely unsuccessful at wholesale, widespread change. This outcome is partially a consequence of the effective suppression by AANDC, obfuscation by the mainstream media, and appropriation of these movements by do-nothing leaders. But I think the most significant factor, especially in more contemporary efforts, is our reactive posture, leaving us always on the defensive. When Canada introduces policy, legislation, or funding changes, we respond with outrage that the mediocre status quo might be upset.

In the best-case scenario, the offending legislation is shelved. The danger of this reactive activism is that it can actually serve to solidify some of the institutions we've come to accept, despite the fact that it is those very institutions that make up a large part of the problem. For instance, while rallying against the *First Nations Transparency Act* or the potential *First Nation Land Ownership Act* is important, it also means defending the existing Band Council system and/or land tenure arrangements on reserve—even though we know that both are extremely problematic and require fundamental change. But instead of working out the shape of that change, we inadvertently entrench an inherently flawed system.

So as we move one step forward, we also effectively take one step back, mistaking inertia for movement. Such unwitting, stubborn idleness allows Canada to push its agenda. So this new and compelling movement presents a unique opportunity. Firstly, it allows us to build on the momentum already created in creative and committed ways to continue raising our collective consciousness (the hunger strike by Attawapiskat Chief Theresa Spence is an active example).

Secondly, it offers the chance to channel energy into considering alternatives. I spoke recently with Anishinaabekwe writer Leanne

The very persuasive Phoenix Sky Cottrelle defending the land at an Idle No More rally in Sarnia and Aamjiwnaang, May 21, 2013. (MIKE ROY)

Betasamosake Simpson about where we go from here; she advocates that we bring together Anishinaabe academics, activists, community members, leaders, etc. to talk about what we want and how we'll achieve it. Generally, this means spending genuine time together to foster national movements and reassert a real concrete plan, not just repeat rhetoric. When the League of Indians, Deskaheh and Great War veterans started causing trouble in the early decades of the 20th century, Indian Agents responded by calling it "annoying" and "advising Indians to have nothing to do with it." When the current Aboriginal Administrator John Duncan was asked about Idle No More, his curt response—"That's social media, so we'll just have to see where that goes"—echoed the same dismissive and arrogant tone of his predecessors.

Canada expects (and hopes) this movement will melt away. Making it sustainable and meaningful requires reflecting on past and current trends in activism among Mushkegowuk, Algonquin, and Lakota peoples. That means honouring and being thankful for them, but also absorbing their lessons.

Originally appeared on MediaIndigena.com, *December 12, 2012.*

TRANSFORMING UNITY:
An Interview with Assembly of Manitoba Chiefs Grand Chief Derek Nepinak

Derek Nepinak with Leah Gazan

LEAH GAZAN (LG): I'm with Assembly of Manitoba Chiefs (AMC) Grand Chief Derek Nepinak, a man and a leader who has never been idle. He has been Chief of his home community of Pine Creek First Nation, served on the governance council of Treaty Four, holds a law degree, and was a graduate student in the University of Winnipeg Indigenous governance program. He was also very active during the winter of 2012-2013 and I want to talk about this today.

On November 1, 2012, along with Chief Wallace Fox and Dene National Chief William Erasmus, you held a press conference where you put Canada on notice that it was no longer acceptable to forfeit

Indigenous sovereignty through actions like proposing legislation without consultation. What was some of the impetus for some chiefs to take a stronger position in opposition to legislative changes by the current Conservative government than perhaps in earlier years?

DEREK NEPINAK (DN): I and others recognized that Stephen Harper's Conservative government has a plan to implement a number of different policies quickly and with very little consultation with Indigenous peoples—such as in the case of Bill C-38 and Bill C-45; the omnibus bills. There are many issues that arose when the Prime Minister introduced these changes, such as the proposed reforms on First Nations on-reserve property ownership which requires our people to be consulted. There is a lot more Canada should be consulting with us on, such as their matrimonial real property legislation, a new law respecting Indian Act elections, and the development of new regulations and opt-in provisions. We know that there is new education legislation coming down the line. All of this legislation was done under the umbrella of the Indian Act—which we don't believe in, we were never a part of, we never agreed to, and we are now finding our feet to once again challenge the false assumptions of Canadian legal fictions. These changes in federal policy and process drive a sense of urgency amongst our people, perhaps to a level as never before. Our actions in December 2012 sought to bring attention to what was being pursued.

At the same time as we are building a strong platform based on our treaty relationships, we also now have a lot of leadership coming along that did not go to residential school. These women and men are not so heavily bound by the legacy of colonialism, the legacy of dependency, and all the negative things that come from many generations of oppressive colonial policy. Of course this takes nothing away from our previous leaders, our ancestors, and our forerunners, for all have withstood these tidal waves of abuse we have endured. Now, however, it is more evident than ever that things are changing amongst the many voices in our communities and there is much momentum to speak strongly about who we are.

LG: On December 2, 2012, you joined other Chiefs in leaving a winter meeting in Ottawa and partook in a march to Parliament Hill and into the House of Commons in an act of solidarity and opposition to the

Conservative Government's proposed legislations. Many also wanted to discuss past colonial atrocities and ask the government to honour treaty obligations, address issues of poverty, water security, missing and murdered women, as well as discuss resource protection, sharing, and development. What happened in the winter meeting to lead up to Chiefs feeling a need to storm Parliament Hill?

DN: The meeting in December had an interesting dynamic, because it had been informed by the Assembly of First Nations (AFN) conference on education earlier that year in October. During that meeting in fact we were talking about the rejection of the concept of federal legislation over education. At the same time however, Department of Indian Affairs minister John Duncan had put out a press release saying that First Nation schools on reserve receive as much, if not more, funding than off-reserve schools. This is a totally false lie and we have seen this government strategically use public media to influence public opinion in a negative way and bolster its own position time and time again. So, on one level there was a great deal of animosity. But, at any AFN meeting there are always two different dynamics. There is a public meeting on the conference floor that is usually broadcast or webcast and so forth, but outside the meeting room there are always other discussions happening where a lot of decisions are made about what we are going to do. This is a significantly different space. The AFN floor is a somewhat structured type system where resolutions are brought forward, resolutions are introduced, individuals make fancy speeches and engage in powerful rhetoric that really hasn't done anything. A lot of the chiefs who attend meetings such as this have become so frustrated with this in fact that they go with the real intention of having the meeting outside of the meeting. I think that's where the move towards marching Parliament Hill came from. I had been discussing some of the implications of the various bills with different chiefs outside of the room and then heard that people wanted to go to Parliament Hill and hold a rally there to instigate action. I said I would be behind that 100 percent. Then, it was just a matter of coming together, with a few key people like Wallace Fox, Isadore Day, and Patrick Madahbee.

LG: At that initial press conference on December 7, 2012, you also publicly endorsed Idle No More and many grassroots people who were holding protests across Canada challenging Bill C-45. Did you feel both Idle No More and the broader grassroots movement could advance the agenda of the Manitoba Chiefs at that time?

DN: I've often pondered what are the fundamental premises of the movement. When we say Idle No More, who is idle? Through several different discussions that have happened, people have said that chiefs are idle. I've always believed that since coming into politics I've never been idle. I've seen the writing on the wall since day one, 'cause I've brought extensive background along with me. When people think that people are coasting with the titles like Chief or Grand Chief, that's not entirely true. Many come into the political arena or system to break through a wall that maintains status quo, keeps people in poverty, and distributes wealth to a small amount of privileged people. I've done my best to try and break that process down from inside the system that we work in, and I've acquired the position of Grand Chief to get into that system, get in and see exactly what is happening. I have never been idle and I have made many sacrifices in my life in order to become effective in my trade. So, my initial reaction was like many other Chiefs—that we were being insulted. Then, though, I said no, let's see where this movement goes and remember that at times the best leadership is not in leading but in following what people are doing and saying. That's the position I took early on, always believing that my role as a Grand Chief is to be a good listener and follow the energies of our people.

There is sometimes a general disconnect between the political elite and what's happening on the ground in our communities and urban environments. When that disconnect becomes apparent, the legitimacy of any political infrastructure is compromised. I'm glad that it is at risk, quite honestly, because we need to see fundamental and transformational change in leadership, governance, and the processes we live within during our lifetime. If we are ever going to break out of this colonial mindset that we are in, this mindset of dependency and deferring responsibility to non-indigenous governments, we need to turn to people most grounded in our communities, the grassroots people. It can't be the political elite because the political elite are comfortable. I've always believed the best thing I can do is break down the status quo walls that have maintained people in poverty for too long. I have been willing to take on the criticism that goes along with being a Chief, because I know what my intentions are: to push for the greater good of everybody. There is admittedly a great deal of negative criticism, a lot of lateral violence, and those who might say: "Nepinak is just in it for himself." I ask those though: If I was just in it for myself, why would I be rocking the boat? Why would I threaten and put our funding sources in such a great threat if I were just coasting along looking for the next big paycheque? So, in the end, I think it is important to stand behind our people 100 percent of the way and this is why I endorsed Idle No More. I saw potential for real change to happen and an opportunity for that disconnect between leadership and grassroots people to transform into something new and strong.

LG: On December 11, 2012, Chief Spence went on a hunger strike to raise public attention about First Nation issues, Bill C-45, and the situation in Attawapiskat. She requested a meeting with Prime Minister Stephen Harper and Governor General David Johnson and vowed she would not break her fast until they agreed to discuss Canada's treaty relationship with First Nation leadership. Shortly after, you went to Ottawa in an act of solidarity to support Chief Spence. Why did you feel her actions were important?

DN: Indigenous people have natural laws. Some are aware of what natural laws are, some do not understand natural laws because they do not carry teachings. You arrive at an understanding of these not just through thought and intellectual understanding but by participation in ceremony and acts at a spiritual level. While on my own search, I quickly understood that Teresa Spence was not just a chief in an impoverished community—she is a mother and a grandmother fasting for her children. At the same time, I know the natural law of the eagle and the love that comes from this powerful relative—so I was aware of what was going on. I've also been through fasts myself, and know that by the fourth or fifth day your life is in jeopardy. I simply could not ignore the gravity of this act.

The Assembly of Manitoba Chiefs have a unity pipe that's been gifted to us through the women. After Chief Spence started her fast I found myself in Ottawa lifting this pipe and forging a bond that we would stand strong with this grandmother, observe the natural law alongside her, and help achieve her goals. My commitment was much more than a political manoeuvre—it was a spiritual responsibility and obligation. What Chief Spence achieved wasn't just a symbolic gesture for her community but had implication on everybody across Canada. Any Indigenous community that understands its natural laws therefore should have been paying attention to what she was doing and demonstrate that understanding by standing with her. It required people to see beyond the limits of the political arena however and some people cannot do that because they are consumed by ambition and the political machines that we have created.

LG: At a press conference on January 10, 2013, the Manitoba Chiefs decided to pull out of the "official" scheduled meeting with Prime Minister Stephen Harper and instead decided to stand in solidarity with Chief Spence. At the press conference you criticized the Conservative government for deliberately trying to discredit Chief Spence, and strongly communicated that the January 10 meeting needed to be on the terms discussed with First Nations and created in a manner that respected nation-to-nation relationships. Why did you feel it was important to take such a strong stance in a time when First Nations were experiencing massive funding cuts, understanding how certain specific and aggressive legislations were a threat to the future of our treaties?

DN: To answer that question you have to be informed by what happened previously a year earlier, in January 2012. I led that discussion by saying "fool me once shame on you, fool me twice shame on me." So, in January 2012, we went into that meeting with a lot of cautious optimism of what would transpire with Mr. Harper and his government. Unfortunately, as we know, nothing really came out of that meeting other than some photograph opportunities. Then Mr. Harper travelled to other countries to try and open up the resource base of the great wealth of Canada by showing his pictures, while saying: "Yeah, we dealt with the Indigenous people. I just had a meeting with them last month. Look, everybody is happy and smiling and shaking my hand." It was really a smoke and mirrors campaign. I saw that right away, and so did the elders I work with. With this in mind, we went to the January meeting in 2013 with a different understanding. It might just be Mr. Harper did too. For this meeting we had to fill out security forms and travel to go the most secure building in Canada, the CSIS building, because this is the only building where the Prime Minister would meet us. Highly secured, they had armed people at every corner, at every door and who knows what other type of security they had in the room where the Prime Minister was sitting with Indigenous people. At the same time, there was a limited amount of seats so bodies like the Assembly of Manitoba Chiefs had to decide—this Chief can go, this one shouldn't, this one should, but this one can't—and this created a political dynamic, in-fighting, and dissension.

That's not how you treat people in a nation-to-nation relationship. When you look at how past Canadian governments have welcomed other nations, they roll out the red carpet and open the front doors of Parliament Hill for dignitaries to walk through. When it comes to Indigenous people, the nation-to-nation relationship that was apparent at the time of Treaty is obviously long forgotten. In January 2013, we needed to remind Canada that there are protocols and responsibilities when engaging with Indigenous peoples. We needed to remind them that there's a show of respect that can be made and that's been completely lost. In January 2013 we had to say no to some Chiefs who wanted to go into the meeting with the Prime Minister to do this. In fact, however, this was a really awful thing, because no Chief representing their community should have to face a situation where they can't go into a room to meet with the Prime Minister... especially when the Prime Minister has opened the doors to meet with people. Many Chiefs that came to Ottawa in January 2013 though said: "I don't want to see us put ourselves in a scenario where we have to agree to a format and agenda prescribed by Mr. Harper's government or his policy people."

At the same time, the AFN already had booked a press conference on Parliament Hill at a certain hour and a certain day but all this was smoke and mirrors. The chiefs of Manitoba saw that, we understood that and that is why we maintained our own caucus room and our own meeting because we needed to clearly and thoroughly decide where we stood. It's important to point out that not every Manitoba hief was in our caucus session but most were. Some had proxies and were participating in the AFN meeting, because they wanted to put their support behind the AFN. There were also some prominent former leaders of the AFN from Manitoba in the AFN meeting, not fully participating

with the Manitoba Chiefs and not fully endorsing what we were doing. But, in the January 10 press conference we were very clear that
we were not going to be subjected to the type of disrespect that had
characterized the January 2012 meeting. I think that message came
across very clear and we also had a grounding through our spiritual
connection to what Chief Spence was doing.

LG: In May 2013 there was a meeting held in Onion Lake to discuss a
national treaty alliance, an entity outside of the AFN. Did the events at the
height of the Idle No More movement in January cause a lot of leadership to lose faith in the AFN and therefore inspire a need to create a sepa-
rate organization to ensure the survival of treaties and inherent rights?

DN: Many across different communities and regions have been concerned for a number of years with what has been happening at the AFN
and what the AFN is all about. When I look at the AFN I see an organization that is federally funded and not far removed from the bureaucracy of the Indian Act. It is, in many ways, designed to enact Indian
Act policy. A lot of resolutions come forward to the AFN, are discussed
and passed as resolutions, and then when we are done—that's where
the political advocacy ends. A lot of chiefs feel that once they have a
resolution on the floor of the AFN then that's good enough, that the
AFN will take it over—and everything will be okay.

Well the truth is that if the resolution goes through, it doesn't go
anywhere because there often isn't any money attached, no resources,
and supporters are unable to fight for it. The money that comes into
the AFN is all policy-driven money intended to implement federal colonial policies and law. At times I've therefore observed the AFN as
nothing more than a lap dog of any particular federal regime in power
at the time. This becomes more apparent as we rid ourselves of the
smoke and mirrors that have characterized the organization over the
last number years and have exposed it for what it is. Another feature
is there's a surveillance mechanism built into the funding structure so
that any political actor within the AFN—whether a national Chief or
regional Chief or whomever—is monitored, every activity that they
engage in has to be reported on in order to keep the money coming in
next month. Simply put, government bureaucrats know exactly what
the AFN is doing every day of the month. It's a surveillance tool, and

we have just had enough of it. Take these omnibus bills too. They are coming through and the AFN is just standing aside, not voicing any significant opposition, not organizing any significant protest to the bills, and allowing Parliamentary process to run its course through Senate and Parliamentary committees. Different leadership come to Ottawa to present, participate, and try to evoke change, but it's not having the effect that we need it to have.

As Treaty People we believe that there is a fundamental relationship built on respect, built on equality, built on an equal recognition of jurisdiction and sovereignty. That position is not being clearly articulated, or presented, or defended by the AFN these days. The treaty relationship has been relegated to an agenda item on a long list of agenda items, as opposed to being fundamental to every activity the AFN does. This is unacceptable in particular to treaty-based communities, who hold a fundamental belief in the nation-to-nation relationship that was agreed upon.

The Onion Lake meeting therefore really represents an opportunity to re-establish fundamentals. My view is that if the National Treaty Alliance materializes, it can't just be a parallel organization. If we are going to break the mould, the status quo, we cannot just recreate a new political organization of chiefs. We have to break down those walls that exist, those walls that protect the status quo, and provoke a fundamental shift away from the existing power structure—a transformation. A treaty alliance movement, not formed in ivory towers or around tables in Ottawa, Toronto, Winnipeg, Saskatoon, Calgary or Edmonton, but in communities has the ability to inspire change from people who have the passion to institute it. That's really what's going to break the mold. As for me, I really see my role technically in this treaty alliance movement is to help strengthen communities build tools of empowerment. That's where change is going to start. Our communities are only as strong as our most dependent and impoverished people because we are all linked. That's as strong as we are. We seem to have made these first steps with the treaty alliance discussion so far and our people are putting their minds towards a new organizational structure as a solution. I believe that a new organization made up of chiefs and leadership is an interim step towards a full decolonization process, and that decolonization process has to include stepping outside of the Indian Act. We all have to bravely step outside the Indian Act; see it for what it is, throw away our status Indian cards, and redefine our identities on something stronger and more fundamental to what it is to be an Indigenous person in this part of the world. When we are willing to do that, and when we are willing to look back at the Indian Act for what it is, then let's hold Canada accountable for its colonial legacy that it created with that Indian Act. Let's hold it accountable to the tune of the billions and billions of dollars it robbed from us while they kept us locked up in that Indian Act system—that's what the treaty alliance to me is all about.

IDLE NO MORE:
Re-storying Canada
Sheelah McLean

> *The truth about stories is that's all we are.*—Thomas King

My identity as a white-settler has been marked by countless number of narratives. Of the many stories that I could choose from, two stand out as framing my own journey towards solidarity work in the Idle No More movement. The first story is of my early experiences as a high school teacher learning about systemic racism, and the second is how I began unlearning the many colonial discourses that constructed my childhood as a settler growing up on the Canadian prairies.

Nothing from my educational experiences prepared me to understand the many forms of systemic racism that Indigenous students in my classes shared with me in my first years of teaching. While I had some background studying the history of colonialism, I didn't have the language or analysis to position these stories within a context of ongoing colonial practices. In fact, I had been taught that racism exists within individual acts of bigotry. The consistency and scale of my students' stories of racism disrupted the foundations of my liberal belief systems. My recognition of the magnitude of violent racism Indigenous students face daily within our school and community propelled me back to university into a graduate program in integrated anti-racist education. This decision was the first step in what has become a lifelong journey of unlearning the many ways that white-settler identity is performed as dominance.

My education in anti-racism allowed me to begin to unpack some of the stories I grew up with regarding what it means to be Canadian. I questioned the myths that nation building in Canada occurred on the foundations of democracy and freedom, multiculturalism, and benevolence. I re-examined the tales I was told of my own success being attributed primarily to work ethic, and how my grandparents built a life from nothing on a family farm. Like other white-settlers, I was socialized into the false logic that my family status was earned through good citizenship and hard work. In reality, state policies secured my family's status as white-settlers by guaranteeing them access to voting rights, land title rights, public education rights, and mobility rights as well as other practices that Indigenous people and people of colour were historically denied. I also learned about the continued theft of Indigenous lands and resources which subsidize the wealth of the Canadian state and recognized the truth: that the many stories of systemic racism my students shared with me were effects of ongoing white-settler colonialism.

Over the last 10 years I have continued to study how inequality is produced and maintained, and have learned that the only way to challenge complicity with ongoing settler colonialism is active day-to-day opposition to it. I continue to deepen my understanding of what it means to intervene in performing dominance in my own thoughts and actions, troubling that I benefit from colonialism even as I try to work against it. I teach anti-racist education as an intervention in my classes, and have become actively involved in organizing with community members using education, gatherings and rallies to challenge oppressions in the school system and community. I also used social media to connect with individuals and groups across the continent who want to fight injustice and inequality. It was my connection to social media which led to my solidarity work with Idle No More organizers.

The Idle No More movement is re-storying Canada—using public gatherings and mass media, it is actively re-telling stories which have been silenced, minimized, and denied, but also provides multiple forums to share stories that inspire hope and promote social and political change. Idle No More seeks to educate the public on how sexism, racism,

Among the most provocative protests throughout Idle No More, hundreds march to and eventually shutdown the Canada-U.S. link, the Ambassador Bridge in Windsor, on January 16, 2013. (GREG PLAIN)

homophobia, ableism, and other oppressions are interconnected to the exploitation of Indigenous lands and resources. Idle No More organizers maintain that Indigenous self-determination must be the foundation for mobilizing towards social and environmental justice in Canada, as well as globally. In the past year the Idle No More movement has inspired millions into action in defence of Indigenous sovereignty, demanding social and political transformation and ecological sustainability.

As we move forward, it is clear that active intervention into white-settler colonialism is essential for systemic change. Those of us who believe in justice must commit to unlearning the oppressive ideologies we currently hold that value the accumulation of profit over life, and find ways to actively dismantle the exploitive systems that reproduced these practices.

Decolonization is a process that requires not only a re-storying of our shared history but a reimagining of our relationships with each other based on respectful solidarity. As author Ben Okri suggests: "In a fractured age, when cynicism is god, here is a possible heresy: we live by stories, we also live in them. One way or another we are living the stories planted in us early or along the way, or we are also living the stories we planted—knowingly or unknowingly—in ourselves. We live stories that either give our lives meaning or negate it with meaningless-ness. If we change the stories we live by, quite possibly we change our lives." The powerful spirit and energy of the people who are the Idle No More movement will continue to transform our future.

IDLE NO MORE IS NOT JUST AN "INDIAN THING"
Wab Kinew

What is "Idle No More"?

It is a loosely knit political movement encompassing rallies draw-ing thousands of people across dozens of cities, roadblocks, a shov-ing match on Parliament Hill between chiefs and Mounties, and one high-profile hunger strike. It is also a meme tweeted and shared about thousands of times a day, for messages about indigenous rights, indigenous culture, and cheap indigenous jokes ("Turn off your ignition #IdleNoMore"). The name Idle No More comes from a recent meeting in Saskatchewan. Sylvia McAdam and three others were mad about Bill C-45, the omnibus budget bill. Their biggest frustration was that nobody seemed to be talking about it. Two provisions in particular upset them: the reduction in the amount of federally protected waterways and a fast-tracked process to surrender reserve lands. In McAdam's view, if Aboriginal people did not speak out it would mean they "comply with [their] silence." So she and her friends decided to speak out. They would be "Idle No More." They held an information session under the same name.

Co-organizer Tanya Kappo fired off a tweet with the hashtag #IdleNoMore—and it struck a nerve. Though Bill C-45 has become law, many of Aboriginal people have voiced their opposition to it. Many of the other tensions in the indigenous community have started to bubble up to the surface and "Idle No More" now encompasses a broad conversation calling for recognition of treaty rights, revitalization of indigenous cultures, and an end to legislation imposed without meaningful consultation. To me this conversation is more than just an "Indian Thing." It is one that Canadians of all backgrounds should pay attention to, if not participate in. The ideals that are underlying this action are ones to which we all aspire, even if we may disagree on how exactly to pursue them.

5. #IdleNoMore is About Engaging Youth

When Grand Chief Derek Nepinak went on national television after he and some other leaders got into that shoving match outside the chamber, he acknowledged the Chiefs were responding to young people calling for action via social media. At the rallies held in cities like Winnipeg, Windsor, and Edmonton, it has been the youth who have done the organizing, and it has been the youth who have made up the majority of attendees. On Facebook and Twitter, "#IdleNoMore" has popped up in the timelines of people who typically discuss Snooki or the Kardashians. Agree or disagree with the message, Idle No More has accomplished something all Canadians want: it has young people paying attention to politics.

4. #IdleNoMore is About Finding Meaning

Much of the talk around Idle No More is about preserving indigenous culture, either by revitalizing spiritual practices, or by keeping intact what little land base we have left. The reason culture is so important is that it provides a way to grapple with the big questions in life: "Who am I?" "What am I doing here?" and "What happens after I die?" Some of the answers have been handed down as words of wisdom. Other times, you are told to go out on to the land and discover them for yourself through fasting or prayer. We need these ways. As I look around and see many fellow Canadians searching for meaning in their own lives, I think to myself perhaps they could use these ways as well.

3. #IdleNoMore is About Rights

What almost everyone carrying the Idle No More banner is calling for is meaningful consultation between the federal government and First Nations people. This is what section 35 of our constitution is all about: Aboriginal and treaty rights are recognized and affirmed, and that means we have to talk. If there is no meaningful conversation happening, it is troublesome. Aboriginal people may be the canary in the coal mine. If we overlook one section of the constitution does that mean others are in similar jeopardy?

2. #IdleNoMore is About the Environment

Idle No More started in part because of outrage that Bill C-45 reduced the number of federally protected waterways. The environment continues to be a regular topic at Idle No More protests. Dr. Pam Palmater, one of the leading voices in the Idle No More conversation, argues this indigenous environmentalism is significant since the Crown has a duty to consult with Aboriginal people before natural resource projects proceed. She says, "First Nations are Canadians' last, best hope of protecting the land, water, sky, and plants and animals for their future generations as well."

1. #IdleNoMore is About Democracy

Democracy thrives when well-informed people are engaged and make their voices heard. Idle No More started with four young lawyers trying to inform the people in their communities about an issue they were passionate about. Now many people are engaged. Even more information is being shared, and even more voices are being heard. There is no one leader or "list of demands" attributable to Idle No More. While this may seem chaotic, this is what democracy is all about. Democracy is messy. Democracy is loud. Democracy is about hearing a wide range of voices and trying to build a path forward among them. It is not about shutting off debate or trying to rush things in through the back door.

Originally appeared in The Huffington Post, *December 17, 2012.*

THE ROUND DANCE REVOLUTION:
Idle No More

Ryan McMahon

> *This is the story*
> *of how we are reuniting our people through*
> *our songs, dances, and cultures.*

The Round Dance Revolution has arrived.

This was supposed to have been written days ago. When I was asked by RPM to do a guest post I immediately said, "Yes, I'll write a guest post: Indigenous... music... culture... #IdleNoMore... Sounds great!" And I hung up the phone. Then I attended the first Idle No More action in Winnipeg and when I got home that night I started writing. Sorta. It was -38 with the wind chill that day—so—I think I drank tea for hours and sat under blankets, but, I'm trying to sound responsible here. *So.* I wrote for a few hours that night. I wrote. And wrote. I heard typewriter keys in my mind. Much like Hunter S. Thompson, I wrote. Sorta. Like Hunter S. Thompson. Well, minus the whisky, the smokes, and the drugs, so, not like Hunter S. Thompson at all, but, dammit, I wrote.

Now, full disclosure—at best, I'm a below average writer. My words, brain, and fingers don't connect. I can't articulate myself very well in this medium (I'm writing two books, by the way, I bet the publishers are stoked I'm saying this publicly) and I struggled to find a clear sense of what I was feeling. But I knew I was feeling something. We all were. We all *are*.

The Idle No More Movement, the politics and the struggle, were providing me with mind-boggling confusion, anger, sadness, and happiness. The fact that mainstream media were ignoring the movement as a whole, the fact that one of our strongest leaders is currently on a hunger strike and the fact that I felt like we were Tweeting and Facebooking into a vacuum...everything exasperated my frustration. I struggled to find something that hadn't been covered yet, when the incredible Métis blogger Chelsea Vowel, my Anishinaabe brother Wab Kinew, and many other journalists and independent media were providing great coverage.

So I struggled. And struggled. No angle. Nothing interesting to say. Nothing informative to add. Then, two days ago I decided that my piece was going to focus on "Revolution Music." I'd call on our Indigenous musicians and artists to find their inspiration in the movement to start building our soundtrack. We have so much talent in our communities—some of the most exciting musicians on the planet are Indigenous, and I was excited about "calling them to action." I talked to many of my musician friends who *are* working on music right now and, although some are working on new music or have released new tracks recently, there wasn't much of a story. It seemed like a lazy idea. Maybe it was too obvious. Too simple. But then it happened.

The Round Dance Flash Mob Explosion

A round dance flash mob was planned and executed in Regina. The next night a round dance broke out inside West Edmonton Mall in Edmonton (North America's largest mall) during the busy Christmas shopping season. Then round dances started appearing everywhere: Saskatoon, Ottawa, North Bay, Regina, Prince Albert... the list goes on and on. There are currently round dance actions, traditional song and game flash mobs, and other peaceful music-based actions planned across Turtle Island. Just look at how many #rounddance posts there are on Twitter. On Wednesday, we saw YouTube video surface of a group of native brothers and sisters from Minnesota singing the "AIM Song" in the Canadian Consulate office in Minneapolis. Incredible. *The round dance revolution.* It's happening. Right? The music revolution is happening. And thank God (if there is a God…c'mon, you know my deal with all that) it doesn't look like Woodstock. Instead, it's a beautiful, peaceful, and inclusive action. We are being led by our drums. It's perfect. It's accessible. It's transportable. It's cheap (hey, we're on budgets, ya know). And it's a whole new form of direct action, protest and resistance. As Metro News Saskatoon reported: With flash mob round dances already occurring in Regina and Edmonton some…say the flash mob has become one of the more effective forms of protest. Compared to traditional methods of protest, the flash mob is a more engaging and welcoming way to spread a message.

Why This Matters

We are the Indigenous Peoples of this land. We have held unique worldviews and cultural and spiritual practices for thousands of years. So many of these practices included drums. As kids, we were told that the drum beat represents the heartbeat of Mother Earth. We were told our songs come from Mother Earth. We were told that our communities are only as strong as the sound of our drums. Then "they" came. And many of our drums went silent. Completely silent. Our songs were banned. Torn from our lives. Forcefully. Violently. But, although they were silent for a time, our old people kept their bundles. Some hid them. Some buried them. Then, slowly, the sound of our drums re-emerged. They started to spread through our communities again. They signalled hope. They signalled our return. Our drums were being used. And we began to gather again. We danced again. And our communities are slowly regaining their strength. It's perfect. It makes perfect sense. *A Round Dance Revolution.* It has reinvigorated and re-inspired our People. It has lifted the spirits of thousands. The act of the "flash mob" can be called "Political/Guerilla Theatre" but it's not politics in and of itself. It's a glimpse into who we are. It is perfect.

One Heartbeat: December 21, 2012

At 12:00 p.m. on Friday, December 21, thousands will gather on Parliament Hill to drum sing and dance—while thousands more will gather in communities across Turtle Island for round dances, songs, and prayers in support of all our relations. IdleNoMore: One Heartbeat Across Turtle Island Idle No More has called on all Nations to drum and sing across Turtle Island on December 21, 2012, at 12:00 p.m. Central Standard time, for a global synchronized Spiritual Awakening. We want to honour and recognize the Drum as it represents the heartbeat of Mother Earth and the heartbeat of our people. Indigenous peoples call on all people and nations to join us in solidarity in "One Heartbeat" through the Drum as we honour the ways of our Ancestors.

We have much to do to sustain this movement. We have long-term and short term planning to get underway. BUT. If we need to #SoundtracktheStruggle: it's already here. Our songs remind us that we're fighting for the land, our languages, our women, our children, and for our lives.

Round Dance Flash Mobs That Have Happened To Date:

Regina, SK
Edmonton, AB
Ottawa, ON
Regina, SK
North Bay, ON
Saskatoon, SK

Round Dance Flash Mobs Scheduled To Happen

Sault St. Marie, ON
Green Bay, WI
Rapid City, SD
Kamloops, B.C.
Prince Albert, SK
Duluth, MN
Fort McMurray, AB
Akwesasne Mohawk Territory

North Battleford, SK
Winnipeg, MB
Victoria, B.C.
Vancouver, B.C.
Kenora, ON
Moncton, NB
Grande Prairie, AB
Sarnia, ON
Tempe, AZ
Hamilton, ON
Brandon, MB
Burnaby, B.C.
Richmond, B.C.
Denendeh, NWT
Halifax, NS
Phoenix, AZ
Seattle, WA
Havre, MT
Billings, MT
Missoula, MT

Now the only question is, "Where will *you* be?"

Originally appeared on Revolution Per Minute *(rpm.fm), December 20,* *2012.*

KISIKEW ISKWEW, THE WOMAN SPIRIT

Nina Wilson

Misikwaskeek[6]

She was sick. All the stars above told her she had a lot to live for yet, but she just didn't know how she would make it to see any more mornings. She lay there looking through the smoke flaps, a star shot across that deep purple velvet backdrop where her relatives twinkled,

6   Drum Spirit

and she wondered if they beckoned her, or did they simply shine that way because there was no more pain there? She was there alone sick and dying. Many sat in council talking of what to do with her and they decided finally they could not risk the whole camp so they isolated her. She lay in sickness waiting for relief that wasn't coming, all alone. However, she was left with all she might need to keep her comfortable, as the people were not cruel, just afraid. She was placed in a lodge that was close to wood, water, and blankets and food. Knowing that her people were afraid of what was making her sick, she watched them all leave in sadness, some looking back at her in tears, before she sank into her bedding and cried herself to sleep. Late that night, she searched the sparkling sky for answers. She knew the stars were her relatives who left this world and they all looked so splendid, like not one of them missed her and a tear slid into her dark hair. Her breathing was laboured and she waited as the pain subsided, before she rolled to her side and watched the embers of the fire dance and roll hypnotically. She wondered how long it would be before she could no longer gather wood for herself. Winter would be coming and she wondered if she would survive that long, only to freeze to death. She drifted into troubling dreams where horses thundered across skies rolling with fire, where children sank into the grass to die. Dreams of lands parched, dusty, angry, as the winds refused to release the rain. Dreams where horses rumbled as they descended and the Earth held out her arms to receive their running beat. Restlessly she shuddered and the sweat on her brow was wiped by no one. No one was left to take care of her.

Like all good men, the sun rose to protect the people and shine on those who voiced those nightmares skyward, for correction. She slowly staggered from her bedding that morning, grateful she did not surrender to the Milky Way during the night. Tearless she sat in silence and prayed for sound. Something to echo throughout the small camp she was left at to say that she was not alone. She sat still, listening, and all she heard was her own steady heartbeat, and she missed her family and community so much that she had a hard time distinguishing the pain from loneliness from the sickness she carried. She rose to look for something to eat and to prepare to haul her water and get her wood for the day. As she gathered wood her energy spiralled and the pain in her chest was so bad, it finished off her ability to do any more. She

Idle No More march through downtown Toronto, January 11, 2013.
(JORDAN SNOBELEN)

lay down carefully in the grass and wept telling the Creator she did not want to die. She begged to be with her family and her friends, her community, and in her exhaustion, she gasped for air and just couldn't go any further. Her dream began and in it her heartbeat grew louder, stronger, until she realized that the vibration she felt did not come from her chest, it was coming from the ground. The beat was pulling her east, where a voice spoke out to her and told her: "Don't be afraid my Grandchild, I have come to give you a gift in which you will heal and live if you decide to accept what I am going to give you." She stirred slightly in her dream state and the voice continued, "I will be back. I have watched you suffer immensely and cry so I want to help you." She awoke to see who was talking to her and no one was around so she got up fast and scanned the area. No one was anywhere near her, so she stood and thought about that dream before she decided to continue on gathering the wood she needed for that day. Suddenly the sound from her dream, the heartbeat, filled the air. Dropping the wood, she tilted her head and listened. There it was again! The noise was coming from an area so she followed it, stopping as the sound stopped now and then, eventually making her way through short bush, shrubs, and longs grass. She stepped into a clearing and stood listening. Just as she was about to turn back because the sound of the heartbeat stopped, it started again and it was now closer than ever. It was drawing her, calling her. She didn't know how she managed to walk so far but she did and she felt no pain. It was then that she heard the voice from her dream. "I am glad you have come to accept the gift I am about to give you. It will heal you and heal others." Once again in her waking state, that beat came again and the sound was so very close. Looking about she finally saw where it was coming from. It was coming from an old tree trunk. The voice introduced itself, "I am Misikwaskeek (Drum Spirit)." A hide lying close to the tree trunk caught her attention and she stood looking at it, wondering where it had come from. The heartbeat sounded all over that meadow, into the shrub, the trees. The sound should have frightened her, but it did not, it soothed her somehow. Kneeling next to the hide and tree trunk, she let that heartbeat sink right into her, into her cells, her bones, her flesh, her heart, her smile, and her hair. She did not know why but the sound amplified her emotions and she wept tears not of sadness, but of love and compassion. She did not understand what was happening to her but she felt so at ease, so calm, so good.

Misikwaskeek told her to make what was about to be shared with her. She was to soak that hide, scrape it, and hollow that tree trunk out for a frame and tie the hide over it. Once she was done this, Misikwaskeek told her to hang it in the sun to dry it. She did all that she was instructed to do and slept fitfully. When Misikwaskeek returned later that night in her dream to check on her, he told her, "You have done well, Granddaughter, now listen carefully and learn." She was taught how to make an offering to the gift she was given, how to smudge it and how to feed it. He taught her how to make the drum stick and what songs were, and how to sing them, and what ceremonies they would accompany. He taught her the teachings of the drum and how to respect it. She was instructed to take the drum home to her people, and pass it down to the men because they cannot cleanse themselves as she could. Misikwaskeek told her the women own the drum, and receives its gift, because they carry that heartbeat of Mother Earth, the unborn, and the tree trunk represents Mother Earth's beings such as plants, medicines. The animal hide represents Mother Earth's children. Misikwaskeek told her she would receive the power to heal through song and prayer, and that drumbeat. For the next four days she sat with the drum and learned the teachings and songs for the different lodges and ceremonies. On the last night, Misikwaskeek told her to get ready and go home to her community and take this gift with her for the people. Before he left her dream he asked her if she noticed how strong she was, how she no longer had pains, how she was no longer weak and sick. By making the drum and doing all that was asked of her, she healed. The healing had started the moment she accepted the offering of healing. "Go now, Grandchild, go teach the man these teachings and these songs and he will become a Drum Keeper, I will live within that drum as long as you all respect and honour me, and I will heal you all in many ways."

At dawn, she awoke and packed her belongings and the drum she carefully bundled, and set off for her camp. When she got close to her community, she was stopped. The scouts said she would not be permitted into the village as she may get everyone else sick and they may all die. The woman said, "Please, look at me! I am well, healed! I brought with me the gift that healed me. I must share this gift with everyone!

Call everyone together, and I will present this gift as I was instructed to share." The camp all gathered around in a large circle and they were nervous, some were crying, some were afraid. She waited for them to be still and she began. She explained how she was given life and how she was healed and how she made the drum after Misikwaskeek spoke with her for several days. She unwrapped the drum and presented it to her people, and she sang all day and gifted them with its sacred teachings. She explained how the mind should work together with the drum and how this frees the people's thinking. After many days, the drum became a sacred gift all the people used in healing and in freeing their minds. Today this is still so.

Nootamew Maciwoyak[7]

It took one young woman to tell a group of her peers, that she wanted to hear the drums in support of Idle No More. She asked many singers if they could do a flash mob round dance, and one singer agreed, so they set out to do what they do best, not realizing how they become part of that flame within people. This was the beginning of the dancing and singing that were signature at the rallies and teach-ins all over the world, in numbers from 500 to 3,000 participants at any one time. Many of the young people who carried out the flash mobs did so in shopping malls and when I asked several of them why there, they said that the shopping malls made sense to them and were a warm place to go. I wondered why they were drawn to the shopping mall, and I attended several all over Canada and the United States. What I saw and experienced has changed me forever. I saw elderly grandmothers openly weep, and hold each other as tears streamed down their faces, and I saw women form barricades around men who sometimes were assaulted. I saw children holding signs and singing along with the adults. I saw white women join the circles and dance with tears streaming down their faces and white men stand with our men, as they were also moved to tears by the drum. On a deep cellular level, they know they too want freedom. They want change. They want to heal and be who they are.

The shopping malls built on stolen lands have been the epitome of consumerism, of capitalism, and of keeping up with what society

7   We Want To Heal

deems necessary in obtaining. The conscious realize that these institutions are part of the game, a manufactured colonial culture that keeps people tied to predatory consumerism, and the illusion of debt. The very basis of why lands were stolen to begin with. To have a young woman tell her peers what should happen, to participate in Idle No More, is a reminder that the spirit of Misikwaskeek is still around, healing and teaching. Women traditionally hold the teachings and the meanings of why the movement is much more than current governmental policy exposure and resistance. The essence of the movement is not about gender, class, race, belief, etc., it is about healing. Original teachings, actions, speaking, are all tied to Mother Earth, and her beings and children. Healing and reconciliation are two different concepts, and one cannot talk reconciliation when there is no closure on the land issues. There can be no healing when our people are still displaced, removed from the land. The land is directly tied to our languages, which guide who we are. We know we are now in that place of prophecy, because the women stood up, and they stepped forward with a gift, so we could all live. We are just beginning and have a lot of work to do as we follow the original instructions of spirit. Writing to change minds, ideas, action, history. To take a story, a teaching of an incident that occurred years ago, is to gift the world with what they will draw from each story for themselves. Kisikew Iskwew, the Woman Spirit, is taking back her power, so the children will live.

WHAT IF NATIVES STOP SUBSIDIZING CANADA?

Dru Oja Jay

There is a prevailing myth that Canada's more than 600 First Nations and native communities live off of money—subsidies—from the Canadian government. This myth, though it is loudly proclaimed and widely believed, is remarkable for its boldness; widely accessible, verifiable facts show that the opposite is true.

Indigenous people have been subsidizing Canada for a very long time.

Conservatives have leaked documents in an attempt to discredit chief Theresa Spence, currently on hunger strike in Ottawa. Reporters like Jeffrey Simpson and Christie Blatchford have ridiculed the demands of native leaders and the protest movement Idle No More. Their ridicule rests on this foundational untruth: that it is hard-earned tax dollars of Canadians that pays for housing, schools, and health services in First Nations. The myth carries a host of racist assumptions on its back. It enables prominent voices like Simpson and Blatchford to liken protesters' demands to "living in a dream palace" or "horse manure," respectively.

It's true that Canada's federal government controls large portions of the cash flow First Nations depend on. Much of the money used by First Nations to provide services does come from the federal budget. But the accuracy of the myth ends there.

On the whole, the money that First Nations receive is a small fraction of the value of the resources, and the government revenue, that comes out of their territories. Let's look at a few examples.

Barriere Lake

The Algonquins of Barriere Lake have a traditional territory that spans 10,000 square kilometres. For thousands of years, they have made continuous use of the land. They have never signed a treaty giving up their rights to the land. An estimated $100 million per year in revenues are extracted every year from their territory in the form of logging, hydro-electric dams, and recreational hunting and fishing.

And yet the community lives in third-world conditions. A diesel generator provides power, few jobs are available, and families live in dilapidated bungalows. These are not the lifestyles of a community with a $100 million economy in its backyard. In some cases, governments are willing to spend lavishly. They spared no expense, for example, sending fifty fully equipped riot police from Montreal to break up a peaceful road blockade with tear gas and physical coercion.

Barriere Lake is subsidizing the logging industry, Canada, and Quebec.

The community isn't asking for the subsidies to stop, just for some jobs and a say in how their traditional territories are used. They've been fighting for these demands for decades.

Attawapiskat

Attawapiskat has been in the news because their ongoing housing crisis came to the attention of the media in 2011. (MP Charlie Angus referred to the poverty-stricken community as "Haiti at 40 below.") More recently, Chief Theresa Spence has made headlines for her ongoing hunger strike. The community is near James Bay, in Ontario's far north. Right now, De Beers is constructing a $1 billion mine on the traditional territory of the Āhtawāpiskatowi ininiwak. Anticipated revenues will top $6.7 billion. Currently, the Conservative government is subjecting the budget of the Cree to extensive scrutiny. But the total amount transferred to the First Nation since 2006—$90 million—is a little more than one percent of the anticipated mine revenues. As a percentage, that's a little over half of Harper's cut to GST.

Royalties from the mine do not go to the First Nation, but straight to the provincial government. The community has received some temporary jobs in the mine, and future generations will have to deal with the consequences of a giant open pit mine in their backyard.

Attawapiskat is subsidizing De Beers, Canada, and Ontario.

Lubicon

The Lubicon Cree, who never signed a treaty or gave up their Aboriginal title, have waged a decades-long campaign for land rights. During this time, over $14 billion in oil and gas has been removed from their traditional territory. During the same period, the community has gone without running water, endured divisive attacks from the government, and suffered the environmental consequences of unchecked extraction.

Sour gas flaring next to the community resulted in an epidemic of health problems and stillborn babies. Moose and other animals fled the area, rendering the community's previously self-sufficient lifestyle untenable overnight. In 2011, an oil pipeline burst, spilling 4.5 million litres of oil onto Lubicon territory. The Lubicon remain without a treaty, and the extraction continues.

The Lubicon Cree are subsidizing the oil and gas sector, Alberta, and Canada.

What Will Canada Do Without its Subsidies?

From the days of beaver trapping to today's aspirations of becoming an energy superpower, Canada's economy has always been based on natural resources. With 90 percent of its settler population amassed along the southern border, exploitation of the land's wealth almost always happens at the expense of the Indigenous population.

Canada's economy could not have been built without massive subsidies: of land, resource wealth, and the incalculable cost of generations of suffering.

Overall numbers are difficult to pin down, but consider the following: Canadian governments received $9 billion in taxes and royalties in 2011 from mining companies, which is a tiny portion of overall mining profits; $3.8 billion came from exports of hydroelectricity alone in 2008, and 60 per cent of Canada's electricity comes from hydroelectric dams; one estimate has tar sands extraction bringing in $1.2 trillion in royalties over 35 years; the forestry industry was worth $38.2 billion in 2006, and contributes billions in royalties and taxes.

By contrast, annual government spending on First Nations was $5.36 billion in 2005 (it's slightly higher now). By any reasonable measure, it's clear that First Nations are the ones subsidizing Canada.

These industries are mostly taking place on an Indigenous nation's traditional territory, laying waste to the land in the process, submerging, denuding, polluting, and removing. The human costs are far greater; brutal tactics aimed at erasing native peoples' identity and connection with the land have created human tragedies several generations deep and a legacy of fierce and principled resistance that continues today.

Canada has developed myriad mechanisms to keep the pressure on and the resources flowing. But policies of large-scale land theft and subordination of peoples are not disposed to half measures. From the active violence of residential schools to the targeted neglect of underfunded reserve schools, from RCMP and armed forces rifles to provincial police tear gas canisters, the extraction of these subsidies has always been treated like a game of Risk, but with real consequences.

Break the treaty, press the advantage, and don't let a weaker player rebuild.

Idle? Know More.

The last residential school was shut down in 1996. Canadians today would like to imagine themselves more humane than past generations, but few can name the Indigenous nations of this land or the treaties that allow Canada and Canadians to exist.

Understanding the subsidies native people give to Canada is just the beginning. Equally crucial is understanding the mechanisms by which the government forces native people to choose every day between living conditions out of a World Vision advertisement and hopelessness on one hand, and the pollution and social problems of short-term resource exploitation projects on the other.

Empathy and remorse are great reasons to act to dismantle this ugly system of expropriation. But an even better reason is that Indigenous nations present the best and only partners in taking care of our environment. Protecting our rivers, lakes, forests and oceans is best done by people with a multi-millennial relationship with the land.

As the people who live downstream and downwind, and who have an ongoing relationship to the land, Cree, Dene, Anishnabe, Inuit, Ojibway, and other nations are among the best placed and most motivated to slow down and stop the industrial gigaprojects that are threatening all of our lives.

Movements like Idle No More give a population asleep at the wheel the chance to wake up and hear what native communities have been saying for hundreds of years: it's time to withdraw our consent from this dead-end regime, and chart a new course.

Originally appeared on The Media Co-Op, *January 7, 2013.*

WE ARE FREE HUMAN BEINGS, PART ONE
Lori M. Mainville

Life presents itself with some very important lessons. As an Indigenous mother and grandmother, and a third generation Residential School Survivor, I am often left to thoughts about healing, identity, and learning. Throughout the recent events of Idle No More, this has been more so. Much in this new legislation will impact the lives of my nation, my community, my family, my life. I sometimes wonder how we can stand up to all of these challenges.

I remember how, as a young reserve girl in Ontario, we would haul fresh water from the lake not too far from my grandmother's house. I remember her getting fish from nets in the same lake. Years later very few can live this way: there is no more clean water to drink from that lake, fewer fish, and limited social connections and interaction. Because of pollution from pulp mills and encroachment of settler communities, the natural law of the waterways was compromised.

In the 70s I attended a youth and elder conference in eastern Ontario. One elder told the audience that water would be sold in bottles in the future. No one could believe it. Selling water? Selling water in bottles? It couldn't be. Water is free, we thought.

Our treaties ensure that we are free, sovereign people. Our identities ensure that we are connected to all living things on the land. Natural law is what we brought to the treaties, it was how we governed ourselves, and how our spirit was connected through relations with the land. Settler governments, in the meantime, valued land in terms of commodity and control.

Now that I am older, and a grandmother, I realize that the free flow of water demonstrated to us that we were just as free as it is. We were guided by land, connected to it through soil and air. This gave us a deep sense of identity. In the present circumstances, and particularly in relation to these omnibus bills, everything is soon to be commoditized, exploited, polluted. It will be like the lake where I grew up. Our natural laws will be compromised, so dichotomized that our spirits will be forced to take on a much different meaning.

Legislation such as Bill C-45 serves to threaten our inherent right to protect our waterways, essentially impacting our right to maintain our connection to our culture and identity. This challenges our ability to maintain what little is left of our freedom as Indigenous Peoples. Woven into this legislation is a threat to our sovereignty. According to international law, treaties are negotiated with peoples who are sovereign. We never surrendered that sovereignty and our spiritual connection that forms our identity is intimately tied to our homelands.

Dene activist Melaw Nakehk'o helped to organize many of Yellowknife's rallies from the earliest days of the movement. (AMOS SCOTT)

Removing our lands, polluting our waters, and inhibiting our freedom as Indigenous people commodifies our spirit—a path in which healing, identity, and learning is radically changed. How do we resolve the continued threat to our existence? How do we enact our spirit? How do we enact our freedom?

The answer lies in the repossession, the protection, and the resilience of our identity, spirit, freedom, and sovereignty. Our freedom cannot be negotiated. We are free human beings governed by our own definition of our reciprocity to the land and to one another.

I am not Canadian, I am Anishinaabe.

"GIVE PEOPLE A HUB":
An Interview with Jarrett Martineau
Jarrett Martineau with Stephen Hui

STEPHEN HUI (SH): Jarrett Martineau calls himself a "grassroots media campaigner" for the Idle No More movement. A 35-year-old member of the Frog Lake First Nation in Alberta, he's a PhD student in indigenous governance at the University of Victoria. Martineau helped build the J11action.com website, which informed people of plans for more than 200 events on the indigenous-sovereignty movement's January 11 global day of action. He also helped organize UVic's #J16 Forum teach-in on Idle No More, which drew 1,200 in-person and online attendees on January 16. As the creative producer of the site Revolutions Per Minute, Martineau spreads the word about talented indigenous musicians. Earlier this month, RPM released *Idle No More: Songs for Life, Volume 1*, a downloadable compilation of songs by various artists. With the growth of Idle No More, RPM is now moving toward becoming an online radio network to support the movement. They're also looking at developing an Idle No More mobile app. Another thing that Martineau is working on is an Idle No More media hub, which will help organizers plan actions and connect with each other, and make it easier for participants to find events. I'm Stephen Hui of *The Georgia Straight* and I reached Martineau by phone in Victoria. I'd like to first ask: Would Idle No More exist without Twitter hashtags and Facebook events?

JARRETT MARTINEAU (JM): Absolutely, it would. But we would not at all have seen the speed with which people have been mobilized in the last seven weeks without it, and that has been fundamental to getting the kinds of numbers and range of activities that we've been seeing in the movement.

SH: What other Internet technologies have contributed to the growth of the movement?

JM: The use of the technology in the movement has reflected the growth of the movement itself. By that, I mean that people have used various forms of networked technology to connect with each other in the same way that different groups in the decentralized movement have self-organized. I think one big thing is the ubiquity of smartphones. That's been a huge part of it. I think you see that phenomenon through all the videos and all the information sharing that's gone on. That's a huge connecting point, especially live streaming. There's been a lot of amazing live streaming.

SH: How are organizers coming together and communicating with each other?

JM: I would say using any and all available means technologically. I've seen, and in my own experience, we've used social media to do further outreach to other people that are involved—you know, coders, hackers, web developers, requests for links to various forms of open-source stuff. There have been a lot of things like sharing Google Docs and various ways of building out collaborative information sharing. That's a really, really great thing that's been taken up by organizers. So people are sharing the information that they have really widely.

SH: You helped put together a website for the #J11 day of action that informed people about dozens of events around the world. How were you able to put that together so quickly?

JM: We started getting some support on Twitter from Anonymous, and I haphazardly threw out a request on my own channel, just saying, "Hey, would anybody be interested in doing some volunteer web

work to help build the Idle No More web presence?" Anonymous sent
it out on their channel, and I got this huge response from people all
offering to jump on board and contribute. I actually ended up getting
connected with a crew out of Toronto called Makook.ca. They had
already started doing the work of mapping out the tweet velocity of
all this stuff as this was taking off. I told them about the #J11 thing,
and they thought it was a great idea. We connected with them, and
we worked volunteer over the course of a couple days to get it set up.

SH: What are the key hashtags you monitor in relation to the movement?

JM: It's changed a little bit. Obviously, the #IdleNoMore one has
been common throughout. There have been other iterations that have
waxed and waned as it's gone on. For a period of time in December,
when this was really taking off, a lot of people were using the
#RoundDanceRevolution tag, which was cool. Obviously, that's still
kind of ongoing. I've since seen several iterations of #IdleNoMore that
have also caught attention. #DividedNoMore, #IdleKnowMore has
been interesting. I've seen people do the straight #INM tag as well. All
the #J tags, as well. So people have jumped off of the #J11 thing that
we did to set the particular day and used it now for the national day
of action, #J16. I've seen some for #J28, for the world one. I haven't
seen any #F ones yet. [There's also the satirical #Ottawapiskat and the
musical #SoundtracktheMovement.]

SH: As a media campaigner involved with Idle No More, what are you
looking forward to next?

JM: One thing that I've gotten a huge response from just in talking to
people—and this came up in our conversation at the UVic forum—is,
because this information is as decentralized as the movement itself,
people are having to go to a lot of different places to get a read on
what's happening. So what we've been talking about doing—and I'm
in the process of talking about this with the guys from Makook—is
building a collaborative media hub for people that want to organize
Idle No More-related events and basically give the opportunity for
people to do their own kind of #J11 site. So if people want to organize an education day or an art project or the various kinds of actions
that people want to do, we'd basically provide a bunch of resources to

set up their own live stream event or Google Docs-sharing collaborative international day of action or whatever it is. Basically, give back the tools that we started to build. Give people a hub where they can take it and run with it, and ideally have a central spot where people can see all the different kinds of Idle No More events that are coming up and that are ongoing.

Originally appeared on Straight.com, *January 18, 2013.*

REVOLUTIONARY ACTS OF NON-VIOLENCE DISEMPOWERS OPPOSITION
Waneek Horn-Miller

Violence is never simple; it is horrific and loaded with long-term devastating consequences. I know this from experience and have lived it up close and personal. Imagine yourself standing on a highway as Canadian armed forces tanks roll towards you flanked by soldiers in full combat gear. Army helicopters hover above with men hanging out the sides; guns are pointed at you. You watch as Warriors scream out in anger as the tanks roll closer and closer. Women are yelling at them to "get back!" and to us, "stay calm!" Your heart is beating so fast, as your body tries to adapt to the adrenaline coursing through your veins. You wait, hold your breath, and listen for that sound, the gunshot that will start and end it all. You are 14 years old, and your summer vacation has taken you to the middle of a war zone. You are scared, excited, and not fully comprehending what is going on. The one thing you do know is, you are unarmed and those guns are pointed right at you. You suddenly understand completely that your life could end at any second, and you wait.

It is August 20, 1990; the Canadian forces have stormed right into the disputed land where a golf course is set to expand onto a traditional burial ground. The Oka standoff would last another 27 days. I would be witness to horrific acts of violence, psychological warfare, and finally I would be stabbed in the chest, two centimetres away from my heart. Memories from that summer have both inspired me to achieve and haunted me. As I write this, my hands begin to shake as I once again feel the adrenaline flooding into me, getting me ready to run or to fight. I am writing this as an open letter. It is a window to my soul and my experiences. It is for anyone who even hinting at violent action. In the post-9/11 world, the consequences of violent action have changed. There are new terrorism laws that have extreme implications for not only the perpetrators, but for all indigenous people across North America.

I am reminded of watching a heated discussion, in the last days of the Oka Crisis, that violent action is not the solution. Some of the men wanted to shoot it out, guns blazing, and the women were arguing against it, telling them to keep a cool head. It was the women's role to remind them, that in the great law, it does not state that you fight till you die, but rather you fight till you win. After a long heated summer of provocation I understood the anger those men felt, and the attractiveness of a martyred death, but I was terrified watching as my life or death was being debated. In the end the debate for life and our future won out. Witnessing that made me understand as an indigenous person we are part of a larger community and we do not exist in a vacuum. All we do as individuals in peace and violence has a huge impact on all of us.

These memories, my new role as a mother, and my overwhelming love of all our children have infected me with a need to ensure no other 14-year-old has to face that kind of trauma. I think violent action is not the solution, and I have made it a life's mission to look for alternate ways of making change. Ones based on peace, cooperation, and inspiration. Over the last few months we have witnessed an awakening of both indigenous and non-indigenous peoples, inspired to stand up, speak out, and act. The power of Idle No More comes from the fact that it is open to all who lend their voices for change. The potent combination of flash mob round dances, social media, and teach-ins, has created a new generation of politicized people. It has done this because the essence of these acts is to raise awareness and because it is peaceful. People from all walks of life are drawn together, have engaged in dialogue and are personally inspired because of the simple message—that the peaceful future of this country matters to all of us.

It is hard to miss the understandable undertone of anger and frustration; I feel this to my core. I feel anger at the incredibly damaging impact of genocidal policies like the Indian Act, intentional mis-education of the Canadian public, and resulting racism. Rage at how they have ripped at the very fabric of our nations, communities and personal lives. It frustrates me that the most damaging legacy left is many of our people's lack of self-worth. How many see themselves only important for their anger, and their lives only worthwhile if given up in a fight. I remember a conversation I had with a reporter during Oka who asked me if I was ready to die. I said yes because if I died today, maybe my life would mean something. Looking back 23 years later, I think I have contributed more with my life than I would have with my death.

The most revolutionary act we could do is not visiting more violence on our communities, but rather to support our leaders in their fight by bringing the passion and power of Idle No More to the dismantling of the legacy of dysfunction, trauma, and violence that plagues our communities. We will disempower our opposition by ending the lateral violence expressed on each other and finally unify our nations by acts of respect, love, and peace. If our ancestors could speak to us today, they would tell us that violent action will never be fully off the table, but for the sake of our children, it should never be the first option, but rather the absolute last.

Peace and Power to all My Relations.

Originally appeared on Dividednomore.ca, *January 25, 2013.*

THE WHITE PAPER AND THE IDLE NO MORE MOVEMENT

Dale Turner

A recent public opinion poll on Aboriginal issues revealed some disturbing, but not surprising results—at least for Aboriginal people: two-thirds of those polled believe that Aboriginal peoples receive too much support from Canadian taxpayers; two-thirds believe that Aboriginal peoples are treated well by the federal government (74 percent in

Saskatchewan and Manitoba); and 60 percent nationally believe that most of the problems faced by native peoples are brought on by themselves (76 percent in Saskatchewan and Manitoba).[8] IPSOS Reid, the market research company that conducted the survey, should have done another poll, one that asked a simple question: Why do the majority of Canadians know so little about their own history? The recent poll demonstrates just how ignorant and uneducated many Canadians are when it comes to understanding Aboriginal peoples, and especially understanding the meaning of Aboriginal rights.

We need only to go back to 1969 to see how a government proposal to solve the so-called "Indian Problem" set in motion an early "Idle No More" political movement that has come to define contemporary Aboriginal politics.

The "Statement of the Government of Canada on Indian Policy, 1969," referred to simply as "The White Paper," laid out clearly and concisely Trudeau's vision of Canada as a "Just Society" and Indians' place in it. "Justice" required that Indians be stripped of their rights, that their lands be turned into private property, and their natural resources exploited for economic gain. In the process, Canadians would welcome and celebrate Indians' assimilation into mainstream Canadian society. Everyone wins. Once and for all, the federal government could get out of the Indian business and save taxpayers countless billions of dollars, and Indians could, once and for all, join the modern world and reap the full economic benefits of Canadian citizenship.

Indian leaders, especially in Alberta, reacted swiftly and passionately. The Chiefs of Alberta's angry response, outlined in the "Red Paper" (later expanded upon in Harold Cardinal's book The Unjust Society), demanded that contrary to unilaterally forcing Indians to assimilate into mainstream Canadian society, the federal government needed to recognize the sanctity of the treaty relationship and live up to its obligations. Indians from across Canada raised angry and frustrated voices in opposition to what they saw as a morally bankrupt view of justice that "killed the Indian to save the state" by unilaterally decimating their political rights.

8 IPSOS, "Fast Fallout: Chief Spence and Idle No More Movement Galvanizes Canadians Around Money Management and Accountability," www.ipsos-na.com/news-polls/pressrelease.aspx?id=5961 (accessed September 6, 2013).

Through the 1970s, this early "Idle No More" movement re-invented Indian politics, culminating in 1982 with the creation of Aboriginal rights in the second part of the Canadian Constitution. Perhaps IPSOS Reid could conduct a poll to see how many Canadians know what Section 35(1) is of their very own Constitution, never mind asking what it means politically.

The reality for Aboriginal peoples is that many Canadians—and I imagine most of those who participated in the poll—consider the 1969 White Paper vision of Canada as a "Just Society" the right way to think about Aboriginal peoples' place in Canadian life. But to say that Aboriginal people receive "too much" of Canadian taxpayers' money ignores the state's obligations to uphold its fiduciary responsibilities. To say that the government treats Aboriginal people well ignores its willful neglect, and its failure to negotiate in good faith and settle the hundreds of outstanding, now intergenerational, land claims. To say that Aboriginal people have brought most of their problems on them-selves is to violate what is fundamental to the relationship between Aboriginal and non-Aboriginal people: the shared belief that peace-ful co-existence is dependent upon our ability to sustain some kind of respectful dialogue.

The Idle No More movement must be viewed as Aboriginal peo-ples reminding Canadians (yet again), just as they did in 1969, that this dialogue has deteriorated and is in danger of disintegrating. This is because the federal government's solution to the Indian problem has not changed: extinguish Aboriginal title, open up Aboriginal home-lands to large multinational resource companies, and exploit natural resources for the economic benefit of "all" Canadians. Aboriginal peo-ples can either participate in this economic venture or be left behind to gradually, and inevitably, vanish from the world (then conclude that they brought their disappearance on themselves).

The root of the so-called "Aboriginal problem" is not money; it is that Aboriginal peoples are demanding recognition of their rights and nationhood and respect for their ways of being in the world. Without this fundamental respect, we cannot hope to find ways of co-existing peacefully. Yes, by necessity, peaceful co-existence is political, and eco-nomic development is central to aboriginal politics. It is also about re-newing our relationship to the environment: our survival, of all of us, is inextricably connected to how treat the world. Aboriginal peoples believe that we cannot possibly sustain the relentless exploitation of the earth's limited natural resources, but they do place the well-being of the earth at the centre of their moral and spiritual universe.

The Idle No More movement is reminding Canadians (yet again), that the federal government has failed to live up to its fiduciary obligations, and that Aboriginal ways of thinking and being-in-the-world lie at the core of Aboriginal understandings of their nationhood. If these understandings of nationhood mean that Aboriginal peoples live in a "dream palace," to use Jeffrey Simpson's condescending term, then so be it. At least it's better than the nightmare most Aboriginal peoples find themselves living today.

Originally appeared on Daleturner.org, *January 29, 2013.*

SINGERS AND DANCERS

The Round Dance Revolution, Ottawa, December 20, 2012.
(NADYA KWANDIBENS)

GIVING A S**T, AN IDLE NO MORE POEM

Janet Marie Rogers

The objective of civilizing us
Is to make Indian history
Become our permanent reality
The necessary objective
Of Native people is to
Outlast this attack,
However long it takes
To keep our identity alive*

We'll give them leather and
    feathers
Whatever gets their attention
We'll give them drums
    and songs
We'll give them stories
To see how long they'll wait
for us to turn angry

We work with an unseen power
Less a weapon More a legacy
An answer to NO MORE
    What now
Simultaneous exhaustion
And exhilaration
Determination thick as
Mineral rich soil negotiations

Not a mob
We are a peaceful people
For now we are the timber
Standing in the way
Getting ready for the grave

How close to death
Do they want us to come
Close enough to smell
What it smells like
We have the answers
And we're showing you
Can't see it you have to
Feel it

Have you nothing to say

The women in their jingles
The fellas in their jackets
The elders in their blankets
And the children
Waving signs
"No More, No More, No More,
    No More"

Flags flowing like
Winter snow
Landing on strong shoulders
Withstanding Blizzards
I see my people
Many shades of the same
So proud
We are the responsible
Incorrigible
Bravery in our veins
Fed by hunger
Writing love letters
Growing in momentum

We are revisiting wampum
We are witnessing commitment
That wasn't legislated by war
Or defense budgets
This is the People's love
For the mother
The movement has just begun

Bring it in
Send it out
Walk it around
Sing it loud
We keep beating
To keep the reality
Of the hate from playing
In our brains
We can take it
For we have good minds
And an army of ancestors
Walking with us

How can they counter that

Blissful ignorance
Sounds like holiday songs
on a Saturday morning
The same day she enters
Day 12 starving
For her people
Starving for attention
When the answers are
Within and right in front
Of us
Protect, react, resist,
Mobilize those to know
Motives working against
Natural law

So what can I do?

I'm going to fuck with
    your money
I'm going to
Talk to your children
Tell them the truth
And influence their reality
Is it true you can love a
    country but not
its government
Is this possible?
When the law says
A country is formed by
A council and registered
Like a baby's birth certificate
Within the courts the same
place that makes the laws,
so what came first?

Is the U.N. knocking at
    your door?
Or the ghosts of those
who circled your abode?
Are you finished dreaming
    of bacon
Are you begging for protection?
Shaking under your blanket
    hiding
From your own ancestors
    saying
"don't shame us"

crossing the line – getting close
closing the gap – moving in
finding the light – standing in it

making the sounds – painting
    in colour
getting it right – taking names
planning for the future
    – re-claim

releasing the medicine –
    pounding the drums
staying connected – stepping
    forward
rooted in humanity – giving
    a shit
reproducing history –
    recognizing equals
slam dancing – gathering
letting the answers find us

saying your piece – providing
helping the cause – craving
stealing home – forcing
    the point

attending to details – walking
    together
shooting craps – taking it
    with you

forward...

*original quote by John Trudell

Originally appeared on Indian
Country Today, December 24,
2012. Visit www.soundcloud.com/
janet-marie-rogers/giving-a-shit
to hear this poem read aloud
by the author.

CANADA, IT'S TIME. WE NEED TO FIX THIS IN OUR GENERATION.

Chelsea Vowel

Today is December 16, 2012 and Chief Theresa Spence has been on a hunger strike for six days. Contrary to what some media outlets are reporting, she is not doing this only to protest Bill C-45 or even the deplorable treatment her community has received since declaring an emergency last year. She has vowed to continue her hunger strike until the Prime Minister, the Queen, or a representative, agrees to sit down in good faith with First Nations leaders to rebuild what has become a fractured and abusive relationship. She is staying in a tipi on

Victoria Island, which sits below Parliament and the Supreme Court of Canada. Many native people across the country have been fasting to show their solidarity with Chief Spence, including Dene National Chief Bill Erasmus. Funds were raised to help three jingle dancers and song carriers from Whitefish Bay (where the jingle dance, a healing dance, originated) get to Victoria Island to honour Chief Spence. About 30 women from various communities participated in this event.

The Assembly of Manitoba Chiefs has issued a statement asking for as many people as possible to converge on Ottawa to support Chief Spence, and to demand that action be taken now to deal with long ignored indigenous concerns. The Assembly of First Nations published an open letter to the Governor General and to Stephen Harper to meet with Chief Spence, saying:

> The Government of Canada has not upheld nor fulfilled its responsibilities to First Nations, as committed to by the Crown including at the Crown-First Nations Gathering January 2012. Canada has not upheld the Honour of the Crown in its dealings with First Nations, as evidenced in its inadequate and inequitable funding relationships with our Nations and its ongoing actions in bringing forward legislative and policy changes that will directly impact on the Inherent and Treaty Rights of First Nations. Treaties are international in nature and further indigenous rights are human rights, both collective and individual and must be honoured and respected.

The Idle No More movement has been busy, with actions occurring all across the country in support of Chief Spence and in support of her message that the relationship between indigenous peoples and the Crown needs serious mending, now. Not all of these actions are being reported, so if you want to know what's actually going on, it's worth your while to follow the #IdleNoMore hashtag on Twitter. People are protesting peacefully and legally blockading roads as well as staging "teach-ins." Many more actions are being planned. We are not going away. These issues are not going to go away. Canada, it's time. We have to fix this relationship in our generation.

We all know that reading comments sections can be hazardous for your mental health, but there are some themes that continue to come up again and again any time native people are discussed in the media, and we need to address these beliefs. I have been trying my best on this blog to refute the myths and stereotypes, but I don't have all the free time in the world that I'd like, and so my "myth-busting list" remains unfinished.

Nonetheless, I am asking for the help of Canadians to combat these ugly lies. I make this plea, because these lies allow people like Stephen Harper to ignore a hunger strike. These lies allow people to throw up their hands in disgust and claim that native people are freeloading whiners who need to shut up and go away. These lies allow a nation to ignore its own history, to erase its own volition, to believe that someone else will fix this problem.

Politicians won't be the ones to fix what's wrong with Canada and its relationship with indigenous peoples. This is a job for regular people, dealing with one another as human beings, and right now indigenous people in this country are not being treated humanely. So I've compiled a list of stereotypes and lies that I think need to stop being spread and passed around as truth. Where possible, I've linked information to help dispel these harmful myths. I'd like to call this list the "READ A BOOK!" list, because I know that a lot of us want to scream this when we read those hateful comments saying these things over and over again.

Here is my "Read A Book" list of some things Canadians absolutely need to stop believing about us:

Native people don't pay taxes, OMG!
Actually, most of the over one million aboriginal people in this country do in fact pay taxes. The tax exemption people apparently know so little about applies to only about 250,000 people in the whole country and is extremely narrow.

Native people get free houses, blaaargh!
There are social housing units available on some reserves, but this is under a program that is also available to other low-income populations throughout Canada, and the number of people actually accessing these social housing units is vastly overrated in the minds of most Canadians. We need Canadians to be Idle No More too.

Native people get free post-secondary education, grrrr!
Only *some* Status Indians actually living on reserve are eligible for
any sort of Federal funding for post-secondary studies. Inuit only receive federal funding if they live outside Nunavut or the Northwest
Territories for a full year. Non-status Indians and Métis are not eligible and a great many Status Indians living on reserve who apply
for this funding are turned down. As of 2006, only three precent of
registered Status Indians had a post-secondary degree compared to
18 percent among the general Canadian population.

Native leaders are all corrupt and super rich and that's why their
people are poor, aaaargh!
This is the most common accusation thrown around it seems, with little in the way of evidence to back it up. Even Stephen Harper let himself rely on this stereotype to point the finger of blame at Chief Spence
back when Attawapiskat first declared its housing emergency. The
logical fallacy invoked in this repeated accusation, which is treated
as common knowledge, is rarely questioned and is tossed out there
even when the Federal Court finds no evidence of such. I have no
idea what it is going to take to get so many Canadians to stop saying
this as though it is established fact, when in fact it is only established
prejudice. In a nation packed to the teeth with political corruption,
it is staggering to witness the vitriol hurled at native communities
when those communities are some of the most highly regulated and
federally controlled places in Canada. I'd love to go into this in more
detail, and at some point I will, but let's leave it at this: these claims
lack evidence and need to stop being presented as established truth.

Native people are lazy, don't work, cry about things long
over and everything that happens to them is their own fault,
RAAAAAAAAAAAAAAAWR!
Indigenous issues affect all Canadians. The relationship between
Canada and indigenous peoples is unlike Canada's relationship with
any other group of people, and needs to be better understood, and
respected. I'm not even going to try to find a source that can refute this blatantly racist belief. There's just too much packed into
it. Stop. Stop using anecdotes about some guy you knew once. Stop

saying you lived by a reserve and you know it all. Stop saying that our concerns are not legitimate. Stop denying the colonial relationship that has never ended in this country. Stop pretending that colonialism is our fault.

Stop pretending you can't do something to change things. There are more ugly things being said about us, all of which will become more and more virulent as the days pass and this movement grows. If you need to confront more of these beliefs, the "Sh*t Canadians say to Aboriginal Women" video will quickly bring you up to speed on the kinds of things some Canadians are saying about us right now any time our issues are raised in the media. Don't let this continue, Canada. Together we need to make a change. That is what Chief Spence is asking for. That is what indigenous peoples are asking for. Many Canadians have been asking, "What can I do to help?" This is something you can do. Understand the issues yourself, and help other Canadians understand them better too. Don't let these beliefs remain "common knowledge" any longer. Challenge them, and challenge the politicians who rely on these stereotypes in order to justify ongoing colonialism. Support Idle No More. Demand that Stephen Harper meet with Chief Spence and other leaders. Demand change. Make change. Live change.

For all our sakes.

Originally appeared on apihtawikosisan.com, *December 16, 2012.*

"WAKING UP TO THE BEAUTY":
An Interview with Chickadee Richard
Chickadee Richard with Leah Gazan

LEAH GAZAN (LG): I'm really honoured to have you here today, Chickadee. I know you have spent a lot of time fighting for Indigenous rights, Indigenous women, and have been a part of political movements for a long time. I'll begin by asking, why did you get involved with Idle No More?

CHICKADEE RICHARD (CR): First of all, I have never been idle (laughs). I started with Idle No More by wanting to see what it was all about. I wanted to meet the founders to see how real and committed they were. In the Anishinaabe world you have to see what is out there, what is real and not, and what you want to be a part of. When I met with the founders, I told them that many have always been on the front lines of many issues. I also wanted to make sure that the young people were able to be involved. There was a time that nobody listened to the Native youth, like when they walked across Canada to bring attention to issues pertaining to all of us. As a result, the Assembly of First Nations (AFN) and the Assembly of Manitoba Chiefs (AMC) now have a youth component. In today's world, our youth are looking for a different kind of leadership. I wanted to make sure they were not dismissed. I believe Idle No More is a different kind of vehicle for them, something they want to be a part of.

LG: One of the things that you have been involved in is the advocacy of Indigenous women. What in Idle No More did you specifically see as the role for women?

CR: I see it as more magnified than ever. While some might have been silenced in the past, women are bringing forth issues and concerns more than ever now. I have especially seen young women stepping up and speaking to leadership saying: "Your leadership is not working and maybe it's time to try something else." They remind us that our traditional governments were based on clan systems with clan mothers. These powerful women chose the leaders, people like headmen who speak for the people during treaty making. Idle No More inspired women to re-enact their traditional roles and responsibilities and to carry this with honour and dignity. Women teach us about the protection of life, water, land, and how we are all walking towards that good life that's not just for First Nation people, but for all. Not to disrespect the men, but women are life givers. We conceive life and carry sacred gifts that can create beautiful nations, beautiful people. There are even some gifts we don't know we even carry, like the ones we might deliver to babies. We experience life distinctly as women, and carry much knowledge.

Once we start to unravel the truth of what colonization has done to us and understand why behaviours are the way that they are, people are going to understand how important the role of women is and how we need this more than ever. Once we comprehend those divide and conquer tactics that have been used against us, we will wake up to the beauty women present to us. We will also begin to understand how women connect us to Mother Earth. Like our Mother, women deliver to us everything we need, they provide for us and nurture us into maturity. This is demonstrated in the work women have always done, especially through the way women take care of water. In ceremony women carry water, teach about it, and study its sacredness—exploring what it means to us. They show us that how we live with water is how we carry our life. Because of this work our ancestors were able to carry on lives, teachings, and ceremonies. It ensured our people were strong, loving, and connected to everything in the Universe. Taking care of water ensured that we were included in Creation.

LG: That's really beautiful what you shared. You mentioned that women have the traditional role of being water carriers, and we are fighting for our waters right now against these omnibus bills. Do you think the Idle No More movement has helped revive a respect for the role of women in our communities?

CR: I think so, some young men out there have been conditioned to believe that women—and in particular Indigenous women—are objects, that they are disposable. We see this in the violence against women across our nations, in the colonization we experience. There is still much work to do, of course, but I've witnessed more men who recognize women as their mothers, aunties, grandmothers and see their relatives as sacred. Many say things like "I respect women," "I walk with women," "I protect women." Some even say: "I want to protect my sisters so no more go murdered or missing," or "I want to support my auntie in fights for her children," or "I want to honour my grandmother who is against development." Because of what men have been taught about women, we have all been marginalized from one another. It takes a lot of courage for men to stand against what they have been taught. We haven't seen this for a long time, it is so moving.

LG: During the Idle No More movement we spent a winter dancing and meeting and now we have now moved into teach-ins and panels. I sometimes hear that the movement is fading. What are your thoughts on that?

CR: Some people say it is redundant, that one rally is like the next rally, and one dance is like the next. I don't believe that. I believe that every day is new, that every dance is new, that each has its own energy and its own life. Each brings forth something that is unseen. I believe every rally opens hearts and minds and this energy comes in waves—from small ones that grow stronger until they dissipate and come back again. Many of the events of Idle No More crossed into so many realms. They connected us to the spiritual movement of Creation; the spirit of Mother Earth, the spirit of the water, the spirit of the land. Some of the mainstream has lost this sense of spiritual connection or lost a sense of what it looks like but it's there. People with spirit can see it, know it, recognize it, and flow with it as it rises and falls. Today some might not see it so clearly, tomorrow others will. Some go with that natural flow, that energy to love, to nurture, to change things that they see is wrong—which is what we saw over the past winter and we will see again.

LG: You have spoken a lot about the active role of woman in the movement. We also know that many women from our nations, for whatever their life reasons (it could be being in abusive relationships, experiencing poverty, stresses, or violence, or something else) may not have had the opportunity to participate fully in Idle No More. Where do they fit in the movement?

CR: They are just as important as the voices we hear, and they are not forgotten. I have a sister lost to the streets and addictions. She lost five babies who are in care. She and my family know what society has done to our sisters and aunties and daughters. When she comes back—and she always does—we welcome her to our circle, to our community, to our family, to our ceremonies, to our drum, to our songs—because they are hers too. Maybe one day she will be free and have strength to speak loudly but when we demonstrate and rally, voices like hers are with us. When we speak about water and land and life everyone is included in this conversation. That's the way our people usually are: everyone is included, everyone is considered. Some sisters may be walking a different path today but all walk towards the same goal of the good life. Maybe one day they will find their voice, maybe one day they will sit with us, maybe one day they will be a powerhouse of strength. Maybe one day they will even lead us. Maybe their experiences will enlighten people and bring reality to the effects of colonization, the effects of residential school, the effects of displacement from our land, displacement of our culture— and we'll all be better off and stronger. They certainly know a lot.

LG: One of the criticisms I have often heard about the INM movement was that there were a lot of divisions and the media focused on this division in leadership, politics, and even at the round dances. What is your perception of the division during the height of the INM movement?

CR: Well, there are lots of things to say about this. First, I think media formed part of the propaganda to divide and conquer our people even further. Second, sometimes our people disagree, for good reasons or not, and we just happened to hear more about it this time. Third, I think some people are so conditioned to believe that if something good is coming along, something bad must be coming too. Lastly, and one of the most important, is that I believe we have been taught to think in a certain pattern and this makes us easier to control. Sometimes our people think that thinking for oneself is wrong, especially if it's against chief and council, government, men, or so forth. Over time you see how media works against certain ideas and in the favour of the government and multinationals, trying to create pretty pictures—when you know there are oil spills, the tar sands, and affected lives. In fact, I think that alternative media is somewhat better than the pretty picture the main-stream media is trying to sell so we should pay some more attention to them. Anyways, we often let people tell us what to think.

We need to see the world for what it really is and we need to refo-cus our actions. We need to reset our goals and this should overcome any division or temptations to deal-make with chiefs or government or whomever. In Idle No More, the focus is the protection of water, land, and the future generations, the unborn. These are our common focus, a common focus for a good and better life. Don't let forces like the media distract from this.

We also need to model this work. The very first time I spoke at INM at the very first rally at the Legislative building, I spoke about life and how we can be unified. We have to be role models and examples of that kindness, that love, that unity. We have to role model this so our young people see that this is possible, that we can make change through words and ideas. You said that change begins with us, and people have been so conditioned by colonization, by the media. You could sit back and think about the disunity, about how people don't want to work together, about how unhealthy we are. I can't do this. The INM movement is about looking clearly in front of us, not behind. We mostly know what happened, all the wrongs that have been done. Sometimes we need to talk about this but today it is about looking ahead and protecting what we have, what is left. We cannot stand by and watch the devastation of our lands, the contamination of our waters, and the deaths of our young ones. We need to take action and make the change we want to see.

LG: If there were something that you could say to all Canadians to inspire a more respectful and kind relationship in this country, what would you say? What advice would you give?

CR: I think one of the original teachings that I express a lot is treat people how you want to be treated. Settlers need to come back to their original teachings, to their faiths, and find that true meaning of compassion, of humanity, of love, of kindness. I think they need to find their faith and walk in it. This will begin a journey into understanding how when they came to this place they were most often met with kindness and respect and this has not always been returned. Many have come to our lands and disrespected who we are as Indigenous peoples. This is not acceptable anymore, and everyone needs to be accountable for their own actions now. Indigenous peoples did not create the devastation of our lands, the contamination of our waters, and the deaths of our young people on our own. It will take all of us to listen, learn, and work together to walk into the future.

EVERYTHING YOU DO IS POLITICAL, YOU'RE ANISHINAABE.
Or, What Idle No More Is To Me
Ryan McMahon

"Everything you do, Grandson, is going to be political. You're Anishinaabe."

Those are the words of my Grandmother. My Grandmother wasn't
a politician or a cultural leader in any sort of way. She was a bead
worker and a master of the various trades that involved moose hides.
She was a good hunter and an excellent fisherman. One of my first
memories I have of my Grandma was her pulling up to my parents'
house in the middle of the afternoon with a dead deer she had shot
while hunting in Minnesota. We lived in Ontario. She drove across the
US/Canada border with a dead buck on the hood of her car. I imagine
the Customs officer had a hard time letting her cross that day. I can
hear her stubborn defence for bringing the deer across the border in
this way—"I'm Indian...I have to eat something." In retrospect, maybe
she was political. Accidently political. But still, political nonetheless.
Stubborn. But politically so.

I loved my Grandmother. I talk about her a lot because I learned
a lot from her. Sure, she could be miserable at times and if you didn't
know her well, her attitude may have rubbed you the wrong way, but
she was always "honest." For better or worse, she let you know what
she was thinking. You knew where she stood on issues—you had no
choice. In her "honesty" you'd get anger, truth, comedy (mostly of the
accidental sort), stories and the pain of a history I couldn't understand.
It's a pain I knew existed but I had no idea why it existed or how it got
there. My Grandma, she's a product of the Indian Residential School
system here in Canada. She lived with the pain and the memories of being abused for years at the Residential School at Fort Frances, Ontario
(Couchiching). She lived the common experience of those that survived
the school systems. Years of wandering. Painful, broken relationships.
A personal mess that was impossible to begin to clean up. The result:
a trail of stories about broken people, families, and communities. A
broken circle. A beautiful, kind, gentle, but broken circle.

It turns out I'm a product of the Indian Residential School system too. I didn't endure what my ancestors did—thankfully. Instead, I
experience it in different ways. I wasn't raised with an understanding
of my culture, language, or ceremony. I was never told "what being
Anishinaabe was." I knew we were "Indian," I just didn't know what
that meant. There was a lot of shame. There was a lot of weird "don't
talk about it-ness." A major scar that I carry(ied) for a long time was
the feeling of "not being enough." Whether it was looking for a hug

Feeling the spirit, Parliament Hill, December 21, 2012.
(NADYA KWANDIBENS)

from my mother (I don't remember too many of these) or trying to fit in during visits to the Rez—I never felt "enough." Through school I was told I wasn't "Indian" by my cousins or other people on the reserve and without a place to "belong to" there was a large empty spot in my heart. A broken circle, if you will. Colonization. You just about beat me. Just about. I've struggled a lot through my life. I've struggled with childhood pain and trauma and I spent years not knowing why I was such a mess. My low point was waking up drunk on the streets of Toronto and not remembering how I got there. I was a mess. I had been a mess for a long time. I was slowly killing myself with booze.

I was saved by an Elder named Roger Jones, an old man from Shawanaga First Nation. He took me in. Nurtured me. Taught me. Talked to me. Told me about the land and what it gives us. He taught me about medicines. He taught me about spirit. As I listened to Roger tell me about the land and the importance of the connection to it, I realized that I *was* "enough" and that I had the connection he spoke of. I realized that the years of not feeling "enough" were a waste. I realized I was Anishinaabe. I had the connection he spoke of. I was raised in the bush. I was raised hunting and fishing. I was taught how to subsist off the bounty and beauty of Mother Earth. Finally, I connected with "being Anishinaabe." I couldn't dance a crow-hop but I could shoot the moose needed to make the drum to sing one. My connection and reconnection to the land is what makes me Anishinaabe. It guides me. It teaches me. Today, when in need, I turn to my bundle, my pipe, my drums, and my medicines, which all come from the land—it is what makes me Anishinaabe. Without the land and without my bundle, I am nothing. Without the land I am not Anishinaabe. So if you take away the land (literally or figuratively) from my people—what are we left with? Being "Canadian"? Being "like everyone else"? Is that not genocidal? The land is my "God" and we as Anishinaabe Peoples are not ready or willing to give you our "God."

The understanding I now have about what it means to be Anishinaabe has brought me back into the circle. It has brought me back to community. Back to walking with values and understanding what it means to be a man, a father, a husband, a son, and a contributing member to the larger conversation. It has helped me repair the circle that was broken in my Grandmother's life. It's not fixed. I don't know that it can be. It's being repaired though. The Idle No More movement is an incredible one. We see people standing up and being counted. We see people participating in resurgence—even if they don't really know what the resurgence is about (yet). The Idle No More movement is not only unsettling the larger Canadian population but it's about unsettling ourselves as Indigenous Peoples. It's my opinion that the aim of the movement must be to continue unsettling ourselves as Indigenous Peoples—the hard work of decolonization is happening right in front of us in real time, on Twitter, Facebook, and in shopping malls. Crazy, huh?

We must continue to unsettle ourselves. The learning and the growth of our Nations depends on putting our collective histories into context so as to move forward while being led by our inherent world views/teachings/traditional governance structures. We have a deep and incredibly poisonous relationship with the Indian Act and the long roots of colonization. The Idle No More movement calls for an end to this relationship. The Idle No More movement is beginning to reawaken the spirits of the People. We have a lot to *unlearn*. We have to find our place in the circle and Idle No More is calling people back to the circle. We're in the process of repairing ourselves as individuals, families, communities, and Nations. Everything we do is political—we are Anishinaabe.

Originally appeared on Decolonization: Indigeneity, Education & Society (*decolonization.wordpress.com*), *January 1, 2013.*

WHY FIRST NATIONS MOVEMENT IS OUR BEST CHANCE FOR CLEAN LAND AND WATER

Winona LaDuke

As Attawapiskat Chief Theresa Spence enters her fourth week of a hunger strike outside the Canadian parliament building, thousands of protesters voice their support in Los Angeles, London, Minneapolis, and New York City. Spence and the protesters of the Idle No More movement are drawing attention to deplorable conditions in native communities and the recent passage of Bill C-45, which sidesteps most Canadian environmental laws.

Put it this way: Before the passage of Bill C-45, 2.6 million rivers, lakes, and a good portion of Canada's three ocean shorelines were protected under the Navigable Waters Act. Now, only 87 are protected. That's just the beginning of the problem, which seems not to have drawn much attention from the general public.

"Flash mob" protests with traditional dancing and drumming have erupted in dozens of shopping malls across North America, marches and highway blockades by aboriginal groups and supporters have emerged across Canada and as far away as New Zealand and the Middle East. This weekend, hundreds of native people and their supporters held a flash mob round dance, with hand drums and singing, at the Mall of America in Minneapolis, again as a part of the Idle No More protest movement. This quickly emerging wave of native activism on environmental and human rights issues has spread like a wildfire across the continent.

Prime Minister Harper's Push for Tar Sands and Mining

A group of natives from Aamjiwnaang First Nation in Sarnia, Ontario, pitched a pickup truck across the tracks of a Canadian National Railway spur and blocked train traffic Friday in support of the Idle No More protest in Ottawa. The blockade began just after Boxing Day, that famed Canadian holiday, and has continued.

The Aamjiwnaang blockade is one of hundreds. A centre of controversy is the proposed Northern Gateway pipeline, which would cost $6 billion and bring tar sands from Alberta to the Pacific. The pipeline will cross over 40 native nations, all of whom have expressed opposition. The legislative changes could expedite approval of this and many other projects—all of which are in aboriginal territories.

"Idle No More" is Canadian for "That's enough BS, we're coming out to stop you," or something like that. Canada often touts a sort of "better than thou" human rights position in the international arena and has, for instance, a rather small military, so it's not likely to launch any pre-emptive strikes against known or unknown adversaries, and has often sought to appear as a good guy, more so than its southern neighbour. More than a few American expatriates moved to Canada during the Vietnam war, and stayed there, thinking it was a pretty good deal. That is sort of passé, particularly if you are a native person. And particularly if you are Chief Theresa Spence. Spence is the leader of Attawapiskat First Nation—a very remote Cree community from James Bay, Ontario, which is at the bottom of Hudson Bay. The community's 1,549 on-reserve residents (a third of whom are under the age of 19) have weathered quite a bit, including the fur trade, residential schools, a status as non-treaty Indians, and limited access to modern conveniences such as toilets and electricity. This is a bit commonplace in the far north, but it has become exacerbated in the past five years.

Enter De Beers, the largest diamond mining enterprise in the world. The company moved into northern Ontario in 2006. The Victor Mine reached commercial production in 2008 and was voted "Mine of the Year" by the readers of the international trade publication *Mining Magazine*. The company states that it is "committed to sustainable development in local communities." But this is where the first world meets the third world in the north, as Canadian MP Bob Rae discovered last year on his tour of the destitute conditions in the village. Infrastructure in the subarctic is in short supply. There is no road into the village eight months of the year; during the other four months, during freeze-up, there's an ice road. A diamond mine needs a lot of infrastructure. And that has to be shipped in, so the trucks launch out of Moosonee, Ontario. Then, they build a better road. The problem is that the road won't work when the climate changes, and already stretched infrastructure gets tapped out.

There is some money flowing in, that's for sure. A 2010 report from De Beers states that payments to the eight communities associated with its two mines in Canada totalled $5,231,000 that year. *Forbes* magazine reports that diamond sales by the world's largest diamond company "increased 33 percent, year-over-year, to $3.5 billion" and that De Beers "reported record EBITDA of almost $1.2 billion, a 55 percent increase over the first the first half of 2010."

As the group Mining Watch Canada notes, "Whatever Attawapiskat's share of that $5 million is, given the chronic underfunding of the community, the need for expensive responses to deal with recurring crises, including one that De Beers themselves may have precipitated by overloading the community's sewage system, it's not surprising that the community hasn't been able to translate its...income into improvements in physical infrastructure." Last year, Attawapiskat drew international attention when many families in the Cree community were living in tents.

The neighbouring village of Kashechewan is in similar disarray. They have been boiling and importing water. The village almost had a complete evacuation due to health conditions, and as Alvin Fiddler, Deputy Grand Chief of the Nishnawbe Aski Nation, a regional advocacy network, told a reporter, "Fuel shortages are becoming more common among remote northern Ontario communities right now." That's because the ice road used to truck in a year's supply of diesel last winter did not last as long as usual. "Everybody is running out now. We're looking at a two-month gap" until the ice road is solid enough to truck in fresh supplies, Mr. Fiddler said.

Kashechewan's chief and council are poised to shut down the band office, two schools, the power generation centre, the health clinic, and the fire hall because the buildings were not heated and could no longer operate safely. "In addition, some 21 homes had become uninhabitable," according to Chief Derek Stephen. Those basements had been flooded last spring, as the weather patterns changed. (Just as a side note, in 2007, some 21 Cree youth from Kashechewan attempted to commit suicide, and the Canadian aboriginal youth suicide rate is five times the national average.)

Both communities are beneficiaries of an agreement with De Beers.

The Lost Boys of Aamjiwnaang

Back at Aamjiwnaang, the Ojibwe have blockaded the tracks. Those are tracks that are full of chemical trains, lots of them. There are some 62 industrial plants in what the Canadian government calls Industrial Valley. The Aamjiwnaang people would like to call it home, but they've a few challenges in their house.

There's a recent *Men's Health* magazine article called "The Lost Boys of Aamjiwnaang." That's because the Ojibwe Reserve of Aamjiwnaang has few boys. Put it this way: In a normal society, there are about 105 boys born per 100 girls. That's the odds for a thousand years or so. However, at Aamjiwnaang, things are different. Between 1993 and 2003, there had been two girls born for every boy in the tribal community, one of the steepest declines ever recorded in birth gender ratio. As the reporter for *Men's Health* notes, "These tribal lands have become a kind of petri dish for industrial pollutants."

This trend is international, particularly in more industrialized countries, and the odd statistics at Aamjiwnaang are indicative of larger trends. The rail line known as the St. Clair spur carries Canadian National and CSX trains to several large industries in Sarnia's Chemical Valley. Usually four or five trains move through each day, all full of chemicals. The Ojibwe have faced a chronic dosage of chemicals for 25 years, and are concerned about the health impacts. They are also concerned about proposals to move tar sands oil through their community in a pre-existing pipeline known as Line Nine.

The Idle No More movement is further spurred by what Clayton Thomas Muller, a representative of the movement, calls "the extremist right wing government of Steven Harper," a government that seems intent on selling the natural wealth of the Canadian (aboriginal) north to the highest bidders in a multinational market. The recent passing of the omnibus budget Bill C-45, which gutted 30 years of environmental legislation, was approved by the Senate in a 50-27 vote.

Aboriginal leaders charge the Conservative government with pushing the bill through without consulting them. They note the bill infringes on their treaty rights, compromises ownership of their land, and takes away protection for Canada's waterways and most of the environment. Since Canada's economy is largely based on exploiting natural resources at an alarming rate, moving into a leading position in the world in terms of greenhouse gas emissions, fracking, and lacing pristine water with cyanide from new mines, it's convenient to gut the environmental laws. It's also convenient to violate the international laws which are treaties.

Start Seeing Indians

In the United States, the native community has been coming out in numbers and regalia to support the Canadian native struggle to protect the environment—drawing attention at the same time to similar concerns and issues here in the US. For instance, Ojibwe from the Keewenaw Bay Community in Michigan rallied against a Rio Tinto Zinc mine project, while Navajo protesters in Flagstaff, Arizona, continued opposing a ski project with manufactured snow at a sacred mountain.

Pamela Palmater, a spokesperson for the Idle No More movement in Canada, urges the larger community to see what is occurring across the country as a reality check.

"The First Nations are the last best hope that Canadians have for protecting land for food and clean water for the future," she said. "Not just for our people but for Canadians as well. So this country falls or survives on whether they acknowledge or recognize and implement those aboriginal and treaty rights. So they need to stand with us and protect what is essential."

Meanwhile, Chief Theresa Spence is still hoping to meet with Prime Minister Stephen Harper, urging him to "open his heart" and meet with native leaders angered by his policies.

"He's a person with a heart but he needs to open his heart," she said. "I'm sure he has faith in the Creator himself and for him to delay this, it's very disrespectful, I feel, to not even meet with us."

The reality is that Attawapiskat, Aamjiwnaang, and Kashechewan are remote native communities that receive little or no attention until a human rights crisis of great proportion causes national shame.

Facebook and social media equalize access for those who never see the spotlight. (Just think of the Arab Spring.) With the help of social media, the Idle No More movement has taken on a life of its own in much the same way the first "Occupy Wall Street" camp gave birth to a multitude of "occupy" protests with no clear leadership.

"This has spread in ways that we wouldn't even have imagined," said Sheelah McLean, an instructor at the University of Saskatchewan and one of the four women who originally coined the "Idle No More" slogan.

"What this movement is supposed to do is build consciousness about the inequalities so that everyone is outraged about what is happening here in Canada. Every Canadian should be outraged."

Actually, we all should be outraged, and Idle No More.

Originally appeared on the blog of Yes Magazine, *January 9, 2013.*

DANCING IN A MALL

Niigaanwewidam James Sinclair

back
in the Beginning
repeating these stories
like a drop
pooling
in fountains of time
linoleum waves
in circles of ancestors

Naanaboozho is here, she is here.
here.here.here.
born with a stone
dropping dripping
into ndns gathered
from children.
of sacrificed mothers
and windy fathers

sent
on journeys
to closed store windows
here
our lives
are born
exploding through breath
into pipes filled with black

two steps
now
don't pause
to
dream see
the
earth move
howa

there is no end
there is no end
there is no end
that is the story when we tell it.
there is no end
the flood
is always a beginning
a return.

writing with our feet
we speak.
in the air
conditioning.
the drum
like petals
on hide
our link

so in the winter we
danced
looking for
mom
and dad
we spoke we walked we danced
we dreamed
and we said no more and

we remade
we remade
we remade
the paper walls.
we remade
we remade
we remade
the world

here, in our repeating
floods
our fables

our births
our families
ourselves
in the hole of fluorescent light
we continue

Ha ya hey ya
   we live
Ha ya hey ya
   we live
Ha ya hey ya
   we live
Ha ya hey ya
   we live

Originally appeared in the Summer 2013 issue of Matrix Magazine.

WE NATIVES ARE DEEPLY DIVIDED. THERE'S NOTHING WRONG WITH THAT

Hayden King

I often find myself surrounded by Mohawks. I've worked in Six Nations territory for the balance of my career and many good friends are Haudenosaunee. In fact, despite being Anishinaabe I often find myself identifying with the two-row wampum or Great Law of Peace. But there are also things I just don't get about those Mohawks (and Cayugas, Oneidas, etc.). They like to claim Anishinaabe land despite overwhelming evidence that it's ours; they make political appeals to peace, power, and righteousness, us to truth, humility, and love; and curiously, when they round dance, they do it in the opposite direction! The point here is that while we share a lot of important traits, there is also much that differentiates us. This fact, or the fact that there are 60-odd unique indigenous nations in Canada (scattered across 600 communities), is lost on Canadian punditry, media, and most of the public generally. Recent attempts to interpret the Idle No More movement have resulted in conclusions of sudden divisions, fracturing, and "chiefs losing control." But in reality the differences of opinion among people, these cleavages, have always existed and some are natural.

Outside of the national political and cultural differences, one of the most noticeable rifts within the Idle No More movement exists between those who see the band council as part of the problem and those who see it as a solution, a debate stretching back to the late 1800s. Many of the former group view band councils as representative of the Indian Act and a system that prevents any real power to affect change (largely due to restrictions in the Act and policy direction required by funding arrangements). Ultimately, it's a system that forces bands to be accountable to the federal government, not community members. Then there are supporters of the band council, who feel chiefs are best suited to lead the transition away from the Indian Act. This is a position taken by band councils that comprise the Anishinaabek Nation in Ontario or the Federation of Saskatchewan Indian Nations. Indeed, there are often good people working towards the resurrection of more authentic governments or the restoration of treaty relationships, but through a less-than-perfect framework.

As for the aforementioned treaties, they are the source of yet another division: communities with a treaty versus those without. The latter are distinct from much of the movement and advocate a better process to create treaties or some mechanism to share the land in the absence of treaties (this latter perspective is a reflection of the growing disapproval of modern treaties). Both non-treaty perspectives advocate jurisdiction over unsurrendered lands. Finally, there are those who have less connection to the band council, the Indian Act, or a treaty. These are Métis and Inuit peoples, but also Dene, Salish and Maliseet peoples in cities and suburbs. Their concerns range from obtaining Aboriginal rights off the reserve, to protection for ecosystems, an alleviation of poverty, a national inquiry on missing and murdered indigenous women, adequate access to education, and on, and on (joining them in the streets are non-Native Canadians expressing solidarity for some or all of the above).

The conclusion of this terse overview of the diverse interests within the movement illustrates that there cannot be a parsimonious message except that federal policies are failing Indigenous peoples. One of the primary reasons for that failure is the continued belief that we're all the same, which is manifesting in one size fits all policy prescriptions. This is a narrative that also leads to misconceptions about factionalism. But as my Mohawk friend and colleague Professor Rick Monture says, "It's strange to call differences of opinion 'factionalism;' we just call it democracy." It's an important point. While we all may dance to a similar beat, our footwork can take us in different directions. And there is nothing wrong with that.

Originally appeared in The Globe and Mail, *January 9, 2013.*

#IDLENOMORE PROVIDES US WITH OPPORTUNITY TO EXAMINE NATIONHOOD

Tara Williamson

I've been starting to feel a little tired. Like thousands of other relatives across Turtle Island and the world, I have been participating in actions and dialogue around #IdleNoMore. I've helped organize events, shown up at events organized by others (in four different cities), written articles, tweeted my thumbs off, performed at events, sent emails, and answered a hundred questions. I don't list these things for credit. I list them so you know that I get it. And, I get that you get it. Lots of us get it. I mean, c'mon, the movement is called *Idle No More*. What did we expect? Lots of us are doing lots of things. That's what mass mobilization needs. But, as I start to feel tired, I think of all of the people I know who are doing even more. And, I know that for many of us, we were never idle to begin with, and so INM has just ramped up our actions to the nth degree. Now that INM is being recognized as a continuous, persistent voice, it is becoming increasingly necessary to consider the sustainability of our work. We don't want people burning out and we do want people doing work that is best suited to their talents.

"It's Time to Put Our Indigenous Governance Skills to the Test."

Traditionally, Anishinaabe nations had shifting, diverse, and emergent leadership. This means that leadership could emerge from various issues—including seasons, diplomacy, and ad hoc responsibilities. There are many benefits to this model. Firstly, leadership is based on context and accounts for a leader's strengths and aptitudes. In this way, leadership is somewhat specialized. I think this makes sense intuitively. Just because someone's a doctor doesn't mean you want her to do open heart surgery on you. Similarly, just because someone's a good orator doesn't mean you want that same person leading you to war. Secondly, having more than one recognized leader disperses power. Thirdly, this model encourages the teaching of leadership skills to a larger segment of society. It does this not only by increasing the "odds" of someone becoming a leader (by virtue of more leadership positions), but also because it is a form of leadership that favours aptitudes and encourages the selection of leaders based on skills instead of social or economic status.

I favour the principles of Anishinaabe governance because I'm Anishinaabe. It makes sense to me. And, the fact that so many of us are at work suggests to me that we still have elements of our traditional governance in our communities—we are witnessing the acting out of a certain kind of diverse and emergent leadership. But, how do we ensure this is sustainable? I think INM offers an opportunity to be more intentional in our Indigenous governance practices. What principles of governance do you take from your nation? What principles do you see being acted out in INM? What kind of leadership is exhibited in your community? How do we foster leadership skills in a broad segment of our communities?

For me, Idle No More is about nationhood. Not nation-state-hood, but nationhood—the ability to take care of the land, our children, and our families in the way we best know how. While the Canadian government currently plays heavily into our ability to function as self-determining nations, we know that true self-governance has to come from ourselves. This could be one of the most tremendous gifts of Idle No More: we have in front of us the perfect opportunity to re-invigorate and re-invent our governance practices from the ground up. The best way to demand self-determination is to be self-determining.

Originally appeared on Dividednomore.ca, *January 15, 2013.*

FISH BROTH & FASTING

Leanne Betasamosake Simpson

A year ago, after the community of Attawapiskat had been dragged through the racist lens of the media for more than a month, I began to write about the situation. I wrote two pieces. One that was published in Briarpatch magazine that was political, and one that was a spoken word piece using the music of Cree cellist Cris Derksen. I am not from Attawapiskat and I've never been there. I wrote because I felt a strong sense of solidarity with the community because like most Indigenous Peoples, I have personal connections and history that links me to all of the same issues. I felt a sense of responsibility to speak out not only on the way the issues where playing out in the media, but on the response of Canadian society. I feel the same way again this year. I am not going to correct all of the slander designed to discredit Chief Spence and her hunger strike—my friends and colleagues have already done a fantastic job of that. Check out the work of Chelsea Vowel and Alanis Obomsawin's *The People of the Kattawpiskat River* if you haven't. The past few weeks have been an intense time to be Anishinaabeg. There is a lot to write about and to process. I felt overwhelmingly proud on #J11 with tens of thousands of us in the streets worldwide, with the majority of our Indian Act Chiefs standing with us in those streets. I also felt the depths of betrayal on that day. But it was during the local #J11 actions in my community that I started to think a lot about fish broth. Fish broth and Anishinaabeg governance.

Fish broth has been cast by the mainstream media as "the cheat." Upon learning Chief Spence was drinking tea and fish-broth coverage shifted from framing her action as a "hunger strike" to a "liquid diet," as if 32 days without food is easy. As if a liquid diet doesn't take a substantial physical, mental, and emotional toll or substantial physical, mental, and emotional strength to accomplish. Of course this characterization comes from a place of enormous unchecked privilege and a position of wealth. It comes from not having to fight for one's physical survival because of the weight of crushing poverty. It comes from always having other options. This is not where Indigenous Peoples come from. My Ancestors survived many long winters on fish broth because there was nothing else to eat—not because the environment was harsh, but because the land loss and colonial policy were so fierce that they were forced into an imposed poverty that often left fish broth as the only sustenance. *Fish broth.* It carries cultural meaning for Anishinaabeg. It symbolizes hardship and sacrifice. It symbolizes the strength of our Ancestors. It means survival. Fish broth sustained us through the hardest of circumstances, with the parallel understanding that it can't sustain one forever. We exist today because of fish broth. It connects us to the water and to the fish who gave up its life so we could sustain ourselves. Chief Spence is eating fish broth because metaphorically, colonialism has kept Indigenous Peoples on a fish broth diet for generations upon generations. This is utterly lost on mainstream Canada, as media continues to call Ogichidaakwe Spence's fast a "liquid diet" while the right-wing media refers to it as much worse. Not *Chief* Spence, but *Ogichidaakwe* Spence—a holy woman, a woman that would do anything for her family and community, the one that goes over and makes things happen, a warrior, a leader because Ogichidaakwe Spence isn't just on a hunger strike. She is fasting and this also has cultural meaning for Anishinaabeg. She is in ceremony. We do not "dial back" our ceremonies.

We do not undertake this kind of ceremony without much forethought and preparation. We do not ask or demand that people stop the fast before they have accomplished whatever it is they set out to accomplish, which in her case is substantial change in the relationship between the Canadian state and Indigenous nations. We do not critique the faster. We do not bandwagon or verbally attack the faster. We do not criticize because we feel she's become the (unwilling) leader of the movement. We do not assume that she is being ill advised. We do not tell her to "save face." We support. We pray. We offer semaa. We take care of the sacred fire. We sing each night at dusk. We take care of all the other things that need to be taken care of, and we live up to our responsibilities in light of the faster. We protect the faster. We do these things because we know that through her physical sacrifice she is closer to the Spiritual world than we are. We do these things because she is sacrificing for us and because it is the kind, compassionate thing to do.

We do these things because it is our job to respect her self-determination as an Anishinaabekwe—this is the most basic building block of Anishinaabeg sovereignty and governance. "We respect her sovereignty over her body and her mind. We do not act like we know better than her." Fasting as a ceremony is difficult. It is challenging to willingly weaken one's body physically, and the mental and emotional strength required for fasting is perhaps more difficult than the physical. So when we fast, we ask our friends and family to support us and to act as our helpers. There is an assumption of reciprocity—the faster is doing without, in this case to make things better for all Indigenous Peoples, and in return, the community around her carries the responsibility of supporting her. A few days ago I posted these two sentences on Twitter: "I support @ChiefTheresa in her decision to continue her hunger strike. The only person that can decide otherwise is Chief Spence." Within minutes, trolls were commenting on my feed with commentary on Chief Spence's body image, diet jokes, calls for "no more special treatment for Natives," and calls to end her hunger strike. One person called her a "cunt."

I understand we need to be positive, I do. We also need to continue telling the truth. The racism, sexism and disrespect that has been heaped on Ogichidaakwe Spence in the past weeks have been done so in part because it is acceptable to treat Indigenous women this way. These comments take place in a context where we have nearly 1000 missing and murdered Indigenous women. Where we still have places named "squaw." Where Indigenous women have been the deliberate target of gendered colonial violence for 400 years. Where the people who have been seriously hurt and injured by the backlash against Idle No More have been women. Where Ogichidaakwe Spence's voice has not been heard. Ogichidaakwe Spence challenges Canadians because no one in Canada wants to believe this situation is bad enough that someone would willingly give up their life.

Ogichidaakwe Spence challenges me, because I am not on day 32 of a fast. I did not put my life on the line, and that forces me to continually look myself in the mirror and ask if I am doing everything I can. This is her gift to me. Idle No More as a movement is now much bigger than the hunger strikers and Bill C-45, but it is still important to acknowledge their sacrifice, influence, and leadership. I want my grandchildren to be able to live in Mississauga Anishinaabeg territory as Mississauga Anishinaabeg—hunting, fishing, collecting medicines, doing ceremony, telling stories, speaking our language, governing themselves using our political traditions, and whatever else that might mean to them, unharassed. *That's not a dream palace—that is what our treaties guaranteed.* We now have hundreds of leaders from different Indigenous nations emerging all over Mikinakong (the Place of the Turtle). We now have hundreds of eloquent spokespeople, seasoned organizers, writers, thinkers, and artists acting on their own ideas in any way and every way possible. This is the beauty of our movement. Chi'Miigwech Theresa Spence, Raymond Robinson, Emil Bell, and Jean Sock for your vision, your sacrifice and your commitment to making us better. Chi'Miigwech to everyone who has been up late at night worrying about what to do next, and then who gets up the next morning and acts. I am hopeful and inspired and look forward to our new, collective emergence as a healthy and strong Anishinaabeg nation.

Originally appeared on Dividednomore.ca, *January 16, 2013.*

DAY 38
Ellen Gabriel

Today is day 38 of Chief Theresa Spence's spiritual hunger strike. Since she started this I have thought of her and prayed for her each day. I worry that some of the "leaders" who profess to represent us— Onkwehón:we, have abandoned their ways and that their actions last week were a symbolic slap in our faces.

Even more disturbing is the fact that the rape of a young woman in Thunder Bay in which her attackers (yes, there was more than one), told her at the end "This is what all Aboriginal people deserve!" has gone unchallenged by our "leadership" and by the public servants whose head is the Prime Minister of Canada.

There is an atmosphere mixed with compassion and grief, fear and hate, but more than ever Hope and Light that all our peoples regardless of faith, creed, and race will unite to protect our Mother Earth.

It is disturbing to see the abuse of the right to "Freedom of Expression" by Sun Media's Ezra Levant whose rants about some of our leaders and indeed about all our peoples to defame, dehumanize

Red Winter, Ottawa, December 21, 2012. (NADYA KWANDIBENS)

and disrespect us—an identifiable group of peoples in ways that promote hate and its crimes against us is reminiscent of the propaganda used by Nazi Germany.

I worry that the most vulnerable group in Canadian society, Onkwehón:we (Indigenous) women, are once again threatened even more than ever, due to the hateful online comments and crimes that have seemingly been condoned by the Prime Minister and Governor General of Canada due to their silence on the matter (check out Amnesty International's "Stolen Sisters" report).

And while the National Chief is taking some time off for mental health reasons, that should not mean that there is a void in leadership. It is well known that I do not approve that he and other chiefs met with the Prime Minister of Canada when the demands by Chief Spence and the grassroots peoples were not met. He and others were asked not to go to the meeting by the grassroots but instead a minority of chiefs decided that this was an "opportunity" not to miss. Why? Nothing was accomplished and the same old buzzwords used like "a commitment to." Same ol' Spin Doctors at work.

In some ways we should not be surprised by their abandonment as Mr. Harper's bullying ways through the use of ECONOMIC TERRORISM have kept some chiefs hopping instead of listening with their hearts to the needs of our peoples.

I wish no ill to Mr. Atleo but instead, I wish him good mental health because I believe that no job is worth losing one's mental health. And because the teachings of our ancestors tell us to pray for those who are weak and need our help and support.

And so on this day 38 of Chief Theresa Spence, a woman who has raised the bar in what true leadership is, we must unite with one heart, one mind to demand that the Governor General and Prime Minister meet with her so she may remain with us to continue the hard work that is ahead of us all.

We must come to peace with Chief Spence's commitment as she has made peace with herself to continue on this path. Our discomfort should not enter into the equation but we must support her and Attawapiskat unconditionally.

Remember, we are nations. We are not minorities or groups. We have self-determining rights as the First Peoples of these beautiful lands to guard against harm to our peoples and lands; to continue our centuries-old resistance to the harmful laws enacted by Canada's colonial government. We must continue to protect our Lands, Resources, and all our relations who live with us and who bring beauty to our lives here on Mother Earth, Beautiful.

Skén:nen Sewakwé:kon—Peace to Everyone

Originally appeared on the Facebook group Turtle Musings *by Ellen Gabriel, January 17, 2013.*

THE SUCKER PUNCH OF JANUARY 11

Alo White

I am wondering if anyone felt like I did this past week: weak, hurt, angry, disoriented, disappointed and downright disgusted at what happened on January 11th in Ottawa. I am sure there are many other men and women who worked twice as hard as I did, but for my part in the month or so leading up to #J11 I spent countless hours up late working for the movement. I spent countless hours thinking, learning, worrying, discussing, praying, and offering tobacco to the spirits. Tweeting, spreading the word about Idle No More; hours talking with family and friends, offering support to people I don't even know, and lobbying my own Chief and Grand Chief. And I also went on two road trips to Ottawa in support of Chief Theresa Spence. For the first time I felt like I was part of something really big. I felt like we had teamwork and I was energized by our shared pride and unity. And ever since #J11, I've been trying to figure out why I was left feeling so down this week. And what I've figured out isn't easy to admit or talk about.

When I played hockey back in the 80s, I played goalie for my community, and everyone gave their heart for the team, including the guys' wives, who were called our "booster club." They would hold fundraising events like bingo, 50/50 draws, and dances so that they could hire a bus and get our fans to come and watch and cheer for us at every hockey game. It was a community lifestyle of friendship and get-togethers. We practised at our outdoor rink, most of the time in 40-below weather. Nobody complained. If we got cold, we just moved a little bit faster. One time a deflected puck at a tournament knocked out my four front teeth. I was bleeding pretty badly and the coach filled my mouth with tissue, put my mask back on, and told me to keep playing. I played the rest of the game, which we won. But win or lose, I've always been a team player and I never let it get me down when I lost.

I'm too old for playing hockey now, but in my younger days once when I was at a tournament I was fighting and exchanging blows with a guy from another team. It was just me and him fighting. It was a fair fight. That was until his teammate came and sucker punched me in the head from behind. I wasn't expecting it and I lost the fight because I was caught off guard. That's how I felt about #J11 and what the AFN did to all of us. As a united team, we were expecting to have opposition from the government, from the media, and even from Canadians. We readied ourselves for it and felt like we couldn't be defeated—*not this time,* we told ourselves. What we didn't expect was betrayal from our own. We didn't expect that the blow to us would come from our own team. The AFN suckerpunched us. Not all the Chiefs. Just 20. Out of tens of thousands who marched on #J11, 20 self-righteous people coasted in on the wave created by the 30-day sacrifice of Chief Spence, and all the countless hours of effort by all of us and stepped on all of us as if we were dirt on their way into the meeting with the Prime Minister.

They abandoned Chief Spence, one of our own, and achieved nothing but to gain another empty promise from a Prime Minister who will most certainly proceed with the very legislative agenda that made us march in the first place. It's so tragic I can't even think about it. The media got it totally wrong. There aren't divisions. There is intense and widespread unity across the country. If a vote for an MP was held today and 9,980 people voted for one person and 20 voted for another, I think the media wouldn't hesitate to call that a landslide endorsement for that person's platform. So there is unity like I have never seen before. But the truth is a very small handful of opportunistic individuals decided to take advantage of their own people. They were not the ones who were hunger striking, they didn't earn the meeting, and there would have been other meetings. That's the truth of it. The betrayal hurts like hell. But, I'll get over it. The events of January 11 may have hurt and thrown us off and also temporarily shifted the spotlight from

Chief Spence to Shawn Atleo but I can already see the people gaining strength again and planning for #J28 and beyond. We aren't giving up. For me, the events of January 11 have also done something else—and this is the positive part. It has made me think really hard about my own community, my territory of Treaty 3, and what I want for my grandkids. I was born and raised on the rez, so my mind and my heart are always at home on our land and on the water of the Lake of the Woods. My community has its hardships: alcohol and drugs and other addictions. The Residential school and day school spared no one—including me and my family. As hard as this is to admit, my community is not healthy. We are dealing with the long-term effects of the loss of power and pride over many generations combined with debilitating poverty. With nowhere for that to go, we act out with jealousy towards one another.

We gossip, we put each other down. We don't like it if someone does well. We say they are trying to be better than us and—in my community—saying that is a putdown. It's not always like that of course—but we have to admit we've been suckerpunching our own for a long time. We can't heal from all of this and have our communities come out healthy if we don't admit first how much we care for one another, and how much we also hurt one another. We have to figure out ways to bring the unity back. We have to support each other and encourage one another. Now is the time for a rebirth of our Nations and our people. We cannot just stand back and feel defeated by a sucker punch. We have to pick ourselves up and keep going. And we have to support Chief Theresa Spence and Raymond Robinson NOW as they are on their 40th day of their hunger strike, and as the Women of Turtle Island led by Ellen Gabriel are calling on us to do.

It's taken 150 years to get here. We are going to have our ups and downs and change is not going to happen overnight. Our people need to heal and that is what we are doing by being involved in Idle No More—it's healing us as we go. We can see this in our youth who are involved already and its filling me with pride. We will always have the type of people among us who are willing to betray their own people for their own personal gain OR because they think they know what is best for everyone. But we owe it to ourselves and our future generations to try to make our communities better than that.

We are better than that.
We always have been.
We just didn't know it.
Originally appeared on Dividednomore.ca, *January 18, 2013.*

RECLAIMING OURSELVES ONE NAME AT A TIME
Christi Belcourt

First Nations, Ojibway, Blackfoot, Indian, Aboriginal, Treaty, Half breed, Cree, Status Indian are all fairly familiar English words but none of them are the names by which we, the various Indigenous Peoples, called ourselves in our own languages. By contrast how many Canadians have heard these names: Nehiyaw, Nehiyawak, Otipemisiwak, and Apeetogosan? Yet, these are who I am because these are the names my grandparents used to describe and call ourselves. Even "Metis" is not the name people called themselves in the language in *Manitou Sakhahigan*, the community my dad was born and raised in. And even that place is not known by its original name but by its English/French name "Lac Ste. Anne." The issue of naming places in Canada is complex. Some would argue that Canada reflects its Indigenous roots because there are many place names which are derived from the original Indigenous languages. Even though the origins and meanings of those names have all been lost to the history that Canadians tell to one another about Canada. Toronto is a case in point.

I would argue that most Canadians are quite comfortable, and even comforted, by the names of the places they call home that are Indigenous in origin—*but only to a point.* As long as they are in name only and don't come with the burden of acknowledging Canada's past colonialist history and the erasure of Indigenous ownership of lands. Canadians seem to hold some quaint and romanticized notion that Canada was founded by the English and French, and Indigenous Peoples' contributions to the country are nothing more than providing some names or assisting in the War of 1812. Regardless, the renaming of lakes, rivers, or areas of land from existing Indigenous names into English or other European names is widely recognized by those who have knowledge deeper than a puddle as a colonialist tool that was used extensively in the claiming of Indigenous lands throughout North, Central, and South America. As famed University of California geographer Bernard Nietschmann put it, "More Indigenous territory has been claimed by maps than by guns, and more Indigenous territory can be reclaimed and defended by maps than by guns." Whether intentioned or not by the people who did the renaming, the collective effect on the Canadian psyche has been the perpetuation of the myth that there were vast empty territories, identified by Europeans as "Terra Nullius," that were there for the taking. Equally damaging is the belief that Indigenous Peoples were immigrants to North America like Europeans and therefore Indigenous ownership over the lands was somehow only temporary until Europeans arrived. Those myths are at the heart of the ongoing conflicts that continue today over land.

It's clear to me the educational system has failed Canadians as much as it's failed us. Sadly, the history Canadians tell one another about Canada is not the history Indigenous people share with one another about this land. Canadian history as it is written by Canadians is so incomplete and devoid of Indigenous history and knowledge, that it is causing many Indigenous people to think that a large portion of Canadians are kind of, well, sorry to say this—dumb. Not dumb generally, just behind the curve, I'll say, when it comes to Indigenous Peoples, the issues, the history and discussing ideas on how to move forward. And I recognize it is not Canadians' fault if they don't seem up to speed on our issues. How can we expect them to know if they aren't being taught?

Renaming the Person

The CBC reported yesterday that there is a girl in Iceland who is simply listed as "girl" on her birth certificate because the name she was given by her parents does not conform to one of the 1,800 or so pre-approved legal names for girls in her country. A CBC online poll asked Canadians if they agree with Iceland's "official name list." Not surprisingly, about 60 percent disagree. Coincidentally, at the same time as

I was listening to the news, my partner asked me to call the Ontario
government office located in Thunder Bay to ask a question about him
legally changing his name. My partner is Anishinaabe.
Like so many Indigenous people in Canada, the name on his birth
certificate and on his I.D. is in English. He has always disliked his surname "White"—not because of anything to do with the word, but
because he said it has never felt like his. Much like the renaming of
places into English names in his traditional territory of the Treaty 3
region, his surname was also imposed on his family. His great-grandfather's name was *Waabshkii'ogin* (pronounced Waab-shkee-o-gun).
That was his name. One name. Not a first and last name. Just one
name. Translated from Anishinaabemowin it means "White Feather."
Perhaps his great-grandfather did have other names, names that were
given to him at different times during his life. But the name that stuck
as the family name was "White" because, as the story in his family
goes, it so happened *Waabshkii'ogin* was the name he had at the time
of Treaty 3. Apparently the person doing the registry was instructed to
list the names in English and not being a fluent in Anishinaabemowin,
the name was shortened to "White" on the official record.

According to the Department of Aboriginal Affairs (AANDC), "As
early as 1850, the colonial government in British North America began to keep and maintain records to identify individual Indians and
the bands to which they belonged. These records helped agents of the
Crown to determine which people were eligible for treaty and interest benefits under specific treaties." Later in 1951, those lists officially
became the "Indian Registry." It further states: "Under the Indian
Act, the Indian Registrar—an employee of AANDC—is responsible for
maintaining the Indian Register. The Registrar is the sole authority
for determining which names will be added, deleted or omitted from
the Register."

Despite the fact that registration for "Indians" is done in Ottawa,
legal name changes are the jurisdiction of the provinces. So on the phone
to Thunder Bay, I tried to explain to the government employee that my
partner wishes to change his name to one name and I was asking if this is
possible. She asked why. I told her it was because in his culture the people traditionally only had one name. She asked which culture. I replied
"Ojibway" and "First Nations." To which she replied, "Which country

is that from?" I kid you not. Thunder Bay is a city where it is estimated one in five residents is Indigenous, the majority being "Ojibway." The amount of educating Indigenous people have to constantly do with the non-Indigenous population never ceases to astound me. I found out also that legally a name in Canada must contain a "first and last name." Therefore, his attempt to reclaim a family name like "Waabshkii'ogin" and return to the traditional way of naming in his community, which is to have first names but not last names, is outlawed in Canada. Suddenly Iceland's policies don't seem all that different.

How can we as Indigenous peoples begin to reclaim our own names and discard our colonialist past if our names are not even considered legally possible unless they conform to the Eurocentric version of what constitutes a person's name and identity? My own attempts at reclaiming are done one name and one word at a time. I always use *Biidewe'anikwetok*, the Anishinaabe name I was given in ceremony, to introduce myself, before English. My daughter was named *Aazhaabikqwe* by her auntie, and then she was given a second name, *Shpegiizhigok*, by the Shaking Tent. I'm trying as hard as I can to learn the language. One by one, I am trying to learn the original names of places around me and speak their names out into words. Awakening into sounds and songs my respect for the places of my ancestors and the sacred ground I walk on.

—Biidewe'anikwetok

Footnote: In Alberta, Manitou Sakhahigan was renamed Lac Ste. Anne by a priest in 1844 when he mistakenly thought the name translated as "Devil Lake." In the case of Manitou Sakhahigan, renaming went hand in hand with the gradual demonizing of traditional ceremonial and land-based practices such as natural medicines and the christianization of the Peoples. During that period and the many years that followed, subsequent generations of my ancestors began to lose the traditional knowledge that went hand in hand with their lands. Christianity ensured that lands that were once considered sacred became something to be dominated. Animals that were considered relatives became commodities. For further reading on original place names please read my post on *"Mapping Roots."*

Originally appeared on Dividednomore.ca, *January 23, 2013.*

NO MORE

Plex (D. Bedard)

Say it loud, we native and proud
We waited it out, the best day to be native is now
It is what it gotta be, hurt the economy
Whatever it takes to get the PM in front of me
Governments, they're the real f**kin' terrorists
Ever since they came to the Americas
Bringing guns to a peaceful protest
Target the hopeless, weak and oppressed
They all cannibals, filthy animals
And if you figure that's cool, it's understandable
But try to walk a block in my shoes
And talk to the cop with the glock behind you
They all cowards, hungry for power
Ain't satisfied 'til the lands been devoured
Vampires, they out for blood
They chop trees and they run pipe right through the mud
They say we drill oil 'cause we need it
They figure we're sheep we'll believe it
They treat treaties like s**t, we're mistreated.
We only want what's ours and that's freedom.

Makin' our move, we ain't gonna Idle No More
Makin' our move, we ain't gonna Idle No More

Call me Christmas, 'cause I'm forgivin'
But I can't forget the state in which native people are livin'
The government would rather see us dead or in prison
And 39 percent of Canadians are with 'em.
The sign of the times is like, "who do you trust?"
They want the whole f**kin' pie, won't even save me the crust
Offerin' us crumbs is some sort of favour to us
They control the terms and we're made to adjust
But we can fight back. Let's see how they like that
After these messages, we'll be right back

When we return, we've crashed and burned
And rise from the ashes, but what did we learn?
S**t's the same, ain't a damn thing changed
500 years of s**t, and we're all that remains
America's history is written in blood
And all the government does is sweep it under the rug
Makin' our move, we ain't gonna Idle No More
Makin' our move, we ain't gonna Idle No More
Originally featured Lase and appeared on Youtube, *January 28, 2013.*

"THE MEGAPHONE GIRL":
An Interview with Jenna (Liiciious) Wirch

Jenna Wirch with Leah Gazan

LEAH GAZAN (LG): Thank you for doing this, Jenna. I wanted to start with a question about your history. Early on in life you were involved with child welfare. For lots of reasons, your trail to leadership began as a leader in local street gangs in the city of Winnipeg. Soon after, though, you chose to take on roles educating and mentoring youth more positively, on issues of social justice. What was it that made you want to change?

JENNA WIRCH (JW): I don't really know when I got my voice, but it was at a point when I ran away from home, around 11 years old. I was being severely abused in my home. I took it until I had enough of it one day. I went to school and my mom was about to hit me and so I said: "No, you're not going to do that to me anymore" and then I ran away. Ever since then I've been on the street. I wasn't taking it anymore. People saw that I was a feisty leader, because I never went back home after that. That's the real point when I found my voice. Nobody would stick up for me, so I had to stick up for myself. When I was in CFS I had no mom or dad, so I started to find that being with a crew made me feel like a family, like I had a home. I became a leader of negativity though. I was headed towards jail, being dead, or becoming a statistic... at the age of 16-17. It's all about choices, right. I chose to go down a better road.

It was when I discovered the drum that I really found some direction. When I was growing up, I didn't understand Elders. I didn't even know I was Native. I knew about headdresses and stuff, but I didn't know there was Aboriginal singing. The teachings that come with the drum really opened my eyes to what was really going on around me. I started learning healing songs and the teachings that come with those songs. I desperately needed those because I needed something to hold on to otherwise I would have just fell through the cracks. I just held onto that for dear life in the group home where I lived. With my peers, I just sat learning these songs from grandmothers who worked with me and for the first time connected to my culture. I discovered that when you are singing those songs, it opens up a hole in your heart and lets in the light. I never wanted to let that feeling go. Since then, whenever I start to think negatively, I go back to those teachings and songs, and it brightens me up. The drum really is the heartbeat of Mother Earth, it connects us all. Without a heartbeat you would be nothing. When singing those songs you are healing and praying to the ancestors for happiness and good health. Since I've come to know that my life has become better. Not better financially, but my self-identity as a person has been better than any other time in my life.

LG: First Nations youth are often stigmatized as being lazy, delinquent, and uninvolved. Idle No More demonstrated the resiliency, strength, and intelligence in our youth, debunking common stereotypes and misconceptions that we often see perpetuated in mass media. You were very involved, becoming known as "The Megaphone Girl." How did you become one of the main youth voices at the rallies held in Winnipeg?

JW: It didn't start at Idle No More but way before that. It started when I got on the drum, and got back to my culture. At the INM rallies, I saw that nobody was standing up, nobody was taking the lead. From my past, I was like, k man, if I don't do it, what's going to happen? These people need to understand the facts, they need to understand why they are here. Before INM rallies there were the "Meet me at the Bell Tower" Rallies to stop the violence on Selkirk Ave in Winnipeg put on by an organization called *Aboriginal Youth Opportunities*. Since that has been happening, the crime rate has gone down 18.7 percent just in the William Whyte area. From those rallies, I remember cheering up the crowd, rallying them up. So, when we went to INM rallies, I really felt the need to get my voice heard so I just started yelling off facts about Bill C-45, water, and what we were resisting. I think me doing that, standing up, really helped other young people. I think it was like, it's okay, there's a young Aboriginal woman, and she isn't afraid to speak up! If that person can do it then why can't I? Now my other friends are starting to stand up as well and do something positive with their lives since the INM movement.

LG: What do you think it was about INM for youth that motivated them to get involved so deeply?

JW: It's in our DNA and it always has been. Our skin is brown; we belong to our Mother Earth. The eighth fire has been lit under our asses, and has woken us up. It woke us from this oppression. We are living out a prophecy right now, in this time and era. I believe that this generation that is born right now is going to grow up and change a lot of stuff. I think what has got everyone inspired is that there is someone up there that looks exactly the same as them. Before, at rallies there were no youth. Before, it was always the elders speaking. Once young people turned up at these rallies, got empowered, and started being on the news all of the time, this really gave them a sense of hope, crushed that hopelessness, and stopped the self-loathing.

LG: When you say self-loathing, where do you think that self-loathing comes from?

JW: From the oppression, the government, the poverty we live in, the day-to-day struggle. All my friends know that I am the same as them, that I live just the same. We're all in poverty, maybe even below the poverty line, whatever that is. They have turned on to the idea that we can never be idle. We were born into the system, and now we are trying to change it.

LG: Did culture and traditions help you fight against stereotypes about yourself and others in the media?

JW: It did help! It gave me the fuel to push even harder against the stereotypes. Coming from where I came from, I didn't want that negativity in my life anymore. I felt like finally I was in control of my life, and those stereotypes were put on me by "uneducated fools"—as I like to call them. Media didn't know where I came from so they kept telling stories from the little bubble of stereotypes they had been taught. I really felt sorry for them, not out of pity, but wanting to help. There's that quote by Gandhi I once saw on a reusable bag: "Be the change you want to see in the world." I remember seeing that and pondering: *I want to be change.* I asked myself what that would look like and that really changed my perspective on how I brought up myself. Hopefully I can pass on this teaching to another young person in the near future, because I'm getting old. (laughter)

LG: You're almost an adult! (plenty of laughter)

JW: Yeah, I'm getting there, I'm 22! (laughter)

I think the INM rallies symbolize a new generation of leaders who are not afraid to stand up against the government and take shit from no one. Youth are tired of the poverty, the child welfare, the abuse, the gangs, the oppression. My generation has had enough and no one should be surprised. What do people expect when you put a bunch of rowdy Neechees together who have gone through the same thing? We're all going to feed off one another. If we have the proper teachings, young Native people are going to go places. That's the mentality that I have. This is why I think happiness and joy are some of the most powerful weapons we have. Laughter is the best medicine. It can defeat any sadness, anger, or despair. I'm a funny person, always trying to make people laugh, brighten up their day, because you never know what they are going through. Every single person I come into contact with, even if it is at a negative rally—like for murdered and missing women—I try to make people smile. That's how we as a people are going to heal, through smiling and laughing and talking and working together. It only takes one person to speak out and help the rest of the crowd.

LG: What is your role in the INM movement going in the future? I know you talk a lot about how you are a "big mouth" on the megaphone, and we know that you are often the entertainment. You come up with these brilliantly witty comments at so many rallies. Where do you see your participation in social movements?

JW: I'll still continue to be the igniter, the big mouth of the crowd. I'll help others find their voices at these rallies. We'll chant big chants, march around, and I'll give people the facts that they need to know. With me being so aggressive on the megaphone, being so straight up, that I hope will get people's wheels turning.

My role will always be to get the crowd going but also organizing, doing research, finding other non-violent ways of protesting, and getting the word and the message out there. As for the INM movement itself, I feel that it needs to move into the schools, and affect the system to educate people about First Nations issues. I'd like to see the INM transform into a political force! We should have our own hub in the House of Commons.

LG: What do you say to youth who are thinking about getting involved with any social movement?

JW: I would give them the facts with what's going on between the government and our treaty systems. I would school them on what's going to happen in future generations if we don't do something. I would explain that all of this work is a collective, that we need a lot of people to come out to these rallies, and we need everyone to stand up for our people and the land. I would say keep going and do lots of research!

THE UNRAVELLING OF A COLONIZED MIND

Jana-Rae Yerxa

Sure, everybody struggles. But to be born an Indigenous person, you are born into struggle. My struggle. Your struggle. Our struggle. The colonial struggle. There are many layers to this struggle. For the longest time, I didn't even know what the true struggle was about yet I couldn't escape it. It consumed me. Colonialism, as I have been forced to discover, is like a cancer. But instead of the cells in your body betraying itself, the thoughts in your mind work against you and eat you up from the inside out. You're like the walking dead and you don't even know it because you are so blinded. You can't see the truth. Here are some of the perverted ways colonialism infects the mind:

- With a colonized mind, I hate being Indian.
- With a colonized mind, I accept that I am Indian because that's who the colonizer told me I am.
- With a colonized mind, I don't understand that I am Anishinaabe.
- With a colonized mind, I believe I am inferior to the white race.
- With a colonized mind, I wish I was white.
- With a colonized mind, I draw pictures of my family with peach-coloured skin, blonde hair and blue eyes because I've internalized that this is the ideal, what looks good and what is beautiful.
- With a colonized mind, I keep my feelings of inferiority to white people a secret from others and even from myself.
- With a colonized mind, I try diligently to mirror white people as closely as I possibly can.
- With a colonized mind, I desperately want to be accepted by white people.
- With a colonized mind, to gain the acceptance of white people, I will detach myself from all that does not mirror acceptable "white" standards, whether it is how one dresses, one speaks, or one looks.
- With a colonized mind, I feel as though I am swearing when I say "white people" in front of white people.
- With a colonized mind, I believe there is no racism.
- With a colonized mind, I believe that racism does not impact me.
- With a colonized mind, I deny my heritage and proudly say, "We are all just people."
- With a colonized mind, when discussing issues pertaining to race, I try desperately not to offend white people.
- With a colonized mind, I do not know who I am.
- With a colonized mind, I believe I know who I am and do not understand that this isn't so because I've become the distorted image of who the colonizer wants me to be and remain unaware of this reality.

- With a colonized mind, I could care less about history and think that our history doesn't matter.
- With a colonized mind, I do not understand how the history created the present.
- With a colonized mind, I do not see how I have been brainwashed to be an active participant in my own dehumanization and the dehumanization of my people.
- With a colonized mind, I do not recognize how others dehumanize me and my people.
- With a colonized mind, I devalue the ways of my people—their ways of seeing, their ways of knowing, their ways of living, their ways of being.
- With a colonized mind, I cannot speak the language of my ancestors and do not care that this is so.
- With a colonized mind, I am unaware of how colonization has impacted my ancestors, my community, my family, and me.
- With a colonized mind, I think that my people are a bunch of lazy, drunk, stupid Indians.
- With a colonized mind, I discredit my own people.
- With a colonized mind, I think that I am better than "those Indians."
- With a colonized mind, I will silently watch while my people are victimized.
- With a colonized mind, I will victimize my own people.
- With a colonized mind, I will defend those that perpetrate against my people.
- With a colonized mind, I will hide behind false notions of tradition entrenched with Euro-western shame and shame my own people, re-creating more barriers amongst us.
- With a colonized mind, I tolerate our women being raped and beaten.
- With a colonized mind, I tolerate our children being raised without their fathers.

- With a colonized mind, I feel threatened when someone else, who is Anishinaabe, achieves something great because I feel jealous and wish it was me.

- With a colonized mind, when I see an Anishinaabe person working towards bettering their life, because of my own insecurities, I accuse them of thinking they are "so good now."

- With a colonized mind, I am unaware that I was set up to hate myself.

- With a colonized mind, I do not think critically about the world.

- With a colonized mind, I believe in merit and do not recognize unearned colonial privilege.

- With a colonized mind, I ignorantly believe that my ways of seeing, living, and believing were all decided by me when in reality everything was and is decided for me.

- With a colonized mind, I am lost.

- With a colonized mind, I do not care about the land.

- With a colonized mind, I believe that freedom is a gift that can be bestowed upon me by the colonizer.

- With a colonized mind, I believe that I am powerless and act accordingly.

- With a colonized mind, I do not have a true, authentic voice.

- With a colonized mind, I live defeat.

- With a colonized mind, I will remain a victim of history.

- With a colonized mind, I will pass self-hatred on to my children.

- With a colonized mind, I do not understand the term "self-responsibility."

- With a colonized mind, I do not recognize that I have choice and do not have to fatalistically accept oppressive, colonial realities.

- With a colonized mind, I do not see that I am a person of worth.

- With a colonized mind, I do not know I am powerful.

The colonial struggle, as I said earlier, has many layers. I am no longer being eaten from the inside. Yet it is no less painful. What is different today is that I am connected to a true source of power that was always there. It's like my friend once said, "I come from a distinguished people whose legacy shines on me like the sun." I now understand this and it is because of this understanding that my mind and my soul are freer than they have ever been. It is because of that gift—that awakening which came through struggle—that I will proudly continue to struggle for freedom.

My freedom.

Your freedom.

Our freedom.

Originally appeared on Lastrealindians.com, *January 30, 2013.*

SILENCE IS NOT OUR MOTHER TONGUE:
Madwewewin, The First Taste of Sound

Lesley Belleau

There is this place called Silence that takes our women by their soft, browned hands and hides them in its long arms and holds them vehemently, wraps these women tightly so tightly and covers their mouths and eyes and feels their strong hearts beating against its dark submersion, its murky breath twining around their tongues, drowning all sounds silent.

Let me curl into my childhood bed, press my dolls against the side of my face and inhale childhood thickly and drift back into yesterday's scents and voices and memories. Find yesterday in today. Once, I sat sprawled against a bed corner while someone from my church consumed my young body as I walked into silent dreaming of picking acorns from the long path behind my house and pulling the tops of each one of them and throwing them into my long, clear river that smelled like morning no matter which season or time of day. Nibi rolling the acorns away to a new shoreline. Anytime these things happened again I could escape back to this pathway so easily, drifting away from them at will, as simply as a dream or a solid door opening toward daylight. But there were never any sounds in these places. Only an underwater humming of pure, flat silence without echoes, without lulls, without a break in between or a parting of the water to ground me. At nights I would line the outside of the bed with my dolls and cover my face with their yarn hair, plastic skin under my finger pads, their small black eyes watching me as I slept.

In creation we expand in the water, form features and eyes and fingers, elongate hourly into human form. Agonde. Floating we form, floating, agonde. The sounds of a mother whispering to her baby, her singing a dream song through the waters, through the taut stomach skin, the sounds of a mother's laughter a trail way toward madwewewin. To the first taste of sound. In creation, we are reaching and turning and growing inside of the underwater humming, arching toward the sound of love, the sound of a voice we base dreams upon. Madwewewin. We learn in the first waters how to hear.

My father had a voice that sounded like syrup. Stories piled up like books through our years. He left long trails against my mind, winding this way and that, and the stories are my inheritance. When we buried him, I carried his voice with me, placed them against my marrow, and embedded them in the soft space of memory where I had him still, long after the nurse's small white hand folded the thin eyelids over his still brown eyes. A memory of protection and strength, knowing that I was on my own now. Sometime later, *maadaagami*—the water swirled, and I was able to whisper myself out of the outer edge of silence. Was able to build long layers of sound wrung out of my own tongue somehow. We lived outside of these voices. My sisters and I walked forward, whispering to each other. Mashkawadin. It is frozen solid until it is warmed by ancient breaths, cracking open, ahki splitting one side to the other, and the clear water flowing underneath.

When the world opened itself to me and I stepped through *endazhi*, that place, the blare of words a trumpet, concrete footsteps cracking, the life paths, the long walk forward, the stepping, we learned the prolonged pull out of silence. The pathway so incessant, the small whispered conversations, the people shaping people, the interchanged shorelines where ideas and visions might survive if we let them. I looked then to the waters. I saw the long bodies swaying beneath the waterline, the cusp of shore a page of memories, the edge of water a secret where strong voices lay flattened, silence holding them under as long as the hands didn't reach too deeply.

Lorelei Williams, of Skatln, expressing a collective sentiment. Vancouver, January 11, 2013. (STEPHEN HUI)

Nibiikaa. There is a lot of water. Everywhere. Dimii. It is deep water. Endaso. So many voices lying in wait. Niibi. The water. Gaadoo. It hides these voices. Pulls it in its wrappings, lets them write underwater stories for the earth to read. These women swimming stories like a scratch of a petroglyph's rock dust settling against itself. We want to keep you here in safety, where they can't find you, where the whole world's careless words fall against the soil. Debinaak. The callous flinging of souls against a rock face, their stories scratching silently because it's the only way to tell it.

Many paths to silence seen in every mirror, crisscrossing over one another like piled limbs heaping against a stark white sky. A blare of noon exposing the stitched lips and even though it is daylight, the people look over our heads, pretending that we might not be there, might not be taped shut and walking down the same streets. *Nibbikaa.* There is a lot of water and we are quickly sinking, the silence entering us in the schools when the teachers tell us that our own stories aren't really happening. When we see our Grandmothers afraid to speak their own languages unless all doors are closed. When there are men who drive us home and think it's okay to pin us down in the front seats and try to rip the buttons off our shirts. When the other children laugh at our grassless front lawns with car parts and bikes and Ski-Doos leaning up against each other, the metal catching light and blinding us until our eyes tear and yet we never cry. We never cry. We never blink when we hear the words "Dirty Indians," we don't flinch when we see one of our own getting bullied for not living on the same city streets as the other good kids. We just keep walking and smiling that hard plastic acquiescent smile. The same blank smile of my baby dolls that got me through the thick nights of childhood dreaming.

And we are the loose buttons dangling tenuously on the shirt, on the wrinkled and forgotten shirt, the hollow closet closing in. And now we are women. Walking through these paths. Choosing the ones we wish to step in, avoiding the ones we are told to accept. Sometimes. We had half-loves; we had faltering minutes where we had to force our tongues to move to say those uncomfortable things that no one else at all wanted to hear. We had the big heavens shift and make us choose things that forced sound out of our mouths and pried words out of the silences that were more comfortable. But we also knew our grandmothers' songs. We remembered her strong hands lifting us. We had her persistence threaded onto our spine walls as tautly as the end knot of Creation. We are women. And because of this, we were compelled to speak, unless the silence held us as they do the still ones. And this is okay, because some of us will speak for them. But for some of us, our tongues are loosened against a long shoreline, stretching as far as imagination can insist. These words that we have dancing against our lips are leaking a strong river over shore and we are wading here, finding solid ground, and deciding to stay.

Some of us like it here where we can entangle our grandmother's spine words and throat them with our own and speak our sounds which are so loud that the daylight doesn't hurt our eyes anymore. Our voices are solid against ahki like the spirals of tree trunks, the eternity of sound stretching forward into a horizon filled with bodies stepping outward, a line of history marching, drumbeats stirring the waters like a large spoon. Maadaagami. Lurid waters curving the whole world open, gathering. When the Idle No More movement came I was speaking, my silence shrugged down my back, my tongue able to move along and beside many other women, youth, and men who saw the need for chiselling spaces where our treaties are honoured and splayed open against settler abuses, where Indigenous women's attacks are spoken about and acted against with due necessity and justice. I have been writing and speaking for some time now and sometimes, because of this, our voices and need for justice are targeted and attacked.

As organizer of several Idle No More rallies and events in my home community of Garden River First Nation and the Bawating area, I received an envelope of hate mail containing my articles from local newspapers that expressed my feelings from an Indigenous standpoint on the Idle No More movement, which were cut out and had lewd pictures and writings, as well as a cut-out of Shawn Atleo, the National Chief of the Assembly of First Nations. On these cut-outs were crude drawings of male sexual organs, horns, guns and semen erupting from the penises, as well as threats such as "Stay away from the soo Lesley Belleau or else," and "The Only Good Indian is a Dead Indian," as well as the words "Yum Yum" beside the penis. I contacted authorities and decided that such attacks were better off in the public eye in order to protect others and to create awareness. Also, it is important to let the perpetrators of such hate crimes know that their actions are being monitored and to not create a bigger gap of silence for us as Indigenous people. This type of attack will never stop me from speaking; will not remove me from my rightful place of sound within ahki.

When we step outside of the gripping silence, the outer world becomes startled and sometimes angry, not seeing the workings for justice, but instead seeing a radical group of people attempting to speak a history that doesn't make sense to some. It is radical to some people when we speak because the silence was so comfortable and easy and quiet, that the soft sounds of our voices creates a humming and drumming along the edges of people's consciousness and awareness that is unwelcome and troublesome to the colonial comfort zone. But we should never stop because of other people's anger or discomfort when we have a great work for the land, for the women, for our children's futures, and for the entire worldscape of Indigenous people, some who are lulled by a comforting silence and others who are drumming sounds globally, the whole world inhaling these sounds as sure as a baby's first suck in of air and exhale their very first taste of sound.

We must not let the hatred and misconceptions that others have within them silence our strong voices. Their hatred and racism is their problem, not our own, and we must continue speaking, acting, writing, and moving to a greater change and justice for Indigenous people worldwide. Silence is not our mother tongue. No amount of hatred, racism, sexism, misconceptions, or stereotypes should act to bring us back to the false safety of silence. Our voices are being heard. And the unwinding from Silence's strong hold, round and round, our hands entwined with others, was not so hard after all. Let's move and speak, from the first sound forward. Madwewewin.

Originally appeared on Decolonization: Indigeneity, Education & Society *(decolonization.wordpress.com), February 7, 2013.*

HOW DO YOU SAY IDLE NO MORE IN ANISHINAABEMOWIN?

Melody McKiver

Looking through the site search statistics on my personal website, I've had a number of readers arrive in recent days wondering "How do you say Idle No More in anishinaabemowin?" Daga aanakanootamawishin. *Please translate it for me.* Perhaps what has hit me the hardest as the Idle No More movement develops is the reminder that I still can't answer that question with confidence. Nin-gagwe-nitaa-anishinaabem. *I'm trying to learn Ojibwe.* I was raised in Ottawa, and my mother was adopted during the Sixties Scoop and raised in a non-Anishinaabe household. My kookum attended Cecilia Jeffrey Indian Residential School in Kenora, and she passed on years before anyone in my family could find her. All of her children were taken from her. Nobody in my immediate family speaks the language fluently. Bangii eta ni-nisidotam. *I can understand only a little.* I hope that my relations living on and near Obishikokaang hold on to the language. Reconnecting with our extended family is an ongoing, long-term process, and there are many relatives I have yet to meet. Many other Indigenous people can share similar stories on how the Canadian state has implemented strategies to rip apart their families and impede the transmission of language between generations. Residential schooling, adoption, hospitalization. Enfranchisement, marrying out. You hear these words and terms over and over again. These are all strategies of colonization, and they have been very, very effective.

    To me, the search engine query "How do you say Idle No More in Anishinaabemowin?" reflects many of these histories of colonization and the damage it has dealt to our Indigenous languages. My website receives little traffic, and when I replicated the query I had to dig through over a page of results before reaching my own site. It is sad to note that none of these pages, mine included, answered the question. And yet, knowing that others are asking leaves me with a great hope. People are seeking to engage with Idle No More, and they want to engage in Anishinaabemowin. How many other people are learning how to say "Idle No More" in their own respective Indigenous languages?

And how, as language speakers and learners, can we work to support those that want to learn?

I first started to learn at 21, taking night classes at Toronto's Native Canadian Centre on my way home from my undergraduate studies. I have since continued to study through print and web resources. I am profoundly grateful to the wonderful people in my life, both in-person and online, that share their knowledge of Anishinaabemowin with those around them. Their guidance, gentle corrections, and insistence on using Anishinaabemowin continuously inspires and challenges me. Chi-miigwech! There are many educators creating language nests and talking circles, compiling dictionaries and workbooks, and developing apps and websites. These are all incredible resources, and we must continue to harness community resources into a targeted effort to restore our languages to the vibrancy that they deserve. I continuously fight against my own internalized shame at speaking English and French fluently while my Anishinaabemowin skills barely rival that of a toddler; I tell myself that I could be doing so much more to learn. Let this be my public commitment. Nindanokii'idiz. *I make myself work.*

The University of Michigan's Nongwa e-Anishinaabemjig language resource posted a poem in Anishinaabemowin and English about Idle No More, and presented their translation as "Kaa Maamda Geyabi Baabiinchigeying!" *No longer are we waiting!* I asked on Twitter how language speakers would translate Idle No More, and received two additional translations. My friend Geraldine King (@JibbyJoos) suggested "gaawiin nii-wiimdbaasiimin minwaa," which translates to *I will not sit again/anymore.* Jeff Monague (@brando44) provided a translation in the Southern Georgian Bay dialect, "kaa wiikaa, kaa gegoo wdaa zhichkesiimin." Note how each speaker provided a different translation based on their own dialect and interpretation of Idle No More. Anishinaabemowin is a complex language and learning it, like decolonization, can't happen overnight. But for both, it is essential that the work be put in.

Originally appeared on Decolonization: Indigeneity, Education & Society *(decolonization.wordpress.com), February 7, 2013.*

MY GRANDFATHER, MY ROLE MODEL
Cara Mumford

I am Métis. In my family, we call ourselves Chippewa Cree because of the group that we travelled with after the Northwest Resistance. My grandfather's family originally signed Treaty 4 but was later discharged from Treaty because of their participation in the Resistance. The Canadian government wasn't particularly fond of Indigenous people standing up for their rights. Some things are slow to change. When I first heard the court decision recognizing the rights of Métis and Non-Status as "Indians" under the constitution, I went through a rapid succession of thoughts and emotions in mere seconds. First was pure heart-swelling pride: *I wish my Grandpa Lou was here to see this!* A Métis elder in Medicine Hat who instilled in me a love of the land and a deep connection to horses, he was a fierce defender of the rights of the underdog. In the factory where he worked, he was the man that women turned to when they were being sexually harassed because he was the only man they knew who would do something about it. And when he was arrested as a union organizer at a strike, it was those women who marched down to the police station to free him. He was so proud when he won his hunting and fishing rights, and he would have been even more proud to be recognized as Indian.

Even though we are from diverse nations and the government has repeatedly tried to disconnect us from our ancestry, we are all connected. As Black Elk said, "In the old days when we were a strong and happy people, all our power came to us from the sacred hoop of the nation, and so long as the hoop was unbroken the people flourished." But the nation's hoop has been broken and scattered. Every child taken from their family, every woman stolen from her community affects us all. Did you know that there are more Native children in state care now than during the time of residential schools? Did you know that while the "official" number of missing and murdered Aboriginal women is 600, the unofficial number is closer to 2,000? Our communities know when our women are missing. We need our women and children for our communities to survive, to mend the sacred hoop. All too recently, a First Nations woman was attacked in Thunder Bay, left for dead

by two men who told her that she "deserved to lose her treaty rights."
When I read about that, I couldn't breathe. *I have to do something*, I
thought. *But what?* You see, my grandfather didn't just instill in me
his love of horses and the land; I also inherited his passion for justice.
My Grandpa Lou. Louis. Named for Riel.
And so I am reminded of Riel's words: "My people will sleep for
one hundred years, but when they awake, it will be the artists who give
them their spirit back." Reminded of who I am. Métis. A Métis artist. I began studying film in 2006 and I knew early on that I needed to
make a film to commemorate the twentieth anniversary of the Montreal
Massacre, a day that made a deep impact on me. Through that event
my eyes were opened to the real danger that women in Canada face
on a daily basis. Just because I had been safe didn't mean other women
were. It hit home in a way it hadn't before... I was a second year science student when those women studying engineering were killed... it
could easily have been me. I worked on that film with spoken word
artist Evalyn Parry, who taught me an invaluable lesson on empowerment. I had become depressed after doing the research for the film. I
knew things hadn't improved for women as much as mainstream media would like us to believe; it seemed like things were actually getting bleaker every year. But Evalyn wouldn't let me wallow there and
ended her spoken word piece with an empowering list of 14 reasons
why you should be proud you are a woman. One of these reasons was:
"You are enough." That really resonated with me.
Another line that Evalyn wrote which haunted me was, "Women's
bodies farmed out, used up, disappeared." It was a specific reference
to the Pickton farm and the missing and murdered women from
Vancouver's East End. Métis dancer Charity Anne Doucette represented
those women in that film. That was when I started to think about creating a film to focus on the missing and murdered Aboriginal women, the
Sisters in Spirit. That was the genesis of "When It Rains." Thoughts of
Charity inevitably lead to thoughts of our mutual friend—Charity's
soul sister—Marsha Ellen Meidow, who worked on the front lines with
at-risk girls in Calgary. Marsha and I were planning a series of writing
workshops for girls at risk, encouraging them to tell their stories. The
majority of the girls were Aboriginal and we had visions of creating a
grassroots Aboriginal version of the Vagina Monologues, connecting

with like-minded writing groups in cities across Canada. Marsha died suddenly from a brain aneurysm shortly after that inspiration, which devastated me, so that project never happened, but maybe there's a way to make it happen after all.

The films I create are intended to draw attention to issues of violence against women, partly in an attempt to shift perspectives and create dialogue, but my primary goal is to empower the women themselves. I believe that Idle No More is an excellent example of how to do both. On the one hand, it is educating people, all people, about the issues. On the other hand, the Round Dance Revolution reminds us the power of our drums. As much as they are a reminder to others that we're still here, they are also a reminder to ourselves. I believe the political goals of Idle No More are of primary importance to the health of this country and this planet, but I believe the long-term success of Idle No More will be seen in a resurgence of Indigenous knowledges, cultures, languages and pride. And I believe that women will continue to lead the way. Our women are vital to healthy communities. Our nation is strong only when our women are strong. And between Chief Theresa Spence and the four women who started Idle No More—Sheelah McLean, Nina Wilson, Sylvia McAdam and Jessica Gordon—our nation is strong indeed. And do not mistake diversity with divisiveness. Regardless of our different approaches, our goal is the same: to mend the sacred hoop. There is a Chinese proverb: "When sleeping women wake, mountains move." I don't know about you, but I can hear the Rocky Mountains rumbling.

Originally appeared on Decolonization: Indigeneity, Education & Society *(decolonization.wordpress.com), February 11, 2013.*

WE HOLD OUR HANDS UP:
On Indigenous Women's Love and Resistance

Dory Nason

Over the past few months, the world has witnessed the boundless love that Indigenous women have for their families, their lands, their nations, and themselves as Indigenous people. These profound forms of love motivate Indigenous women everywhere to resist and protest, to teach and inspire, and to hold accountable both Indigenous and non-Indigenous allies to their responsibilities to protect the values and traditions that serve as the foundation for the survival of the land and Indigenous peoples. These ways of being also provide a framework that ensures Indigenous women's relationship to the land and their human right to bodily sovereignty remains intact and free from violation. Specifically, women in the #IdleNoMore movement seek to protect the waters, the environment, and the land from the threat of further destruction. Indeed, they seek protection not only for themselves but for those values, practices, and traditions that are at the core of Indigenous women's power and sovereignty—concepts that have been and remain under attack, and which strike at the core of a settler-colonial misogyny that refuses to acknowledge the ways it targets Indigenous women for destruction.

This point is an important distinction when we discuss what Indigenous women want for themselves and their communities. I would humbly ask all of us to think about what it means for men, on the one hand, to publicly profess an obligation to "protect our women" and, on the other, take leadership positions that uphold patriarchal forms of governance or otherwise ignore the contributions and sovereignty of the women, Indigenous and not. But that is another subject for another time. What I want to focus on is what the women in #IdleNoMore have shown us all—that Indigenous women's love is powerful. It is a love that can inspire a whole world to sing and dance and be in ceremony for the people. This has always been so. Yet, I would be mistaken to not address how this love has also made Indigenous women targets. Indeed, popular backlash against women in the #IdleNoMore movement demonstrates how Indigenous women's love is countered in patriarchal settler colonialist societies—with epidemic levels of violence, sexual assault, imprisonment, and cultural and political disempowerment.

Because the colonizer has always known that to counter the power of Indigenous womanhood, you need to make acceptable the practice of hating Indian women. To normalize this hatred and violence, Indigenous women's power to love and to inspire is turned into something insidious; their powerful love for who they are and where they come from becomes distorted in mainstream consciousness and those distortions become the narratives and images society pulls from in times like these. When Indigenous women's love inspires a nation to round-dance, question destructive environmental policy, or demand justice for children living in substandard conditions, other forces counter with vitriolic hate. It is at this point that we see the power of Indigenous women's love turn into something ugly in the mainstream media—this love becomes self-serving, opportunistic, and a lie—or as Anishinaabe scholar Leanne Betasamosake Simpson has shown us in her beautiful piece "Fish Broth and Fasting" about Chief Spence's sacrifice, settler colonial misogyny can turn something as sacred as a Native woman's ceremonial fast for her people into a publicity stunt, a cynical smokescreen, and a Senator's ugly joke.

It is what makes it acceptable to run political cartoons such as Malcolm Mayes' recent piece in *The Edmonton Journal*,[9] mocking her love with an image of death and words that are meant to put all Native women leaders in their places. Mobilizing this hate seems alarmingly easy in the popular consciousness. Indigenous women have always known of its presence and the violence it provokes. This kind of violence has a history, one that in 1883 led Paiute activist Sarah Winnemucca to write these words:

> My people have been so unhappy for a long time they wish now to disincrease, instead of multiply. The mothers are afraid to have more children, for fear they shall have daughters, who are not safe even in their mother's presence.

Violence against Indigenous women is so normalized in settler society; it even becomes a category of desire in the public consciousness. For that we don't have to look far. Even in popular so-called homages to our womanhood, violence and sexual degradation saturate the picture.[10]

But, I do not want to dwell on this darkness. Movements like #IdleNoMore are more than a response to oppressive conditions that structure all of our lives. These movements are about the profound love that Indigenous women have for the future stability and health

9   View the cartoon at www.edmontonjournal.com/7865425.bin, printed on
    January 24, 2013—the day she ended her hunger strike.
10 See No Doubt's 2012 music video "Looking Hot" for an example of this.

of their families, their land, and their nations. And of this love there are countless historical and contemporary examples. I want to close with just a few that are specifically about the love Native women have for one another despite the pervasiveness of settler colonial misogyny and violence.

There is the example of Dakota writer and activist Zitkala-Ša who went to Oklahoma in the 1920s to investigate the rampant violence against Indigenous women and girls in Indian Territory. To conduct this investigation, Zitkala-Ša spoke with women in these communities, listening to their stories of the ones who had gone missing or turned up murdered, the girl-children whose oil money and head rights made them targets of lawyers, judges and other white men in power. This work underscored the love Zitkala-Ša had for Indian women and for this research; she too became a target. Indeed for naming a prominent judge's criminal behaviour in her final report, she was threatened with imprisonment if she ever stepped foot in Oklahoma again.

In this vein, I think of the many Indigenous women activists, scholars and artists whose love for murdered Mi'kmaq activist Anna Mae Aquash have made sure she is not forgotten in our histories of resistance. There are the Indigenous women writers such as Marie Clements, Linda Hogan, Louise Erdrich, and countless others who never let us forget the power of women's love. And there are Indigenous women filmmakers such as Alanis Obomsawin, Elle-Máijá Tailfeathers, Christine Welsh, Catherine Martin, and Sandy Osawa, whose films tell the stories of women warriors in our lifetime.

In recent weeks, we have seen the letter of the Women of Turtle Island in support of Chief Theresa Spence that reminds us all that "as mothers, aunties, sisters, grandmothers, our concern is for the safety and well-being of all peoples." On February 14, there will be the Women's Memorial March committees in Vancouver and other cities that will show love for the murdered and missing across Canada and the world. Profound love of the kind that moves nations, starts movements, and inspires action does not go away; it deepens and becomes stronger with time. It is of a generous spirit and one that is captured in the words of Nancy Ward, Nan-ye-hi, Beloved Woman of the Cherokee Nation. I close with her words to the US Treaty Commissioners in 1781, words that remind all of us, Indigenous and settlers alike, the true meaning of building a lasting and loving relationship based on kinship and a respect for women's rights and obligations: *We are your mothers, you are our sons. Our cry is all for peace; let it continue. Let your women's sons be ours; our sons be yours. Let your women hear our words.*

Originally appeared on Decolonization: Indigeneity, Education & Society *(decolonization.wordpress.com), February 12, 2013.*

MORE THAN A POSTER CAMPAIGN:
Redefining Colonial Violence

Sarah Hunt

Nineteen years ago, when I started my undergraduate degree, I was introduced to Indigenous women's writing for the first time. Until then, the words in my own personal journal were the only reflections of Indigenous women's lives available to me. Reading the stories of Lee Maracle, Jeanette Armstrong, Beth Brant, Patricia Monture-Angus, and others, I was struck by both the prevalence of violence in their lives and the strength of resistance to this violence. Their stories of resilience sprang off the page, transforming moments of shame and silence into ones of strength and survival. After a family member took her own life, these stories inspired me to focus on issues of violence in our communities, and I've taken my direction from this calling ever since.

Over the years, much has changed in how violence against women is talked about. With the emergence of a discourse around "the missing women," gendered violence is being recognized as a widespread reality in our homes, schools, cities, and streets. The conviction of a serial killer in Vancouver's Downtown Eastside solidified the reality that our aunties have been preyed upon for far too long. But in talking with other Indigenous people across Turtle Island, I know the daily reality of interpersonal violence continues despite this increased awareness. After close to 20 years of talking about this issue, what unsettles me the most is the similarity of stories from girls in small towns and large cities, in urban centres and remote villages. Across this land, our daughters continue to be targeted for physical, mental, and emotional abuse on a daily basis, by people from both inside and outside our communities. Something needs to change in our strategies to stop this violence. Colonialism relies on the widespread dehumanization of all Indigenous people—our children, two-spirits, men and women—so colonial violence could be understood to impact all of us at the level of our denied humanity. Yet this dehumanization is felt most acutely in the bodies of Indigenous girls, women, two-spirit, and transgender people, as physical and sexual violence against us continues to be accepted as normal. Our strategies to name gendered violence can themselves become part of the problem, as the language of "the missing women" masks the brutal reality of how they become "missing." Girls and women don't simply disappear—they are beaten, murdered, kidnapped, violated, and raped. The language of "bullying" in our schools also serves to mask the nature of this violence, which is not simply about online taunts or threats but about targeted assaults. It may be more palatable to use softer language to raise awareness, but, as the girls in our communities can tell us, the realities we're trying to change are anything but soft. We're fighting for our lives here, as our aunties and grandmas have been doing since colonialism began.

News stories of girls being killed or kidnapped continue to surface momentarily on the local newspaper and radio, without any follow-up or outrage. Our "disappearance" is still easily dismissed as mere blips on the radar of most Canadians. And, as those of us working with families and communities know, many more daily incidents of violence go untold, unheard, or unnoticed. Despite the national Stolen Sisters campaign, local marches, vigils, and other events to remember girls and women who've been killed, our efforts have yet to change the acceptance of daily violence enacted on the bodies of our loved ones. Many of the strategies to address violence have further strengthened broad systems of colonial power, which are themselves inherently violent. We continue to appeal to the Canadian legal system to address physical violence, calling for more policing or better laws, while knowing this system is set up to oppress, rather than help, us. The same colonial mentality that created the Indian Act to privilege the rights of men over women, and instituted residential schools to break down our family systems, serves as the foundation for the Canadian legal system.

Surely we must engage with this powerful system, but appealing to law alone will not stop the violence.

So how do we begin to change norms around gendered violence without reinforcing its roots in colonial power? As we strategize, we must be careful not to reproduce the systems and ideologies that colonialism has introduced. Sexist, racist, and homophobic ideas have been internalized at many levels, but colonialism's stealthy ways make them hard to recognize.

As an example, one consequence of developing broad public awareness about the prevalence of violence against Indigenous women has been the privileging of some women's voices over others. Moving from Vancouver's Downtown Eastside to offices in Ottawa and other urban centres across Turtle Island, efforts to name gendered violence have shifted from grassroots discussions to slick poster campaigns. In these moves, certain voices have been left behind, enacting a form of silencing that I believe is in crucial need of reparation. Rather than calling on our sisters in the sex trade to speak for themselves, others are asked to speak on their behalf. We must ask ourselves how colonial values continue to shape whose voices are seen as legitimate, while working to centre the voices of the most marginalized women in our communities rather than only those of us with a colonial education.

So colonial violence can be understood as more than just interpersonal abuse—it is inherent in the systems that have shaped how we define ourselves and relate to one another as Indigenous people. It should go without saying that healing from violence requires rebuilding our individual and collective strength rather than reinforcing the power of the state. By centring local Indigenous knowledge in our understandings of leadership, honor, strength, and love, we can redefine "power" as well as "violence." This requires relearning our stories and our cultural teaching in order to raise up the girls in our communities and respect them as leaders, mothers, warriors, and knowledge keepers.

Transforming our dehumanization must move beyond just poster campaigns and court cases, because their ability to enact change only goes so far. I believe it is only through building stronger relationships with one another, across the generations and across differences in education, ability, sexuality, and other social locations, that we can break down the stigma and shame resulting from generations of colonial violence. As we reinstate the roles of women and two-spirit people in systems of Indigenous governance and law, ending gendered violence can be understood as integral to self-determination. In the words of the late Patricia Monture-Angus, "Self-determination is principally, that is first and foremost, about our relationships. Communities cannot be self-governing until members of those communities are well and living in a responsible way. It is difficult for individuals to be self-determining until they are living as part of their community" (*Journeying Forward: Dreaming First Nations Independence*, 1999, p.8).

Originally appeared on Decolonization: Indigeneity, Education & Society *(decolonization.wordpress.com), February 14, 2013.*

"I HAVE WAITED 40 YEARS FOR THIS. KEEP IT GOING AND DON'T STOP!":
An Interview with Siku Allooloo

Siku Allooloo with Leanne Betasamosake Simpson

LEANNE BETASAMOSAKE SIMPSON (LS): I'm with Siku Allooloo, a Haitian Inuk whose mother was from Haiti (Taino/French/Spanish/African descent) and father is from Mittimatalik, Nunavut. She was born and raised in Denendeh and is also a member of a large Dene Sųłiné family. Miigwech for joining me.

Siku, I realize you were back home (in Denendeh) for a large part of the Idle No More movement but you did join with some close Dene friends who were leading the charge (and continue to) in Somba K'e (Yellowknife). I am aware that you and your group organized teach-ins, rallies, and drum dances as well as travelled to support Idle No More events that were held in other communities and also that you worked closely with other community members, drummers, teachers, and current and former Dene leaders. I also know that you have expressed appreciation that many leaders were generous in their support—both by stepping aside to let others lead the way and in providing guidance and assistance when asked. At the same time, you did some creative work too, right?

SIKU ALLOOLOO (SA): Yes, my friend and I created a short documentary about the Idle No More blockade at the Deh Cho Bridge. That was an incredibly joyous and very powerful event where people demonstrated and drum danced throughout -40°C weather in Denendeh.

LS: We'll include the link so people can watch it.[11] There is a very long history of resistance in your homeland. How does Idle No More fit into that context?

SA: There are long histories of resistance in Indigenous homelands worldwide, and certainly in all three of my homelands as well. For now, I will talk about Denendeh, although my knowledge only goes back about 100 to 150 years. It was the Dene who insisted on making treaties with the British Crown in order to set the terms of the relationship and to protect the freedom and ways of life of both their people and all living beings of the land. They explicitly denied land as a topic for negotiation, thus deliberately excluding the cessation, surrender, or sale of land and extinguishment of their rights from the agreements. However, the agreements were made orally and the colonial government bent this to their advantage, ensuring that cession, surrender, and extinguishment became the primary terms on the written documents for both Treaties 8 and 11.

This history was taken up in the late 60s/early 70s during the American Indian Movement, when two pivotal events took place that sparked enormous resistance in the North: the discovery of oil and natural gas in Prudhoe Bay in 1968, and the proposal of the 1969 White Paper. The Mackenzie Valley Pipeline was at the time the largest private construction project ever proposed, and it promised certain destruction of the land, animals, and Dene way of life. The White Paper attempted to do away with Indigenous peoples entirely by eliminating our legal rights and our relationship with the state, which propelled the Dene to establish the Indian Brotherhood of the NWT (now the Dene Nation). My Dene father, Francous Paulette, and 16 other chiefs in the Brotherhood promptly sued the Crown, filed a caveat against the pipeline (the Paulette Caveat), and won. They exposed the Treaties as

11   Available at: vimeo.com/56886462

fraudulent documents and secured Aboriginal Rights to over 400,000 square feet of land. Construction of the pipeline was halted for over 40 years, (though sadly, a new pipeline has been approved and will now be underway very soon). Idle No More was a continuation of that struggle to protect our lands, communities, cultures, and existence as Indigenous peoples from further attempts at annihilation, in Denendeh as well as in every other Indigenous homeland that has suffered colonization. That struggle has been ongoing for several hundreds of years, and for my generation this was our time of awakening to our power in taking action. At the time, my Indigenous brothers and sisters and I were aware of taking our own steps along a path that we have inherited from our parents and ancestors, and which we will one day pass on to future generations. Many of our parents were those active leaders and our group was lucky to have their support. Several of them expressed how they have waited all this time for the younger generation to take up the charge and drive it forward. They welcomed us into the struggle and said "At last!" Or as my papa said to me and my partner: "I have waited 40 years for this. Keep it going and don't stop!"

LS: What did it mean to you to participate in Idle No More?

SA: For me, it meant the arrival of my time to step in and join my Indigenous sisters and brothers in breathing life into our collective sense of being; to raise ourselves up and support one another in asserting our vitality as Indigenous peoples; and to take up our power in our own hands. We all experience the oppression and suffering that colonial systems continue to impose on us, and there is much to be done. Participating in Idle No More at the time meant pooling our energy and resources to help one another in our respective and collective struggles, and building strong connections across all kinds of borders. For me, it was a starting point, a way to put myself forward, to join forces with other like-hearted people, and to set our energies in motion towards what we most believe in: the strengthening and empowerment of Indigenous nations and instatement of balance in our relationships on every level.

LS: What are the big issues in your homeland that you think motivated yourself and others to take action?

Stanley George Jr., Johnny Abraham, David Kawapit, Raymond Kawapit, Geordie Rupert, Travis George were the original six Wisjinichu-Nishiyuu. Along their 1,600km journey from Whapmagoostui to Ottawa to promote Indigenous unity, hundreds joined them. Ottawa, March 25, 2013. (MELODY MCKIVER)

SA: Massive resource extraction is a huge, long-standing concern in the North, and all of the problems that go with it—destruction of the environment and animal populations, increased substance abuse, increased violence against women, deterioration of respectful relationships with the land, between people, and with other forms of life due to the culture of exploitation, etc. Knowing the successful history of resistance in Denendeh and having a great love for where I come from inspired me to join my brothers and sisters in taking action. The first week that Idle No More took off, I saw photos of my friend and her small kids holding Idle No More signs out on the main street in Yellowknife at -40°C, just the few of them, and I was hugely inspired. As soon as I arrived in town, I joined my friends in the organizing, and then none of us slept for the whole month during the height of the movement!

Personally, I have always been inspired by my ancestors and by those who are driven by love for their people and homeland. I was lucky enough to be raised with those stories, so I am proud of who and where I come from. I feel that as an Indigenous person, as part of a community of people who are systematically oppressed, it is of the upmost importance to know that those who came before us fought for our existence, and that the vitality of our nations, homelands, and ways of life are worth loving immensely enough to stand up for with our every inch of strength. There are many people in the North and all over who demonstrate that through their hard work in the communities, and their presence at the rallies gave us a deep sense of fortitude.

LS: Idle No More was led by women and youth—how did this play out in your territory?

SA: It was true to form in Denendeh too. We knew that Indigenous movements in the 70s were forefronted exclusively by men, and our group (which is made up mostly of strong-minded women) were definitely not going to have any of that! Women were (and continue to be) the leading force both in our actions and others that took place in Denendeh. I think highly of the men in the group too, they are incredibly respectful and respectable people who fully supported our lead and stepped in to lead in their own ways as well. Also everyone in our group is of a younger generation (mid-20s to mid-30s), and those who have children involve them in everything from making signs to sitting in during meetings to marching on the street. It's still very important to have the voices and actions of Indigenous women and youth held up so highly, as both groups continue to experience a great deal of marginalization, even within our communities.

I must point out that what I appreciate about the forms of organizing I have been a part of is the balance of women and men working together equally, taking different leads and providing mutual support. Everyone has their own strengths, abilities, and resources to contribute and it's best when that can be coordinated harmoniously, regardless of gender, age, or any other identifier.

LS: Your work is very strongly rooted in nationhood and resurgence. Does Idle No More move these issues along for you?

SA: For me, Idle No More was a catalyst—it propelled me into action and set in motion work that I have always felt compelled to take up though hadn't yet found a direct avenue for. It was a major catalyst for my Dene friends too, who are still going strong in their organizing work and raising awareness about pressing issues in their territory, especially regarding proposed fracking projects.

I myself have always been passionate about Indigenous peoples, particularly women and youth, and my work is driven by a desire to hold up and encourage our people to find strength, pride, and empowerment in who they are and the homelands they're from so that we can raise up our nations and live well again on this earth, in both the ways that have been given to us and also in new ways that affirm balance and nurture well-being. For me, this is about Indigenous nationhood, meaning actively directing my energy toward the revitalization of our nations, our homelands, ways of life, systems of governance and values, the restoration of healthy families and communities, and the restoration of our respective nations' autonomy. These are the things that I care about.

LS: Both art and social media played an important role in Idle No More. How did this play out in the North?

SA: Social media was of course what facilitated the movement, and it was hugely important in the North because it connected our actions with what was happening in the rest of the country and the world. Because of our distance, isolation and low population the North is often overlooked by Canadian society, even amongst Native populations in the South. But Northerners are very active and are sure to stay informed, so when Idle No More blew up on the scene we were quick to take action and represent in our communities. We did it the Dene way, by drum dancing, having feasts at our teach-ins, seeking advice from our parents and elders over tea, and initiating respectful collaborations with Native leaders and community members. Some of our group members work in media as well, so we were able to spread the news throughout Denendeh on the radio (in English and Dene languages), also through film, photography, and online. We connected ourselves with active Natives in other parts of the country and supported one another, as everyone else was doing as well. It was really incredible.

LS: What do you want Canadians to know about your people?

SA: That we are present, proud, and growing stronger. Our peoples remain resilient as ever, and we will continue to take action to protect our homelands, restore our nationhood and autonomy, and live with dignity as Indigenous peoples. I want Canadians and Native peoples alike to learn from our histories, and to choose to live with integrity and respect, as our peoples have struggled to do since European settlers first arrived.

LS: What are your hopes for the youth of your nation?

SA: I hope that all Indigenous youth find great strength and pride in their cultural heritage, their people, and their homeland so that they can lead with their hearts and ensure that their lands and communities are taken care of. I want our peoples to grow strong and to be fuelled by the love of our ancestors who struggled for hundreds of years to ensure our existence, despite enormous adversity. I want our youth to know through our actions that their future and their children's future is of the upmost importance. And that we carry this love and this struggle for them.

IDLE NO MORE RULES FOR ALL ETERNITY FOREVER AND EVER TAPWE AND AMEN MAHSI CHO!

Richard Van Camp

December 10, 2012, is when I set aside my mostly worry-free ways and decided to use social media (Facebook and Twitter) to face my fear and growing concern of what I was hearing about Canada and where it was headed. I could not believe what I was reading about the Prime Minister of Canada and these omnibus bills that were being proposed. I could not believe that so many scientists were being let go from their jobs. These were the specialists who were trained to monitor the waterways for Canadians. Here was my first social quote: "Mr. Harper, you are now in the way of clean and safe water for all Canadians. It may be the Treaties that save Canada, after all." It received 57 likes.

I think it's safe to say many Aboriginal people and Canadians were suddenly realizing that things that seemed unthinkable with the omnibus bills were actually going to happen. Chief Theresa Spence started her 30-day hunger strike on December 11. As word started to spread online and in newspapers about what the omnibus bills were truly all about, I decided to post this on Facebook on December 15, 2012. It was shared several times and I received 158 likes.

You know what would be awesome? If a human led Skynet sent Elijah Harper into the past to also become the Governor General of Canada and on Monday—eagle feather in his gorgeous Cree hands—he turned to the House and to the world and said, "Traditionally, the Head Man of a Nation received direction from the elders and the mothers of that Nation. Somewhere along the way, this has been lost. It has been said when you break the treaties, you break the law. Before us are these Omnibus bills, which you, Mr. Harper, opposed yourself in the past. What elected leader jeopardizes the water of its Nation for not only this generation but for generations he or she can't even imagine? Did you not hear the warning that future wars will not be about gold or oil, but they will be about water? Sir, you have given me no choice as I, once again, raise the same eagle feather that I held up at the Meech Lake Accord hearings and say, "No. No to all that you propose right now. Canadians have asked you not to jeopardize the safety of this great nation for your greed and third party interests, and because you did not listen, it came to this: Harper versus Harper and I say, No. May this great Nation continue to grow and prosper and share its abundance with the world in a good way. A ho. I have spoken. Tapwe. The truth has been spoken here." Now wouldn't that be cool?"

Again, I received more "likes" and shared posts on Facebook. I think it's safe to say that many of us were horrified that the first omnibus came to pass. We couldn't believe it!

On December 16 as word of a grassroots movement titled Idle No More started to grow and rumours of flash mobs across Canada and in different parts of the world started to spread, and as I read more and more about what Prime Minister Harper was wanting to do with Canada, I decided to post the following Facebook post attached to a YouTube link titled "The Lord of the Rings: The Two Towers (2002)— Gandalf Releases Theoden." I wrote:

Awwwwwwww you know what would be so awesome? It would be so awesome if Elijah Harper was Gandalf and Theodon was Stephen Harper and Gandalf's staff was his Eagle feather and Elijah smudged Stephen Harper and our Prime Minister woke up and said, "I know your face. Elijah?" And Elijah said, "Breathe the free air again, Brother." And then Stephen Harper said, "Dark have been my dreams of late." And then Elijah said, "Your fingers would remember their own strength better if you grasped your pen." Stephen Harper would remember everything in his heart for living in a good way, and he would realize what he was about to do to Canada and he would say, "NO. NO! We have to stop what's about to happen with these ridiculous Omnibus bills. Why did I allow opposition only one minute in the House of Commons to state their business? They could really have something to say. Okay, where do I sign to 'undo' all I've done that would jeopardize our happiness as a great and giving nation? Sign here? Okay. Done! Voila! Thanks, Elijjah. Holy cow, man. That was close. Hai Hai." Then Stephen and Elijah would go see The Hobbit and they'd be smiling after going "Dude. Dude." :)

Here's the link: www.youtube.com/watch?v=PY9eRkdIeuk

On December 18, 2012, Keavy Martin, my neecheemoos, and I decided to go to our first outside flash mob, which ended up turning

into a full-on downtown Edmonton drum dance. I posted, along with
this photo:

I saw this young man at the Idle No More gathering in Edmonton on
Dec. 10th. I should have asked his name. I hope Canadians know
Aboriginal people are not only fighting for our Treaty rights but for water
and resource protection across Canada for all our
future generations. This is a terrifying time for Canada and greed seems
to be the order of the day. Mahsi cho!

It turns out this was Boppajay Lafleche. I love this picture! Look
at the pride in his eyes. What made me so happy about this gathering
is there were so many young people there and they were genuinely so
mad about what was happening in our country. I kept thinking, "Prime
Minister Harper, we're willing to fight for Canada. Why aren't you?"
I was also aware that Harper had stirred up the fastest growing demographic in Canada.

On December 21, I was home for my dad's birthday in Fort Smith, NWT, and I saw our leaders unite with a drum song and a ceremony of "Feeding the Fire" in the middle of town. Many trucks honked as they rode by and there were so many of us dancing together as Fort Smithers for the very first time. This is when it hit me that the federal government had now united Canadians and Aboriginal people: "Praying for Canada at the drum dance in Fort Smith as we honour our ancestors, the land and all future generations #Idlenommore."

One thing I will always remember is Elder Mike Beaver saying that the agreements with the treaties are not with the Prime Minister. These are peace treaties between the Crown and sovereign nations. He's right. Prime Minister Harper is counting on Canadians not knowing their history and getting Canadians, once again, to blame Aboriginal people for standing in the way of "progress" (i.e., fracking, the tar sands, pipelines, etc.)

On December 27, I wrote:

You know what Idle No More deserves? We need an anthem that unites us all. Take, for example, this incredible song: "Eye of the Tiger" by Survivor. Holy cow, does the lead singer ever look like Clinton Kathrein! (**a very cool dude that I grew up with) Check it out! And 'member when Midnight Oil's "Beds are Burning" came out? Holy cow! That stirred our blood like crazy!

So here's my call to all musicians: please upload your song and perhaps yours will be the one that is sung all over the world in support of what everyone is trying to do with this revolution. Here's the link to "Eye of the Tiger" if you want to rock out! www.youtube.com/watch?v=btPJPFnesV4

On December 30, 2012, I wrote:

Mr. Prime Minister, can you feel the drum thunder of a revolution that you and your leadership have started by underestimating us? Meet with Chief Spence and end this time of international disgrace. It's time to build a bridge back to a transparent partnership that honours the treaties and our future together. Mahsi cho!

I linked this to Rage Against the Machine's song "Guerilla Radio." I also wrote on that day:

Edmonton, see you at the Idle No More Revolution at 1 pm today at the Alberta Legislature Grounds. The sun is shining. Let us honour Day 20 of Chief Theresa Spence's hunger strike. This is a day for all Canadians to join us in a peaceful demonstration saying we've had it with a leadership that's leading a culture of extinguishment for Aboriginal people and unsafe waterways for all of our future generations. Mahsi cho!

At this time, IdleNoMore was in the papers, online, being acknowledged by the Canadian media in press and in news broadcasts, so I started to incorporate more of my Tweets and Facebook posts with their hashtag.

On January 10 (at the U of A round dance outside), I Tweeted:

See you in the circle! See you at the round dance with our breath rising as one! Every little crow hop is a stand against greed! Our march and drum thunder are growing! Join us! **#idlenomore**

On January 11, I Tweeted:

Everyone who's dancing, marching, singing and praying in this **#idlenomore** revolution is a warrior in my eyes. Mahsi cho!

Chief Theresa Spence was our hero and was bringing national shame to the Prime Minister (who was now being openly called "The Crime Minister" because rumours of his participation in automated "Robocalls" that diverted 7,000 voters to the wrong polling station in Guelph, Ontario, were starting to grow). Had he won the election illegally? How was any of this possible in Canada? Why wasn't he fighting for all Canadians? Why wasn't anyone stopping him? There were so many opportunities for Stephen Harper to address the nation and outline why he was doing what he was doing, but there wasn't a single one that I remember. In fact, rumours were starting to grow that federal employees had received a gag order and that they were not to speak to the press without authorization.

On January 12, I had the pleasure and joy of Round Dancing at the West Edmonton Mall in a flash mob with my neecheemoos, Keavy Martin, and my mom, Rosa Wah-shee, and with thousands of other dancers. I wrote:

So this is what a revolution feels like: the scent of sweetgrass blanketing us all; holding an elder's hand in the Round Dance with my mom and my neecheemoos at my side; children learning about their ancestry and inheritance; Canadians asking how to help; international and national support; awareness; unity; taking a stand for Mother Earth; the power of our aunties leading us on. See you in the growing circle! #idlenomore

On January 28, I wrote:

Prime Ministers will come and go, but this paradise called Canada shall remain with all of her gifts and generosity. Let's protect her for each other and the generations on their way. Mahsi cho. #IdleNoMore

On January 28, I wrote:

Where will Big Industry be when you can't trust the water in your taps? Where will the corporations be when loved ones, neighbours, and future generations get sick from the water and food around us? Canada is worth protecting. I support the #IdleNoMore Revolution!

On May 18, I saw how Harper was losing ground in the eyes of so many Canadians and on a national level. I Tweeted:

thatspiritofgreedandbackalleydealshasnowturnedagainstyou
#idlenomore

and I posted this picture:

I don't want to believe that the prime minister won this election through fraud, but if this is true, why isn't there a mechanism to impeach him? And if this is true, then I want these omnibus bills to be a fraud and, therefore, illegal, and I want to wake up and know that this was all just such a horrible and sad dream.

Idle No More isn't just fighting for Canada: it's about fighting for government transparency—which Stephen Harper promised before he became Prime Minister—and it's for a public awareness to what exactly third party interests entail for all Canadians. This government is counting on our apathy and our lack of understanding history. The best part of Idle No More is it woke so many of us up and it informed and will continue to inform and inspire us all. See you in the Circle!

SCAPEGOAT FOR A MOVEMENT?

Ethan Cox

Of all the myriad and varied actions, blockades and events which have taken place since the Idle No More movement came together late last year, only one has resulted in charges being laid. This is the story of the only person in the country facing legal consequences for his role in Idle No More, and his efforts to raise enough money to pay for his defence.

On December 21 of 2012, members of the Aamjiwnaang First Nation, located near Sarnia, Ontario, began a peaceful blockade of CN tracks as an expression of solidarity with Chief Theresa Spence's hunger strike and the broader Idle No More movement.

On the morning of the 22nd they were served with an injunction ordering them to dismantle the blockade by CN police. Later that day Ron Plain, a member of the Aamjiwnaang First Nation, arrived home from a trip and became the spokesperson for the blockade.

Plain is now the only person in Canada charged as a result of Idle No More related actions, and faces catastrophic fines, which he says would cause him to lose his house, and even the possibility of *indefinite* detention.

Raul Burbano, a Toronto-based organizer, has launched an *Indiegogo* campaign to raise funds to help Plain cover his rising legal fees.

"I got involved in helping Ron because I'm very concerned with the criminalization of dissent," said Burbano. "I think this is a clear case of such criminalization, where the courts are being used as a tool against peaceful protesters who want to bring attention to community issues." With ten days left the campaign has raised only $3,528 of a goal of $10,000, which itself would only cover a fraction of the legal fees Plain will incur if the case drags on. Burbano however remains hopeful that the public will come through to help Plain defend himself.

"I think if people know about his story, they'll be moved to support him."

In an interview with *rabble*, Plain explained that after arriving, he advised the mostly young members of his community to move the blockade from one crossing to another to nullify the injunction and force CN to seek another one.

"The judge who issued this injunction, David Brown, had not only worked for CN in the past as a lawyer, he had also been an expert witness for them. The ties to CN are twofold and deep, and yet he failed to disclose this past relationship with CN, which he was required to do."

The first injunction which was served on the 22nd ordered the blockaders to appear in court on the 24th of December if they wanted to appeal; otherwise, they could appear in court in Toronto on the 27th.

"It was all very strategically done. There was no way we could find a lawyer on two days' notice on Christmas eve. On the 24th, Judge Brown upheld his injunction and expanded it to apply to the tracks where we were at that point. He also ruled that if we wanted to appeal on the 27th we would have to give the CN lawyers twenty-four hours' notice. Of course there weren't 24 working hours between then and the 27th, because of the holiday, so it was impossible for us to appeal."

At the hearing on the 27th Judge Brown changed his injunction from an immediate injunction to a 30-day injunction. This meant that taking down the blockade and immediately setting it up again would no longer satisfy its terms.

At the same hearing, according to Plain, Judge Brown publicly complained that police were not enforcing his injunction, and suggested that the OPP and Sarnia police ignore the recommendations of the Ipperwash inquiry, which they had been following, and which called for police to not interfere with blockades.

On January 1, Plain says he received an email from CN's lawyers telling him he had to appear in court in Sarnia the next day, along with his band chief and the chief of police in Sarnia.

"Everyone agrees that I had no obligation to go. This was an email, from CN's lawyers, giving me barely 12 hours' notice. But I did, and in 12 hours I produced 250 pages of government documents which show that the tracks are there illegally. This isn't a land claim issue—in a land claim there is a dispute over ownership, here there is no dispute. No permit was ever issued to cross that road, and that makes the crossing illegal. But I was not allowed to present this evidence in court."

CN has now dropped the charges against the chief and council out of a desire to maintain good relations with the band. This leaves Plain alone, facing the prospect of dire consequences.

Because the charge is civil contempt of court, a complaint brought by CN, Plain cannot be sentenced to jail. However he can be ordered to pay a fine of an indeterminate amount and to pay the legal fees incurred by CN. He can also be sentenced to indefinite detention, if CN argues that they fear he will repeat his actions and he needs to be jailed to prevent him from blockading their tracks.

At the hearing on the 2nd of January CN offered to drop the charge, if Plain would agree to donate $5,000 to a charity of their choice, an offer he refused. According to Plain, the Sarnia judge, whose name Plain could not recall, then warned him that if he didn't accept the CN offer, he would be forced to pay their legal fees which could be as high as $200,000. For Plain this was a clear indication that the judge had already determined his guilt, and had prejudged the outcome of his case.

He says the judge told him that the blockade was coming down that day no matter what. Plain then tried to explain that he had no control over the blockade, which he didn't start and wasn't responsible for. The decision to remove it had to be made by the community.

That evening, in consultation with Sarnia police, Plain was able to negotiate a face-saving means of removing the blockade. Nevertheless, he remains at the mercy of the justice system.

"CN objected to my request for a fall court date, and insisted on May 24, which is now the date of my next hearing. None of my lawyers are available on that date, so we'll petition for a fall trial. We will also be filing a complaint against Judge Brown for failing to disclose his past relationships with CN, and filing to have the injunction quashed because it was illegal. But at the end of the day I am still in contempt of a court order, even if that order is illegal and is quashed, I still violated a court order."

Plain says that Canadian Auto Workers President Ken Lewenza intervened on his behalf with higher-ups at CN, getting them to agree to drop the case if Plain signs an agreement not to block any rail tracks, something Plain is unwilling to do.

"If my community decides to block the tracks, I will stand with my community. I can't sign a paper saying that I won't."

Originally appeared on rabble.ca, *March 15, 2013.*

NISHIYUU WALKERS:
In Restlessness, There Is Power
Paul Seesequasis

> *What did we say to each other*
> *that now we are as the deer*
> *who walk in single file*
> *with heads high*
> *with ears forward*
> *with eyes watchful*
> *with hooves always placed on firm ground*
> *in whose limbs there is latent flight*
> —N. Scott Momaday, "Simile"

When the Nishiyuu Walkers arrived in Ottawa on March 25, 2013, 68 days and 1,600 kilometres from the start of their journey, they were fulfilling a time-honoured Cree tradition of walking. It is not a small thing, this tradition. For thousands of years, the Cree, and other First Nations, have walked, paddled, or, in the west, ridden vast distances. That act of motion was, in its essence, the balance of tradition and necessity combined in a way of existence that was sustainable and life-affirming.

The "Original Seven," as they became known—David Kawapit, 18; Geordie Rupert, 21; Raymond (Bajoo) Kawapit, 20; Stanley George Jr., 17; Travis George, 17; Jordon Masty, 19; and Johnny Abraham, 19—were following in that ancestral movement. Guided by 46-year-old Isaac Kawapit, the "white wizard," they faced an arduous challenge and met it head on. Their example captivated tens of thousands, primarily through social media, Facebook, and Twitter, who followed the journey from its beginning on a frigid, January 16 day in northern James Bay. But more than this, the walk was an affirmation from Indigenous youth, at first young men, then later young women, that they could no longer be "idle."

Towards a New Vista

Bruce Chatwin once wrote that "travel does not merely broaden the mind. It makes the mind." There is no better example than the Nishiyuu Walkers. By the end of the trek, and a trek it was, more than 270 Indigenous youth had joined. They were called by a simple message of hope and unity and by the example of walking with a goal in kind. It was giving the youth purpose. It was giving the youth a sense of their collective power.

There was likely not a single one of those nearly 300 youth who had not witnessed, or felt first-hand, the debilitating effects of reserve life: boredom, dysfunction, isolation, addiction, abuse, or suicide. These are all too prevalent in the sedentary enclosures that we call the "reserve" and that affect so many northern communities. Added to this is the loss of knowledge of how to live off the land, the boom and bust cycles of mining and its despoliation, and the fact that there is simply "nowhere to go." Take all this under consideration and perhaps one can begin to grasp the essential relevance of the Nishiyuu Walk.

The Nishiyuu Walk was every bit as evocative and powerful a statement as the Zapatista Walk of Silence on December 21, 2012, when 40,000 Mayans marched through the cities of the Mexican state of Chiapas without a word. They came and left in silence. Similarly with the Nishiyuu who walked south, across open country and highway, a long column inspired by the idea of the journey. David Kapawit felt the need to walk, inspired by Chief Theresa Spence's hunger fast on

Victoria Island in Ottawa. By the time they arrived, the fast was long over but the idea of being "Idle No More" lived on. Spence was there to greet the walkers.

Step by Step

In February, hereditary Chief Beau Dick walked from Quatsino to Victoria with supporters for a copper-shaming ceremony on the steps of the legislature. In the wake of the Nishiyuu journey, there are now walkers on the move from Saskatchewan and Manitoba, heading to Ottawa. There will be others.

We are witnessing youth in motion. And in the simple act of walking they are doing much. They are moving away from colonial confines, from their own fears, from their own insecurities. It is a move away from the reserve, both metaphorically and physically. In each step, there is a new vista offering a better future.

The most difficult transition now for the Original Seven Nishiyuu walkers and for all who joined them is adjusting to being back home. Back to normalcy. It will not be an easy transition for they who have felt power.

It is the power of walking. The restlessness that does not abate. They are like the deer in Scott Momaday's "Simile."

Originally appeared in The Tyee, *April 6, 2013.*

FRIENDSHIPS

Round dance, Cumberland House, Saskatchewan. (JENNIFER STEWART)

BLIND JUSTICE
Lee Maracle

Ts'leil Waututh, Chaytoose, Snauq'w
The mountains rise behind my ancestors
And disappear in the sale of them
Orchestrated by a department that seeks
Their vanquishment—$25.00 becomes millions in the
blink of an eye
    $25.00 becomes hunger in the next blink
Becomes inadequate in the next blink
Becomes the murder of cedar, sea vegetables, Ouske,
whale and sockeye
As I struggle to mature without food
I am sorry too Mr. Harper

Sustained Violence
We could have recovered from smallpox
We had Xway-Xway
We had medicine
We had healing songs and dances
But they were banned

Violation
We could have recovered
We had friends
Christian friends
But they too were banned
My relations were banned from speaking
    Organizing or fighting for land rights
    Fishing rights,
The right to sing and dance
To raise our children
To educate them
We could have included you in our ceremony
Of facing ourselves,
Recovering ourselves

Transforming ourselves
But our ceremonies were banned.

Still, I am not tragic
Not even in my addicted moments
A needle hanging from the vein of my creased arm I was not tragic
Even as I jump from a boat in a vain attempt to join my ancestors
I am not tragic

Even in my disconnection from song, from dance,
I am not tragic
Even in seeing you as privileged,
As an occupier of my homeland in my homeless state
Even as men abduct as I hitchhike along these new highways
To disappear along this lonely colonial road
I refuse to be tragic

My body has always understood justice
Everyone eats and so we included you
There is no word for exclusion, So your whiteness is not threat

We have lived for 11,000 years on this coastline
This is not the first massive death we have endured
We girded up our loins,
Recovered and rebuilt

We are builders,
We are singers,
We are dancers
We are speakers
And we are still singing
We are dancing again
We are speaking in poetry
In story, in film

In the millennia that we have lived here there are
constants
The tide will retreat and it will return
The fishes that are threatened will return
The people who died during those epidemics are
returning

The plants, the trees, the animal world will recover
It may take another tsunami of the sort that nearly
killed us all
It may take earthquakes and storms
But the earth, the waters, the skies, the plants and
the animals will return

I am a witness
I am inspired by the earth's response to her
desecration
A tsunami cleanses the earth
A hurricane rearranges rivers
An earthquake is an objection
And we will all have to face ourselves,
Face our sense of justice
To include all life

We will need to nourish our imagination
To include a new equality
And summon our souls, our hearts and our minds to a
justice,
which includes all life

Originally appeared in Decolonization: Indigeneity, Education &
Society *Vol. 2, No. 1, 2013, p. 134-136, and* Buffalo Shout, Salmon
Cry: Conversations on Creation, Land Justice and Life Together,
edited by Steve Neinrichs, Herald Press, Waterloo, ON, 2013, p. 124-126.

WHY IDLE NO MORE IS GAINING STRENGTH, AND WHY ALL CANADIANS SHOULD CARE

Jeff Denis

In a December 16 editorial, *The Star* rightly called on Prime Minister
Stephen Harper to meet with Chief Theresa Spence, now in her 10th
day of a hunger strike. It rightly drew attention to the ongoing housing

crisis at Attawapiskat First Nation. Yet, it missed the big picture. Spence's hunger strike is not just about Attawapiskat. It is not just about housing or school funding. And it is not just about the omnibus budget Bill C-45, which eliminates federally protected waterways and facilitates the surrender of reserve lands without consultation. It is about all of that and more. Spence's hunger strike is part of the Idle No More movement, which, in a matter of days, has become the largest, most unified, and potentially most transformative Indigenous movement at least since the Oka resistance in 1990.

The fundamental issue is the nation-to-nation treaty relationship with Indigenous peoples that Canadian governments repeatedly flout by passing legislation without free, prior, and informed consent. Harper and the Governor General (as Crown representative) must meet with Chief Spence and other First Nations leaders, to not only discuss this relationship but take concrete action to repair it. Idle No More is not a sudden case of "mass hysteria." If one were paying attention, one could feel the movement brewing for years. On June 11, 2008, Harper apologized for the residential school system and promised to forge "a new relationship" based on "partnership" and "respect." Some people believed—or wanted to believe—that things would change.

Unfortunately, actions speak louder than words. Since 2008, the Harper government has cut aboriginal health funding, gutted environmental review processes, ignored the more than 600 missing and murdered Indigenous women across Canada, withheld residential school documents from the Truth and Reconciliation Commission, abandoned land claim negotiations, and tried to defend its underfunding of First Nations schools and child welfare agencies. When some dared call attention to poverty, "corrupt" chiefs were blamed. Although the minister of Aboriginal Affairs, John Duncan, claims to have visited 50 First Nations communities and conducted 5,000 consultations, he and his staff clearly have not gained the First Nations' consent on the fourteen currently tabled (or recently passed) bills that Idle No More activists oppose. Meanwhile, Indigenous peoples are the fastest growing population in Canada. They are young, ambitious, and well aware of historical and contemporary injustices. Like others abroad, they are revitalizing their languages and cultures, rebuilding their nations, and supported in these initiatives by international law, including the UN

Declaration on the Rights of Indigenous Peoples, which Canada reluctantly endorsed in 2010.

On Friday, December 21, thousands of Indigenous peoples and their allies will converge in Ottawa for a mass rally. This event follows two weeks of direct action from coast to coast to coast, including round dances and sit-ins, highway blockades, and drumming and prayers for change. Indigenous elders across the land have joined Chief Spence in her fast. Why should non-Indigenous Canadians care?

First, it is a matter of social and environmental justice. When corporate profit is privileged over the health of our lands and waters, we all suffer. When government stifles debate, democracy is diminished. Bill C-45 is just the latest in a slew of legislation that undermines Canadians' rights. In standing against it, the First Nations are standing for us too. Second, as Justice Linden of the Ipperwash Inquiry said, "We are all treaty people." When our governments unilaterally impose legislation on the First Nations, they dishonour the Crown, they dishonour us, and they dishonour our treaty relationship. We are responsible for ensuring that our governments fulfill their commitments. If our governments do not respect Indigenous and treaty rights, then the very legitimacy of the Canadian state—and thus of all our citizenship rights—is in doubt. That's what Idle No More is about. So, yes, Harper should meet with Spence. But a meeting alone will not suffice. Change requires action. It requires a shift in public consciousness. It requires all of us being there, December 21 and beyond, to "live the spirit and intent of the treaty relationship, work toward justice in action, and protect Mother Earth."

Originally appeared in The Toronto Star, *December 20, 2012.*

AWAKE, HUNGRY, AND IDLE NO MORE
Naomi Klein

I woke up just past midnight with a bolt. My six-month-old son was crying. He has a cold—the second of his short life—and his blocked nose frightens him. I was about to get up when he started snoring again. I, on the other hand, was wide awake. A single thought entered my head: Chief Theresa Spence is hungry. Actually it wasn't a thought. It was a feeling. The feeling of hunger. Lying in my dark room, I pictured the chief of the Attawapiskat First Nation lying on a pile of blankets in her teepee across from Parliament Hill, entering day 14 of her hunger strike. I had of course been following Chief Spence's protest and her demand to meet with Prime Minister Stephen Harper to discuss the plight of her people and his demolition of treaty rights through omnibus legislation. I had worried about her. Supported her. Helped circulate the petitions. But now, before the distancing filters of light and reason had a chance to intervene, I felt her. The determination behind her hunger. The radicality of choosing this time of year, a time of so much stuffing—mouths, birds, stockings—to say: I am hungry. My people are hungry. So many people are hungry and homeless. Your new laws will only lead to more of this misery. Can we talk about it like human beings?

Lying there, I imagined another resolve too—Prime Minister Harper's. Telling himself: I will not meet with her. I will not cave in to her. I will not be forced to do anything. Mr. Harper may relent, scared of the political fallout from letting this great leader die. I dearly hope he does. I want Chief Spence to eat. But I won't soon forget this clash between these two very different kinds of resolve, one so sealed off, closed in; the other cracked wide open, a conduit for the pain of the world. But Chief Spence's hunger is not just speaking to Mr. Harper. It is also speaking to all of us, telling us that the time for bitching and moaning is over. Now is the time to act, to stand strong and unbending for the people, places, and principles that we love. This message is a potent gift. So is the Idle No More movement—its name at once a firm commitment to the future, while at the same time a gentle self-criticism of the past. We did sit idly by, but no more.

The greatest blessing of all, however, is indigenous sovereignty itself. It is the huge stretches of this country that have never been ceded by war or treaty. It is the treaties signed and still recognized by our courts. If Canadians have a chance of stopping Mr. Harper's planet-trashing plans, it will be because these legally binding rights—backed up by mass movements, court challenges, and direct action—will stand in his way. All Canadians should offer our deepest thanks that our indigenous brothers and sisters have protected their land rights for all these generations, refusing to turn them into one-off payments, no matter how badly they were needed. These are the rights Mr. Harper is trying to extinguish now.

During this season of light and magic, something truly magical is spreading. There are round dances by the dollar stores. There are drums drowning out Muzak in shopping malls. There are eagle feathers upstaging the fake Santas. The people whose land our founders stole and whose culture they tried to stamp out are rising up, hungry for justice. Canada's roots are showing. And these roots will make us all stand stronger.

Originally appeared on Naomiklein.org, *December 24, 2012.*

#IDLENOMORE EVENTS AND POSTERS ACROSS THE WORLD

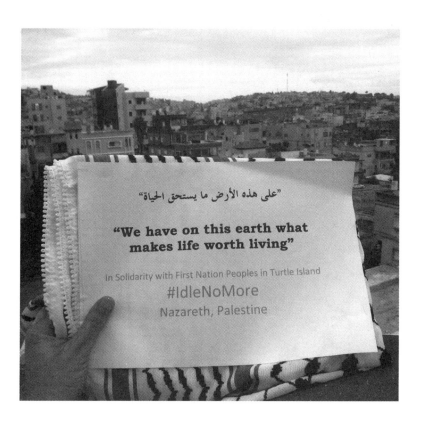

#IDLENOMORE:
Settler Responsibility for Relationship

Stephanie Irlbacher-Fox

Being at the Idle No More drum dance in Yellowknife this past week was moving in many ways. It was led, in part, by strong young Indigenous women who have moved in their own decolonization journeys from frustrated anger to empowered loving action. In the cold afternoon air, the sun shone bright as more than a dozen drummers spoke loud and clear with a unified beat. Dancing to the drum in the middle of the city brought a hush over the dancers: the land was fed by the closeness and spirit of the people, receiving the offering and affirmation made by the drummers and the circle. The drum dance transcended the political context, revealing a spiritual bond that lives and breathes through Dene being indivisible from the land.

Many settler allies support Idle No More on the grounds of moral responsibility, or self-interest. These are legitimate bases from which to act. But the calls from Idle No More organizers where I live are ones that are premised on recognizing and acting on relationship: calls that say "We need everybody." Relationship: it's a constructive approach to harnessing settler support for achieving this movement's goals. Everyone is needed. Its effectiveness rests on requests for specific settler actions to be taken in the context of recognizing and creating relationships. Relationship is fundamental to meaningful co-existence and an antecedent to motivating change within settler society over the long term.

Co-existence through co-resistance is the responsibility of settlers, and we achieve it in part by making change in our own systems and among other settlers, taking our cue from Indigenous action and direction. For settler allies, having a place to land relationally creates a stronger rationale for unsettling established systems: knowing and being with Indigenous peoples, even if it is just to be welcomed to stand alongside at marches and rallies, or to join the drum dance circle, creates a tangible bond. Relationship creates accountability and responsibility for sustained supportive action. This does not mean requiring Indigenous energies for creating relationship with settlers; it means settlers taking initiative to live on a personal level what they claim on a political one.

What Idle No More highlights in part is not simply neglect and actions of the Harper government. What it highlights is that Harper's extreme legislation is only possible because successive generations of settler Canadians have normalized looking to government rather than themselves to resolve "the Indian problem." Canadians don't tend to get riled when Canada gets it right (such as impetus toward such initiatives as a residential school apology, the Kelowna Accord); nor do they get riled when the appalling undoing of decades of slow progress on Indigenous issues occurs, as has been accomplished by the Harper government over the past few years. For the most part, settlers simply have no clue, are not engaged in relationship with Indigenous peoples, and assume that the government is following the rule of law and doing right by Indigenous peoples.

I am somewhat skeptical about the willingness of settlers to support a movement in a sustained way on the basis of either moral responsibility or self-interest. I have found that even the most supportive settlers have a privilege line they refuse to cross. It is the existence of that line and the refusal to cross it which requires long-term effort. Erasing that line is predicated on personal transformation. In the short term some settlers may show support as a way to leverage Indigenous unrest to achieve their own social or environmental agendas. But over the long term, settlers must engage in personal transformation to entrench meaningful decolonization. Idle No More may assist in moving such settlers past merely supporting their own interests toward the more difficult task of supporting interests of decolonized justice.

I am convinced that such a shift needs to start early: it has been said that it is easier to build strong children than repair broken men. As the mother of two boys I am convinced that they are the key to settler change: they and all the other settler children in Canada who will in future people Canadian institutions and society. A critical settler responsibility is consciously educating our kids away from the constant barrage of social, educational, and structural influences that reinforce an omniscient patriarchal heterosexual white male birthright. This task is crucial because children are open; their "normal" is created by us as parents. What this means is parenting in a consciously decolonizing way. So far some basic rules for me include supporting my boys' developing relationships with people and places that are decolonizing; fostering their respectful spiritual and physical relationship with the land; and supporting them in developing critical thinking faculties necessary for an ethics of compassionate discernment. In this task, a movement such as Idle No More is a lifeline.

Idle No More has the potential to motivate societal change in so many ways. It is an opportunity to shift awareness among settlers and so shift the context on which settler privilege is premised. Over the long term it has the potential to contribute to changing how and what settler children learn about Indigenous peoples, and the history and current Indigenous-state relationship. It will stand as part of a longer record of documented injustices and Indigenous responses, opening young minds to understanding the complexity of injustice in which settlers live and prosper. A gift that it stands to impart to settler society is one of both awareness and self-awareness, sustaining a basis for a fundamental shift toward decolonizing settler consciousness, creating a tool for fashioning a shared future of all of our children in the shape of justice.

Originally appeared on Decolonization: Indigeneity, Education & Society *(decolonization.wordpress.com), December 27, 2012.*

LETTER TO CHIEF THERESA SPENCE
Canadian Union of Postal Workers

The Canadian Union of Postal Workers honour Chief Theresa Spence of Attawapiskat for her courageous stand in defence of the land against the moral bankruptcy of the Canadian state. We recognize the racist and genocidal history of Canada and that the attempts to assimilate and silence Indigenous voices have been rife with failure and abuse. The ongoing theft of Indigenous lands, the refusal to honour agreements made in the name of the British Crown reveal a sadly dishonest and indefensible relationship. It seems nothing is sacred in the eyes of the greedy.

Now this latest government after their so-called "apology" without substance are making another kind of attempt to forever extinguish rights and title to your land while continuing the poverty, illness, homelessness, disappearances of Indigenous women, and imprisonment that it has wrought. Everyone who identifies as "Canadian" should be deeply ashamed of this sad performance but shame is not enough. Our organization will not lend our name to that destruction or defend a morally bankrupt government and system. We will not be a party to traumatizing whole populations and can no longer deny or remain silent over the fact the homes of the settlers were built on the ruins of others. No rewriting of history will change what we all know. These territories were unjustly seized and exploited while accompanied by ongoing attempts to erase history. We hope that we will learn better to develop customs and practices to guide our relationship. When Indigenous peoples stand to defend the land and Mother Earth it is our duty to stand with them in order to decolonize ourselves and recognize this complicity of silence that has occurred for generations is not acceptable.

We honour you, Chief Spence, driven to this measure, and with humility and gratitude thank you for your courageous defence of the knowledge you have kept alive, for trying to protect places that future generations will enjoy and though it is maybe not your intent, to know that your actions are now speaking for all of us, for everyone who wants and deserves a sustainable way of life in harmony and respect with the earth. We add our name to those who will not stand for taking away sovereignty and the inherent right to land and resources from First Nations peoples in this abusive and indefensible relationship.

In solidarity and gratitude,

Denis Lemelin
National President
Originally appeared on cupw.ca, *December 17, 2012.*

I AM CANADIAN!
(Because of Treaties with Indigenous Nations)
Toby Rollo

As Chief Theresa Spence continues her hunger strike, her request that Prime Minister Stephen Harper and the Governor General meet with First Nations Chiefs to discuss treaties has many Canadians wondering what relevance treaties could possibly hold today.

Anticipating this uncertainty, I wrote a pamphlet with the Mohawk scholar Taiaiake Alfred, which was widely distributed both in the US and in Canada during recent Idle No More events. The pamphlet laid out in clear and concise language the concrete practical and legislative steps necessary to advance the goal of reconciliation. The outline was based on the recommendations laid out in the 1996 *Royal Commission on Aboriginal Peoples*. This Royal Commission, the most comprehensive and expensive in Canada's history, determined that achieving the goal of reconciliation necessarily entails the restoration of a "treaty relationship."

I recall being a bit confused but mostly just ambivalent the first time I heard Indigenous peoples in Canada invoke the concept of a "treaty relationship." I was 12 years old and it was the height of what would come to be known as the Oka Crisis. To me, treaties were boring relics—artifacts excavated from Canadian history—of interest to history teachers. As I grew older, I was fairly certain that treaties were irrelevant to modern Canada and to modern citizens like myself. What relevance they *might* hold did not seem to bear on my life in the same way as did taxes or elections.

That youthful confusion and ambivalence was displaced over the years by a realization in my adult life that if Canada was to claim legitimacy as a *nation* as opposed to a complex colonial *encampment*, that legitimacy must derive from the founding treaties that made Canada possible. Accordingly, I recognized that my identity as a Canadian as opposed to a mere occupier or colonizer was dependent on the status of those treaties. The stakes could not be higher.

I had always understood that agreements made before I was born formed the conditions of my Canadian citizenship and identity. I am Canadian by pure accident of birth, yet still I recognized that I was born into a society constituted by certain historical events, acts, and agreements that more or less structure the obligations I have to others.

Take our relationship to the United States and to Americans, for example. I acknowledge that Canada has no right to impose any territorial, political, or cultural arrangement upon them. Likewise, they have no right to impose upon us. Why? Because of treaties and agreements, some old and some new. Specifically, because of the 1814 Treaty of Ghent, the Convention of 1818, the Webster-Ashburton Treaty of 1842, and the Oregon Treaty of 1846, which established the territories and borders of Canada. Within this context, Canada was constituted as a nation through various acts and declarations, e.g., The Royal Proclamation of 1763, the British North America Act of 1867, and the Constitution Act of 1982.

These treaties and constitutional events reflect historical compacts between peoples—agreements that established our right to exist autonomously as Canadians rather than as British subjects or American citizens. Of course, there are still a handful of disagreements over the details of the treaties between the US and Canada (e.g., the Dixon Entrance), but the lack of precise territorial borders, or of cultural borders for that matter, does not take away from the binding spirit of the agreement. There are a number of international agreements that detail our right to cultural integrity as well. The US is obliged by virtue of being a signatory to various international treaties and UN declarations not to organize any political assault on other cultures. We are distinct nations—our covenants are nation-to-nation. Our disagreements, some of which concern our very borders, are not settled even after centuries of dialogue. Yet we respect each other as legitimate and autonomous in the absence of perfect borders and perfect agreement.

I see now that the legitimacy of Canada and of Canadians as a people is constituted by historical treaties and agreements that contemporary citizens did not consent to but nevertheless benefit from and are obligated to uphold. We recognize that the violation of such treaties is unjust. Imagine if citizens in Washington state decided that because they did not *personally* sign the Treaty of 1818 that they could unilaterally assert ownership over the majority of its northern neighbour British Columbia. Ridiculous, right? Or imagine if the United States decided to divest Canada of its traditional political structures and impose its own, arguing that the treaties that safeguard our borders and cultures were established in a distant past and so cannot be taken seriously today. Imagine if the US interpreted our historically defining treaties in the manner of China's so called 'Seventeen Point Agreement for the Peaceful Liberation of Tibet', which is recognized by most as China's transparent attempt to justify the imperial, colonial occupation of Tibet. Consider China's claim that Tibet is unfit to govern itself, or that something called "unity" is always preferable to divisiveness. Sound familiar?

I see now that a similarly ridiculous and transparent disregard for official treaties and more informal conventions is reflected in our dealings with Indigenous nations, whom we once acknowledged as autonomous political and legal jurisdictions. Understanding this *present* means coming to terms with the fact that we stand today in violation of our original agreements, in violation of the 1763 Royal Proclamation/1764 Treaty at Niagara; in violation of international declarations such as the 2007 UN Declaration on the Rights of Indigenous Peoples, and in violation of our own 1982 Constitution Act sec. 35(1). I was struck by the realization that you and I as non-Indigenous Canadians are involved in a criminal neglect of the very treaty obligations undertaken in the course of identifying ourselves as a people. So long as we ignore our obligations we can only exist on this land as illegitimate occupiers.

Instead of taking responsibility and recognizing the foundational status of its treaties, Canada continues to enforce a form of colonial rule over Indigenous peoples, most straightforwardly through legislation contained in the archaic Indian Act. Problems abound in First Nations politics defined by the Indian Act, a fact that is entirely predictable and unsurprising. Is there any doubt that Tibet, too, has problems with political corruption? And is there any doubt that any subsequent demand for greater "accountability" or "transparency" in local Tibetan governance misses the point that Chinese colonial interference in Tibet is the problem?

But lest you think the situation is too far gone—and before you acquiesce to the permanence of injustice while shrugging your shoulders at such seemingly vast and intractable problems—remember that the research has already been done, the difficult conversations have already taken place, and the solutions are in the books waiting to be instituted. They exist in the spirit of the original treaties and agreements, and even in our Constitution, but they are also delineated in concrete institutional terms in the four-year *Royal Commission on Aboriginal Peoples*. The practical recommendations articulated in the RCAP offer a path forward. It is not perfect, but then no agreement is. Just as current disputes between Canada and the US are informed and constrained by an old treaty relationship that defines us, the dialogue that will necessarily unfold between Canada and Indigenous nations in the future must be informed and constrained by the treaties we have made—the very treaties that establish the legitimacy of Canada and of being Canadian.

Originally appeared on Toboldrollo.com, *January 1, 2013.*

ACADEMICS IN SOLIDARITY WITH CHIEF SPENCE AND IDLE NO MORE
Open Letter to the Right Honourable Prime Minister of Canada Stephen Harper and the Right Honourable Governor General David Johnston

We, as academics teaching in universities, witness the courageous and honourable actions of Attawapiskat First Nation Chief Theresa Spence to defend the land and Indigenous peoples of Canada. Chief Spence has said that she is willing to die for her people, and we will not stand silent while she starves to death on the doorstep of our Parliament. We call on our government to meet immediately with Chief Spence and to initiate a comprehensive plan to address the urgent situation in Aboriginal communities across this country.

On December 11, 2012, Chief Theresa Spence began a hunger strike, calling the Right Honourable Prime Minister of Canada Stephen Harper and the Right Honourable Governor General David Johnston to "initiate immediate discussions and the development of action plans to address treaty issues with First Nations across Canada." Chief Spence wishes to raise concerns about the disregard of First Nations peoples by the Government of Canada, such as the continued failure to address poverty experienced in Indigenous communities, especially those living in rural and isolated communities. Chief Spence also wants to discuss recent bills that were passed in the legislature without First Nations consultation, including the omnibus Bill c-45 which included changes that removed all environmental protection from the vast majority of Canadian waterways, along with many other attacks on the environment. In addition to endangering the future of all Canadians, these changes violate Aboriginal and treaty rights by permitting the destruction of hunting and fishing economies. These concerns and others are clearly expressed in the Idle No More movement manifesto, which we encourage all Canadians to read and discuss in their communities.

We have been saddened and ashamed to witness the way that Chief Spence has been ignored by our government. We have been deeply disappointed to observe the refusal of both the Prime Minister and the Governor General—the Queen's representative—to meet with her or acknowledge the importance of her concerns.

We stand in solidarity with Chief Theresa Spence's attempts to change the abusive manner in which the Canadian Government has ignored, threatened, and bullied Indigenous peoples. As teachers interested in contributing to a just and sustainable future where the rights of all Canadians are respected, we recognize that Canada's history is one of exploitation, dispossession, and marginalization of Indigenous peoples, denial of their rights and sovereignty, indifference to their suffering, and in many cases the destruction of their land. We also recognize the strength, resilience, and profound respect for Mother Earth that exist in Indigenous communities and welcome this current mobilization against the government-sponsored destruction of the environment.

We urge all people of Canada to enter into respectful dialogues about Aboriginal rights and treaties, and to take meaningful action in your communities to ensure the honouring of our treaties, respect for self-determination, and the protection of our environment for the generations to come.

While we are publishing the following list of academics who have signed the letter, we will continue to republish it as we gather additional names. If you would like to sign this letter go to

www.facebook.com/AcademicsInSolidarityWithChiefTheresaSpence?
ref=stream

and post your name, position, and departmental/university affiliation or email the information to Academics4ChiefSpence@gmail.com.

Thank you so much for standing in solidarity with Chief Theresa Spence. For more information about the Idle No More Movement go to idlenomore1.blogspot.ca.

This letter has been translated into French and Spanish. Should you wish to translate the letter into another language please do so and send it to Academics4ChiefSpence@gmail.com.

We, the undersigned, endorse the open letter written on Friday, December 21, 2012, to the Right Honourable Prime Minister of Canada Stephen Harper and the Right Honourable Governor General David Johnston:

1. Roewan Crowe, Associate Professor, Women's and Gender Studies & Co-Director, Institute for Women's & Gender Studies, University of Winnipeg.

2. Catherine Taylor, Professor, Faculty of Education and Department of Rhetoric & Communications, University of Winnipeg.

3. Robin Jarvis Brownlie, Associate Professor, Department of History, University of Manitoba .

4. Angela Failler, Chancellor's Research Chair, Associate Professor, Women's and Gender Studies, Research Affiliate Institute for Women's and Gender Studies, University of Winnipeg.

5. Adele Perry, Associate Professor and Canada Research Chair, Department of History, University of Manitoba.

6. Rachel Zolf, Assistant Professor, Department of English, University of Calgary.

7. Rachael Van Fossen, Part-time Faculty, Department of Theatre, Concordia University. Faculty, MFA in Interdisciplinary Arts, Goddard College.

8. Tracy Whalen, Associate Professor, Department of Rhetoric, Writing, and Communications, University of Winnipeg.

9. Laura Ishiguro, Assistant Professor, Department of History, University of British Columbia.

10. David Churchill, Associate Professor, Department of History, University of Manitoba.

11. Pauline Greenhill, Professor, Women's and Gender Studies, University of Winnipeg.

12. Alex Wilson, Opaskwayak Cree Nation, Associate Professor, Department of Educational Foundations, University of Saskatchewan.

13. Heather Milne, Assistant Professor, Department of English, University of Winnipeg.

14. Erin Wunker, Assistant Professor (limited term), Department of English/Canadian Studies Program, Dalhousie University.

15. Karis Shearer, Assistant Professor, Department of Critical Studies, UBC (Okanagan).

16. Chloe Brushwood Rose, Associate Professor, Faculty of Education, York University, Toronto.

17. Elise Chenier, Associate Professor of History, Simon Fraser University, Burnaby, B.C..

18. David Camfield, Associate Professor, Labour Studies, University of Manitoba.

19. Mary Jane McCallum, Assistant Professor, Department of History, University of Winnipeg.

20. Elena Basile, Contract Faculty, Department of English, York University; Sexual Diversity Studies, University of Toronto.

21. Wendy Pearson, Assistant Professor, Department of Women's Studies and Feminist Research, University of Western Ontario.

22. Heather Snell, Assistant Professor, University of Winnipeg .

23. Christopher Keep, Associate Professor, University of Western Ontario.

24. Kevin Fitzmaurice, Associate Professor Indigenous Studies, University of Sudbury/Native Laurentian.

25. Ashok Mathur, Canada Research Chair in Cultural and Artistic Inquiry, Thompson Rivers University.

...and 2,059 other academics.

For the full list and translations of the letter, go to academicsinsolidarity.wordpress.com.

Yonge and Dundas Square, Toronto, December 28, 2012. (HAYDEN KING)

IDLE NO MORE:
A Profound Social Movement That is Already Succeeding
Judy Rebick

I haven't written about Idle No More yet because I am inspired by the plethora of Indigenous voices that we are finally hearing across the country, including of late in the mainstream media. If I learned anything from the women's movement it is that we have to speak for ourselves, not be represented by others, however well-meaning and supportive. Instead I have devoted my support for the movement to sharing the many brilliant and informative articles, the announcements and reports of events and the beautiful graphics and photos from Idle No More to my rather large social media network. The spurious attacks against Chief Theresa Spence over the last couple of days have made me decide to speak out. I don't know if Theresa Spence is a good chief. It seems to be that is up to the members of Attawapiskat to decide. Others more informed that I, including most eloquently Chelsea Vowel who writes the blog âpihtawikosisân, have countered the attacks against her by pointing out, among other things, that most of the problems reported in the audit happened before she was elected chief in 2010. A fact that most media is ignoring.

What I do know is that Chief Theresa Spence's hunger strike has inspired a generation of Indigenous youth to stand up, organize, and speak out. "She is prepared to die for us," one young man explained. Whether or not she is a good chief to her reserve is irrelevant to the fact that she is a courageous and inspired symbol for her people. What's more, she has accomplished what no one else has been able to do, including the premiers. She has forced Stephen Harper to do something he didn't want to do. The other thing that is driving me crazy is this constant questioning of whether Idle No More is a movement, whether it is the new Occupy, what it can possibly accomplish. Yes, Idle No More is a movement. I've been part of and studied social movements all my life, and it fits the description of a movement perfectly. Of course, it looks different than the movements people of my generation, like journalist and environmentalist Terry Glavin, are used to. It is a 21st-century movement decentralized and deeply democratic in the sense that much of the initiative belongs to the grassroots.

In that way, it looks like Occupy but as Pam Palmater, now a spokesperson for Idle No More, has explained, it is a movement of a group of people with a common identity and despite the different history and cultures of their nations, a common history in relation to Canada. In this way, the Idle No More movement is better compared to the civil rights movement and women's movement. As to whether they will be effective, my answer is they have already been effective. First and foremost, they have mobilized Indigenous people, the most oppressed group in our country, by showing them that they can organize and make change; that many non-native people will join them; and that their culture is beautiful and worth celebrating. This is always the most important feature of a social movement. This was what the black liberation movement, including both the civil rights movement and the Black Power movement, did for African Americans. They did not achieve full equality but who amongst us would claim they didn't achieve anything. Similarly with the women's movement of my generation.

The most important change we made was not the rights we won or the laws we changed, however important they are, but the change in women. When I was young, women didn't think they could be politicians, journalists, musicians, artists, carpenters, lawyers, doctors, professors. We were supposed to support men to do all those things. It was when the women's movement started organizing and demanding equal rights that our consciousness was changed. The consciousness-raising groups of the late 60s and early 70s, much ridiculed in the media at the time, showed us that what we thought were personal problems were really political and social problems and that women were capable of solving those problems collectively. Oppression only works when the oppressed internalize the idea that they are inferior to the dominant group. Breaking out of that paralyzing internalized oppression is central to any movement. Idle No More is breaking out of internal oppression, both through celebrating Indigenous culture and through providing hope of change.

For the first time I can remember we are hearing and seeing multiple Indigenous voices in the media. Last night TVO's *The Agenda* had a panel of four speakers, three of whom were Indigenous. They had many agreements and some differences but it was a great discussion and I learned a lot. On the same night, the *National* had a panel with two Indigenous people, promising the first in a series in the "countdown to Friday." I have seen individual Indigenous leaders in the media, usually the Grand Chief of the Assembly of First Nations, but I never remember hearing from this many Indigenous people. That's another accomplishment of Idle No More. Idle No More is being led by women, which is amazing and wonderful. Perhaps they are also providing a direction of change for the women's movement. It may be time for women to move much more into the lead of bringing change to our communities, our countries, and our planet. I think the mostly female leadership has provided a very different approach than men often do. The unity they have achieved, the non-violent nature of the actions, and the focus on relationships all reflect this difference.

What Idle No More wants is as significant, if not more significant, a change to our culture and our country as the black liberation or the women's movement. And just as white people and men have to recognize their privilege and how they benefit from the oppression and discrimination of black people and women to be true allies, so we settlers have to recognize the great privilege each of us has, as a result of the colonial exploitation of First Nations historically and today. The problem of the relationship between First Nations and Canada is not just a government problem, not just a problem of a right-wing philosophy; it is our entire problem. This means trashing the stereotypes, learning the history and the real economics of the relationship between Canada and First Nations. This too Idle No More is accomplishing by inspiring through blogs, Facebook, Twitter, articles, and teach-ins as well as alternative and mainstream media coverage. I have provided some links at the end of this article.

Idle No More builds on a proud history of Indigenous struggle for self-determination at a national and international level. The UN Declaration on the Rights of Indigenous Peoples, the Royal Commission on Aboriginal Peoples, Section 35 in the Charter of Rights and Freedoms are all the result of those struggles upon which Idle No More is building. The American Indian Movement, the struggle led by George Manuel for Section 35 to be included in the constitution, the successful battle to defeat Meech Lake, inspired by Elijah Harper and Oka as well as numerous local and regional battles. But so far, the achievements of these movements and struggles and the laws and reports produced have not fundamentally changed the conditions of First Nations or their relationship with Canada. Idle No More is saying "enough." The time has come to end the broken promises and recognize the rights of the first people of this land. I must say that Idle No More is much more generous to us settlers than we in the women's movement were to men. As a result, the support from progressive Canadians has been extraordinary and hopefully will grow. The other reason there is so much support from non-native Canadians is because Idle No More is posing the struggle as in our interests as well. As Pam Palmater has said so eloquently, "Canadians need to realize that we are their last best hope at saving the lands, waters, plants, animals, and resources for future generations because our Aboriginal and treaty rights are constitutionally protected."

It is Jeffrey Simpson and others who support the current neoliberal economic system who are living in a dream palace (whatever that is). They believe that we can continue exploiting the planet in the interest of profit, putting economics before survival. If that isn't living in a dream world, I don't know what is. We have to make a sharp turn away from the politics of Stephen Harper and his like not only by electing someone else the next time but by changing our relationships to each other and to the planet. From what I've seen, Indigenous people whether in Bolivia or in Canada seem to have a better idea of how to do that than anyone else. If that makes me a romantic, so be it.

Originally appeared on rabble.ca, *January 8, 2013.*

#OTTAWAPISKAT

Compiled by Hayden King

One of the lighter, yet still very political, moments of activism throughout the Idle No More movement emerged, not surprisingly, from Twitter. In a collective effort to pushback against the narrative of corrupt and freeloading Indigenous peoples that government politicians (with the help of the media) had crafted, Twitter users laid the hypocrisy and irony of those same politicians bare.

It was the Edmonton-based Metis artist Aaron Paquette who is credited with starting the months-long trend of exposing Canadian dishonesty that became one of the most creative expressions of activism throughout the Idle No More movement. As Paquette tweeted on January 12, "#Ottawapiskat is a word that popped in my head last night as I was painting. I literally laughed out loud and had to share it. #IdleNoMore." He followed it up with a call to action:

Aaron Paquette@aaronpaquette *13 Jan 2013*
Can we get **#Ottawapiskat** going? As in, Parliament sure is wasteful in
#Ottawapiskat ;) just some good natured satire

From there the idea gathered steam, began to trend on Twitter in Canada, and according to *Hashtags.org,* from January 12 to January 17 there were over 1.3 million tweets posted with the #Ottawapiskat hashtag. Below is a curated collection of a few dozen of those tweets:

Kenneth Yurchuk@JKennethY *13 Jan 2013*
In **#Ottawapiskat** unelected elders make huge salaries for no useful
work. They call it the Senate.

Settler Colonial@SettlerColonial *13 Jan 2013*
We should just take all those people in that barren hell-hole
#Ottawapiskat and move them to the city where they can work for
a living.

Christine Myrden@cmyrden *13 Jan 2013*
A million people from their tribe use foodbanks each month, while their
Grand Chief GG serves 10 course meals in his palace. **#Ottawapiskat**

Tim Catcheway@TimCatcheway *14 Jan 2013*
In **#Ottawapiskat** if you question the chief and council, they discredit
you and start rumors that you aren't even a real band member.

Melody McKiver@m_melody *14 Jan 2013*
Residents of **#Ottawapiskat** sit in cubicles in their band offices all day
playing Solitaire. They should get real jobs!

Silvaine Zimmermann@greenthinkers *14 Jan 2013*
When asked about repairing native relations, **#Ottawapiskat** Chief **@PMHarper** replied, "I'll doublecross that bridge when I come to it."

Arlene Adamo@ArleneAdamo *14 Jan 2013*
Those poor ignorant people of **#Ottawapiskat** and Chief Harper! All they need is to be educated and assimilated in with civilized people.

Beari8it@Beari8it *14 Jan 2013*
In **#OTTAWAPISKAT** $50M for Gazebos without a paper trail and fake lake expenses are considered good accounting practices. **#cdnpoli #CPC #roft**

Chris Wright@ChrisNotWrong *14 Jan 2013*
$16 for a glass of orange juice?! Something needs to be done about food prices in **#Ottawapiskat | #IdleNoMore #CdnPoli #GlassHouses**

Janice Makokis@bearclannation *14 Jan 2013*
I heard the **#Ottawapiskat** chief is corrupt, withholds info. from his ppl & doesn't consult them when making decisions affecting them.

Tara Williamson@WilliamsonTara 14 Jan 2013
You can become the majority leader of **#Ottawapiskat** with only 33% of band members voting for you.

Hayden King@Hayden_King *14 Jan 2013*
#Ottawapiskat debt hovering around $600,000,000,000. Might be time for a third-party manager.

Su@Urban_Su *14 Jan 2013*
#Ottawapiskat Chief refuses to talk to media.

Ryan McMahon Comedy@RMComedy *14 Jan 2013*
In **#Ottawapiskat** they smudge w/the smoke & stench from oil sands tailing ponds. The dizziness incurred cited as "financial spirit helpers."

David William@nrvscrcts *14 Jan 2013*
I'm sick and tired of my hard-earned tax dollars paying for the housing of **#Ottawapiskat** residents. Why do they deserve all the breaks?

IMAGE WARRIORS

CURATED BY WANDA NANIBUSH

Sonny Assu, *There Is Hope, If We Rise* #*1-12* (archival ink on rag paper, digital print)

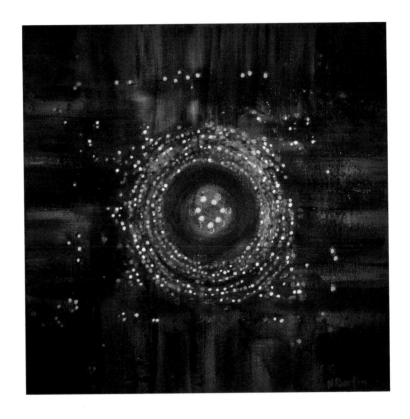

Nathalie Bertin, *Round Dance* (acrylic on canvas)

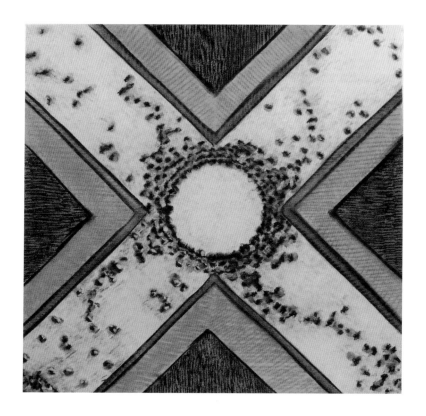

David Garneau, *Idle No More II* (pastel on paper), 2013

David Garneau, *Restless* (photograph), 2001

David Garneau, *Canadian Flag* (oil on canvas), 2004

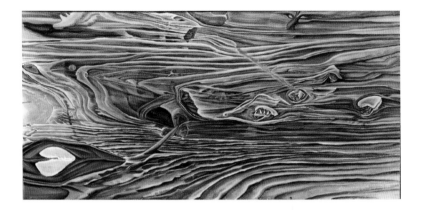

TOP: LauraLee K Harris, *Hunting Windigo* (painting on wood)
BOTTOM: LauraLee K Harris, *Oh Kanata, We Are* (painting on wood)

LauraLee K Harris, *Spiritual Awakening* (painting on wood)

Erin Konsmo, *Still Wading* (poster)

Erin Konsmo, *Traplines Not Pipelines* (poster)

Erin Konsmo, *Land Body Conquest* (poster)

Tannis Nielsen, *Idle No More Toronto* (poster)

Tannis Nielsen, *Bill C45* (poster)

Tannis Nielsen, *Parliament Hill* (poster)

Tannis Nielsen, *Nation to Nation Now* (poster)

Michael Wesley, *Omnibus* (mixed media painting)

Tannis Nielsen, *Water Walk* (poster)

Nuliayuk@Nuliayuk *14 Jan 2013*
Where are my tax dollars Harper? WHERE ARE THEY?!?!?
#Ottawapiskat

OJIBWAYMAN@deejayndn *14 Jan 2013*
Chief of **#Ottawapiskat** used **#robocalls** to win an election and has
yet to be held accountable for election fraud.

Jeff Monague@brando44 *14 Jan 2013*
in **#Ottawapiskat** the Chief wields absolute power and muzzles his
council. They cannot display dissent. We must teach them democracy!!

Kevin Gonzaga@speakfaithfully *16 Jan 2013*
#Ottawapiskat Chief sees "As long as the sun shines, the grass grows
and the rivers flow" clause as loophole in treaty. Destroys environment

Jeff Corntassel@JeffCorntassel *24 Jan 2013*
Chief of **#Ottawapiskat** once waved to protestors from his
limo—it was recorded as his first community consultation
#ConsultingFirstNations

At the time of writing, the hashtag continues to endure. Twitter
users attach it to the seemingly endless examples of federal, provincial,
territorial, and even municipal (#Torontowapiskat) politics that indi-
cate corruption, waste, lack of transparency or accountability, and so
on. In fact, at this point the original #Ottawapiskat hashtag should
probably be replaced simply with #Ottawa.

Yet, like many hashtags, and possibly Twitter itself, #Ottawapiskat
is not a trend. Rather it has been yet another example in the very long
history of Indigenous peoples resisting in whatever ways they can. As
Twyla Baker-Demaray noted (on Twitter):

Twyla@Indigenia *14 Jan 2013*
#Ottawapiskat is further proof of how Natives have always used hu-
mor; as medicine, as a shield from negativity, and as a weapon of truth.

THE TERMS OF ENGAGEMENT WITH INDIGENOUS NATIONHOOD

Eric Ritskes

What are the terms of engagement for the resurgence of Indigenous nationhood? In an Idle No More forum hosted by the Indigenous Governance (IGOV) program at the University of Victoria (hashtagged on Twitter as #J16Forum), Kahnawake Mohawk scholar Taiaiake Alfred responded to a commenter who was distraught by the term "settler" with this comment:

As a visitor, you can't demand to be respected on your own terms.

This, along with Taiaiake's earlier-in-the-night assertion that Idle No More needs to be in tandem with a movement towards Indigenous nationhood, made me think: for decolonization to happen (something I define as—in short—resurgent action towards Indigenous sovereignty), what are the terms of engagement?

For myself, a settler in a settler-colonial state such as Canada, I believe what Stephanie Irlbacher-Fox lays out clearly, that one of the tasks of decolonization is "co-existence through co-resistance." What are the terms of engagement and what is it that I am resisting to create?

This is important in a micro context and in a larger, global context as well. As Taiaiake reminded the forum, even as a Mohawk entering into Lekwungen homelands the terms of engagement might change or shift, depending on the relationship. For those of us on Indigenous territory—yours or others—do you know the land you're on and the Indigenous people's terms of engagement with nationhood? What is it that you're engaging with and for? Globally and locally, these particularities need to be clear; it is these articulations of Indigenous sovereignty that disrupt the universalizing and homogenizing flow of globalization and reveal it for it is, and always has been: colonial.

From the forum, and from many other sources, I think there are two basic principles of engagement that need to be examined and thought about. They are:

Land

At the forum, Wab Kinew summed this connection up beautifully when he stated:

> *Our resistance is not abstract, this is about our ways of life, about the integrity of being Anishinaabe. If the land's integrity is compromised, our integrity is compromised.*

In Indigenous cultures around the world, land sustains the people, the culture, the spirituality, and their very existence. Haunani-Kay Trask, a Hawai'ian scholar and activist, argues in her book *Notes from a Native Daughter*: "As Indigenous peoples, our nationalism is born of a genealogical connection to our place." *(59)* The land contains everything there is to know about Indigenous peoples. As Trask states powerfully:

> *To know my history, I had to put away my books and return to the land. I had to plant taro in the earth before I could understand the inseparable bond between people and 'aina (p. 118).*

Focus on land as a site of engagement is important, not only because it is the centre of Indigenous nationhood and resurgence, but because as Tuck and Yang (2012), as well as many others, remind us—land is the primary object of settler colonialism. Colonial wealth is based on land, colonial power is based on land and, even more pivotally, the very legitimacy of settlers is based on their erasure of Indigenous peoples to lay claim to 'virgin' land, *terra nullius*. There is no Indigenous sovereignty without recognition and repatriation of Indigenous land.

Culture

Culture is such a loaded term and can be mobilized in so many detrimental ways, but Indigenous culture or consciousness is so intimately connected to land that you cannot desire repatriation and sovereignty over Indigenous land without centring and resurging Indigenous culture. It doesn't happen. To be even clearer, you can't resist without resurging and centring Indigenous thought and action. Thinking and acting as Indigenous peoples is highly political in colonial contexts where assimilation for the purpose of erasure is the colonial goal.

As mentioned at the beginning, there is no one Indigenous nation. Speakers at the forum reiterated numerous times that the strength of

Drawn to the sound of the drum, a downtown employee snaps a photo of the New Year's Eve round dance at Portage and Main in Winnipeg on December 31, 2012. This image was one of many that inspired artists such as Nathalie Bertin and David Garneau (see colour insert) in their representations of Idle No More. (EMAN AGPALZA)

Indigenous movements is the diversity of nations, the diversity of cultures, the diversity of thought. On a global scale, this diversity is magnified. It is these diverse Indigenous cultures that represent resistance to the predatory consumption of Western culture that "smooths over" difference in its quest for universal domination.

So, what are the terms of engagement? They depend on the Indigenous land and culture that you are co-existing and co-resisting with. This is not a benign, universalizing "We are all one" project that is devoid of power relations. There must be a conscious engagement with the domination of colonialism and the active resurgence of alternative, Indigenous ways of thinking and acting in the world. Resistance is lived out through everyday acts of resurgence (Corntassel, 2012). We must actively apply the theories of decolonization to our daily acts of creation and resurgence. As Taiaiake Alfred (2009) calls it in his book *Wasase*, we must engage in "creative contention."

What is presented here is obviously a simplified answer to what is a very complex way forward. Forums, such as the one discussed here, highlight the difficult challenge of forging a way forward and the many discussions and challenges it entails. One thing is certain though, this engagement and recognition of Indigenous nationhood is a necessary goal, one that demands resistance to colonialism and the creative resurgence of Indigenous sovereignties.

References

Alfred, T. (2009). *Wasase: Indigenous pathways of action and freedom.* Toronto:University of Toronto Press.

Corntassel, J. (2012). Re-envisioning resurgence: Indigenous pathways to decolonization and sustainable self-determination. *Decolonization: Indigeneity, Education & Society, 1*(1), 86-101.

Trask, H.K. (1999). *From a Native daughter: Colonialism and sovereignty in Hawai'I (Revised Edition).* Honolulu: University of Hawai'i Press.

Tuck, E. & Yang, K.W. (2012). Decolonization is not a metaphor. *Decolonization: Indigeneity, Education & Society, 1*(1), 1-40.

Originally appeared on Decolonization: Indigeneity, Education & Society *(decolonization.wordpress.com), January 17, 2013.*

WHITE NOISE
Shane Rhodes

And the drums

will beat

and the people

will chant

MMMMMMMMMMMMMMMM!

LET OUR VOICES BE HEARD!

NO MORE LAND!!
NO MORE MONEY!!
No solutions,
no perspective,
no empathy,
No need for this treaty BS
no more indian bombast
no deal for whitey
red man
Happy now, you freeloader?

I for one feel know "historical guilt".
Oh and your little school thing. Who cares?
EVERY single person has a grievance
SOMEWHERE'S in their family tree.
hahahahahahaha !!
How is meaningful discussion possible
when no one knows what they are talking about??
Your comments are a random
spray of words

TOOT TOOT

You are nothing but unorganized grabastic pieces
of amphibian sh*t!!
I was sitting with an elder one day
During on speech, he whispered
"Where do these young people get this
'mother earth' sh1t from?
That's nothing we taught them."
Lol. That's awesome.
You owe me a new keyboard!
Canada cannot be complete
until a Native flag flies with the Maple Leaf
tribalist baloney

How do you type in a strait jacket?

Time to go home and leave Canada to the Canadians!
go back to India
Count the silverware after they leave.
And the crystal.
And the Scotch.
Racist? Me

Oh waa

I am rendered speechless by impeccable sentence structure.

Idle No More
is an opportunity to find
a new compromise .
scattered to the wind forever
RIght HERE.
No, here. Hang on,
Here, Yes,
definitely right HERE.
Huh?
Oh ok, over here then.
Wow, this gets 24 thumbs up?
Because it was awesome.
I think allowing comments
has allowed the journalists to see
we're capable of depth
Woof!
and know just where to stick the shiv
The papers will not print
what Canadian TAXPAYERS think
about the latest indian crap.
Almost all of my posts have been removed !
A note to the editorial staff: you are evil
Quite the tantrum wot?
tiny fists clenched in fits of rage
Keep at it - migwetch!.
Honey. Lets be honest.
They have awakened a giant.

Yawwwwwnnnnnn.

fatuous dimwit
Reality doesn't play a large part in your life, does it?
No sire, he is totally oblivious to that!
What life?
freeloading ,stealing,

As for you liberal Suckholes…you disgust me.

waa waa waa

More inane bleatings from a socialist sheep

Oh please. That's just incredibly foolish.

Very well said

You sound hot!

That's sexist

You're sexy!

phoney " Native" posers   please note

these comment boards are running 100 to 1 against you.

the Canadian government has been

raping and pillaging first nations lands for years

Someone has finally stated the OBVIOUS.

Brilliant comment.!! Great post

Raped and pillaged!?

Yeah, they must feel REAL raped and pillaged.

Nailed it!

Bravo. can't say any more than that.

I'm a native Canadian…so don't get on my case dudes!

not at all surprised ,

We banned potlatch ceremonies.

We took their children without permission.

What a wonderful way to destroy the culture.

.if you get your information from "Dances with Wolves",

departure from the truth will be a regular occurrence.

JUST SAYING.

Actually That's what I read about potlatch too.

And now we cut cheques to natives

thousands of mini potlatches

Every time "residential schools" are brought up

all I hear is excuses

over and over and over and over and over again

Monkey

That is such an excellent display

of stupidity and bigotry.

Huh??

….blah,blah,blah……

Reserve natives are basically pets.
We feed them, house them
and occasionally scoop the poop.
hahaha...
gawd you guys are funny
We are all SETTLERS, now!
is 'face-palm' one word or two?
boo hoo
gimme gimme gimme
the new paradigm shift in the language
I have tried to be factual
in the face of a monumental pile
of opinion laced garbage.
Wrong. Utterly wrong.
Problem is fn peoples can't face the truth.
No one needs a Treaty
to understand murder

This is an excerpt from the longer poem, *White Noise*, which was originally published in *X* (Nightwood Editions, 2013).

White Noise was composed of material harvested from 15,283 public comments posted in response to fifty-five online news articles from the *Globe and Mail*, the *National Post*, the Canadian Broadcasting Corporation, Aboriginal Peoples Television Network, Sun News, the *Ottawa Citizen*, the *Province*, and the *Calgary Herald* between December 20, 2012, and January 28, 2013. All news articles were in relation to the Idle No More protest movement and the beginning and end of the hunger strike of Theresa Spence, Chief of the Attawapiskat First Nations reserve.

LETTER TO PRIME MINISTER HARPER FROM INDIGENOUS WOMEN OF TURTLE ISLAND

Indigenous Women of Turtle Island

Re: *Respectfully requesting Prime Minister Stephen Harper and Governor General David Johnson to meet with Chief Theresa Spence as soon as possible*

January 18, 2013

Dear Prime Minister Harper and Governor General David Johnson:

We, the Indigenous women of Turtle Island, respectfully ask you, as head Crown Representatives of the Commonwealth of Canada, to commit to a meeting with Chief Theresa Spence and Indigenous women leaders as soon as possible, in order to end Chief Spence and Raymond Robinson's fast. We are genuinely concerned with the health of Chief Spence who is close to reaching day 40 of her fast. Chief Spence has demonstrated a sincere will to help her people and her fast, firmly rooted in her traditional spirituality, has demonstrated strong leadership, and has galvanized the grassroots Indigenous peoples' movement.

The key issues that have caused Chief Spence to undertake her fast are rooted in the long-standing historical grievances of Indigenous peoples and must be addressed in an atmosphere of respect and openness. We, the Indigenous women of Turtle Island, insist that a meeting take place to begin respectful and honest dialogue to help the community of Attawapiskat emerge successfully from their State of Emergency which has been in place now for over one year.

We, the Indigenous women of Turtle Island, assert that this meeting be grounded in the fundamental principles of nation-to-nation dialogue and do firmly believe that establishing this relationship as the basis for discussion which will benefit both our peoples in the long term. As we have stressed, the urgency of this meeting is paramount to the health and welfare of Chief Spence, but also for all our peoples given the determination of the grassroots peoples to continue demonstrations under the banner of Idle No More.

The problems experienced by Indigenous peoples in Canada are deeply rooted in colonial ideology. However, given the Government of Canada's Indian Residential School Apology and its endorsement of the United Nations Declaration on the Rights of Indigenous Peoples, we believe that this is a genuine opportunity for the Government of Canada and the Crown to show good will towards Indigenous peoples and foster a healthy process of reconciliation and restitution.

The Indigenous women of Turtle Island remain firm in our support for Chief Spence and her goal of adequate housing for Attawapiskat. As mothers, aunties, sisters, and grandmothers, our concern is for the safety and well-being of all peoples. We remain dedicated to finding peace and harmony for all of society.

We are dedicated to preserving our lands and resources for future generations. Our ancestors' teachings instruct us and oblige us to do so. It is within those teachings that our moral and spiritual obligations to the All Our Relations and Mother Earth are founded. WE are compelled by those same teaching, to request that you open your hearts and minds to attend a meeting with Chief Theresa Spence and Indigenous women leaders at the Governor General's residence as soon as possible.

We the Indigenous women offer our support to Chief Spence in facilitating this meeting with the Prime Minister's Office and the Governor General of Canada, to address Attawapiskat's State of Emergency and to discuss honouring the intent of Treaty 9. We would like to thank the Anishinaabeg Nation for their kind generosity and kinship which they have provided for Chief Spence and her team on Victoria Island since she began her hunger strike.

We hope that you will welcome this opportunity to meet and look forward to your response.

In peace,

Ellen Gabriel	Beverly Jacobs
Cheryl Maloney	Tantoo Cardinal
Christi Belcourt	Marilyn Buffalo
Leanne Betasamosake Simpson	Kim Anderson

INDIGENOUS JOURNALISTS NEED APPLY:
#IdleNoMore and the #MSM
Waubgeshig Rice

A modern Indigenous movement is sweeping the country and a lot of Canadians don't understand it. Idle No More has captured the hearts and minds of people of all walks of life from small communities to big cities. At its core, the movement's objective is to protect treaty and land rights and strengthen Indigenous culture. But for the most part, that basic message hasn't permeated the conscience of everyday Canadians, much to the frustration of the people driving the movement. To the latter, mainstream media as a whole has yet to effectively capture and convey the essence of what Idle No More is. National newsrooms initially ignored it. Then they scrambled to cover it. Now the spotlight is moving away from it. While Idle No More was born at the grassroots and proliferated through social media, in order to properly educate regular Canadians about it and wider ongoing Indigenous issues, mainstream newsrooms need more Indigenous journalists.

Idle No More began last fall when four women in Saskatchewan came together as lawyers and academics to teach others about the impacts of the federal government's omnibus budget bill, or Bill C-45. The initiative spread quickly via social media and evolved into a comprehensive awareness movement that sparked rallies in cities across (mostly Western) Canada on December 10. While local mainstream news outlets covered those demonstrations, this collective effort largely didn't make it into the lineups and layouts of national news broadcasters and newspapers. That prompted an immediate backlash from Indigenous communities. Movement leaders hinted at a general mainstream media bias against First Nations issues. Some even floated the ridiculous myth that there was a federal government-imposed media blackout on Idle No More. The more likely unfortunate reality is that many news decision-makers just didn't take note or understand what happened that day, and there weren't enough Indigenous people in their newsrooms to convince them otherwise.

But in the weeks that followed, the mainstream national news media eventually caught up. All the while, Idle No More leaders, activists, and academics continued to fuel momentum by generating discussion with blog posts and elevated coverage in community and social media. That mainstream coverage peaked in the week that led up to the ill-fated meeting between chiefs and the Prime Minister on January 11. In the lead-up, national television and radio news shows devoted large segments of their programs to features and panel discussions on Idle No More, while the developments took over the front pages of national newspapers with deeper context inside. That coverage is now fading, even though the movement itself shows no signs of slowing down.

As Idle No More evolves, it's up to mainstream news media to tell Canadians why it still matters to the mass of people speaking up for it. In order to advance the story, Indigenous journalists are potentially key resources needed in the newsroom. Aboriginal people (First Nations, Métis, and Inuit) are the fastest growing demographic in the country, especially in urban centres. Because these communities are closely connected, a journalist with the same background, knowledge, and understanding can intricately reflect what's really happening at the grassroots. Right now, many non-Aboriginal people who have been following coverage of the movement likely only associate it with images of rallies and round dances.

But there are many other creative outreach initiatives happening at the local community level, like teach-ins and art workshops to help strengthen the relationship between First Nations and the rest of Canada. Journalists with Indigenous backgrounds can help find those stories and advocate for them in the newsroom in order to foster a better understanding in the wider community. And at the most fundamental visual level, seeing and hearing Indigenous reporters in broadcast or reading their names in print goes a long way in fostering a positive sense of trust and understanding among First Nations viewers, listeners, and readers.

While inconsistent (and sometimes inaccurate) coverage of Idle No More has soured many First Nations people on mainstream news media in Canada, they shouldn't reject it as an outlet for their voices. The movement gained momentum and continues to thrive on social media. Articles, essays, and videos still go viral across networks. Interactive online discussions draw thousands at a time. But relying solely on social media to move understanding forward runs the risk of creating an echo chamber. Ideas and stories are being shared on a scale never before seen, but in social media they're more prone to stay within the same networks (i.e. Twitter followers and Facebook friends) of like-minded people. The much wider scope of mainstream media can help extend these unique stories to the unaware. Also, in a world of evolving information sharing, social media and mainstream media aren't mutually exclusive when it comes to raising awareness. Both can benefit from one another.

As a video journalist for CBC News in Ottawa, I've been able to cover local Idle No More events regularly. The newsroom has been very receptive to the stories around it because the producers understand how much these developments mean to people here. Still, I've heard ongoing frustrations from my peers in the community that wider coverage is falling short. Other viewers in the city may call my objectivity into question simply because I'm a visibly Anishinaabe person reporting on an unprecedented Indigenous cultural movement. But being able to tell these stories critically is the reason I wanted to become a journalist. When I was growing up, I never saw any other Indigenous reporters on TV or in print (although there were many blazing trails at the time, unbeknownst to me) telling the crucial stories I saw happening around me. I got into media to get the story out there. Now that awareness is on the rise, it should inspire a new generation of young journalists to ensure the story's done right. Instead of spurning the media, become it.

Originally appeared on waub.ca, *January 21, 2013.*

THE WORDS WE HAVE INHERITED

Niigaanwewidam James Sinclair

On January 22, 2013, writer and Assistant Professor of Native Studies Niigaan Sinclair travelled to Morris, Manitoba to speak with the publisher of the Morris Mirror, a newspaper which printed an editorial that called First Nations "corrupt" and "lazy" and "acting like terrorists in their own country" during the Idle No More movement. Editor

Idle No More Across the World

CLOCKWISE FROM TOP LEFT

Yale University, New Haven, Connecticut, USA, January 28, 2013.
(NIIGAANWEWIDAM JAMES SINCLAIR)

Guovdageaidnu/Kautokeino, Norway, January 28, 2013.
(BRITT HALONEN)

Buckingham Palace, London, United Kingdom, December 21, 2012.
(ALEXI MARCHEL)

Kobe, Japan, January 7, 2013. (ENSHOU YAMADA)

Reed Turcotte refused to meet with him, but other residents welcomed Sinclair and encouraged him to keep this conversation going. This was the letter Sinclair taped to the door of the Morris Mirror.

To the Editor of the Morris Mirror,
    I want to give you something.
    A gift. A story, maybe.
    A piece of our home.

I offer this in the way I would bring food to a feast—if you and your family organized that sort of thing—and invited my family and me to enjoy all we had brought.

This is, perhaps, an unlikely vision—but I offer it nonetheless.

I give this so that you might know a little about the land where you and I now reside. The earth, water, and wind have seen far more than you or I—and will be here far after we have gone. They have witnessed far better than us.

I also give this as a rejection of what has passed for communication in our home: a cacophony of anonymous Internet commentaries with name-calling and tired, predictable stereotypes based on little more than a passing glance. In editorials, rich in generalizations and lacking in accuracy.

I give this so that we might find a way to live together meaningfully, in the vision established by the agreement that made this place. This is a treaty that—while never fulfilled—promises mutual benefit, non-interference, and peace. These are words promised by the man who your town is named after, Alexander Morris. As Morris and those who oversaw the formation and delivery of Treaty One remind us: the vision of this agreement is a map marked with signposts of honesty, bravery, patience, and listening. We now have to trust that these are still there—even if the brush has grown over them.

I give this to ask you to consider what could make a human being come to be seen as "lazy" and "corrupt." I ask you whether these traits are some inherent, savage deficiency or the product of a constant barrage of words driven by the belief that second-rate, dying cultures exist. That these words became laws that locked people into unsustainable areas, made it impossible to make a living, and threw them in jail if they resisted. I ask you to think about those who promised much during treaty time and then supplied their friends with handfuls of welfare, told them how to run their community and then, finally, removed their children and put them into schools where they were physically and emotionally abused.

These children learned that they were inferior and how important it was to destroy the languages and cultures they came from. Many resisted, but were left with the gap of years away from their parents and communities. Returning home, if any did, there were understandable feelings of confusion and disjunction.

I ask you to think about how, at the same time and in schools nearby, Canadian children learned the same curriculum and that they were superior. These children were taught the same words as what the other children endured: they were abused too.

I ask how you or your children might have turned out if any of this happened to you. Now, call them "lazy" and "corrupt."

Human beings are obviously more than this. I give this to you to honour a grandfather who fought for this country, lying about his age so he didn't have to return to residential school, and was injured, never to be healed again. I give this to recall how the government he fought for abandoned him and told him he was no longer an Indian. How he was left completely on his own, to struggle with alcohol and disability, with children to feed and bills to pay. I have no doubt that for Grandpa the vision of the treaty that promised him much was a blurry sight. It was probably made invisible when he lost the only woman he ever truly loved to illness and his first son was killed by Canadians who were never punished.

I give this to you to ask whether dependency is more about those dependent, or those who created the system of dependence. I ask where most questions need to be asked: to those who benefit incredibly through privilege and exploitation, or to those who trust promises and endure more about repairing the imbalance. Whether it is to those who hand systems of dominance to their children, or those invested in escaping this abusive relationship. Whether it is to those who want to call people dancing in a mall "terrorists," or to those who want to find another way, another path.

I give this to you to remember a man who quit drinking when his grandson was born. This man, defined by so many as broken, lazy, and dangerous, chose to give this little boy the greatest gift he could give: love. He gave it not in the hopes that he could repair the past but that he could give him a chance to see something better, something beautiful. Something more than the violence that had been rained down on him. This man, a member of Treaty One—just like you and I—chose to end cycles that had shaped so much of his life. This man chose to stand up, to be more than words and policies, and to tell a new story. I know this. I'm living it.

It is time that we all learn a little history about who we are and maybe, if we're lucky, make some new paths. I believe that we are more than the words and images we have inherited. I know that we can make a better home than this, that we can expect more of ourselves if we are brave, honest, patient, and if we listen. It is time that we give each other gifts of responsibility.

I ask you to be more than the words we have inherited. And, I ask you to talk. Share food. Discuss how we can be more.

You have said that you are not ready. That's OK. Change is hard. I am ready. I will wait for you.

Our home is too important.

Miigwech, ekosi, thanks, merci.

Originally appeared in The Winnipeg Free Press, *January 24, 2013.*

WA'TKWANONWERÀ:TON AKWÉ:KON TETEWÁ:NERA—GREETINGS ALL MY RELATIONS

Ellen Gabriel

Yesterday I was honoured by Femmes Autochtones du Québec/Quebec Native Women's Association with a ceremony to present me with the Queen Elizabeth's Diamond Jubilee medal.

I refused the medal because I could not in good conscience accept this honour considering how the current Crown Representatives —Prime Minister Stephen Harper, the Governor General of Canada David Johnson and the Government of Canada—have acted this past month. They have shown a complete lack of humanity and lack of re-spect towards Chief Theresa Spence during her spiritual fast and a lack of commitment to her request for a simple meeting to discuss how to restore the intent and spirit of Treaty 9. None of these were acts wor-thy of being called the "Honour of the Crown."

I am also refusing to accept this medal be-cause PM Harper has refused to repeal Bill C-45 and C-38. His silence continues to condone rac-ism against Onkwehón:we through his pass-ing of amendments to hate crimes legislation in Canada and his crippling of the Canadian Human Rights Commission's jurisdiction to ad-dress these crimes.

This generation continues within a 500-year-old inherited struggle to search for peace and justice for the First Peoples of this land and All our Relations, and so it is for this reason as well that I could not accept this medal. My refusal was not meant to insult or be disre-spectful, but was done so with respect and love to all our Ancestors, and with the intent that it was given by my sisters at QNW/FAQ.

I want to say Niawenkó:wa—a big thank you to president Vivianne Michel and the board of directors of Quebec Native Women's Association for the honour of nominating me. As I told them words cannot express the happi-ness and gratitude I have in their simple and kind gesture of acknowl-edgement. I raise my hands to all of the QNW, its president, board and of course the staff who carry out the important work of advocacy for our communities, families and women.

You have made this Onkwehón:we sister in our shared struggle very honoured and humbled.

Skén:nen—Peace to All my Relations

Originally appeared on the Facebook group Turtle Musings *by Ellen Gabriel, January 26, 2013.*

KAA MAAMDAA GEYABI BAABIINCHIGEYING, NO LONGER ARE WE WAITING!

Miskwaasining Nagamojig (Swamp Singers)

Here in Ann Arbor, Michigan we are thinking of relatives, borders and history. Wenesh enendamaan Anishinaabemong? What are your thoughts in Anishinaabemowin?

Here are some sentences about this movement:

Kaa Maamdaa Geyabi Baabiinchigeying!
No longer are we waiting (Idle No More)!

Wii bi naawchtoonaa'aa maanda Anishinaabemwin.
They are messing with aboriginal culture.

Gojitonaa'aa Zhaaganaashigaabwiwaad eta.
They are trying to make them Canadian only.

Gaawiin gikendasiinaa'aa minik Anishinaabem gaa bi wiijigaabwitagwaad.
They don't know how much the Anishinaabe have stood by them.

Gaawiin gego piitenmaasiiaan Anishinaabem.
They are not respecting tradition.

Nendaanaa'aa gaa bi ezhiwebag chizhaazhagwa.
They forget what happened long ago.

Zhaganaashag g'miwidoon kewin nitam gii miigaading miinwaa ekwa niizhing gii miigaading
Canadians, they carried your flag in WWI and WWII

miinwaa niibina Anishinaabe Zhimaaganishag gii aapidendwag
and many Anishinaabe soldiers were lost.

Giintamwaa noongwa Zhaganashag wiijigaabwitooshinaang.
It's your turn today Canadians to stand with all aboriginal people.

Originally appeared on Noongwa e-Anishinaabemjig, People Who Speak Anishinaabemowin Today, *January 28, 2013.*

CANADIAN ARTISTS STATEMENT OF SOLIDARITY WITH IDLE NO MORE

We, the undersigned Canadian writers, filmmakers, dancers, musicians, and artists call on all Canadians to join us in unequivocally supporting the demands and actions of the First Nations' Idle No More movement for healthy, just, equitable, and sustainable communities.

We recognize that our identity as Canadian artists is coloured by the shameful and continued history of injustice and colonialism, and support the Idle No More movement's demands that Canadians honour and fulfill Indigenous sovereignty, repair violations against land and water, and live the intent and spirit of our Treaty relationship.

We also call on Prime Minister Stephen Harper to meet with First Nations peoples and their representatives in the intended spirit of the original Treaties, as sovereign nations. We agree with Idle No More's contention that recent legislation proposed and passed by the Canadian Government, including Bill C-45, violates those sacred and sovereign Treaties.

We encourage all Canadians to visit www.idlenomore1.blogspot.ca to learn how they can support Idle No More in their communities.

DÉCLARATION DE SOLIDARITÉ DES ARTISTES CANADIENS AVEC LE MOUVEMENT IDLE NO MORE

Nous, écrivains, artistes, réalisateurs, danseurs et musiciens, soussignons et demandons à tous les Canadiens et Canadiennes de se joindre à nous et d'apporter leur irrévocable et inconditionnel support aux requêtes et aux actions initiées par Idle No More, le regroupement par l'entremise duquel les Premières Nations réclament un environnement sain, juste, équitable et durable pour leurs communautés.

En tant qu'artistes canadiens, nous reconnaissons volontiers qu'une grande partie de notre identité est teintée d'une longue et honteuse tradition d'injustices coloniales infligée aux Premières Nations. C'est une des raisons pour lesquelles nous supportons les demandes faites par

Idle No More afin que les Canadiens et les Canadiennes respectent et reconnaissent pleinement la souveraineté aborigène, réparent les tords fait par l'exploitation illégale de leurs terres et leurs cours d'eaux ainsi qu'ils honorent toujours et en tout lieu l'essence et les intentions des relations établies par les Traités précédents. Nous demandons également au Premier Ministre Stephen Harper d'aller à la rencontre des communautés des Premières Nations et de ses représentants en reconnaissant d'emblée leur statu de nations souveraines, tous comme le stipule les Accords originaux. Nous nous rangeons également derrière Idle No More lorsque ces derniers affirment que certains projets de loi, récemment proposés et adoptés par le Gouvernement Canadien, incluant le loi c-45, enfreignent les précédents Accords.

Nous incitons également tous les Canadiens et les Canadiennes à visiter le site : www.idlenomore1.blogspot.ca afin de voir ce qu'ils peuvent faire pour aider la cause de Idle No More au sein de leur communauté.

Signed,

1. Ryan Ash, Stand Up Comedian, Winnipeg, MB
2. Karen Asher, Visual Artist, Winnipeg, MB
3. Paul Aucoin, Musician, Toronto, ON
4. Rebecca Bain, Musician, Montreal, QC
5. Sharlene Bamboat, Artist/ Artistic Director of SAVAC, Toronto, ON
6. Steve Bates, Musician, Montreal, QC
7. Nicole Bauberger, visual artist and storyteller, Whitehorse, YK
8. Michael Belitsky, musician, Toronto, ON
9. Dave Bidini, Musician, Toronto, ON
10. Sheldon Birnie, Musician, Winnipeg, MB
11. Jonas Bonnetta, Musician, Toronto, ON
12. Ian Blurton, Musician/ Producer, Toronto, ON
13. Christopher Bolton, Writer/ Director, Toronto, ON
14. Craig Boychuk, Recording Engineer, Winnipeg, MB
15. Amanda Boyden, writer, Moosonee, ON and New Orleans, LA

16. Joseph Boyden, writer, Moosonee, ON and New Orleans, LA

17. Shary Boyle, Visual Artist, Toronto, ON

18. Tyler Brett, visual artist and musician, Bruno, SK

19. Christopher Brown, Pianist/Composer/Producer, Wolfe Island, ON

20. Susie Burpee, Contemporary Dance, Toronto, ON

21. Brendan Canning, musician, broken social scene/cookie duster, Toronto, ON

22. Stefan Christoff, musician/activist, Montreal, QC

23. Bruce Clark, Writer, Palm Springs, CA and Winnipeg, MB

24. Jason "Keebler" Colwill, Tour Manager, Montreal, QC

25. Judith Coombe, Music, Toronto, ON

26. Cassandra Cronenberg, Writer, Painter and Filmmaker, Toronto, ON

27. Jim Cuddy, Musician, Toronto, ON

28. Scott Da Ros, Music, Montreal, QC

29. Mary Ellen Davis, documentarian, Montréal, QC

30. Sean Dean, musician, Toronto, ON

31. Kris Demeanor, songwriter, Calgary poet laureate, Calgary, AB

32. Charles Demers, Author/Comedian, Vancouver, B.C.

33. Bazil Donovan, musician, Toronto, ON

34. Stacy Douglas, Lecturer, Carleton University, Ottawa, ON

35. Anita Doron, Filmmaker, Toronto, ON

36. Gord Downie, Singer, Toronto, ON

37. Kevin Drew, Musician, Toronto, ON

38. Coral Egan, Singer/Songwriter, Montreal, QC

39. Leslie Feist, Musician, Toronto, ON

40. Christine Fellows, musician, Winnipeg, MB

41. Nick Ferrio, songwriter, Peterborough, ON

42. Jon Paul Fiorentino, Writer, Montreal, QC

43. Kelly Frazer, Writer, Winnipeg, MB

44. Randy Frykas, Documentary Filmmaker, Winnipeg, MB
45. Steven Galloway, Writer, New Westminster, B.C.
46. Bill Gaston, Writer, Victoria, B.C.
47. Carla Gillis, Musician/ Writer, Toronto, ON
48. Lynette Gillis, Musician, Toronto, ON
49. Dallas Good, musician, Toronto, ON
50. Travis Good, musician, Toronto, ON
51. Noam Gonick, Filmmaker, Winnipeg, MB
52. Dave Guillas, Musician, Winnipeg, MB
53. Freda Guttman, visual artist, Montreal, QC
54. Rob Haacke, film/theatre, Winnipeg, MB
55. Rawi Hage, Writer, Montreal, QC
56. Billy Hamilton, Musician, Toronto, ON
57. Chris Hannah, Musician, Winnipeg, MB
58. Sarah Harmer, Musician, Kingston, ON
59. Emma Healey, Writer, Montreal, QC
60. Lee Henderson, Writer, Victoria, B.C.
61. Jeremy Hiebert, Musician, Winnipeg, MB
62. Veda Hille, Musician, Vancouver, B.C.
63. Derek Hogue, Web Designer, Winnipeg, MB
64. Clive Holden, Visual artist, Toronto, ON
65. Jason Hooper, writer, artistic director, Winnipeg, MB
66. Brett "Limo" Hopkins, Musician, Gibsons, B.C.
67. Simon Hughes, Visual Artist, Winnipeg, MB
68. Gemma James-Smith, Actor, Toronto, ON
69. Jeremy Jansen, Visual Artist, Toronto, ON
70. Dean Jenkinson, Writer/ Producer, Winnipeg, MB
71. Stewart Jones, Visual Artist, Wellington, ON
72. Tim Jones, cultural worker, Toronto, ON
73. Afie Jurvanen, Musician, Toronto, ON
74. Charley Justice, musician/ activist, Winnipeg, MB
75. Greg Keelor, musician, Toronto, ON
76. Don Kerr, Musician, producer, Toronto, ON

77. Vish Khanna, Music/
    Arts Journalist/Musician,
    Guelph, ON
78. James A Kilpatrick,
    Musician, Brandon, MB
79. Wab Kinew, Rapper,
    Winnipeg, MB
80. Alice Klein, writer,
    Toronto, ON
81. Daniel Koulack, Musician,
    Winnipeg, MB
82. Steven Lambke, Musician,
    Toronto, ON
83. Eusebio Ricardo Lopez-
    Aguilar, Musician/Artist,
    Winnipeg, MB
84. Maggie MacDonald,
    Writer/Musician,
    Toronto, ON
85. Colin Mackenzie,
    Documentary radio/video
    maker, Montreal, QC
86. Arne MacPherson, Theatre
    artist, Winnipeg, MB
87. Erika Macpherson, video
    artist, Winnipeg, MB
88. Greg Macpherson,
    Musician, Winnipeg, MB
89. Keith Maillard, novel-
    ist, poet, and educator,
    Vancouver, B.C.
90. Heidi Malazdrewich,
    Theatre Artist,
    Winnipeg, MB

91. Mandy Malazdrewich,
    lens based artist,
    Winnipeg, MB
92. David Marshak, Painter,
    Cannington, ON
93. Tonni Maruyama, Music,
    Toronto, ON
94. Nancy McLennan, poet/
    writer/decolonizer,
    Minitonas, MB
95. Alex McMaster, Musician,
    Toronto, ON
96. Casey Mecija, Musician,
    Toronto, ON
97. Colin Medley,
    Photographer, Toronto, ON
98. Maurice Mierau, Writer,
    Winnipeg, MB
99. Glenn Milchem, Musician,
    Toronto, ON
100. Howie Miller, Stand-up
    comedian/actor/writer,
    Edmonton, AB
101. Greg Millson, Musician,
    Toronto, ON
102. Barry Mirochnik, Musician,
    Vancouver, B.C.
103. Alexis Mitchell, media
    artist, Toronto, ON
104. jake moore, intermedia
    artist, educator & cultural
    worker, Montréal, QC
105. Freya Olafson, Multi-
    disciplinary Artist,
    Winnipeg, MB

106. Heather O'Neill, Writer, Montreal, QC
107. Mike O'Neill, Songwriter, Film writer, Halifax, NS
108. Ethan Osland, Musician, Winnipeg, MB
109. Steven Page, Musician, Manlius, New York, NY
110. Debbie Patterson, Theatre Artist, Winnipeg, MB
111. Sandro Perri, Musician, Toronto, ON
112. Natasha Peterson, Photographer/Cultural Worker, Winnipeg, MB
113. Maya Postepski, Musician, Toronto, ON
114. Greg Pratt, Writer, Victoria, B.C.
115. Andrew Pyper, Writer, Toronto, ON
116. Simon Racioppa, screen-writer, Toronto, ON
117. Al Rae, Television and Radio writer/Comedian, Winnipeg, MB
118. Najat Rahman, Professeure, Université de Montréal, Montreal, QC
119. Kerri Reid, visual artist, Bruno, SK
120. Tanis Rideout, novelist, poet, Toronto, ON

121. Ed Riefel, Percussionist, Toronto, ON
122. Shelagh Rogers, Broadcaster, Nanaimo, B.C.
123. Justin Rutledge, Musician, Toronto, ON
124. The Sadies, Musicians, Toronto, ON
125. Jord Samolesky, Musician, Winnipeg, MB
126. Sheila Sampath, designer, musician, writer, Toronto, MB
127. John K. Samson, Musician/Publisher, Winnipeg, MB
128. Rebecca Schechter, screen-writer, Toronto, ON
129. Rob Schmidt, Radio, Winnipeg, MB
130. Deborah Schnitzer, writer, editor, and filmmaker, Winnipeg, MB
131. David Seymour, writer, Toronto, ON
132. Alicia Smith, Producer, Winnipeg, MB
133. Samuel Smith, Artistic Director, Winnipeg, MB
134. Sylvie Smith, Musician, Toronto, ON
135. Karen Solie, writer, Toronto, ON
136. Katie Stelmanis, Musician, Toronto, ON

137. Linda Svendsen, Writer, Vancouver, B.C.
138. Katie Swift, Theatre Maker, Toronto, ON
139. Sarah Tacoma, Photographer, Cannington, ON
140. Madeleine Thien, Novelist, Montreal, QC
141. Miriam Toews, Writer, Toronto, ON
142. Dave Tough, Musician, Peterborough, ON
143. Philippe Tremblay-Berberi, Fimmaker, Montreal, QC and Brooklyn, NY
144. Suzanne Ungerleider, Musician, Toronto, ON
145. Caelum Vatnsdal, filmmaker, writer, Winnipeg, MB
146. Andrew Vincent, Musician, Ottawa, ON
147. Bry Webb, Musician, Guelph, ON
148. Bob Wiseman, composer/ filmmaker, Toronto, ON
149. Dorian Wolf, Musician, Toronto, ON
150. Vahé Yegoyan, Performance artist, Montreal, QC
151. Alissa York, Writer, Toronto, ON
152. Karen Young, musician, singer, composer, Verdun, QC
153. Cristina Zacharias, musician, Toronto, ON
154. Leanne Zacharias, Cellist and Music Professor, Brandon, MB

J28

Rita Wong

last year, i never imagined we would be
round dancing in Glenmore Landing
round dancing in Chinook Centre
round dancing in Olympic Plaza
round dancing in Metrotown
round dancing in West Edmonton Mall
round dancing outside the Cayuga courthouse
round dancing on Akwesasne
round dancing on Strombo

huychexa!
mahsi cho!
welalin!

drumming at Waterfront Station
drumming at the United Nations
drumming at Columbia University
drumming at Granville & Georgia
drumming at Dalhousie University
drumming at the Peace Arch
drumming on Wellington Street
drumming on Lubicon lands
drumming in Owen Sound
drumming in Thunder Bay
drumming in Somba K'e
drumming in Chicago
drumming in Chilliwack
drumming in Kitimat

taking a much needed pause for thought
on tarsands Highway 63
on the 401
on CN rail tracks
with Aamjiwnaang courage
a human river on Ambassador Bridge
time to stop & respect
remember we are all treaty people
unless we live on unceded lands
where rude guests can learn to be better ones
by repealing C45, for starters

we have to stand together in many places all at once
J11, J16, J28
Indigenous spring
Eighth Fire summer
autumn wisdom
winter sleep to
renew Indigenous spring
again & again

it is Gandhi we need to align ourselves with
Gandhi and Gaia and Vandana and Maude *and marbled murrelets and*
mycorrhizal mats
Winona and Ward and Jaggi and Arundhati *and phytoplankton and*
peregrine falcons
Naomi and Oren and Toghestiy and Jeannette and Lee *and bittermelon*
and bees
Percy and Shiv and Jack and Elizabeth *and chrysanthemum greens and*
canola, now radiated
Yoko and Yes Men and Chrystos and Dionne *and dolphins and*
prairie dogs
Theresa and Melina and Pamela and Rosa *and salmon and cedar*
Wab and Harsha and Clayton and Eriel *and eider ducks and water bears*
Takaiya and Roxanna and Glen and David *and wolves and whales*
there is a time for pies and there is a time for rocks *and beavers*
and snowy plovers
there is a time for poems and a time for rifles *and coral reefs and*
caribou
there is also a time for the Haudenosaune Wampum Belt
two rivers running side by side
(as long as one party doesn't try to dam and mine and kill the
other's river)
and a time for spinning wheels
it is Super Barrio, who stopped 10,000 evictions in Mexico, who
I look to
it is the Zapatistas, the Mohawks, the KI, the Lhe Lin Liyin
the Mother Earth Water Walkers, the 20-year-olds suddenly in
Parliament, the grannies and the grandkids
it is the children I will never see, but who I hope will live and
drink clean, wild water

with gratitude to Chief Spence, whose life I celebrate and honour

Originally appeared on Decolonization: Indigeneity, Education &
Society *(decolonization.wordpress.com), January 28, 2013.*

IDLE NO MORE ORGANIZERS REACH OUT TO QUEER COMMUNITY

Laura Zahody

Two-spirit organizers of the Idle No More movement say they're looking for more allies from the queer community in order to maintain momentum.

Indigenous peoples who oppose parts of the federal government's omnibus Bill C-45, which they say ignores existing treaties and will negatively affect First Nations, Métis, and Inuit communities, as well as the environment, lead the grassroots movement. Idle No More protesters gathered in Ottawa January 28 as MPs returned to the House of Commons.

"We're talking about human rights and sovereignty," says Alex Wilson, an organizer and a professor of social justice and indigenous education at the University of Saskatchewan. "I think that's a place where the LGBTQ community can connect. This is a global issue that affects all of us."

Queer people have histories of mobilization for social justice similar to Idle No More, says Melody McKiver, an administrator and videographer working with the movement in Ottawa. Wilson says she is frustrated that many people who are normally involved in politics have not asked about Idle No More.

"I wonder if they feel excluded or if they just don't know enough, so they don't feel comfortable asking," she says.

Idle No More is not limited to indigenous peoples, McKiver says.

To welcome queer people as allies, artist Thomas Bruyere has created a graphic logo that includes them in the movement. "The graphic uses the lambda symbol that has been used in the past as a gay pride symbol. I thought it looked like a teepee," he says.

The four teepees in the image symbolize the four founders of the Idle No More movement. At the bottom is a rainbow flag.

"What is also important is that it says ally. This is so anyone can use this symbol and feel included," Bruyere says.

In Ottawa, queer-friendly sex shop Venus Envy spent four days collecting clothes, food, canned goods, blankets, letters of support, wood, and cash donations for Idle No More, says Lara Purvis, the shop's education coordinator. This was done in response to a call for supplies to help support participants, she says.

Most of the supplies were brought to hunger-striking Attawapiskat First Nation chief Theresa Spence's camp on Victoria Island, Purvis says. But some of the extra clothes were taken to blockades outside of the city, she adds.

The response to the shop's collection has been positive, she says. "People seemed happy to have a way to contribute to a cause that many might support, but aren't and weren't sure what they could actually do."

One thing people can do is go to a rally or flash mob round dance, McKiver says. "Putting your body on the line with others is a really powerful message, just going and offering your presence," she says.

In fact, it's crucial to have people who hold different points of view participating, Wilson says.

The founders of Idle No More are committed to a range of social-justice principles because sovereignty is impossible without the undoing of systemic forms of oppression like sexism, racism, and homophobia, Wilson says.

Although two-spirit people have different roles depending on the particular indigenous community they belong to, a general understanding is that they encourage open-mindedness, Wilson and McKiver agree. They are necessary for a community to be balanced, Wilson adds.

McKiver, who is Anishinaabe with roots in the Lac Seul First Nation of northwestern Ontario, says that for her, being two-spirit is as much about gender roles as sexual orientation.

"If you look back to living on a trapline, you wouldn't have had the moment to think of whether a woman were to go out and hunt or tend to a fire or if a man were to—you do what you need to do to survive, and there shouldn't be such rigidity in different gender roles."

Anishinaabe cultural teachings emphasize a profound ethic of non-interference, McKiver says. In this climate, two-spirit people find ways to serve their communities that make best use of their talents and interests, regardless of existing gender roles, she says.

"It's an issue of personal sovereignty and presenting yourself in the way that you feel comfortable. It can be a way of shaping dialogue and bringing other viewpoints to discussions," she says.

Two-spirit people can help encourage political and personal transformation, Wilson says.

"There needs to be people that can kind of have that vantage point of standing in a doorway and you can kind of see the two sides. By two sides I don't mean male/female; I mean the two sides of any kind of discussion that we're having," Wilson says.

Ultimately, Wilson and McKiver agree that Idle No More is about education. Before growing to include flash mobs and protests, it started with teach-ins that provided information about Bill C-45, Wilson says.

"For me, what's been really energizing about Idle No More is creating dialogue in places where there hasn't been a lot of dialogue," McKiver says. "There's so much ignorance about indigenous issues within Canada, and I think Idle No More is working to bring that to light."

Originally published on dailyxtra.com, *January 28, 2013.*

IDLE NO MORE, THE BLACK EXPERIENCE, AND WHY IT IS THAT WHAT WE SAY ABOUT OTHERS REVEALS SO MUCH ABOUT OURSELVES

Daniel Tseghay

"Well, I know this and anyone who's ever tried to live knows this: that what you say about somebody else, you know, anybody else, reveals you," said the author James Baldwin in a 1963 documentary entitled *Take This Hammer.* "What I think of you as being is dictated by my own necessity, my own psychology, my own fears and desires. I'm not describing you when I talk about you. I'm describing me." Baldwin was exposing America's habit of investing certain qualities—its own worst characteristics which it dare not acknowledge—onto black people. People who look like us are habitually depicted as angry, lazy, dumb, decrepit, in the grips of a deep and unjustified sense of entitlement, and all the rest. But those qualities aren't really us. Whatever America refused to admit about itself, it projected onto black people.

"I think that the guilt complex of the American white man is so profound," said Malcolm X during an interview for the Canadian Broadcasting Corporation's television show *Front Page Challenge*, "that he tries to cover it up by accusing his accusers of teaching hate."

Like too many regrettable features of our social landscape, this habit is as apparent today as it's ever been. We are as prone as anybody before us to seeing in others the characteristics we can't stand to face in ourselves. "They put their club upside your head," Malcolm X thundered in one speech, "and then turn around and accuse you of attacking them." Baldwin's words have travelled—taking hold in, and speaking to, America's northern neighbour, where the Idle No More movement (protesting the many violations of Indigenous rights) marches on. His declaration "that what you were describing was not me and what you were afraid of was not me" is equally resonant and relevant here, in Canada.

Too many people here in Canada have taken to calling Indigenous people lazy and their community leaders corrupt and wasteful with government money. This is meant to serve as some kind of explanation for the impoverished conditions many of them are in. Discredit, disparage, demonize. When Theresa Spence, the Chief of a town called Attawapiskat, undertook a hunger strike in December, Christie Blatchford, a prominent Canadian columnist, called it an act "of intimidation, if not terrorism." Blatchford once referred, dismissively, to the "broken state of Aboriginal culture... which is pathologically ill." Blatchford, and many others who think like her, betray a blinkered and myopic vision. Even one of our former prime ministers, Paul Martin, recently said that Canada has been, and continues to be, a colonial power in its relations with Indigenous peoples.

The effects of colonization are apparent. In December, Amnesty International Canada released a report entitled *Matching International Commitments with National Action: A Human Rights Agenda for Canada*. The report noted that "the fundamental right to water within First Nations communities continues to be cavalierly disregarded across the country"; and that most of the water and sewage systems they use are contaminated. Their land and resource rights are going unrecognized and unprotected. A fifth of the country's prison inmates are Indigenous, even though they make up only about three percent of the population. On January 28, there were rallies and demonstrations across Canada. Flash mob dances in Halifax, Montreal, Vancouver, and Ottawa. Solidarity movements echoed across the u.s. in Texas, Washington State, Oregon, Florida, Massachusetts, Minnesota, Montana, Alaska, Michigan, Colorado, Nebraska, New Mexico, Nevada, Connecticut, Oklahoma, New York, North Carolina, and other locations. Around the world, more than 40 Idle No More events took place. The movement's even grown large enough to enter the field of the United Nations' vision, with the un Special Rapporteur on the rights of indigenous peoples, James Anaya, voicing his concerns. These concerns have led to the four founders of the movement to be invited to speak in May at the United Nations.

Four lawyers from Saskatchewan began Idle No More when they planned a teach-in to protest the omnibus budget Bill c-45, which ended up passing without public consultation in early December, withdrawing protection of waterways and facilitating the sale of reserve lands without consultation. The creeping presence of corporate interest in Canada's political affairs is often felt first by Canada's First Nations people. And this time they've pushed back. "When corporate profit is privileged over the health of our lands and waters, we all suffer," wrote Jeff Denis, assistant professor of sociology at McMaster University. "When government stifles debate, democracy is diminished. Bill c-45 is just the latest in a slew of legislation that undermines Canadians' rights. In standing against it, the First Nations are standing for us too." As a reward for this noble effort to protect all our interests and to direct attention to some of their concerns (like poverty and imprisonment and the many broken treaty agreements), many Canadians have amplified murmurings of prejudice long kept muffled.

Racism directed towards Indigenous people is greater now—and more out in the open—than it was before Idle No More. "I keep thinking, who are these people who write these things?" a Toronto aboriginal artist named Keesic Douglas said about the anonymous readers posting in the comments sections of articles. "Is that my next-door neighbor?" The Facebook page for one newspaper, the *Thompson Citizen*, for instance, had to be shut down because of the racist remarks against Indigenous people. It's common to hear a Canadian call Chief Spence lazy or corrupt and seem to forget that our Prime

Minister, Conservative Stephen Harper, isn't exactly a paragon of just leadership. The charge of mismanagement of funds, for one, is misguided. Their communities are subject to strict accounting and control by the federal government. "Many people seem to be labouring under the misapprehension that First Nations have self-governance and run themselves freely," wrote Chelsea Vowel in the *National Post*. "Most First Nations have to get permission before they can spend money. Bands are micromanaged to an extent unseen in nearly any other context that does not involve a minor or someone who lacks capacity due to mental disability."

The narrative of entitled, wasteful freeloaders is born of little more than prejudice and the unwillingness of the government to accept its involvement. "There is a prevailing myth that Canada's more than 600 First Nations and native communities live off of money—subsidies—from the Canadian government," writes Dru Oja Jay in The Media Co-Op. "This myth, though it is loudly proclaimed and widely believed, is remarkable for its boldness; widely accessible, verifiable facts show that the opposite is true." But the facts are uncomfortable and are difficult to integrate into the consciousness of a society which steadfastly believes it's all good. This communal coping mechanism to manage (read: reject) inconvenient facts has deep roots. "There's a long history of coloured perils. There's the 'red peril'," said Professor Charles Mills in a BBC documentary called *Racism: A History*. "There's this idea of the non-white 'Other.' The non-white 'Other' is threatening, the non-white 'Other' is scary, and the non-white 'Other' is maybe coming to attack. And it comes out, you could say, of a bad conscience."

By continually calling out Aboriginals for their supposed imperfections, they are working to avoid a discussion about their very real, and continued, involvement. As Harsha Walia put it, "the theft and appropriation of Indigenous lands and resources subsidize the Canadian economy rather than the other way around." Ultimately, this is just individual psychology writ large. Canada, as a whole, is doing what immature individuals—or all of us at our most immature—do best. "This mechanism of projection—or, if one prefers, transference—has been described by classic psychoanalysis," Frantz Fanon wrote in *Black Skin, White Masks*. "In the degree to which I find in myself something unheard-of, something reprehensible, only one solution remains for me: to get rid of it, to ascribe its origin to someone else. In this way I eliminate a short circuit that threatens to destroy my equilibrium." It's an incredible feat of the imagination when you really think about it. We are complex and cowardly enough to be treacherous and brutal towards others and still find a way to convince ourselves that it's actually our victims who are treacherous and brutal. "That is why he [Obama, in the eyes of the far right] is the out of control spender when they sat on their hands through all of Bush's malfeasance," wrote one anonymous commenter on Andrew Sullivan's blog. "That is why his talking to schoolchildren is dangerous when our government wiretapping its citizens wasn't. That is why saving the financial system from years of Republican regulation is taking away our future." So what do a people do when their fellow citizens consistently project their worst qualities onto them? How do you respond to this? Well, one move is to go with satire and to simply make fun of those so petty and so small that they must mutate reality in such ways. This attitude inspired the #Ottawapiskat hashtag (merging the capital, Ottawa, with Chief Spence's Attawapiskat). The idea's been to have Indigenous people (and others in solidarity with the movement) write the kinds of things about "Chief" Harper they had gotten all too accustomed to hearing about their own leaders.

These disparaging Canadians, the reasoning goes, can't keep pretending that only our communities or our leaders are flawed. "#Ottawapiskat chief is living in a mansion while many of his people are homeless," reads one tweet. "Have you seen #Ottawapiskat on Canada Day? They all gather in a tribal celebration and they drink so much!" reads another. I contributed one myself with this one: "#Ottawapiskat Chief lazily refuses to walk the short distance to meet our leader." (Though Spence was conducting her hunger strike near Parliament, where Harper worked, she couldn't secure a meeting with him.) It's comedy rooted in observations of the absurd, of the inconsistent and the incongruous. But it might also be the kind of comedy that only some of us can even see as funny. Those who project might have a difficult time seeing how obvious it is to us that they're revealing more about themselves than about anybody else.

I hope the fight continues. I hope that they continue to mock the attempts of others to demean them, and to deem them things that better describe them. I hope the rest of us can mature enough to admit that we, too, aren't above the kind of criticism we habitually only mete out to black people and Indigenous people. The myth that there's some neat division between one sect of people and another, between nobler and more righteous characteristics and their debased inversions, impedes spiritual and social growth. "[E]everyone," said Vaclav Havel, "has a small part of himself in both." How it'll turn out in the end is anybody's guess—but, by continuing to reject the old narrative, Idle No More has already won. The movement and Spence's courageous hunger strike will one day command something approaching universal respect and recognition. In facing the cold winds of governmental indifference and societal projection, their fight speaks to the importance and the power of wearing the cloth of self-knowledge.

Baldwin, at the end of the segment I mentioned above, said he would not accept what his society was trying to tell him about himself. They tried to construct a caricature, or pin their own problems, onto him—but he wasn't having that. "Well, he's unnecessary to me," he said, pointing to this caricature, this scapegoat, this shadow that America needed him to be, "so he must be necessary to you."

"I give you your problem back."

Originally appeared on rabble.ca, *February 27, 2013.*

IDLE NO MORE:
Where the Mainstream Media Went Wrong

Leanne Betasamosake Simpson

You didn't have to look hard to find racist comments and biased coverage on the Idle No More movement and Chief Theresa Spence's hunger strike over the past couple of months. Christie Blatchford's racist column in the *National Post* on December 27, 2012, referred to Chief Spence's fast as "hideous puffery and horse manure." A week later, it was Jeffrey Simpson's column "Too many first nations' people live in a dream palace," in *The Globe and Mail* on January 5, 2013. Neither column surprised me, nor were they unique with respect to reporting about Indigenous issues and our peoples in the mainstream media. As a writer and an academic, I felt a responsibility to intervene in the conversation that was taking place.

As though Indigenous Peoples had left the room, mainstream media voices continued in their attempts to discredit Chief Theresa Spence's hunger strike action. Chief Spence's 44-day hunger strike might have just ended, but the fight for Indigenous nationhood, sovereignty, and a fair and just relationship with Canada has not. With the intention of correcting the misconceptions spread through mainstream media about Chief Spence's strike, I wrote a piece in mid-January for the blog dividednomore (www.dividednomore.ca) to explain the cultural significance of Chief Spence's fast. The title of the post was "Fish Broth & Fasting," and it was well received by the readership of that blog. A few days later, the *Huffington Post* contacted me and asked to re-post it.

I felt conflicted. On the one hand, I knew this offer presented an opportunity to reach a large Canadian audience not accessible to me with the original post. But on the other hand, I knew *Huffington Post* allows a substantial amount of racist comments on its site, and I suspected it would sensationalize my article's title. Finally, after lengthy discussions among friends in the Idle No More movement, we agreed the benefits of reaching a larger audience outweighed the risks of sensationalism and racist comments. So I gave the *Post* permission to run my piece on their site. Their new title for my piece? "Think Chief Spence Is on a 'Liquid Diet'? I Think You're Ignorant."

The title was written by a *Huff Post* blog editor and published without my permission. Apparently, the article had to be in the realm of accusation rather than respectful dialogue for consumption in the mainstream media. Herein lies one of the challenges with the media representation of the Idle No More movement—Indigenous Peoples have little agency to represent themselves within mainstream media, which has boxed our peoples inside the confines of the same recycled stereotypes it insists upon invoking. And that challenge hasn't stopped us; in fact, it has only served to inspire us further. With few exceptions (and the *Huff Post* is one of them because they regularly re-blog Indigenous voices), the mainstream media reports Indigenous issues through the lens of the colonial ideology that permeates every aspect

Indigenous women leading a movement...again. On the way to Parliament Hill in Ottawa on December 21, 2012. (NADYA KWANDIBENS)

of Canadian culture. Since the beginnings of Idle No More, they have consistently chosen to exaggerate and manufacture controversy and crisis, rather than to create open dialogue. They've promoted fear over understanding and have amplified potential divisions as a way of destabilizing the movement.

Worse, a few networks (including Sun News) have even promoted Indigenous protesters as "terrorists" and questioned if Idle No More is a rise in a "more fundamentalist view of First Nations politics." Once the movement started to take hold, as with other social movements involving people of colour or women, racism and misogyny were used to discredit it, with columns like Christie Blatchford's leading the way. Idle No More has consistently rejected the framing of protesters as fed up and angry, or of the mobilization as "new." The movement is in fact a continuation of 400 years of resistance. We have also rejected the media's need to focus on a single leader or spokesperson, and on a concise list of short-term demands. Instead, Indigenous Peoples have consistently brought in the historic and contemporary legacy of colonialism, occupation, and dispossession as context to our deepening movement.

There is also a problem with expertise, or lack thereof, in mainstream media. Repeatedly, I've listened to pundits and panelists with no expertise on Indigenous issues contribute to the already overwhelming body of misinformation about us. For example, while CBC Radio's Q host Jian Ghomeshi's opening essay on Idle No More was warmly received on December 21, 2012, that same episode's media panel discussed the movement with no Indigenous representation. Instead, the nearly 10-minute discussion relied on its regular panel of Judy Rebick (rabble.ca), who did an excellent job, Jonathan Kay (*National Post*), and John Cruickshank (*Toronto Star*). There is no excuse for this. We have hundreds of political scientists, academics, analysts, journalists, and experts within Indigenous communities. Just like Canadians, we don't all agree. If your media panel is discussing Indigenous issues and you do not have at least one Indigenous expert on the panel, you are doing something wrong. Period.

The colonial narrative in the media only intensifies when one brings gender into the analysis. Chief Spence has been repeatedly questioned about whether continuing her fast is in the best interests of her children. I don't remember the parenting of a male leader coming under scrutiny because of his ceremonial and political actions. This, in the context of a colonial legacy that has manipulated public perception of Indigenous women in order to justify cultural termination policies through residential schools and, later, the child welfare system. But through all the mainstream media coverage of Chief Spence's strike and the Idle No More movement, Indigenous Peoples have not been passively silent.

Indigenous media outlets such as APTN have worked diligently to disrupt and challenge the mainstream perspective. As Anishinaabe journalist Waub Rice observed online, there isn't a critical mass of Indigenous reporters working within mainstream media, but the few who do have been quite vocal in transforming mainstream representation and understanding of the movement. One of those few is Duncan McCue, Anishinaabe journalism professor and producer for CBC's *The National*. McCue is an Indigenous journalist who has produced in-depth stories on the movement for CBC's *The National* and *The Current*, and has developed a website for non-Indigenous journalists covering Indigenous issues at www.riic.ca. To add to the few are Indigenous women such as Connie Walker and Angela Sterritt, who have brought the stories of our women to the mainstream through CBC's *8th Fire* series and its website.

People within the movement have also engaged in an extensive self-representation media campaign as an alternative to the mainstream press, aimed at both educating Canadians on Indigenous issues and inspiring our youth. There is an impressive array of high-calibre writing about the movement in various blogs such as:

- *dividednomore*
- *Decolonizing: Indigeneity, Education & Society*
- *mediaIndigena*
- *Decolonizing Media*
- And of course from our allies in the independent media including *The Media Co-op* and *rabble.ca*

Jarrett Martineau is a grassroots media campaigner for Idle No More and member of Frog Lake Cree Nation in Alberta who writes online at culturite.wordpress.com. In an email, he said to me, "I think we've reached a critical mass in our peoples' media literacy and online presence, and we're empowering multiple generations to join the movement, share knowledge, and get down to organizing the work that needs doing."

Métis artist Christi Belcourt started the blog *dividednomore* in response to mainstream media coverage of Idle No More. Also in an email to me, she wrote, "DividedNoMore is a space that was created to share ideas that could be expanded beyond 140 Twitter characters about the Canada we want and believe our children deserve." Belcourt was pointing to the educational component of the movement, which has included hundreds of teach-ins across Canada geared towards both Native and non-Native peoples on topics ranging from treaties, the Indian Act and Indigenous resurgence to the omnibus Bill C-45 and community organizing. One recent teach-in at the University of Victoria attracted 300 people from all different backgrounds; 300 more were turned away; another 400 participated online. A series of online town hall meetings has assembled more than 300 participants at each.

Over the past six weeks, we have also seen an artistic outpouring, including podcasts, edgy logos and posters, zines, pamphlets, solidarity concerts, short films, poetry and new music by DJs, rappers, and singer-songwriters, including new tracks by A Tribe Called Red, Cris Derksen, Derek Miller and Star Nayea. RPM.FM has released two free album downloads called *Idle No More: Songs for Life* with donated tracks from Derek Miller, Digging Roots, John K. Samson, Plex, and Jenn Grant.

And the National Film Board offered a week of free online viewing of Abenaki filmmaker Alanis Obomsawin's *The People of the Kattawapiskak River,* chronicling the wider context in which issues in Attawapiskat take place. Without fair mainstream media coverage, very little of this work will reach most Canadians. It is our hope that by reflecting our own stories back to ourselves, we will validate and pass them along to our young people. It is our hope that we will both inspire our youth when they see themselves and their relations represented in a positive manner across multiple media, as well as provide Canadians with different stories, angles, and voices. Idle No More is not just a fight for Indigenous nations, land, culture, decolonization, language, treaties, and the environment; it is also a fight for the fair and accurate representation of Indigenous Peoples and our issues. It is a fight for a better relationship, and that begins with truth, dialogue, and respect.

Originally appeared on leannesimpson.ca, *February 27, 2013.*

AS LONG AS THE WATER NEVER IDLES:
Movement in Grassy Narrows First Nation
Ryan Duplassie

As water flows, so is Idle No More a movement. Important conversations have started, weaving information, history, steadfastness, courage, and love into loops of social networking, journalism, television and radio. Round dances, rallies, and hunger strikes brought us together through weeks of winter snow and into the summer. All of this movement has tripped the wires of complacency and we move—we are Idle No More—as we learn and fight for our treaties, lands, and waterways.

Of course, none of this is new. Take the resistance at Asubpeeschoseewagong Netum Anishinaabek, or Grassy Narrows, now in its third generation, a struggle that began when it was confirmed that fish in the community were heavily contaminated with mercury. The grassroots has since been embroiled in a public struggle to protect their lands and waters, to restore the vitality of bodies, spirits, and local economies.

More than eleven years ago, a handful of youth felled a tree to block the logging road leading into the traditional territories of the Asubpeeschoseewagong Netum Anishinaabek. They started a blockade that was joined by adults and elders and garnered almost overnight international attention. The blockade still stands today. For the community at Grassy Narrows, concerns around the ongoing effects of mercury—owing to logging and pollution—are more potent than ever. This might be why Idle No More appealed so deeply to the youth; both are deeply about the water—and both are about our future.

But Idle No More is also about building and revitalizing community. Like all Indigenous communities, there are 21st century distractions in Grassy Narrows—alcohol, internet, drugs, television, consumer messaging, video games, and suicides. Few spend time on the land and water. More and more are not going outside at all. This separates us from the sacred teachings the land holds; to teach us of the pace, simplicity, creative problem-solving, and how to communicate with our immediate relations and honour the gifts of wood, fish, sun, and rain.

Inspired by Idle No More and particularly by the situation at Grassy Narrows last summer, I and Andrew Keewatin (trapper, hunter, craftsman, volunteer educator, and addictions counsellor are amongst his many roles) began a project bringing small groups of young people 45 minutes across Indian Lake to build a large trapper's cabin on the Kokokopenace family trapline. Participants learn how to build a cabin, but also much more. They learn how to pitch tents, construct a weatherproof camp kitchen/eating area, fetch drinking water and dish water, collect wood and start a fire, feed one another, take care of each other, and how to always make tea first. Our time on the trapline is not just about work, it is about swimming in the lake, playing with garter snakes and frogs, marvelling at the moss, sleeping on the grassy shore, and sharing stories under moon and starlight.

In our own simple way, we are defining and refining the meaning and significance of "occupation." Our work is decolonizing. These young people learn to enjoy working hard in the bush and earning senses of stewardship and responsibility. It is hoped that they will eventually host visitors as they experience Indian Lake and perhaps even find comfort in the cabin. At the same time, these young people gain a closeness with the land that teaches them that it is sacred in its relationship with us; Mother Earth is our protector and our life-giver. Actions like clear-cutting severs that tie. Finally, our earth also teaches the importance of politics. The grant that funds this program is co-administered under the auspices of federal Aboriginal Affairs and the Ontario Ministry of Natural Resources, who have clear agendas of their own. These sometimes run in opposition to the health and well-being of land and water, as seen in MNR clearcut logging plans. Youth learn not only about this history, but how choices come with impacts and more choices. Without question, these participants cannot help but learn a complex sense of land, sharing, and Treaty.

My doctoral research explores the significance of water for us Anishinaabe, and the meaning and interpretation of Treaty 3. Like many treaties, Treaty 3 was meant to remain sacrosanct "as long as the water flows and the sun rises."[12] In Treaty 3 however, these words take two interrelated and interesting interpretations. One, that Treaty will be upheld as long as rivers run. The second is that Treaty will last as long as "the water flows" from childbirth; in other words, as long as we Anishinaabe exist. How long we will exist in these climactic times is for us to determine, but we cannot forget that water demonstrates through flow and denotes purpose. It is all around us—it *is* us. We must take care of it to take care of each other.

This summer in a little bay across "Indian Lake" from the Grassy Narrows reserve, there is a handful of young Asubpeeschoseewagong Netum Anishinaabek engaged in resistance and renewal. They—rather, we—are exercising our "rights," yes. But our work is more than that. We are, through movement, carrying out our obligations under Treaty.

So we give thanks to those who learn, act, and live with us... as we Idle No More.

Presentation given at the "Globalization and 'Minor' Cultural Groups: the Role of 'so-called' Minorities in Rethinking the Future of Modern Societies" Conference at the University of Versailles in France, June 20, 2013.

12 Promised during Treaty 3 talks by Alexander Morris, Lieutentant-Governor of Manitoba and the Northwest Territories, as published in 1880 in his *The Treaties of Canada with the Indians of Manitoba and the North-West Territories, Including the Negotiations on which They were Based, And Other Information Relating Thereto.* Morris "negotiated" Treaties 3, 4, 5, 6, and revised Treaties 1 and 2 on behalf of the Crown. He often deployed this borrowed diplomatic phrase—used by many First Nations across Turtle Island—in an effort to assuage fears by appearing familiar in spirit to the First Nations whom he addressed. Morris's full publication is freely available online at www.gutenberg.org/dirs/etext04/tcnnd10h.htm. Last retrieved August 9, 2013.

NEW DIRECTIONS

Warrior Tantoo Cardinal's voice echoed off Toronto skyscrapers throughout Idle No More. January 2, 2013. (IRINA POPOVA)

HIS FEAST: HER BROKEN FAST

Rosanna Deerchild

Harper doesn't need to worry
About the woman on the hill

She's already dead
From the arrows in her back

Those headdresses & handshakes
Did the trick a treaty real good

Slip a token promise
Of more talk in their tea

They pack up her tipi
Even sweep up her mess

He's not responsible
For what desperate men will do

Smiles in all the pictures
Says nothing of honour

Thinks of what he will eat
After all this is over

Theresa of the hill
Far away & forgotten

He doesn't know
About the others

Just reaching
The horizon

The girl who danced
All the way

In a storm her blue regalia
Flashes lightning

In the open plain
Her sisters' drum

Song is thunder
Across the land

Young men walk
Talk in new languages

Carry new weapons
Learned from history

Alongside the highway
An old woman carries a sign

An old man marches
Just as he did in war time

The women bang on the door
Followed by leaders

Who refuse to fall
For the same old tactic

Of divide
Subtract and distract

Harper doesn't know
The round dance is not over

Until the circle
Is complete

Until all the people
Are dancing

As one
We are here

To dance at your feast
Sing the story of your lies

Stand with our ancestors
We are hungry

Originally appeared in kimiwan zine, *March 2013.*

IDLE NO MORE:
Where Do We Go From Here?

Chelsea Vowel

> *Canada is a test case for a grand notion—the notion that dissimilar peoples can share lands, resources, power and dreams while respecting and sustaining their differences. The story of Canada is the story of many such peoples, trying and failing and trying again, to live together in peace and harmony. But there cannot be peace or harmony unless there is justice. It was to help restore justice to the relationship between Aboriginal and non-Aboriginal people in Canada, and to propose practical solutions to stubborn problems, that the Royal Commission on Aboriginal Peoples was established.*—page ix,
> "A Word From Commissioners"[13]

The quote above comes from a publication that is 150 pages in length, and in my opinion should be read by every single Canadian. This publication is called *People to People, Nation to Nation: Highlights from the Report of the Royal Commission on Aboriginal Peoples*. If you never manage to wade through the five volumes of findings and recommendations published by the Royal Commission on Aboriginal Peoples (RCAP), please at least make your way through the Highlights.[14]

Backing up a little...the RCAP was established in 1991 and engaged in 178 days of public hearings, visiting 96 communities, commissioning research and consulting with experts. In 1996, the RCAP released a five-volume report of findings and recommendations.

> *We directed our consultations to one over-riding question: What are the foundations of a fair and honorable relationship between the Aboriginal and non-Aboriginal people of Canada?*—page x,
> "A Word From Commissioners"

13 All references in this article are taken from the full report of the *Royal Commission on Aboriginal Peoples*. The full report can be found online at: www.collectionscanada.gc.ca/webarchives/20071115053257/www.ainc-inac.gc.ca /ch/rcap/sg/sgmm_e.html.

14 If you want something even less dense, there is a 51-page PDF document that does a bang-up job of summarizing the report and its main recommendations. Included at the end is a nice breakdown of financial estimates for implementation of these recommendations.

This was the central purpose of the RCAP. To figure out what went wrong, how it went wrong, and what can be done to correct the problems identified. A lot of people seem to feel lost when it comes to the huge diversity of issues faced by indigenous peoples in Canada, and with the obviously dysfunctional system of relationships between natives and settlers. You will see this reflected in comment sections, or falling from the mouths of politicians and reporters, or yelled out in frustration over and over again whenever there is conflict between us. What you are witnessing is hopelessness. Helplessness. Confusion does this to people, and that is why I think the RCAP is so incredibly powerful and important. You see, people really do sit down and identify the problems and try to come up with solutions, and if you feel like you have no idea where to begin to address these problems, then I want you to know that you have a good place to start. You don't need to reinvent the wheel here, folks. So much work has already been done to come up with practical solutions to identifiable problems and it's a damn shame that most Canadians have never read a single word published by this Royal Commission. So let's get to it, shall we?

What's the Big Picture Here?

Our central conclusion can be summarized simply: **The main policy direction, pursued for more than 150 years, first by colonial then by Canadian governments, has been wrong.**—page x, "A Word From Commissioners"

I know a lot of people reading that conclusion are going to roll their eyes and say "Well, duh! We know that things weren't done in a fair fashion, but holy! Let's get over the past and live in the present already!" Except that's not what the Commission is saying. They have not absolved current government policy, or indicated that things have been fixed and now we have only historical injustices to address. Please understand this very clearly. Current government policy continues to be wrong. The RCAP was quite adamant about this when they released their final report in 1996, and not enough has changed since then to warrant a pat on the back for making things all better.

I recognize that this is too vague for you right now, but I want you to understand that it is incredibly important to simply admit this one thing. Admitting that historical AND current government policy towards indigenous peoples is wrong is no light thing. You will find strong resistance to this concept, particularly in the contemporary context. The Canadian government certainly does not accept this as true. The vast majority of Canadians probably do not accept that this is true. So before you ask "Why belabour the obvious, âpihtawikosisân?", I want you to remember that getting people to accept this premise on a wide scale is something we have yet to accomplish, and that the rejection of this as truth is the number one reason we have yet to resolve our problems, people to people, nation to nation.

So What Do I Need to Know?

I think the first thing all Canadians need to have firmly rooted in their consciousness is…we're not going away. Ever. Never ever ever.

> *Successive governments have tried—sometimes intentionally, sometimes in ignorance—to absorb Aboriginal people into Canadian society, thus eliminating them as distinct peoples. Policies pursued over the decades have undermined—and almost erased—Aboriginal cultures and identities. This is assimilation. It is a denial of the principles of peace, harmony and justice for which this country stands—and it has failed. Aboriginal peoples remain proudly different.* **Assimilation policies failed because Aboriginal people have the secret of cultural survival. They have an enduring sense of themselves as peoples with a unique heritage and the right to cultural continuity.**—page x, "A Word From Commissioners"

Many Canadians are still clamouring for assimilation. You can see this again in all those comment sections, in all of the dialogues about "how to fix the Aboriginal problem." The solutions are invariably:

- Make them more like us!
- Private property!
- Get them out of isolated communities and into the cities with the rest of us!
- No special rights!
- No differences!
- Treat them the same! and so on.

It's all been tried. It really has. You might not know all the history yet, so perhaps you think your ideas are novel. Pretty much every suggestion currently being given to assimilate native peoples has been actively tried before, with disastrous results and ultimately, a failure to actually assimilate us.[15]

Stop it. It didn't work, and it isn't going to work, no matter how much cooler you think you are than the policy-makers of the past. Accept the fact that we are here, and we aren't leaving, and that we recognize you aren't leaving either. It would do us all a world of good if we could be on the same page on this one.

Where Do We Go From Here?

After some 500 years of a relationship that has swung from partnership to domination, from mutual respect and co-operation to paternalism and attempted assimilation, Canada must now work out fair and lasting terms of coexistence with Aboriginal people.—page 1, Looking Forward, Looking Back

The truth is, the *status quo* isn't working. I have repeatedly talked about the need to form new relationships, but I'm not just pulling this out of thin air. This is something many people have recognized over the years as they have examined the history and the current reality of Aboriginal and non-Aboriginal relationships. The Commission quite conveniently outlined *four reasons* to commit to building this new relationship:

1. Canada's claim to be a fair and enlightened society depends on it.
2. The life chances of Aboriginal people, which are still shamefully low, must be improved.
3. Negotiations, as conducted under the current rules, have proved unequal to the task of settling grievances.
4. Continued failure may well lead to violence.

Don't buy it? Then perhaps you can explain how repeating the mistakes of the past (assimilation, relocation, etc.) is a more intelligent approach? I don't know about you, but I'm definitely ready to try something different.

15 I suggest starting with Volume One of RCAP, titled *Looking Forward, Looking Back*. Go ahead and skip to the sections on the Indian Act, Residential Schools, and Relocation of Aboriginal Communities.

"The first and perhaps most important element is the need to reject the principles on which the relationship has foundered over the last two centuries in particular—principles such as assimilation, control, intrusion and coercion—and do away with the remnants of the colonial era. As a beginning, we need to abandon outmoded doctrines such as terra nullius and discovery. We must reject the attitudes of racial and cultural superiority reflected in these concepts, which contributed to European nations' presumptions of sovereignty over Indigenous peoples and lands. The renewed relationship needs to be built on principles that will return us to a path of justice, co-existence and equality.—Chapter 14 of Part 3, Volume 1

I know I keep coming back to this, but it's important. The way forward needs to be guided by accepting these two related points as true:

I. The main policy direction, pursued for more than 150 years, first by colonial, then by Canadian governments, has been [and continues to be] wrong.

II. We need to reject the principles on which the relationship has foundered over the last two centuries in particular—principles such as assimilation, control, intrusion, and coercion—and do away with the remnants of the colonial era.

Until we have that firmly set in our minds, we are all going to spin our wheels, because a great many of the people "coming to the table" will continue to hold on to ideas that will actively sabotage any attempt to create new relationships. But let's pretend we all agree, and move on.

Volume Two of the RCAP final report deals with precisely how to restructure the relationship. The Commission makes concrete suggestions about restructuring and renewing treaties, for example, to return them to living agreements rather than historical artifacts. This includes changing the approach to so-called "modern" treaties which are still very much based on a model of "we talk about this once, we sign, and we never ever discuss it again." No other kind of treaty works that way and the Commission provides some good recommendations about how to change the process both of addressing historical treaties, and approaching modern treaties.

In-depth discussions and recommendations related to governance, lands, and resources, economic development, can also be found in Volume Two. If you are curious about any of these things, please use this resource to learn more about the issues. Again, the important thing about this report is that it does not just leave you with the problems identified (a step that is undoubtedly important), but also provides you with concrete solutions that you can roll around in your head for a while to see how you feel about it. Volume Two is very much about building a vehicle for change.

Some might ask: even if we change the relationship, how is that going to fix the problems Aboriginal communities face? Volume Three of the RCAP is titled "Gathering Strength." It deals with many of the issues that have been raised recently in the context of Attawapiskat, such as housing, education, and health. It also addresses family, arts and heritage, and social policy in general. Volume Three is about how where we're going to drive that vehicle for change. Volume Four provides us with a diversity of indigenous perspectives on a range of issues, providing us with historical information, current issues and needs, and recommendations for integrating these different perspectives in a way that ensures any sight-seeing we do along the journey doesn't leave anyone out.

So is there a roadmap for how any of this would actually work? Volume Five lays out a 20-year plan to implement all the recommendations of the Commission. It provides the sort of cost/benefit analysis that seems to tickle some people to no end, so if that's your thing, feel free to skip straight to the "nitty gritty." If you simply want to overload on practical suggestions for identified problems, then mosey on over to Appendix A, which contains all 444 recommendations for change proposed by the RCAP.

So if this was a 20-year plan and the report was released over 15 years ago, surely we're close to implementing all these recommendations... right? No. Unfortunately we have seen precious little improvement in 15 years.

The Assembly of First Nations released a Report Card, 10 years after the RCAP, detailing the dismal implementation record to date[16]. I also attended a conference in 2006 that basically discussed Life After

---

16 Available here: www.cbc.ca/news/background/aboriginals/pdf/afn_rcap.pdf

THE WINTER WE DANCED   313

the RCAP, which was pretty disheartening. That conference provided some very interesting information on what impact the RCAP *has* had, even absent full implementation, so if you want a quick discussion on the pros and cons of how the Commission went about fulfilling its mandate, and on how the report has been received non-officially in the courts and so on, please take a gander![17]

In particular, I suggest reading the summary of Alan C. Cairn's breakdown of some of the inherent problems with the Commission's approach to nationhood. The RCAP was not without its flaws.

The central question is: Why hasn't there been more progress? This is why I take you back to those points I kept hammering away at earlier. You know, these ones:

- The main policy direction, pursued for more than 150 years, first by colonial, then by Canadian governments, has been [and continues to be] wrong.

- We need to reject the principles on which the relationship has foundered over the last two centuries in particular—principles such as assimilation, control, intrusion, and coercion—and do away with the remnants of the colonial era.

It is my firm belief that Canada has not yet accepted these two points as true, and because of this, there has been little in the way of progress. If you actually believe that native culture is inferior, then you don't value it and you sure as heck aren't going to take it seriously. If you don't understand the history of relations between indigenous peoples and settlers, then you aren't going to believe that current conditions faced by native peoples aren't almost entirely self-imposed. If you know nothing about indigenous governance and think Indian Act governance is "traditional," then you probably aren't going to have much faith in native self-government. If you don't know what has been attempted before (assimilation, relocation, etc.) then you're going to think that you're coming up with something really radical when you suggest similar things in the current context.

This country is woefully ignorant, on a grand scale, and we will never succeed in rebuilding relationships until we address that

17 Available here: www.indigenousbar.ca/pdf/2006%20IBA%20Final%20 Conference%20Report.pdf

ignorance. I can't stress this enough: without education, there can be no justice. And until there is justice, there will be no peace. My purpose here was to introduce people to the RCAP, both as a starting point for further investigation into the many issues faced by native peoples in Canada, and also as proof positive that practical solutions *have* been suggested. That latter part is important, because people need to stop believing that there is no other way "out" besides just assimilating us once and for all. It might seem so much simpler to just legislate us out of existence, make us all "the same" to satisfy liberal notions of equality, but it won't actually solve anything. The RCAP is a good place to start if you want to know why such attempts are doomed to fail, and what alternatives have been proposed.

Originally appeared on apihtawikosisan.com, *December 26, 2012.*

RESETTING AND RESTORING THE RELATIONSHIP BETWEEN INDIGENOUS PEOPLES AND CANADA

Taiaiake Alfred and Toby Rollo

We bear witness today to an inspiring resurgence of Indigenous consciousness directed at injustices within the Canadian state. History demonstrates that such events constitute the necessary preconditions of social and political change. Two decades ago, Indigenous resistance to colonialism moved Canada to establish the Royal Commission on Aboriginal Peoples (RCAP). The goal of the commission was to establish the steps necessary for restoring a just relationship between Canada and Indigenous peoples. RCAP was comprehensive and inclusive, with its recommendations reflecting an extraordinary consensus between Indigenous and non-Indigenous peoples, an agreement arrived at through processes characterized by mutual respect, friendship, and peace.

Twenty years later, Indigenous peoples and settler Canadians find ourselves in a new, profound moment of resistance and resurgence. The sense of urgency and of possibility may be unprecedented. Perhaps there is no better time, then, to press forward with a restoration of the relationship delineated in RCAP. In the spirit of mutual respect, friendship, and peace, we have provided concise accounts of what we feel to be the most crucial and immanently needed recommendations:

1. **Declaration of Responsibility.** To restore this relationship, the Government of Canada must acknowledge the systematic nature of Canada's colonial past and present. Recent governments have issued apologies for specific colonial programs, such as the Residential School System, but have yet to acknowledge responsibility for the full range of colonial institutions, including legislation currently enforced under the Indian Act.

2. **Legislated Recognition of Political Authority.** The Government of Canada must enact legislation that recognizes the inherent rights of Indigenous Nations to designate political authority according to their own laws, governing principles, and customs. The law will provide guidance and give expression to the already existing recognition of the right of self-determination found in Section 35(1) of the Canadian Constitution and the nation-to-nation relationship established by previous treaties and agreements. In addition, it will allow systems of political authority and accountability to take root in Indigenous communities that will correct the democratically defective and dysfunctional Indian Act system.

3. **Legislated Devolution of Governance.** The Government of Canada must devolve control over social, cultural, economic, housing, health, and educational services to Indigenous governments, in accordance with Section 35 of the Constitution of Canada. The current "duty to consult" must be replaced with federally structured shared-jurisdiction over lands considered for urban and economic development. Indigenous jurisdiction will provide a stopgap measure against the erosion of environmental protections under external pressures.

4. **Legislation of Crown Fiduciary Duty.** The Government of Canada must provide funding, training, and resources sufficient to assist Indigenous nations while they re-establish their capacities and autonomy as Indigenous Nations. As these capacities

are realized, the cost to Canada will diminish sharply until it is no longer needed.

5. **Unrestricted Modern Treaty Process.** The Government of Canada must remove formal and informal restrictions placed on treaty negotiations with Indigenous governments over rights to land and culture. A refusal to negotiate in good faith amounts to a bare assertion of colonial sovereignty, which stands as an affront to international law and to the Constitution of Canada itself.

Originally distributed as a pamphlet at several Idle No More events, including those held on Coast Salish Territory and in Victoria, British Columbia.

SEEING STRENGTH, BEAUTY & RESILIENCE IN OURSELVES:
An Interview with Eugene Boulanger

Eugene Boulanger with Leanne Betasamosake Simpson

LEANNE BETASAMOSAKE SIMPSON (LS): I'm with Eugene Boulanger, who is a Shutaogotine Dene artist, hunter, community organizer, and cross-media producer currently living and working in both the Unceded Coast Salish Territories of the Squamish, Musqueam and Tsleil-Waututh Nations, and Somba K'e, located in Chief Drygeese Territory in the Akaitcho Region of Treaty 8 in Denendeh. Miigwech for joining me. I'd like to start by asking what was your personal motivation to participate in and organize Idle No More events?

EUGENE BOULANGER (EB): My personal motivation to participate in and organize Idle No More events stemmed from my commitment to meaningful, culturally relevant community development and youth engagement. I hope that my actions during Idle No More helped to inspire young leaders to move further than their comfort allows when a sense of justice compels them to action. My intention has always been to empower youth to take leadership in their communities, and

Idle No More proved to be a powerful vehicle to initiate that process in many young people's lives.

LS: There's long history of resistance in Denendeh. How does Idle No More fit into that context?

EB: In Denendeh, resistance to colonization has been a long-standing tradition. From the formation of the Indian Brotherhood of the Northwest Territories in response to the White Paper in the late 60s, and its subsequent evolution into the Dene Nation, the resistance to the Mackenzie Valley Gas Pipeline during the Berger Inquiry of the 1970s, and the Dene Nation's hardline negotiations with the federal government in attempts to establish culturally appropriate governance in Denendeh, many historical examples of resistance to settler colonialism in Denendeh exist. In the context of Idle No More, resistance efforts to non-renewable resource extraction and the ongoing assimilative practices manifest in Aboriginal policy can be seen as a renewed effort to break from a politics of recognition to one of authority and jurisdiction over our own lives. Idle No More has brought back the term "self-determination" in the north, and has forced us to examine what this means in the second decade of the 21st century.

LS: As a young Shutaogotine Dene, what did it mean to you to participate in the Idle No More movement?

EB: Idle No More was an opportunity for me to participate in what I believe might become a lasting movement for genuine reconciliation and social justice for Indigenous peoples around the world. My participation in Idle No More was an exercise in surrender; my commitment to the resurgence of traditional Dene values while being proficient in the skills required to achieve the goals of cultural resurgence in the dominant Euro-western society demanded my time and energy to effectively deliver actions in two territories. While organizing protests in Vancouver, I allowed myself to be vulnerable to people I didn't know and with whom I may never have a chance to talk—a feeling that most times is unsettling and uncomfortable, however necessary the task may be.

LS: What are the big issues in your homeland that you think motivated yourself and others to take action?

EB: With an enhanced interest in the non-renewable resource sector in Denendeh comes superficial agreements promising community prosperity, however, these agreements rarely offer community members with opportunities for educational or career enhancement in sectors other than petro-energy and mining. In Denendeh, issues ranging from traditional land use to language and cultural revitalization to sustainable economic prosperity reflect the values of a growing population of Indigenous northern youth unsatisfied with the current socio-political conditions in which they live. Mental health, addictions, community wellness, and prosperity for Indigenous peoples in the north are secondary and tertiary in priority to the needs of the mining and oil and gas sectors which operate in the traditional territories of the Dene and Gwich'in peoples. This inconsistency between the needs of Indigenous peoples resisting cultural assimilation, the leadership of Indigenous and non-Indigenous northerners, and the needs of Canada's energy sector result in a dissonance that is reflected in incarceration, suicide, violent crime and high school dropout statistics. Effective, culturally relevant solutions to these issues are presented without historical context and the frustration which fuelled Idle No More in the north can be attributed to living with these issues and being denied justice for the historical wrongs that resulted in the oppression, internalized racism, and legacies of abuse that are playing out today.

LS: Idle No More is often framed as a movement that was led by women and young people. Is this true in your territory?

EB: Idle No More in Denendeh, namely in Somba K'e (Yellowknife), was largely organized by young women, with the assistance of a group of young men. Direction and guidance were provided by the women in the group, with men helping to coordinate logistics and providing resources and materials needed to produce events in coordination with larger, national events happening around the country. Members of Aboriginal leadership, upon realizing that events had been organized without their "blessings," behaved in manners typical of a generation raised to believe that the role of women is literally to be behind men. What they hadn't acknowledged throughout the speeches was the huge role that women had played in organizing supporters, drummers, venues, schedules, and transportation—and if these efforts were acknowledged, it was in a condescending, dismissive, and patriarchal manner. That being said, those who were aware of the tremendous energy put forth by female organizers and the chronic marginalization of Indigenous women had illustrated for them a cross-section of Aboriginal politics in the north. Many viewed this uncomfortable experience, however disrespectful, as an important illumination of the deficiencies in northern Aboriginal leadership, and a measure from which to continue to work to build inclusive, respectful, and capable leadership.

LS: Your work is very strongly rooted in nationhood and resurgence. Does Idle No More move these issues along for you?

EB: Idle No More served to bring to my generation a renewed interest in collective Indigenous struggles for self-determination, a tradition that has waned in recent decades in the north. Whether this decline in Indigenous activism can be attributed to increasing pressures of assimilation is hard to tell; it is fair to say that Idle No More was the Oka or the Gustafsen Lake or the Burnt Church or the Wounded Knee for many young people in North America today.

LS: Both art and social media played an important role in Idle No More. How did this play out in the north?

EB: Social media provides us a space in which we can broadcast our own narratives—from a grassroots level. Rather than waiting and working within the confines of corporate broadcast media, clear narratives were communicated between diverse groups across the world in mere seconds. Given this ability to see and be seen, the opportunities for self-analysis and for reflexivity were accelerated, creating a dynamic social fabric capable of addressing the needs of its constituents—Indigenous and non-Indigenous participants of the movement. The role of visual art in these movements has always been a way to instill pride in one's culture, to communicate the diversity of the people of the north, and to create unity despite cultural divisions. Like the blue drops that anti-oil activists wear on the west coast, to the red squares worn by Quebec protesters last year, symbolism works to unite people despite their differences. If we can agree on certain values, we can work together and work through these values in pursuit of common interests. In the north, everyone can appreciate the beauty of moose hide mitts with native beadwork, which represent resourcefulness, creativity, and resilience.

LS: What do you want Canadians to know about your people?

EB: Canadians need to know more about their own history before they study the history of Indigenous peoples in Canada. Canada's own educational system does not prepare its citizens for engaging with Indigenous people or communities, and in doing so creates cultural barriers which limit cross-cultural engagement on critical issues such as protection of land, water, and air. Canadians should know that without their major investors, the formation of this country could never have happened. Rather than being seen as investors in the state of Canada, Indigenous peoples were seen as labourers. Looking back at the fur trade era shows that the founding of this nation was reliant on the co-operation of Indigenous peoples and settling colonists. Drawing on the original partnerships that founded the nation in which we live today, we find lessons vital for moving forward together as diverse peoples in a culturally pluralistic society, rather than the assimilative, multicultural paradigm of today.

LS: What are your hopes for the youth of your nation?

EB: My hopes for the youth of my nation are that we can create a culture of criticality, curiosity, and empowerment. I hope to see more young people in positions of leadership, organizing their communities and asking hard questions about the economies that they're creating or participating in, the health and wellness of their communities, and the wealth of their lands and how that is defined. Primarily, I hope that the youth of my nation have the opportunity to see the strength, beauty, and resilience in themselves that I see in them.

LS: What do you see are the next steps for action?

EB: As with any long-game strategy, I see the next steps for action being strategic visioning and network building. If Idle No More was an excited flexing of one muscle, we need to work together to coordinate the movement of arms and legs. People working in their communities to build support for different initiatives need to be supported by other groups doing similar work in other communities, and all of us have different roles to play in organizing stronger, more focused actions for the betterment of our communities, and in ways that we agree are beneficial for all things—plants, animals, and human beings. This requires commitment, imagination, and creativity, but I believe that we're capable of finding the solutions we need because we always have.

FIRST NATIONS:
Working Towards Fundamental Change
Chief Theresa Spence and Supporters

In the true spirit of commitment to initiate dialogue to discuss both Treaty and non-Treaty Indigenous issues on behalf of our First Nations Peoples of Canada, Chief Theresa Spence of Attawapiskat First Nation and Mr. Raymond Robinson of Cross Lake, Manitoba will continue their Hunger Strike, pending outcome of this written Declaration. We also like to acknowledge Mr. Jean Sock of Elsipogtog, New Brunswick and all other Fasters who have shown their deep dedication and courage in support of protecting and honouring both Treaty and non-Treaty obligations as written, entered into or understood by all Peoples, with the Federal Government of Canada including each Provincial/Territorial signatory.

Further, we agree the self-sacrifice and the spiritual courage of Chief Theresa Spence, along with Elder Raymond Robinson and all other fasters, have made clear the need for fundamental change in the relationship of First Nations and the Crown. We fully commit to carry forward the urgent and coordinated action required until concrete and tangible results are achieved in order to allow First Nations to forge their own destiny.

Therefore, we solemnly commit to undertake political, spiritual and all other advocacy efforts to implement a renewed First Nations/Crown relationship where inherent Treaty and non-Treaty Rights are recognized, honoured, and fully implemented as they should be, within the next five years.

This Declaration includes, but is not limited to, ensuring commitments made by the Prime Minister of Canada on January 11, 2013

Danny Metatawabin, Chief Theresa Spence's Oshkaabewis and constant presence on Victoria Island. (JOHN PAILLÉ)

are followed through and implemented as quickly as possible as led by First Nation on a high-level priority with open transparency and trust. Furthermore, immediate steps are taken working together to achieve the below priorities:

1. An immediate meeting to be arranged between the Crown, federal governments, provincial governments and all First Nations to discuss outstanding issues regarding the Treaty Relationship, as well as for non-Treaty area relationships.

2. Clear work plans that shall include deliverables and timelines that outline how commitments will be achieved, including immediate action for short-, medium-, and long-term goals. Addressing the housing crisis within our First Nation communities shall be considered as a short-term immediate action.

3. Frameworks and mandates for the implementation and enforcement of Treaties between Treaty parties on a Nation-to-Nation basis.

4. Reforming and modifying the comprehensive claims policy based on inherent rights of First Nations.

5. A commitment towards resource revenue sharing, requiring the participation and involvement of provinces and territories currently benefiting from resource development from traditional lands.

6. Commitment towards ensuring a greater collective oversight and action towards ensuring the sustainability of the land through a sustained environmental oversight.

7. A comprehensive review and meaningful consultation in regards to Bill C-38 and C-45 to ensure it is consistent with Section 35 of the Constitution Act (1982).

8. Ensure that all federal legislation has the free, prior, and informed consent of First Nations where inherent and Treaty rights are affected or impacted.

9. A revised fiscal relationship between First Nations and Canada that is equitable, sustainable, and includes indexing and the removal of arbitrary funding caps.

10. A National Public Commission of Inquiry on Violence Against Indigenous Women of all ages.

11. Equity in capital construction of First Nation schools, including funding parity with provincial funding formulas with additional funding support for First Nation languages.

12. A change in how government operates that would include direct oversight, a dedicated Cabinet Committee, and Secretariat within the Privy Council Office with specific responsibility for the First Nation-Crown relationship to ensure implementation.

13. The full implementation of the United Nations Declaration of the Rights of Indigenous Peoples—UNDRIP.

As expressed from time to time by Chief Theresa Spence, "Our Treaty Rights continue to be violated and ignored." Elder Raymond Robinson says, "Treaties were entered into on a Nation-to-Nation basis and we need to do our best to re-bridge that balance to walk and work together as was the original intent of the treaties." Far too long, we have been denied an equitable stature within Canadian society. The time is ours and no longer will we be silenced and idle. We will continue to call upon the insistence of truth, justice, fairness for all our First Nation Peoples.

As fully endorsed and supported by:

Assembly of First Nations National Executive Committee
Native Women's Association of Canada
Liberal Party of Canada Parliamentary Caucus
New Democratic Party National Caucus

Released to media and the public on January 24, 2013.

MIIGWETCH, THANK YOU, CHIEF SPENCE
Wab Kinew

Ahow Ogichidaakwe Theresa, nimiigwetchiwiyin. Aazhaa kigi-igichiminochige. Kidaagiigiiwe noongom. Gegoo chaaniminoken. Gigaminoayaamin. Kidaagiimawadisaag kidaanisag nongom. Miigwetch ndikid. [Translation to follow]

To Chief Theresa Spence,

    I am writing to you to tell you that when you break your fast and end your hunger strike there should be no shame in your heart. You should hold your head high, for you have done a good thing for our people.

    Our Anishinaabe people have a word "Ando-bawaajige," vision quest, which refers to the ceremony where we fast in order to seek a dream. Our sister Leanne Betasamosake Simpson has pointed out that this is similar to the spiritual journey that you, Ray Robinson, Jean Sock, and the other hunger strikers have been on.

    Through some mysterious process the universe has chosen you to take on your important work at a unique moment in our people's history. All of our peoples' history. First the media frenzy about living conditions in Attawapiskat a year ago. Then the court challenge against your community's third party manager. Now the hunger strike. When the forces of history have called your name, you haven't backed down. You stood up for environmental and social justice. It is for this reason we call you "Ogichidaakwe," a term that literally means "Warrior woman," but is colloquially used to mean "Saint." You may not be perfect, but you have become a hero.

    You will be indelibly linked to "Idle No More." You began your hunger strike shortly after the people's movement began. You helped to galvanize support. The role you played in making our people care about their futures cannot be understated. Your work, in conjunction with "Idle No More," helped also to bring about a renewed focus on our issues on the political level which resulted in the meeting between the Assembly of First Nations and the Prime Minister's Office on January 11. You also led the delegation of treaty chiefs to meet with the Governor General that day, thereby showing continued good faith in dealing with our crown treaty partners.

    Beyond the politicians, you helped to bring the issue of Indigenous rights back to the forefront of the national collective conscience within Canada. Whether people agree with the goals of "Idle No More" or not, they have been forced to consider our cause and to hold their existing views of Aboriginal people up to the light. Many of our non-Indigenous brothers and sisters are now taking it upon themselves to learn about the issues and find ways to get involved to help us all succeed together. This will alter the course of Canada over the coming generations.

The media needed a character with which to tell the story of Idle No More. You became that figurehead. As the backlash mounted, your prominence made you a target. The audit of your community caused many to question your integrity. Many of the comments degenerated into vulgar character assassination. You maintained your dignity throughout. While there must be greater accountability for public funds it does not appear as though anything criminal happened. I have spoken with qualified First Nations managers who are willing to help your community chart a course to fiscal stability, if you choose to reach out to them.

I hope you know that even in the midst of these attacks many of our own people raised you up to great heights. I have travelled the country and seen little children holding signs featuring your name. I have met young women with T-shirts and earrings emblazoned with your face. You became the hero that many people needed, a testament to the dignified, quiet strength so many of our people possess. You helped those young ones find their voice.

The most compelling reason to end your fast is not a political one, however, but a personal one. At the meeting at the Governor General's residence, I was struck by the presence of your three daughters. I thought to myself, these young women need their mom. Indeed, your daughters need a mother more than your people need a martyr.

One month ago I said goodbye to my Father for the last time. The time we spent together before he passed will be held in my heart forever and has made me a better person. This helps me to appreciate how much you and your daughters deserve the chance to create more of your own memories together. I pray you now have the chance to do so, and that many more moons pass before you have to think about saying "goodbye." In the words of our great Shawnee brother Tecumseh "Seek to make your life long and its purpose in the service of your people." You have served the people. You should also make your life long.

So go now and be with your family. Enjoy many good meals together and each other's warm company. You can rest now knowing that others will carry your work forward. The National Chief, the leaders of the opposition, and even the Prime Minister have committed to action for the benefit of Indigenous people. The thousands of young people, mobilized and engaged by "Idle No More," myself included, will work to hold them to account. We will try to ensure they produce real change for all of our children, in a way that respects who we are.

Our Anishinaabe people have another term that relates to dreams that I would like to share: Izhii'oon. This says that after we receive a dream in a spiritual setting we should work hard to make it come to pass. You have helped bring the vision to our people. All of our people. It is up to the rest of us now to make it reality.

Ahow, Miigwetch. Thank you.

[Translation of opening]: Oh Chief Theresa, I thank you. You have done a very good thing. You should return to your home now. Don't worry. We will be all right. You should spend time with your daughters now. I say thank you.

Originally appeared on wabkinew.ca, *January 24, 2013.*

IDLE NO MORE:
A Revolutionary Love Song
Alex Wilson

Idle No More is a global grassroots movement of Indigenous peoples and their allies that focuses on honouring and reaffirming Indigenous sovereignty and protecting land and water. A relatively young movement with ancient, deep-reaching roots, Idle No More came roaring to life in Canada in 2012 and is the latest expression of a long history of Indigenous resistance in the Americas.

Idle No More was started by women, and I am one of many who have joined them in this peaceful revolution. My family clan name (passed down through my grandmother and the women who preceded her) is *Wassenas*, "related to light." I am from the Opaskwayak Cree Nation, a sovereign nation centred on a large river system that reaches into and links it with the surrounding country of Canada, and now one of the most endangered fresh water systems in the world. Our family lives on the Saskatchewan River, in a part of our traditional territory called *Pamuskatapan*, a term that has a few meanings. It is used to refer to the point in a journey where the only way to move your canoe forward is to step out into the water and pull it. The term can also refer to a place a little off to the side.

What I have learned from the place and people I come from has helped me find my way to Idle No More. Those of us who have worked as activists for most of our lives are familiar with the experience of being pushed out or pushed off to the side, and the need to reclaim our place or renegotiate our paths. We understand, too, our responsibility to share our knowledge, experiences, and understandings with those we are connected to—and that this bright collective light that will show us our place and our path. And like the river I live beside, our connections extend well beyond the banks that might seem to confine us in the here and now of this moment.

Idle No More is guided by understandings and philosophies shared by most Indigenous cultures on these continents—in particular, the very old knowledge that we are all related. Within these relationships, we are accountable to and share responsibility for the well-being of each other and the lands, water, and earth that we rely on and that sustain life.

I say this is old knowledge and I look to Idle No More to give it new meaning. Our peaceful revolution draws forth the teachings of our ancestors, reaching back to the stories, songs, and ceremonies that record our origins. *We are peoples who originated in these lands.* My people, the Swampy Cree, *Neyinowak Inniniwak,* tell the story of how we came to be—a story too long to tell on these few pages, but one that begins in the earth and then traces our lineage from tiny sparks of life to single-celled organisms through emergence as plants, animals, and people. This story is also the story of these lands, how this place that some call North America but we call Turtle Island exists because in the time of water Muskrat was able to dive deep enough to reach the bottom and bring up mud and place it on the back of Turtle, slowly building this land mass.

So as Cree people we know that we cannot live without water, without Muskrat, or without *Weegess* a plant rhizome found in the peaty bottom of swamps and the favourite food of muskrats. *Weegess* is a spirit medicine and the soft peat bogs where it can be found are places of transformation. The rhizome throws down roots to draw fuel and energy from the bog's decaying matter, pushes up sprouts to catch the light, and grows laterally in every possible direction to form vast and interconnected systems. Every bit of *Weegess* has been nurtured by and holds within itself the past and when we take that root into our bodies as medicine, it is our past—our origins—that brings us back to wellness.

Like *Weegess,* Idle No More is a rhizome, nurtured and nurturing in an intricately connected non-hierarchic system of land, water, and people. This revolution grew quickly, reaching out through social media, reclaiming public spaces with our bodies and our voices, spinning out new connections with people, and reaching down roots to draw up the ancestral knowledge that each of us carry in our bodies. That knowledge is bringing us back to the practice of relational accountability. Those of us who are part of Idle No More recognize that there is no us or them. All of us (regardless of cultural, gender, sexual, or class identity or expression) are welcome and all of us are connected. We acknowledge the collective sovereignty that Indigenous people have over the territories they have traditionally occupied, and the individual sovereignty that each of us has over our own bodies, minds, hearts, and spirits. We bring our bodies, spirits, and energy together, our voices united so all can speak and all will be heard, and we know our path.

We are here to make change. We are here to restore balance. We are here to care for the land, for water, and for life. In Cree, we say *Sahkihiwawin*—we commit ourselves to love in action.

THE OGIMAA MIKANA PROJECT

The Ogimaa Mikana Collective: Susan Blight, Hayden King, Connor Pion, Alex McKay, Craig Tough, and Julia Hepburn

The Ogimaa Mikana Project is an effort to restore Anishinaabemowin place names to the streets, avenues, roads, paths, and trails of Toronto—attempting to transform a landscape that often obscures or makes invisible the presence of Indigenous peoples. The Project was born in the midst of the Idle No More movement with the goal of bringing language, language-learning, and the revitalization of Anishinaabe cultures into focus amid the variety of calls to action among activists across the country. Starting in late January 2013 with a small section of Queen St., renaming it Ogimaa Mikana (Leader's Trail) in tribute to all the strong women leaders of the Idle No More movement, the Project has expanded across the city of Toronto:

TOP: Queen St. at McCaul = Ogimaa Mikana (Leader's Trail)

BOTTOM: Indian Rd. at Bloor St. = Anishinaabe Mikana (Path of the original people)

TOP: Spadina Ave. at Queen St. = Ishpadinaa (Place on a hill)

BOTTOM: Bathurst St. at College St. = Gikino'amaagegamig (Place of learning and knowledge)

TOP: Queen's Park Heritage sign = Piitaapocikewaatikakocin (Place where the logs flow)

BOTTOM: Dufferin Bridge = Gwayakochigeg (Make it right/honour the apology)

AFTER THE RALLIES:
Where do we go from Here?

Michael Redhead Champagne

The last few months, the Canadian public has been witness to large demonstrations focusing on Indigenous issues accompanied by peaceful protests, educational workshops, and ceremonies. Many people see or attend the rallies as a way of getting involved in the beginning and that is great, we're doing it, the movement is alive. But at the beginning there were more people attending, there was more media attention, seemed like more people talking in person and online. But now there are rumblings that the movement is fading and our opportunity to participate in lasting and meaningful change towards our issue leave us scared and heartbroken. There will be more rallies, which is great...but we have to ask the question: where do we go from here? What more can we do?

Next Step: Bring the ACTION

There was a rally. You just attended it. Chanted, sang, danced, and spoke from your heart about the issue you believe in. But at the rally they mentioned that WE ALL had to do something to make this change real. You even learned that there will be another rally in a month's time. Because you are committed to the core issue being protested, you write the date in your calendar and feel good knowing that you are doing something. And then you wait one month and repeat this cycle? Attending rallies and helping to mobilize and educate the masses at rallies is a great and necessary step in raising awareness. But are these rallies going to change the negative realities that we collectively oppose? I would say no. So what exactly can we do to help?

Not only do we have to DO something in terms of action, we have to be smart and strategic about which actions we choose to undertake. We have to think creatively about how we can use our gift to help the movement. Can we help organize, motivate, communicate in any way that others may not be able to? This is also a time to emphasize education. We must continue to educate ourselves on the issues, sharpen our own understanding and practise delivering it in very accessible, easy to understand and correct language. It is not easy, and it takes time and practice. I always think that I need to talk in a way that even little kids can understand my message and why they can/should get involved too. Think about it like this, when you are talking to someone about the movement, try to deliver what is the movement, why is it important to you and what are we trying to achieve into a 30-second "elevator speech" that you can share with others!

Because I always have to break everything into steps, here are the steps I would take/have taken in between rallies:

1. **Do Your Homework:** We are not helping our movement if we ourselves do not know the background of the issue we are involved in. "Stephen Harper sucks" is not a good answer to why others should get involved. There are many ways to do this— Google is our friend here. But also look outside the box and ask the people directly involved and affected by this issue. *(e.g., research the issue, learn historical facts, study other causes/movements, write down strategies, brainstorm with others)*

2. **Take Initiative:** A movement is made up of various events and activities that ultimately contribute towards a collective goal or objective. In most cases, if you ask yourself "When is the next event?" and you can't find an answer, that's an opportunity for you to take initiative and set one up. Also, try to be considerate of others' planning—try to not compete with others that are advocating for the same issue—unity is integral to successful movements. *(e.g., create/join a Facebook page, write a blog post, organize a group planning meeting, inquire about others' planning meetings, draw a picture, write a letter to your elected officials, schedule a meeting to talk ACTION & NEXT STEPS with anyone and everyone who is willing to help you further your goal)*

3. **Ask For and Accept Help:** In a movement, we work together and share the load. When we are able to we help others, but we also have to ensure that we are taken care of as well. If we appreciate all of the gifts around us we'll always have a lot to be thankful for—so showing gratitude and saying thank

you are so very important. We want to take care of the people who are helping us, so we offer our support when and where we can! This also includes taking care of yourself as much as you can. You are no good to any cause if you are not well physically, mentally, emotionally and spiritually. *(e.g., recognize when you need help, ask someone for help, have a phone call/coffee with a friend and chat, write thank you cards/letters, smudge)*

4. **Creatively Build Momentum:** Use people's unique skills and abilities to help network, make cool connections (aka partnerships), find creative ways to build awareness. I like to think of this part as EDU-TAINMENT (I learned that one from Chris Crocker lol), which as you can imagine is a combination of education and entertainment. People learn better when they are engaged and feel valued. This is a great time to try new things and don't be afraid of failure—if you learned a lesson it was all worth it! *(e.g., flash mobs, make funny videos, create dances, create strategies, create public awareness, go on the radio; people love laughter, humour, and accessible activities).*

We must maintain our integrity and maintain our positivity. There are several reasons for this, but the main two are that when we are positive we attract others to the positivity, and secondly, thinking positively allows us to see others' gifts and abilities! This is where you offer others help.

Originally appeared on northendmc.wordpress.com, *February 19, 2013.*

THROUGH OUR EYES—WHO LEADS?

Mary Ellen Turpel Lafond

The trajectory of Aboriginal protests over the past few months followed an uneven course. Some non-Aboriginal Canadians were initially engaged by the spontaneity of the protest events, enjoying the drumming flash mobs in shopping malls and other public spaces. The Idle No More events appeared to be joyful celebrations of culture, involving families and people of all ages, and were more performance than pure political rallies with speeches and "messages."

But many Canadians grew increasingly perplexed, and decidedly less sympathetic, as other strands of protest developed: hunger strikes and the blockage of roads, rail lines, and ferries that aimed at economic disruption. While a slight majority of Canadians continues to support the need for the federal government to improve the living circumstances of Aboriginal peoples, the absence of solutions to the wider problem of the relationship between Aboriginal peoples and other Canadians bedevils the country. The atmosphere of threats and the complexity leave a trail of despair, the sense of a conflict stuck in stalemate, while the goodwill evaporates.

But the events surrounding the emergence of Idle No More have resulted in one fundamental change: it irrevocably damaged the legitimacy of Indian Act chiefs to speak on behalf of First Nations. And the new leadership, forged in large part by young women with their own grievances from living under the existing power order, represents a different kind of leadership with the creative potential to change the course of history.

In reality, the political legitimacy of the elected Indian Act chiefs has been in serious trouble for a long time within the First Nations community, weakened by divisive battles on membership, voting, financial, and governance issues. Those battles left the Assembly of First Nations (AFN), and its ineffectiveness in leading First Nations out of the Indian Act, in a diminished state. The issue is not whether the Act is finished—it most certainly is finished and so too are those who think they can use it as a base from which to govern or lead effective change. Any such strategy will be met with escalating protests from the grassroots. The Indian Act and the system it created is toxic (the provisions to force children to residential schools under threat of physical punishment remain in the Act, even if they are in disuse). The Indian Act represents a failed policy that should have ended long ago, especially in the modern era of human rights.

But here is the nub of the problem. If the Indian Act chiefs have been overtaken, who leads? Who speaks for whom? Is there a transition process, or any ratification process, to confirm new political arrangements?

The answer for the time being is no, but this does not mean nothing new will emerge. Political means will have to be found to make the break a strong and clean one, and reconfirm a preference for a negotiated process with some stability. Innovative ideas will need to be considered, including possibly a civil society process of engagement with young people and a meaningful commitment to improving their lives through a rigorous and effective education system that respects their identity and culture.

The alternative is unsustainable. The Prime Minister brought a glint of hope to many with his residential school apology. It held promise that the failed policies that gave us residential schools would end. Five years on, the Indian Act still sits on the books, a testament to a corrosive era that delivered so much harm to Aboriginal people and families. The agenda of Aboriginal issues has not moved forward, and the result of five stalled (some would argue retrograde) years is Idle No More. The Indian Act chiefs have been overtaken by protest they haven't led and freely join in it, acknowledging they are on a tightrope without a net.

One of the reasons why former Grand Chief Matthew Coon Come could easily engage in discussions with the Prime Minister and his executive was that the Cree communities have been out of the Indian Act for so long that it bears little meaning for them other than as a historical artifact. The Cree have been free of the Act's influence since the 1975 James Bay Northern Quebec Agreement, and a few years ago they concluded a 20-year bilateral agreement with Canada and a 50-year agreement with Quebec.

Coon Come is almost not speaking the same language as the Indian Act chiefs, which may explain why his own tenure as national chief lasted just one term. The vast majority of chiefs are not at all familiar with the distinct kind of relationship with a provincial and federal government that is taken for granted by a generation of leaders of the Cree of Northern Quebec. Even with their political strength, they struggle with operating effective public services, like educating children for success—the graduation rate for Cree children is only 10 percent. But the while the larger issues facing the Cree are profound—secession and territorial integrity—they no longer have to contend with the colonial artifact of the failed Indian Act, which imposes the administrative and reporting requirements of a federal bureaucracy.

Things could hardly be more different for Shawn A-in-chut Atleo and the chiefs in his home base from British Columbia. Working largely under the 250-year-old Royal Proclamation and without treaties (apart from the few adherents to the Douglas treaties and some Treaty 8 adhesions, there are three modern treaties and one federally legislated self-government arrangement), the British Columbia chiefs have seen glacial progress on their issues but enjoy one of the highest levels of public support. Collaboration with the province and hard work on public services has improved the education for First Nations children in B.C., with a graduation rate close to 50 percent.

But the B.C. chiefs find themselves dealing with an industry of consultants that has mortgaged the participant bands' possible settlements through unsustainable loans to fund their participation (more than 60 processes are technically underway, but few are functionally promising). Many bands have liabilities they will certainly never repay, which hampers their chances of participating in economic opportunities today. B.C. First Nations have engaged in more court battles over rights than any other region, with mixed successes. Every court wants to redirect the parties back to the negotiating table. But there is very little progress happening at the table. And the threat of "extinguishment" of rights effectively reinforces the arrangements of Indian Act politics.

Many Canadians prefer Atleo's conciliatory approach, but Idle No More has made it clear it is not interested in preserving personalities or endorsing his positions. Even Atleo seems to realize that the only contribution the AFN can make is to bring about the transition away from the Indian Act and the AFN as we have known it, effectively leading itself out of existence.

The Idle No More leaders were loath to endorse violence as a means to any end. Young, educated First Nations women who were among its leaders are struggling to raise children and support families. They are hardly going to lead a violent movement nor yield their voices to the advice and direction aimed at them from the Indian Act dynasty.

This is one of the most encouraging aspects of the protests. At event after event, in malls, streets, and elsewhere within Idle No More, there are mothers and grandmothers, children and youth. These caregivers have been left with the lion's share of building a future—for themselves and their communities—out of such deep economic and social difficulties. Many have faced tough life experiences. The younger women have struggled to find support for post-secondary education, and they have raised children without the comforts of child support (there is no enforcement of child maintenance on reserves, and matrimonial property rights are essentially unenforceable).

In the absence of a responsive government family policy, with no properly functioning education or child welfare system or any serious investment in helping women and grandparents raise families dealing with intergenerational trauma and abuse, we should recognize how much the women have achieved. And the women know well how many did not and will not make it unless things change. Just mention the missing and murdered Aboriginal girls and women and you will see a steely determination to prevent a future generation of vulnerable citizens from being inhumanely treated.

The Indian Act system has provided no recognition of the need to reconcile these women's caregiving responsibilities with their broader potential as citizens and participants in the labour force. Many bands resisted allowing women whose Indian status was restored by the courts to return to the community. They starved these women of resources for additional housing and tried to deny them the right to vote in band elections. (Chiefs put the blame on the federal government for not providing enough resources to respond to a surging rise in membership after the 1985 amendments to the Indian Act.) Distrust of local band government has required women and their children (male and female) to battle in their communities and in court for what is rightfully theirs—participation in the band, and a fair share of programs and resources.

The burden these younger women have assumed is significant, and they do not accept a jackboot political approach or the expectation of blind loyalty from their leaders. Many more First Nations women than men are working to complete their education. They are striving to improve their life circumstances, seeking to protect and confirm their cultural identity and transmit it to their children—almost against all odds. These caregivers don't like what they see as horse-trading over control of resources, worried that deals could be struck to reallocate the resources or to allow more of the swindles and unfair processes that the Indian Act has permitted since colonial days.

Idle No More arose with scant planning—using social media and tapping into the deep sense of unfairness and the political abandonment of their voice felt by educated Aboriginal women. It has resonated with many others, including men, and generations young and old, because it speaks a bitter truth about Canada—it has failed to deliver on human rights and equal opportunity for Aboriginal peoples. This brings us back to the key point about the Indian Act. Why hasn't it changed or transitioned into a more meaningful government regime designed to be effective or responsive to the needs of First Nations citizens, especially those in crisis? I reflect back on the failed constitutional renewal process that followed the conclusion of the Charlottetown Accord. This accord offered a transition process out of the Indian Act to a new arrangement that preferred an obligation for a negotiated settlement but clearly recognized a legally enforceable and existing inherent right of self-government, as well as a fiscal arrangement to support that transition. Those provisions, and the protocols that supported them, would have represented a new path forward, but it was quickly put to rest when constitutional reform politics was shut down.

Some First Nations women had deep suspicions about the Charlottetown Accord at the time and felt they were mistreated when the Native Women's Association of Canada was not represented at the discussion table. They worried self-government might not address issues such as caregiving support and equality, or redress their grievances about their treatment at the hands of band leadership. They were right to be worried. Twenty years later there is still no improvement in meaningful government services or policies to make caregiving and raising children easier than it was then.

I'm not advocating a new constitutional round. The constitutional discussions ended because of the unworkable amending formula and a lack of public appetite for them. The *Report of the Royal Commission on Aboriginal Peoples* recommended a nonconstitutional reconciliation approach with a negotiated process for change. Its recommendations have merit and deserve thoughtful consideration, but it too has been ignored, either because of the scope of change required or a lack of political will at the national level. Crucial issues about the scale and viability of First Nations communities and economies require a broad and pragmatic discussion in an appropriate political forum.

So where does that leave us? The Prime Minister and his government do not appear to have suffered any major setback in popular opinion from Idle No More and other protests. But not even the most Machiavellian of strategists can be sanguine about the uncertainty that now characterizes the relationship between Aboriginal leaders and their grassroots. We are in uncertain terrain and a state of stasis, and the system that maintained it can no longer be counted on to keep the peace. The failed policy of the Indian Act era has run its course, and no one can make a deal without the support of the people.

The glimmer of hope lies with the women. They understand that solutions lie in forging relationships that respect the rights of all and that address the social and economic issues that blight the lives of so many of our most vulnerable. With Idle No More, they have shown they are prepared to make noise. Canadians would be unwise to think the drumming and celebratory atmosphere of Idle No More has no substance or will soon subside. Aboriginal politics will never be the same.

Originally appeared in Policy Options/Options Politiques, *February 2013.*

IDLE NO MORE:
Strong Hearts of Indigenous Women's Leadership
Wanda Nanibush

On January 26, 2012, I found myself marching down a busy Toronto street beside grandmother Pauline Shirt and a number of Indigenous women in front of hundreds of marchers. As a water carrier, I was holding a part of lake Ontario in my hands. This water walk and ceremony was called together to bring attention to the Idle No More movement and the fight against the changes to the Navigational Waters Protection Act under Bill C-45 that legalized resource development's precedence over environmental protection. We weren't protesting—we were speaking the spirit of the water. We were attempting to heal her from the pollution choking her life force, which in turn chokes our own.

The actions under the Idle No More banner have largely been peaceful and ceremonial in nature, thus markedly different from any other massive international Indigenous-led movement in history. It is a movement led largely by grassroots Indigenous women. The movement exhibits a post-Cartesian Indigenous ethos where the mind, body, spirit, and emotions are engaged together. Like the drum at the centre of the round dances is the heart of the mother earth, the women maintain the heart at the centre of the movement. It's a rare feeling to go to a political action and want to hug every stranger around you, to feel vulnerability at the centre of life and a desire to protect it.

Indigenous women's leadership has always been at the grassroots level, having historically been shut out of Indian Act-based leadership until 1952. Many have forged their leadership skills in ceremonial spaces where pre-contact cultural values around the roles of women have allowed us significant influence and power. The teachings gathered at the skirts of our grandmothers have also required a different set of principles for working cross-culturally. While a return to and education about the Nation-to-Nation relationship that exists between Canada and the many Indigenous nations on whose soil this country was birthed has been the centre of the movement, it has also required understanding how we are to work together now and in the future. When the relationship is not defined from thought alone but also includes the spirit and the heart the work takes on a different character. Wampum belts hold the history of our treaties with other Nations and speak of these Nation to Nation relationships being based on peace and friendship with the values of trust, integrity, honesty, and truth as the basis for interaction. This is not a written contract to be analyzed and assessed but a contract of spirit and heart to be lived together.

Women who have worked at the ground level healing their communities from historical trauma, who deal with large socio-economic disparities and have counteracted cultural discontinuity—all brought on by colonialism and racism—bring a considerable knowledge base to the movement. Cross-cultural conflicts that are quite common in Canada come to the fore in an Indigenous-led movement like Idle No More. Canadians have been denied access to an education, which leads to deep mistrust and misunderstanding between Indigenous and Non-Indigenous participants in a struggle to protect the earth and water.

Unity has been stressed and yet unity in difference is the goal. For this movement to work we must remain unified. This means no behind-the-back talk against each other. It means putting aside petty jealousies, envy, dislikes, and old grudges. It means not having an ego. Indigenous concepts of the human that are non-ego based become important. It means true humility that listens before speaking, and that understands before judging, it means letting go of negativity and holding the fragility and dignity of fellow humans close.

It does not mean that we will all agree but the way we disagree is the main question. If I disagree I choose to disagree openly in front of the person, without anger or passive aggression as a form of peace offering towards understanding. I choose to ask questions and seek understanding, to deliberate before forming opinion. I choose to care for strangers. I choose to set aside my own desires for the larger picture. I choose to step forward and share my knowledge and skills for others. I choose to take the heat. I choose peaceful disobedience. I choose to obey ancient laws of respect. These tenets, if you will, are women's teachings that they bring to the movement and affect how it operates. The earth, for us, is considered a mother; mothering and creation is foregrounded for our identity. This does not mean that women cannot choose men's roles or have sexual relations with women. It does mean that there are specific knowledges within the acts of creation for both earth and women that are essential to the sustenance of our world and humanity. Creation is also an act of futural imagining which is what is at the heart of women's work. The creativity of the actions and the focus on our children's children's etc. future is part of what is expected of a woman living in a good way. Humanity is the weakest link in all of creation because it relies on all of creation to exist—that is why they must ultimately protect it. The focus on male leadership under colonial rule has not quieted the voices of Indigenous women leaders. There is a strength derived from the attempted silencing in their closeness to the community, ceremony, children, and creativity.

Originally appeared in Women in a Globalizing World: Transforming Equality, Development, Diversity & Peace. *Ed. Angela Miles. Toronto: Inanna, 2013.*

Khelisilem Rivers, an Idle No More Vancouver organizer, cracks up the crowd during the January 11 Day of Action, 2013. (STEPHEN HUI)

WE ARE FREE HUMAN BEINGS, PART TWO

Lori M. Mainville

"We do this for our future generations" are words describing legacies. It suggests presence and, depending on the tone and inflection, it suggests action. These words are sounds of life, of choice, of freedom. I was privileged to listen to the late elder Peter O'Chiese, who spoke of such things as the power of sound. Our original language had this built right within it, it was co-relational to the vibration of sound of the land. Our words not only sound like the world around us, but so did the spaces between the words. One need only sit in silence near water or trees to understand the deep sense of connection we carry in sound.

Our voices are sacred binds with one another. The oral tradition demonstrates that to us, it is a relational reciprocity of speaking, listening, and witnessing as a group. It also demonstrates how a nation can interact with another nation. Language connects us, it teaches us to maintain our social connections with living beings from all over the world, and the universe. Sometimes we speak different words, but we must keep trying to communicate. We can close that gap of understanding with action.

Part of this is found in Idle No More, an awakening of this very opportunity. The past months have been challenging. This may have been by the leaderless nature of the movement, which made it at times tough to negotiate and communicate widely. It may have been the challenging nature of bringing so many nations into a complex discussion involving so many key issues. Another might have been some of the concerns around "copyrighting" the movement. It's impossible to control energy and harness it under a couple sets of fingers. Our original governance resided with clans, societies, and collectivities, not a few.

It is now that we have opportunities to make sounds of our own, and explain these to others. They must understand too. It is time to think of what will happen next to ensure that we do this for our future generations. It is my prediction that in the coming months we will:

- Reflect and discover the lessons learned from the movement.

- Discover the direct impacts of the bills and experience first-hand how they impede relationships with ancestral laws.

- Re-enact our Sovereign rights, discover what this means, and engage in a dialogue to define them.

- Strategize and exercise our rights over things like air quality control, water quality control, provisions, governance, and develop policies invested in ancestral laws.

- Formulate mass education programs on the purpose and intent of treaties, and return to our oral histories to uncover our original and unique definitions surrounding land and title.

- Demand Canada adopt UNDRIP and the preamble validating Indigenous authority over stewardship of the land, reminding Canada that it could not be built without treaties.

- Learn which parts of our nations will co-opt themselves by agreeing to provisions of the various bills, thus threatening their identities in laws not of their own making. At the same time, helpers will come to these people to remind them that original laws will always supersede unnatural ones.

- Become a stronger, more unified, and complete people.

The tsunami is coming so we must be ready. We all feel it, sense it. All our voices are essential in this moment.

We need our peacekeepers, our wisdom holders, our Elders, our strategists, our up-and-coming leaders to sit amongst us all. From the lady who stood alone in her traditional regalia on a cold winter day in a small Manitoba town during Idle No More to the young man who hitchhiked to Ottawa for a rally to the flash mob round dances seen across the land to those observing in silence—all of this was a testament that we need one another. We must gather stronger, we must strategize more intently together around our kitchen tables, powwow grounds, ceremonies, and wherever else we gather to come up with solutions to promote unity and solidarity. No one person holds the answers, it belongs to the collective.

We are free human beings taken care of by the natural law of this land, given to us by the Creator. No tree stands alone for long—it needs the biodiversity of its relatives to live in relative harmony and peace.

The answers are within our land title and our collective reciprocal relationship to the land and to one another. Idle No More is here to stay. We can never go back to not knowing and we know more than we can imagine. We have within our grasp the lessons learned, we are scholars by virtue of culture and identity. We know ourselves. We are here, and we are here to stay.

I am not Canadian. I am Anishinaabe and a proud free member of the Anishinaabe Nation. I believe in the spirit of Nation, will you believe in yours? We are stronger by believing in who we are so let us make these sounds.

IDLE NO MORE AND INDIGENOUS NATIONHOOD
Taiaiake Alfred

Our collective action in Idle No More has shown that there is support among Canadians for a movement that embodies principled opposition to the destruction of the land and the extension of social justice to Indigenous peoples. When we as Indigenous people have a political agenda that's consistent with our Original Teachings—to have a respectful relationship with the land and the natural environment and to have a respectful relationship among all of the nations that share this land—we have seen that this is a powerful draw for many people in our own nations and in the broader society. But it is clear too that the movement has plateaued. Much of the passion, urgency, and attention Idle No More generated is dissipating in the wake of Chief Theresa Spence's fast and the "13 Point Declaration" supported by Chief Spence, the Assembly of First Nations, and the two Canadian opposition parties—which to many people in the movement represents a cooptation of the movement's demands by the chiefs of the Assembly of First Nations in support of their ongoing negotiations and long-running bureaucratic processes. The question in the minds of many people in the movement who are committed to more serious and transformational goals is how do we revive the momentum driving us towards fundamental change that we had at the start of the movement? I think that the only way to keep this movement going is for us to see our actions in Idle No More as part of a larger and long-standing commitment to the restoration of Indigenous nationhood.

We need to focus our activism on the root of the problem facing our people collectively: our collective dispossession and misrepresentation as Indigenous peoples. Now is the time to put ourselves back on our lands spiritually and physically and to shift our support away from the Indian Act system and to start energizing the restoration of our own governments. Our people and our languages and our ceremonies should be saturating our homelands and territories. Our leaders should answer to us, not to the Minister of Indian Affairs or his minions. Our governments should be circles in which we all sit as equals and participate fully and where all of our voices are heard, not systems of hierarchy and exclusion legitimized and enforced by Canadian laws. Restoring our nationhood in this way is the fundamental struggle. Our focus should be on restoring our presence on the land and regenerating our true nationhood. These go hand in hand and one cannot be achieved without the other. Idle No More has been a good and necessary thing. Like thousands of others over the last couple of months, I am proud to have been a whole-hearted participant in educating the wider public, making the connection between our Native rights and the democratic rights of all citizens, and arguing for the protection of the environment under the Idle No More banner. But the limits to Idle No More are clear, and many people are beginning to realize that the kind of movement we have been conducting under the banner of Idle No More is not sufficient in itself to decolonize this country or even to make meaningful change in the lives of people.

Those of us in the movement need to ask ourselves this hard question: what have we accomplished through Idle No More? There's been politicization of some Native people. There's been some media attention. There have been rallies and demonstrations. Great art and music has been produced. These are all good. But in terms of meaningful change in the lives of people and the struggle for justice, things are no different now than when this whole thing started. The federal government has not responded or felt the need to address in any way the challenge we've presented so far. We are in danger of becoming institutionalized and predictable as a movement, or worse, becoming kind of a giant Facebook rant that like all Facebook rants is a closed circle easily ignored which has no real relation to things actually happening in people's lives. What this means if we are committed to making change and achieving justice for our people is that we need to alter our strategies and tactics to present more of a serious challenge on the ground to force the federal government to engage our movement and to respond to us in a serious way. I believe that what our movement needs is a mobilization of people on the basis of Indigenous Nationhood, led by traditional chiefs and clan mothers, medicine people, elders and youth, to start acting on our inherent rights on the land and to demand respect for our traditional governments. In practical terms, we need to go beyond demonstrations and rallies in malls and legislatures and on public streets and start to reoccupy Indigenous sacred, ceremonial, and cultural use sites to re-establish our presence on our land and in doing so to educate Canadians about our continuing connections to those places and how important they are to our continuing existence as Indigenous peoples.

If we do this we can, once again, make the Assembly of First Nations, the mainstream media, the opposition parties hear the true voice of Indigenous people in this country and if we are strong and tenacious in demonstrating our commitment to these goals, we can force the federal government to take us seriously. Now is the time to transgress, reoccupy, rise...as Original Peoples.

Originally appeared on Taiaike.net, *January 27, 2013.*

PAUWAUWAEIN:
Idle No More to The Indigenous Nationhood Movement
Lesley Belleau

People are contemplating if the rush of a new revolution called Idle No More is bubbling down to a whisper. There are news articles asking if this is the end of Idle No More, and there are people wondering if the Indigenous nations have gotten the protests and rallies out of their systems and have gone back to life as usual. I read the tweets and the Facebook posts suggesting that Idle No More is in its final gatherings, using the very last energies of a fury of activity that was short-lived and powerful only at its peak; its power diminished now that Chief Spence has finished her hunger strike and Grand National Chief Shawn Atleo has fatefully—despite great resistance—undercut the movement by meeting on January 11 with Stephen Harper and other elected officials. Despite all of this, from my vantage point as an Indigenous woman, mother, academic and activist, I see fully that just the opposite is true because the idea of Indigenous Nationhood must also be considered and understood.

Bill C-45 and resistance to it, particularly the hunger strike by Chief Theresa Spence of Attawapiskat First Nation, catapulted Idle No More into the public spectrum at an opportune moment in history. Fueled by Indigenous voices, cultural renewal, and acts of resistance, and led by the rise of Indigenous women and youth, treaty discussions, political engagement and resistance spread through social media and many new ideas, both academic and creative, sprung up as quickly as a camera shooting in quick succession. *Click. Click. Click.* So rapidly that people were in constant motion. It was the breaking of a long sheet of ice and the overpour that hits the shore; a thaw during the onslaught of winter. A soaking of history and immediacy that attracted the attention of people globally. A wide screaming of the earth against the hand of a Prime Minister who callously ignored the pleas of a starving and desperate Indigenous woman whose voice lay protectively over all of the earth and the bones beneath in her singular action toward justice and accountability. An accumulation of voice and resistance that rose to meet the parting of history and justice that lay swallowed deep underwater. The remnants that lay in wait within the water.

After some time, things quieted. The media and outside world heard the quieting ebb. When those on social media began to discuss other issues, when the urgency of the movement was not on the forefront, the mass media began to insinuate that this was just another movement like Occupy, or merely another Oka or just one more Native issue. When the flash mobs and round dances became spaced further and further apart, when the screams fell into humming, and there was a feeling that the urgency has ended. When there was a lapse between the drumsounds, between the urgent gathering of a country holding hands and dancing round and round and round.

Idle No More was the moment of release, the flurry of activity before a great flight, the prayer before the takeoff, the stretch of breath before a new mother pushes a first baby from her body. Think of a woman in labour: the creation of the new life is a period of gathering, of nurture and preparation. The labour is immense work and action where the mother and child are working together intensely to produce and to shift into a new way of being and life; her physical body needs to undergo a great transition in order for a new life to come into the world and to begin to live and thrive inside of the world that she already knows. But she has to endure the loud action in order to be able to hold the fruits of her labour. In transition, the last stage of labour, the woman often goes into herself and her will and uses the very last morsels of her strength and resilience in order to help her baby find its way into the world. This is a moment of great willfullness and strength, often much quieter and more intense than the previous hours of labour. And then, shortly after, she imparts the final strength onto her own body and onto her baby birthed, and she can hold this new life in her arms as her body regains momentum and begins the building up of strength once again. All great movements come from a moment of sacrifice and great inner working to produce and birth something vital, earth-changing, and necessary.

Something extremely significant happened during the months of December 2012 and January 2013. It was a time of great action, of a great collective voice that rose together to work toward resistance, decolonization, cultural revival, and to hold hands within a new and possible hope that was only seen in fragments and small and scattered pieces before this, although we have had many significant historic and strong moments inside of our history. We held hands with other nations, other cities, other cultures, and other countries for the same purpose during these months. For justice, for future generations, for the possibility of a new world and new voice for Indigenous peoples, for protection of our lands and waters because their voices matter and we must speak for them and work with them to sustain our future. During this time, Pauwauwaein happened on a large and collective scale. Pauwauwaein is described by John Burrows as "a revelation, an awakening, a vision that gives understanding to matters that were previously obscure." By understanding the idea of Pauwauwaein, the future of Idle No More seems at once clearer and more realistic, and

352 THE WINTER WE DANCED

the reality of the actions of Indigenous Nationhood that has been at work for a long time can be observed more clearly. Pauwauwaein as a revelation, an awakening, or a vision has deep implications for the future of Indigenous peoples and Mother Earth globally in terms of the Idle No More movement. The last couple of months, during the flash mobs, the rallies, and protests, we began discussions on the honouring of our treaties, we took a long look at our future if we do not protect our lands and waters, and we opened our hearts, minds, and spirits to a place of awakening where we could accept the potential of a new vision. This is no small occurrence and holds the very future of Mother Earth and Indigenous peoples within it.

In *Dancing on Our Turtle's Back* Leanne Betasamosake Simpson writes, "The act of visioning for Nishnaabeg people is a powerful act of resurgence, because these visions create Shki-kiin, new worlds." The Idle No More movement's beginning months did just this: created acts of visioning for Indigenous people worldwide, and from this created Shki-kiin, a New World. In this New World it is possible to break free from colonial thought and speak what you know is true. In this New World you are able to express yourself culturally in public places, strengthening your own sense of the power of expression and the very beauty and joy of declaring your culture after a history of colonial powers silencing and denying such things. In this New World peoples use their individual and collective strength to protect their children's futures by acting today, and use their strengths to protect Mother Earth against the powers that wish to destroy her. This New World has been initiated on a large scale over the last couple of months through Idle No More. A New World opened and the public outpouring of action was the celebration to the opening of this New World. Shki-kiin. What the world saw as Idle No More was a much needed awakening, a return to and speaking of that long history of action our people have. When Shki-kiin's doors sliced open, the Indigenous Nationhood Movement was seen. This movement has always existed in the hearts of our people, but has gone unrecognized at times. It exists and always has. We are Indigenous Nationhood.

Now that this New World has opened its door, there is another step that comes next. Leanne Betasamosake Simpson writes, "In terms of resurgence, vision alone isn't enough. Vision must be coupled with intent; intent for transformation, intent for re-creation, intent for resurgence."

Now that Idle No More has created an activated vision, we, the people, must follow this vision with a conscious intent for transformation, for Indigenous Nationhood. We must move from the initial celebratory and birthing stages of Idle No More and urgently create and continue to transform the New World of the Indigenous Nationhood Movement through strategizing with other people. We must continue to find justice for our missing and murdered mothers, sisters, and daughters. We must continue to protect our earth. We must continue with a consuming desire to walk into history and take back what is ours—because we have to—while at the same time seeking to find our way toward a stronger and more just future. Simpson writes that will require "sacrifice, commitment, and countless selfless acts. It requires strategy, commitment, and a one-mindedness built from the diversity of our perspectives and understanding."

We must not be content to live a life that holds us down in restless corners, that writes our stories for us, that continues to belittle our cultures and languages, that offers our children, lands, waters, and everything we hold sacred a future of destruction. Each of us must keep this New World alive by personally and collectively acting. We must never let go of our languages, cultures, children's futures, love for the land we stand on, and waters we drink. We need to rewrite a history of colonial silencing. We have to understand that the Old World that held our voices and personhood down no longer exists for us. When we see reminders of oppression against ourselves and our lands, we must remember that these are the actions and thoughts that are still alive and thriving in the Old World, and we must not let them affect our walkings through Shki-kiin, our new and powerful world.

Idle No More did so many necessary things and will continue to do so through the Indigenous Nationhood Movement. Idle No More activated a dormant seed. Idle No More created leaders out of people who did not know they were meant to be leaders, those who have powerful and righteous work to do within the Indigenous Nationhood Movement. We have always had strong leaders, active workers, academics, and artists who were working toward a more just society for Indigenous people and our earth. However, on a large scale, Idle No More created a collective leadership focused on moving forward. Indigenous people saw allies rise up from those who heard our cries for justice, those who related to our voices, who heard us, and who walked with us from around the globe. The most important seeds have sprouted over the last couple of months and will continue to create a harvest unlike anything that would have been possible otherwise. Idle No More created springtime during a long winter. Idle No More is unlike anything that has ever occurred before and it cannot be compared to any other revolution, because *it is not a revolution!* This is not a revolution. It is more than that; it is an awakening that will forever progress. Idle No More has unleashed a responsibility that was living inside of us, but needed prompting and awakening. We are responsible for our earth and our children's futures and we must intently hold on to our responsibility. Idle No More opened our spirit doors and eyes to a New World and it is up to us what we do inside of this New World.

Pauwauwaein. We have awakened to the Indigenous Nationhood Movement. Now there is work to be done to harvest and plant new seeds in this world which has been visioned for us. INM is throbbing and living and expanding by the second, like the sprouting of a new plant, perfect and arching toward maturity and vitality, a strong green root sunk deep into a rich and ancient soil, breathing the breath of the newly birthed, yet held tight by the ancestors' thick memory and lovesong. Pauwauwaein: We are together, inhaling the dreams of our future.

Originally appeared on *Decolonization: Indigeneity, Education & Society* (decolonization.wordpress.com), March 4, 2013.

INDIGENOUS NATIONHOOD MOVEMENT— STATEMENT OF PRINCIPLES

Who We Are

We are a movement for land, life, languages, and liberation.

We are fighting for the survival and independence of Indigenous nations.

We are an alliance of mutual support and coordinated action that branches out in all Four Directions.

We are an Indigenous-led movement that includes women, men, and two-spirited people of all ages, colours, and nationalities.

What We Believe

We will protect the land, water, and air that provide the basis for all life.

Indigenous cultures, spiritualities, and governments are the foundation for our continuing survival.

It is our responsibility to take action and to live according to our original teachings and natural laws.

Colonial laws and systems must be abolished.

Restitution must be made for the theft of our lands and the failed attempt to exterminate our peoples.

What We Stand For

Indigenous self-determination and autonomous nationhood.

Re-empowering traditional governments, hereditary and traditional chiefs, and clan mothers.

Defending and protecting the natural environment and all living beings.

Reclaiming, renaming, and reoccupying Indigenous homelands and sacred spaces.

Restoring nation-to-nation relations with Settler people and governments.

Learning and teaching Indigenous languages, traditions, ceremonies, and knowledge.

Eliminating all forms of violence within Indigenous communities, including violence based on gender and sexual orientation.

Edited as of September 10, 2013.

IDLE NO MORE SOLIDARITY SPRING:
A Call to Action
Idle No More and Defenders of the Land

Idle No More has sparked an awakening of Indigenous and non-Indigenous peoples internationally in support for democracy, human rights, and environmental protections. In three short months, the movement has succeeded in raising global consciousness through education, cultural resurgence, and democratic political activism. We have shaken the foundations of inequality in Canada, and invited communities to join in a movement for social and environmental justice. We now need many more people to stand with us. The Harper government's agenda is clear: to weaken all collective rights and environmental protections, in order to turn Canada into an extraction state that gives corporations unchecked power to destroy our communities and environment for profit. Harper is trying to extinguish Indigenous Peoples' Inherent, Aboriginal, and Treaty rights to their territories, because these rights are the best and last protection for all Canadians.

Idle No More has confronted these policies, and Harper supporters such as ex-Minister of Aboriginal Affairs John Duncan, suspended Senator Patrick Brazeau, resigned minister Peter Penashue, and Tom Flanagan have been called into question by grassroots people. Idle No More will help rebuild the nation-to-nation relationship that is the foundation of this country. This means deepening democracy, respecting Indigenous sovereignty, and protecting the land and waters from further resource extraction without the affected Indigenous Peoples' free, prior, and informed consent. We know it will take a lot more to defeat Harper and the corporate agenda. But against the power of their money and weapons, we have the power of our bodies and spirits. There is nothing that can match the power of peaceful, collective action in the defence of people and Mother Earth.

Idle No More and Defenders of the Land, a network of Indigenous communities in land struggle, have joined together to issue this common call for escalating action. Our demands are clear and in accordance with the principles of coexistence and mutual respect between Indigenous and non-Indigenous Peoples. We demand that Canada, the provinces, and the territories:

1. Repeal provisions of Bill C-45 (including changes to the Indian Act and Navigable Waters Act, which infringe on environmental protections, and Aboriginal and Treaty rights) and abandon all pending legislation which does the same.

2. Deepen democracy in Canada through practices such as proportional representation and consultation on all legislation concerning collective rights and environmental protections,and include legislation which restricts corporate interests.

3. In accordance with the United Nations Declaration on the Rights of Indigenous Peoples' principle of free, prior, and informed consent, respect the right of Indigenous peoples to say no to development on their territory.

4. Cease the policy of extinguishment of Aboriginal Title and recognize and affirm Aboriginal Title and Rights, as set out in section 35 of Canada's constitution, and recommended by the Royal Commission on Aboriginal Peoples.

5. Honour the spirit and intent of the historic Treaties. Officially repudiate the racist Doctrine of Discovery and the Doctrine of Terra Nullius, and abandon their use to justify the seizure of Indigenous Nations lands and wealth.

6. Actively resist violence against women and hold a national inquiry into missing and murdered Indigenous women and girls, and involve Indigenous women in the design, decision-making, process, and implementation of this inquiry, as a step toward initiating a comprehensive and coordinated national action plan.

Calls To Action:

March 21 International Day for the Elimination of Racial Discrimination—We are calling for decentralized actions across the country.

April 22 Earth Day—Indigenous Peoples and Indigenous rights are in many cases the best defence against environmental destruction by unchecked greed and industrial development. This Earth Day we are calling for nationwide autonomous local protests—and a mass non-violent direct action in Ottawa to be announced soon—highlighting the importance of Indigenous rights in combatting the Harper and corporate agenda. We are asking people to prominently include messaging on Indigenous and Treaty rights in their actions.

Sovereignty Summer—Indigenous communities have the right to determine the development on their traditional and treaty territories. In defending their right to say "No" to unwanted development, First Nations like Barriere Lake, KI, Grassy Narrows and many others are advancing alternatives that help us reimagine our relationship to the environment. Across the country, people are increasingly supporting First Nations who are trying to protect lands, waters, and air for everyone, and to win recognition of marine protections, of sustainable forestry, of local, just economies, and of the principle that we must respect the environment that we are a part of.

We are calling on non-Indigenous people to join Indigenous communities in coordinated non-violent direct actions in the summer. Alternatives will only come to life if we escalate our actions, taking bold non-violent direct action that challenges the illegitimate power of corporations who dictate government policy.

SIGNED BY:

Idle No More Founders, Lead Organizers, Provincial And Territorial Chapters, And Working Groups

Defenders Of The Land

Kitchenuhmaykoosib Inninuwug First Nation

Algonquins Of Barriere Lake

Ardoch Algonquin First Nation

Judy Da Silva—Grassy Narrows Women's Drum

Chief Candice Paul—St Mary's First Nation*

Dini Ze Toghestiy—Hereditary Chief, Likhts'amisyu Clan, Wet'suwet'en

Mel Bazil—Lhe Lin Liyin Co-Founder, Grassroots Wet'suwet'en

Rebeka Tabobondung, Publisher—Muskrat Magazine

Audrey Huntley—No More Silence

Melina Laboucan-Massimo—Lubicon Cree First Nation*

Carol Martin—Downtown Eastside Women's Centre*

Russell Diabo—Mohawk Nation (Kahnawake)*

Arthur Manuel—Secwepemc Nation, Indigenous Network On Economies And Trade

Clayton Thomas-Mueller—Pukatawagan Cree Nation*, Indigenous Tar Sands Campaign

Released to media and the public on March 18, 2013.

THE PKOLS RECLAMATION:
Saturating Our Land With Stories

Leanne Betasamosake Simpson

On May 22, members of the Tsawout (SȾÁUTW) nation, with support from the Songhees and the other local WSÁNEĆ nations, including Tsartlip (WJOȽEȽP), Pauquachin (BOḰEĆEN), Tseycum (WSIKEM), Malahat (MÁLEXEȽ) and allied supporters from the Greater Victoria community, led an action to reclaim the original name of PKOLS, now known as Mount Douglas, in what is now known as Victoria, in what is now known as British Columbia.

I live 3,400 km from PKOLS, and I am not apart of the SȾÁUTW, Songhees, or the WSÁNEĆ nations. As an Anishinaabekwe however, I know intimately the importance of standing in one's territory, freely practising our ceremonies at our sacred places, harvesting our foods, and telling our children their stories of creation in the exact spot creation happened and is happening. I know that living as Anishinaabe is one of the most important things we can do, on reserve, off reserve, in the middle of the bush or in the middle of the city. So I know that the reclamation of PKOLS is an extraordinarily important act for the SȾÁUTW, Songhees, and the WSÁNEĆ because it physically connects them to a powerful place, alive with story, and breathing with history. I hope for non-Natives living in Victoria that it instills in them a sense of responsibility to the land and to the peoples whose homelands they live in—a responsibility to learn what that means on the terms of the SȾÁUTW, Songhees, and the WSÁNEĆ nations. I hope it reminds every non-Indigenous visitor to PKOLS that we are still here—as living, breathing, intelligent, creative peoples committed to living in and protecting our homelands.

This process of renaming is a prominent part of colonial dispossession. Naming within western thought is a signifier of occupation and ownership, and mapping is a highly political act, deliberately designed in a colonial context to erase Indigenous presence, history, and connection to the land. English and French place names reflect a narrow, constructed view of history that erases any question of Canada's claim to territory. Looking at a map of Canada, it is as if Indigenous Peoples never existed, except to infuse the odd anglicized word from a Native language in a series of otherwise disconnected place names taken from colonial homelands, and white hero-ized men who are celebrated only for dispossessing Indigenous Peoples of our lands.

Peaceful co-existence requires much more.

Indigenous Peoples name places for much different reasons. In my own homeland, the Mississauga Nishnaabeg part of the larger Anishinaabeg nation, places are named for the connection our people have to that particular place. Our place names are holders of story, history, teachings, events—our collective and individual intimate connections and interaction with place. The stories and cultural meanings embedded in our place names connect our people to the land spiritually. They link our children to both their future and our history, and to a time when our environment was intact. Sometimes they mark events—political gatherings or ceremonial and sacred sites. Sometimes they are poetic descriptions of our affection for the natural features of our land. Although these names rarely appear on the topographical or road maps of Ontario, they continue to exist in the oral tradition.

A few days ago, I was visiting Doug Williams, an Elder at Curve Lake First Nation in Ontario. Together we've begun to record Mississauga Nishnaabeg place names on topographical maps. I began asking him about Buckhorn Lake on the west side of the reserve. Using his finger, he drew a circle around the water surrounding Wagosh Minis, or Fox Island, and told me that this part of the lake is called "Omiimiinens Zaaghigan." I asked why. He explained that in the past, large flocks of passenger pigeons flew over this part of the lake. The

flocks were so large that the sky was dark for three hours. Another place was named because there were lots of cranberries there. Another, because if you paddle towards it from the south, it looks like a curve. Then I read him a few names I'd found in old history books and the archives. At one point he said "Leanne, imagine yourself in a canoe, paddling in the lake, looking for an entrance to the river. You see what might be one, but it looks too marshy—it looks like it's going to be too difficult to get in, but you go anyway. When you get there, it's actually easy to get in. I think that's what that place name is telling us." That's key to understand Mississauga Nishnaabeg place names—you almost always have to look at it from the perspective of paddling a canoe, and that makes sense since our ancestors spent so much time on the water travelling through our homeland.

In 1993, some of the Elders at Curve Lake First Nation, led by Gladys Taylor, launched a complaint to the Ontario Geographic Names Board to have the name of the Squaw River changed back to its original name Miskwaa Ziibi (meaning Red River), for reasons that should be obvious to everyone. The Ontario Geographics Name Board agreed. Miskwaa Ziibi is now one of the only original place names on topographical maps of Ontario.

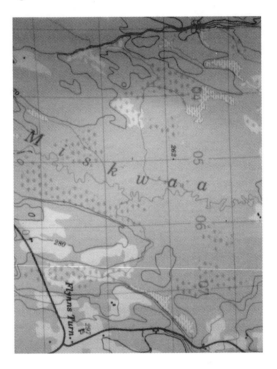

Reinstating Indigenous presence is not just happening in rural areas. This winter, the Ogimaa Mikana Project emerged as an effort to restore Anishinaabemowin place names to the streets, avenues, roads, paths, and trails of Chi Engikiiwang/Tkaranto/Toronto. A small section of Queen Street was renamed Ogimaa Mikana (Leader's Trail) in tribute to all the strong women leaders of the Idle No More movement. Another street sign was installed along Spadina Avenue, restoring the name Ishpadinaa, meaning a hill in Anishinaabemowin.

The dispossession and removal of Indigenous Peoples from our homelands so that these homelands can be exploited for large-scale natural resource development is the end goal of Canadian colonialism whether it's 1876 or 2013. Building a strong, connected Indigenous

Nationhood Movement rests on reclaiming the lands and sacred sites we have been removed from. It involves using the original names of these places, not symbolically or as an act of semantics, but as a mechanism for reconnecting our peoples to the land, our histories and our cultures. At the core, our responsibilities to our homelands, whether they are urban or rural, require a substantial number of us to inhabit them, to maintain relationships with their features and to pass that presence down to our children and grandchildren.

For every body of water—lake, river, stream, creek, spring; for every mountain, prairie, peninsula, bay, island, ridge, portage; for every trail, portage, place of birth, or burial ground, and for all the places our ancestors or our families gather, there is at least one Indigenous nation that has a name for that place, and there are often several. It is time to find these names, learn them and as Taiaiake Alfred says, saturate our homelands with our peoples, our languages and our ceremonies. We all have within our territories our PKOLS, many PKOLS—sacred places waiting to be restored to their place within the fabric of Indigenous societies. Whether it is a mountain, burial ground, hot springs or spring water, buffalo rubbing stone, tipiiring, teaching rocks, a medicine picking spot, or a travel route, or a city street, the PKOLS reclamation provides us with impetus to not just feel inspired, but to act.

Originally appeared on leannesimpson.ca, *May 22, 2013.*

THE MOVEMENT THAT SHOOK THE INDIGENOUS GLOBE
Andrea Landry

The feeling of family can be felt in a small community of 100, up to the world's population of over 7 billion; this is what the movement has aided in the development of. Indigenous peoples from New Zealand, Australia, Canada, the United States, Finland, and countless other countries have created a global community through one simple outlet: fighting the same fight.

What began as a movement based out of Canada has grown and erupted across landscapes, through rivers and oceans, and eventually into the hearts and minds of those we never thought it possible to reach. Demonstrations against enslaving the earth to create mining corporations; round dances showcasing how honouring the treaties within Canada can create viable, healthy relationships; and blockades significantly valuing the land for what it truly is—a living entity—are growing globally. It is through these demonstrations that we begin to see how strong the heartbeat of mother earth truly is, how this prophecy will never sleep, and how all Indigenous peoples around the world are honouring their realities, their truths, and the lives of their ancestors.

An international community is quite difficult to contain. Yet, while stepping onto the land of the Maori, and hearing the stories of how they feel the same struggle we do, or listening to the truth from a young Sami man, discussing the fights they fight based on the life of the land, the truth unfolds. No matter how large the distance is between us as Indigenous peoples, we live similar realities. Not only has this movement proved this true, but it has allowed us to join in complete solidarity, to reach out to one another, and to share in a way we may have never shared before.

Because of this movement, an understanding of global Indigenous issues has developed outside of using the United Nations system. We do not need a declaration to show us that treaties in other countries are not being honoured, we do not need a United Nations system to provide us space to share stories of our traditional livelihoods, we do not need governmental bodies trying to tell us they are fixing the problems, we need one another. There is strength in numbers, as this movement is showing us. We gain partnerships without colonial, indoctrinated processes. We gain unity through ceremony, through traditional knowledge, through language, through storytelling. We are continuously honouring our oral traditions globally in spite of the difficulties we are facing throughout the development of this movement. And we stand side by side with our future generations and ancestors, honouring one another internationally and decolonizing public spaces universally.

There is one more thing that stands out within this international revolution: the voices of youth. These youth are leading the way by speaking up at the rallies, by organizing the demonstrations, and by transforming public space into traditional space. Partnered with ceremony, the youth are truly the voices behind, and in front of, the movement. Whether the event is taking place on a small reservation in Northwestern Ontario, on the steps of Parliament in the capital city, coordinating events for Sami Parliament, or in an academic space within a university in New Zealand, we see the youth at the microphone. It is through this that we know that this movement is prophecy, but it hasn't been encased within the colonized borders of Canada—it has surpassed those borders, it decolonizes those borders, and it reaches out to the brothers and sisters globally.

The youth are engaging in global prophecy, global ceremony, and global traditions. This revolution embodies traditional livelihoods, oral traditions, stories from our ancestors, and the heartbeat of mother earth in a multitude of ways; and this is why it's growing and thriving. This movement has become us, we have become this movement. International barriers implemented by colonial governments will not keep us apart and we have united by indigenizing and decolonizing global space. The strength and power stems from ceremony and traditions, and the voices that are heard around the world come from our younger generations, understanding why they're doing what they're doing, and why we fight the same fight globally. For this we put our hands together, and recreate the war cry that was so often portrayed in Hollywood movies. This war cry is our truth, and this movement is our reality.

Originally appeared in Redwire Magazine, *Spring 2013.*

THE RISE OF THE NATIVE RIGHTS-BASED STRATEGIC FRAMEWORK:
Our Last Best Hope to Save our Water, Air, and Earth
Clayton Thomas-Muller

Years ago I was working for a well-known Indigenous environmental and economic justice organization known as the Indigenous Environmental Network (IEN). During my time with this organization

I had the privilege of working with hundreds of Indigenous communities across the planet who had seen a sharp increase in the targeting of Native lands for mega-extractive and other toxic industries. The largest of these conflicts, of course, was the overrepresentation by big oil who work—often in cahoots with state, provincial First Nations, Tribal and federal governments both in the US and Canada—to gain access to the valuable resources located in our territories. IEN hired me to work in a very abstract setting, under impossible conditions, with little or no resources to support grassroots peoples fighting oil companies, who had become, in the era of free market economics, the most powerful and well-resourced entities of our time. My mission was to fight and protect the sacredness of Mother Earth from toxic contamination and corporate exploration, to support our Peoples to build sustainable local economies rooted in the sacred fire of our traditions.

My work took me to the Great Plains reservation, Three Affiliated Tribes of Fort Berthold to support a collective of mothers and grandmothers fighting a proposed oil refinery, which if built would process crude oil shipped in from a place called the tar sands in northern Canada. I spent time in Oklahoma working with Sac and Fox Tribal EPA under the tutelage of the late environmental justice warrior Jan Stevens, to learn about the legacy of 100 years of oil and gas on America's Indian Country—Oklahoma being one of the end-up points of the shameful indian relocation era. I joined grassroots on the Bay of Fundy, in an epic battle against the state of Maine and a liquefied natural gas (LNG) producer who wanted to build a massive LNG terminal on their community's sacred site known as Split Rock. The plant, had it been built, would have provided natural gas to the City of New York for their power plants.

I worked extensively with youth on the Navajo reservation in America's Southwest, who were fighting the Peabody Coal mining company, trying to stop the mining of Black Mesa, a source of water and a known sacred site in the Navajo Nation. On the western side of the Navajo Nation, I worked to support Dine/Navajo who were fighting an attempt to lift the ban on uranium mining, which would have seen the introduction of a dangerous form of uranium mining called in situ or "in place" extraction that could've poisoned precious groundwater resources in the desert region. Uranium had already left a devastating legacy on the Dine/Navajo in the 40s and 50s. I worked in the Great Lakes at a community of Walpole Island (Bkejwanong First Nation) to stop an oil company from drilling for oil in their community—a place where First Nations peoples harvest for wild rice, muskrat, and fowl grains. It had also become a place of local economic importance as ecotourism from American duck hunters, providing income to the community. Walpole Island was already dealing with the impacts of 60 petrochemical facilities within 60 kilometres of their nation. I worked to support groups in Montana's Northern Cheyenne and Crow Indian reservations who were fighting massive expansion of coal bed methane in their region. The encroachment was decimating local ground water resources. I worked in Alaska and was a co-founder of the powerful oil-busting network known as Resisting Environmental Destruction on Indigenous Lands (REDOIL) that was created to take on the corrupt Alaska Native Corporations and big oil who had been running roughshod trying to start development in fragile places like the Arctic National Wildlife Refuge (ANWR). I worked with groups in British Colombia's Northeast, where natural gas companies were ripping apart the landscape with massive gas developments. I worked in dozens and dozens of other territories and places across the globe, many not mentioned in this story.

During my five years as an IEN Indigenous oil campaigner (2001–2006) I learned that these fights were all life and death situations, not just for local communities, but for the biosphere; that organizing in Indian Country called for a very different strategic and tactical play than conventional campaigning; that our grassroots movement for energy and climate justice was being led by our Native women and, as such, our movement was just as much about fighting patriarchy and asserting as a core of our struggle the sacred feminine creative principle; and that a large part of the work of movement building was about defending the sacredness of our Mother Earth and helping our peoples decolonize our notions of government, land management, business and social relation by going through a process of re-evaluating our connection to the sacred.

In the early years I often struggled with the arms of the non-profit industrial complex and its inner workings, which were heavily fortified with systems of power that reinforced racism, classism, and gender discrimination at the highest levels of both non-profit organizations and foundations (funders). It was difficult to measure success of environmental and economic justice organizing using the western terms of quantitative versus qualitative analysis. Sure, our work had successfully kept many highly polluting fossil fuel projects at bay, but the attempts to take our land by agents of the fossil fuel industry—with their lobbyists pushing legislation loopholes and repackaging strategies—continued to pressure our uninformed and/or economically desperate Tribal Governments to grant access to our lands.

The most high-profile victory came during the twilight of the first Bush/Cheney administration when our network collaborated with beltway groups like the Natural Resources Defense Council and effectively killed a harmful US energy bill containing provisions that would kick open the back door to fossil fuel companies, allowing access into our lands. The Indian Energy Title V campaign identified that if the energy bill passed, US tribes would be able, under the guise of tribal sovereignty, to administer their own environmental impact assessments and fasttrack development in their lands. Now this sounds like a good thing, right? Well, maybe for tribal governments that had the legal and scientific capacity to do so, but for the hundreds of US Tribes without the resources, it set up a highly imbalanced playing field that would give the advantage to corporations to exploit economically disadvantaged nations to enter into the industrialization game.

Through a massive education campaign and highly negotiated and coordinated collaborative effort of grassroot, beltway, and international environmental non-governmental organizations (eNGOs)—as well as multiple lobbying visits to Washington DC, led by both elected and grassroots Tribal leaders—we gained the support of the National Congress of American Indians who agreed to write a letter opposing the energy bill to some of our champions in the US Senate, most notably the late Daniel Akaka who was Hawaii's first Native Senator. Under the guidance of America's oldest Indian advocacy group he would lead a vote to kill the energy bill in the Senate. This was my first view into the power of the Native rights-based strategic and tactical framework and how it could bring the most powerful government on earth (and the big oil lobby) to its knees. Of course upon the re-election of the Bush/Cheney administration we lost the second reincarnation of the energy bill and the Title V was passed.

What I learned in these battles is that our sacred treaties outlining our priority rights and the fiduciary obligations governments have to us, are an important tool in this fight. We are the keystones in a hemispheric social movement strategy that could end the era of big oil and eventually usher in another paradigm from this current destructive time of free market economics.

The challenge would be to get people with power, both real and falsely perceived, to understand this reality. It is a task not easily accomplished. For example, with the passing of the US energy bill under the second Bush/Cheney administration, the US climate movement began to ramp up its attempts to have the administration pass a domestic climate bill. A massive investment by the administration focused on strategies developed by the foundations and individual donors; most of it was earmarked for policy makers instead of building an inclusive movement for climate justice that would take into account the environmental and economic justice framework in the struggle to force the US to lead the world in emissions reductions.

This movement saw the rise of mega-labour/eNGO coalitions like the Blue/Green Alliance, Apollo Alliance and mega-eNGO groups like 1sky and 350.org. Citizen groups like the US Public Interest Research Group (US PIRG) received millions of dollars to try to organize people to put pressure on President Bush, and later President Obama, to adopt some form of climate policy. However, the strategy screamed that age-old saying "what goes around comes around." There would be no climate bill under Bush and, to the surprise of the people who voted for him, no climate bill under Obama (yet).

The groups that ended up receiving resources from that limited pot of climate funding did what they did best, which was to invest in top-heavy policy campaigns. They did not focus on mobilizing the masses to get out in the streets to target and stop local climate criminals or build a bona fide social movement rooted in an anti-colonial, anti-racist, anti-oppressive foundation to combat the climate crisis. Instead, they kept the discourse focused on voluntary technological and market-based approaches to mitigating climate change, such as carbon trading or carbon capture and storage. I would argue that this frame is what kept this issue from bringing millions of Americans into the streets to stop the greenhouse gangsters from wrecking Mother

Jean Sock from Elsipogtog and Shelley Young from Eskasoni begin fasting to protest a lack of leadership in their communities. March 1, 2013, Millbrook, NS. (BRYSON SYLIBOY)

Earth. Groups like the Indigenous Environmental Network, Southwest Workers Union and others fought tooth-and-nail to try and carve out pieces of these resources to go towards what we saw as the real carbon killers, which were local campaigns being led by Indigenous Nations and communities of colour to stop coal mining, coal-fired power, and big oil (including gas).

During the early hours of the Obama administration there was a massive effort to "green" the economic stimulus, a package of job creation funding that was to be doled out by the Obama administration to counter the recession which had crippled the US economy. I had the opportunity to sit with some of the leaders of some of the biggest NGOs and foundations at a New York City round table, including members of the Obama White House team. High-profile individuals like former Green Jobs Czar Van Jones, and Energy Action/Mosaic Solar founder Billy Parish were also in attendance. At this table I told a story.

In the 80s and 90s America was in the grips of a recession, and groups rose up from all sectors to create a strategy to combat the crisis. Alliances were formed between the trade unionists and the NGOs and social justice groups. When the negotiated target of funding was in sight and Congress was about to write a cheque, groups became divided, and what was plentiful turned to scarcity and in the end AmeriCorp was born. Unions, NGOs, and social justice groups. And more importantly, the unity they had created, was shattered. Political games and divisive tactics were used by those in power. They used race, class and gender politics to divide a movement. I said that we were in the exact same moment in time, that we were seeing big oil ram through an energy bill loaded with corporate welfare for the one percent during the collapse of Americas middle-class and the stalling of a US climate bill, would impact the most vulnerable to our rapidly destabilizing climate—poor communities of colour and Native American communities.

America's wealth, and more directly, America's energy infrastructure was built on our backs. Efforts should be made to invest locally first—from training green jobs workers locally to using local building materials to producing energy locall. This would close the financial loop and help revitalize Native America's strangled economies, making them less vulnerable to volatile external costs while maximizing the positive impact of the new green revolution.

A green jobs economy and a new, forward-thinking energy and climate policy would transform tribal and other rural economies, and provide the basis for an economic recovery in the United States. In order to make this possible we had to encourage the Obama administration to provide incentives and assistance to actualize renewable energy development by Tribes and Native organizations and our allies. I made the argument that we could use the attributes of a predatory economic paradigm that had disproportionately targeted our communities, to flip the script on our enemies and that Native Americans, with our unique rights-based and trust relationship with the US government, could be a strategic and tactical asset to a diverse social movement trying to lobby for an economic stimulus bill that would actually help empower the most vulnerable while not exacerbating an ecological crisis. For this to work we would have to make moral agreements and not, under any circumstances, be denied. On the table was $750 million earmarked for green jobs and the task at hand was to determine how to equitably share the pot. In the media, the numbers of jobs created versus the amount of workers unemployed went from one million to five million and then back to one million and again. Once we got to the point where Congress was ready to write a cheque, we saw the downfall of mega groups like the Apollo Alliance and the absorption of 1SKY by 350.org. Many groups that started off at the table fell, one by one, with the first being groups representing racialized constituencies. Meanwhile in Indian Country, Tribes saw Congressional allocations from this economic stimulus packaged in the billions (rightfully so) and kept on keeping on.

The point of the story was that if we could truly understand the aspects of our struggle that kept us united, and more importantly, understand our unique contributions to a successful social movement paradigm, we could effectively expand the pot from $750 million to billions. By converging struggles in a solidarity framework rooted in anti-racism, anti-oppression, and anti-colonialism and by creating economic and political initiatives uniting urban and rural centres, we could wield a power never seen by our oppressors and actually gain economic independence and community self-determination. We could develop economies that didn't force people to have to choose between clean air, water, and earth or putting food on the table. I did not attend this meeting to ask for handouts, but rather as an ambassador of a strategic framework that I had come to know as the Native rights-based approach, which could be used to bring to an end what Native American activist, author, and Vice Presidential candidate Winona LaDuke described as "predator economics" and what activist and author Naomi Klein rightfully describes as "shock doctrine" economics.

Little did I know that all of these experiences were preparing me for what would be one of the biggest battles of my life. During the IEN Protecting Mother Earth Summit in 2006 in Northern Minnesota, three women from a small mostly native village called Fort Chipewyan, Alberta came to share their Dene people's struggle. Years later it would be known as the most destructive industrial project on the face of the earth, the tar sands mega-project. These three women were related to each other and represented three generations of one prominent family in Fort Chip known as the Deranger clan. They listened to the dozens of stories told in the energy and climate group about the injustices happening because of oil companies and complicit governments across Turtle Island. They told us about a project so large, so devastating that you had to see it to believe it. They spoke of a wild west of sorts, one of the last bastions of earth were big oil was ramping up, and they spoke of the deaths in their community from rare cancers, auto-immune diseases, and boomtown economics that plagued people living downstream from the tar sands. They said that we needed to go up to Fort Chipewyan and help.

I was taking time off from organizing and living in Ottawa with my wife and newborn son, Felix. My lifetime mentor and friend Tom Goldtooth, Executive director of the Indigenous Environmental Network, took this invitation from the Deranger matriarch Rose Desjarlais very seriously. IEN immediately organized a fact-finding mission in the Athabasca region of the tar sands with our Native energy and climate director, Jihan Gearon, and Rainforest Action Network campaigner, Jocelyn Cheechoo, from the James Bay Cree in Northern Quebec. I was invited because of my experience in fighting big oil across Turtle Island.

When we flew into Fort McMurray, the boomtown in the heart of the tar sands, I was immediately struck by how much it reminded me of Anchorage, Alaska. That was the only other city I had ever been to that also reeked of oil money. The town had an infrastructure to support 35,000 people but was bursting at the seams with a population of 75,000. Most were men between the ages of 18 and 60 and all working directly or indirectly for the tar sands sector. We took a tour of the infamous Highway 63 loop to Fort McKay Cree Nation that carves though man-made desert tailings ponds so big you could see them from outer space. We marvelled at the 24-hour life of the city and the incredible traffic jams at shift change. I think what struck me most was the level of homelessness in a town where there was a six-figure salary for anyone who wanted it. To see the tar sands themselves was devastating, to fly over endless clear cuts, open-pit mines and smokestacks surrounded by pristine Cree and Dene peoples' homelands was gut-wrenching. When we drove through and walked in the tar sands the smell of bitumen filled our noses and lent to the trauma that locals live with every day.

We got on a bush plane at the Fort McMurray airport and flew to Fort Chipewyan. We flew the route of the Athabasca River—a critical life path of the people of that land, a source of water, fish, and transportation and a spiritual connection to a past. We were told of how the river had changed, become poisoned, was no longer safe and how every year the water levels became lower due to industry use. When we got to Fort Chip we were well taken care of, and we met many elders, the elected leadership and youth who all told the same stories of hardship, the untimely sickness and death, and the destruction of a subsistence way of life—all by the tar sands. We heard about the history of the peoples going out into the Athabasca Delta and on to Lake Athabasca for food and medicine and how that was becoming impossible due to the massive regional contamination by industry. Again, we were told that we needed to help local grassroots people magnify this scandal to the world by amplifying their voices as the face of the issue.

After we took in the horrifying science fiction of the tar sands— and more importantly the power, beauty, and resiliency of the people of this land they call Athabasca—Tom Goldtooth asked me to build the Canadian Indigenous Tar Sands Campaign. The first thing we did was raise funds for an action camp in Fort Chip where we could do a proper power mapping and skill share with community members who were leading local campaigns and wanted to scale them up. Our first action camp had around 15 community members, including tar sands

warriors and climate movement folk heros like former Mikisew Cree
Nation Chief George Poitras, local Dene activists Mike Mercredi and
Lionel Lepine, Melina Lubicon Massimo, a Lubicon Cree activist, and
Eriel Deranger, a Dene woman also of Fort Chipewyan.

We brought in resource people from the NGO sector. With the direction of local Indigenous leaders we organized a series of workshops on
Aboriginal law, organizing, campaign planning, power mapping, and
the Native rights-based approach. The outcome of the camp formed
directives to launch a Native-led campaign to stop the expansion of the
tar sands; to utilize a treaty and Aboriginal rights-based framework;
to ensure that Indigenous peoples on the front line were the face of the
campaign; to raise the human health impacts as a moral issue; and to
follow the money financing the tar sands and to target those control-
ling it. Also, we were to advocate in the non-profit industrial complex
that a meaningful proportion of funding and resources earmarked for
tar sands work go directly to First Nations.

What came next would consume most of my waking time on
Mother Earth for the next seven years. When IEN launched our tar
sands campaign we knew that this issue was about to become one of,
if not the most, visible campaigns on the planet. The local grassroots
peoples were engaging with the most ruthless, powerful, well-resourced,
and just plain old evil corporate entities on the face of the planet. We
knew that these companies had bought every level of colonial government, and many were in bed with our own First Nations governments. But we knew that if executed properly we would see victory.
This multi-pronged campaign would contain elements of legal intervention, base-building, policy intervention (at all levels of government,
including the United Nations), narrative-based story-telling strategies
in conventional and social media, civil disobedience and popular education, and a whole lot of prayer and ceremony.

Again, I found myself at a table of funders and eNGO directors discussing a massive campaign that would impact every segment of our
society including our biosphere. I found myself viewed by my peers as
without power and that perhaps I was at the table for handouts rather
than with something to offer. The same old tricks of top-heavy, pol-
icy-focused pitches by the usual suspects happened again. And I found
myself repeating the need to take the time to understand and work in

solidarity with the Native rights-based strategic framework. I talked about how in the last 30 years of Canadian environmentalism there had not been a major environmental victory won without First Nations at the helm asserting their Aboriginal rights and title. This included many of the victories that those in the room counted in their own personal careers. I argued passionately that we should agree on the fact that we needed to dedicate meaningful resources to this approach and the decision would mean the difference between a fight lasting years or decades. During that meeting the facilitator representing the collective of foundations and donors that had contributed to a pot of money to fund anti-tar sands work became noticeably frustrated with our platform and things escalated to a point where he was yelling and swearing that our IEN campaign was "in the way" of plausible strategies that were actually going to work. Once the chastising was over I proceeded to say, "Well, now that I know where you're coming from and you know where IEN is at, how much of this funding are we going to get?" We walked out of that meeting with $50,000 seed money to start our campaign.

From that moment to now, our Indigenous heroes, or should I say, "Sheroes," have successfully built an international movement to stop the Canadian tar sands. Supported by thousands of Native and non-Native allies, the campaign is now active in the United States, Canada, and Europe with hundreds of First Nations, unions, NGOs, private-sector companies, municipalities, foundations, and individuals participating and elevating First Nations and our rights-based strategic approach as the keystone to the campaign. Part of this success was achieved through some seriously gutsy moves, one being a visit of high-profile Hollywood director James Cameron to tour the tar sands right when his block-buster movie *Avatar* had become the highest grossing film in history.

Cameron's tour was done at the time when IEN was pushing hard for our Keystone XL campaign to be funded. It was an uphill battle since everyone knew that pipeline fights historically have usually been defeats. We had done an analysis on the viability of victory in a Keystone XL campaign for the funders, because we were one of the few groups that had taken on the Keystone pipeline. Our analysis told us a couple of things. In the US, the Oglala aquifer would be the primary ecological card, as millions depended on this source of water and the pipeline was right through the heart of it. We knew that the dozen or so US Tribes could be educated to use the power of their unique rights-based approach to fight the pipeline. We also knew that no one in the US, especially in the heartland of the Dakota states, Nebraska, Oklahoma, and Texas knew what the tar sands were. We knew by bringing James Cameron to the tar sands, and by having him talk about the human rights scandal unfolding in First Nations communities, during a time when *Avatar* was on every theatre screen on the planet, would be huge boost to our cause.

Jim Cameron came, he saw, he met with the tar sands industry, the Alberta government, and with First Nations. He made a lot of promises about direct support of the legal strategies of First Nations against the oil sector and the government of Canada. As an avid supporter of technological remedies, he did not condemn the tar sands. He spoke highly of nuclear energy as an alternative—as well as the emerging theoretical carbon capture and storage technologies. What he did do was to say in front of the international press "I did not make *Avatar* until the technology was available for me to tell the story right, and the Canadian government should not develop the tar sands until they have the technology to not poison and kill First Nations people with cancers."

Avatar parts 2 and 3 are set to come out in 2015. I have a feeling that Cameron and his commitments to First Nations about directly funding the rights-based strategic framework are yet to be tested. The fallout from his visit was that every newspaper, television, computer, and smartphone in America was comparing the story of *Avatar* to the real-life situation unfolding between First Nations in the tar sands. The result was the emergence of the Keystone XL campaign as the lightning rod of the US environmental movement, a fight that's still raging today and it was done through the lens of human rights.

The tar sands campaign of IEN started at a time when direct community funding was in the tens of thousands but over time and through pressure it is now in the millions. We're still dealing with a non-profit industrial complex that is its own worst enemy. But Harper's corrupt, totalitarian federal government—with its extremism—is pushing a larger base of non-Native allies to our side of the equation.

With the current Harper government and the passing of recent omnibus legislation, Canada has seen 30 years of environmental, social, and economic policy thrown out. In response, we seen the rise of Idle No More, a catchy social media and education campaign launched—again by First Nations woman—and the result was a quickening of Canadian reconciliation with its own violent history of colonization as well as the rapid politicization of tens of thousands of Indigenous peoples occurring not just in Canada, but in all occupied lands across Mother Earth. Left without a pot to piss in, the conventional non-profit industrial complex and their supporters are trying to figure out their next steps in dethroning Harper, a daunting task after the unsuccessful bid to elect the New Democratic Party in British Colombia.

The one area where the Harper government has not been able to stack the cards is the courts, and a Native rights-based tactical and strategic framework—supported by labour, NGOs, students, and other social movements scaled up to the proportions of the 1960s US civil rights movement—is what's going to not only dethrone Harper, but is the last best effort to save our resources from Canada's extractive industries sector and the banks that finance them. This rights-based approach has been tested time and time again, it is enshrined in section 35 of the Canadian constitution, it has been validated by more then 170 supreme court victories, it is validated by all of the Indian treaties, it is validated by the United Nations Declaration on Indigenous Peoples, it is validated by the ILO convention 169 and many, many other legal instruments. The racism that Idle No More has met in the media, reminiscent of a 1950 Mississippi era, toward Native peoples and our winning rights-based strategy has driven even the most conservative of Canadians to our side and even toppled some of the biggest architects of the free market neoliberal agenda such as the infamous US-trained lawyer and mentor to Canadian Prime Minister Harper, Thomas Flanagan. We have come too far as Indigenous peoples to give up who we are. We have always been kind and again we will share the wealth and abundance of our homelands with our relatives from across the pond. Instead of lessons on how to survive the harsh winters of our lands, today we are offering lessons on how to be resilient and to overcome the oppression from the archaic oil sector and in our own government who have lost their minds with power.

We are faced with tremendous odds, the end of the era of cheap energy, the loss of ecosystems to sustain unfettered economic growth and, of course, the global climate crisis. We must understand that these are all symptoms of a much larger problem called capitalism. This economic system was born from notions of manifest destiny, the papal bull, the doctrines of discovery, and built up with the free labour of slaves, on stolen Indian lands. We have much to do in America and Canada to bring our peoples into a meaningful process of reconciliation. I have learned that our movement is very much led by women. This is something I am very comfortable with given the fact that I am a Cree man and we are a matriarchal society. There is a powerful metaphor between the economic policies of this country Canada and the US and their treatment of our Indigenous women and girls. When you look at the extreme violence taking place against the sacredness of Mother Earth in the tar sands, for example, and the fact that this represents the greatest driver of both Canadian and US economies, then you look at the lack of action being taken on the thousands of First Nations women and girls who have been murdered or just disappeared, it all begins to all make sense. It's also why our women have been rising up and taking power back from the smothering forces of patriarchy dominating our economic, political, and social, and I would say spiritual institutions. When we turn things around as a people, it will be the women who lead us, and it will be the creative feminine principle they carry that will give us the tools we need to build another world. Indigenous peoples have been keeping a tab on what has been stolen from our lands, which the creator put us on to protect, and there is a day coming soon where we will collect. Until then, we will keep our eyes on the prize, organize, and live our lives in a good way. we welcome you to join us on this journey.

Originally appeared on canadiandimension.com, May 23, 2013.

THIS IS A CEREMONY

Tara Williamson

The children and adults are scattered across the small clearing gathering wood. There is the sound of crunching leaves and the snapping of twigs and branches, mingled with laughter, and the soft soothing voices we use to teach our children. Every dried-out twig that fell has a purpose as we start a small pile on a piece of the path that is close to the opening where we can see the sun reflecting on and off the lake. The pile grows. Somebody has birch bark. Somebody has asemaa. Somebody has a match. Boozhoo shkode, we say. This is a ceremony.

We are here to feast and sing songs and give offerings to remember our loved ones. We are here to support each other. We are here to share and laugh and help each other remember the rhythms and words for the ritual. We are here to eat. And, so we do all of those things. Together. And, when it is time to be alone, we walk out into the sun— through the opening in the trees—and go the direction our hearts lead us. We stop when our feet tell us to stop and we take the time to be alone with our relatives. We take our time, all of us, individually and collectively. There is never a rush. The children do not know how to be impatient. They have learned to play in any place. It is beautiful. And, it is not lost on their teachers that the mounds that they roll down are made of our stories and our ancestors. And, so I roll down a mound too. This is a ceremony.

When it is time to put out ishkode and go away from this place, we offer water to the flames and heat. We are careful not to let her burn longer than we are able to take care of her. We watch as the smoke turns to steam turns to air. The crispness on this day—the first day we woke up to a light sheet of snow on the ground—returns where it used to be warm and we walk back to where we parked and we give hugs and kisses and wish each other well. This is a ceremony.

I choose to tell this story with grace. And so, I intentionally leave out the part where the zhaaganash man told us we were on private property so we couldn't park there. And, I omit that the reason we were in a small clearing by an opening is because we had to hide our fire and our offerings. I am happiest to forget about the police who showed up and the one zhaaganashkwe officer whose first words to us were "Did you not see the 'No Trespassing' sign?" And, it is heartbreaking to remember that it was hard to get to the lake because the orange snow fence was in the way.

I was taught that you do not talk about the most sacred parts of the ceremony when it is done. You do not tell people what your family said or what you experienced or how you went about preparing and practicing the ceremony. Those sacred parts are for you and your spirit and for the spirits of the people who were there. So, while I still smell like smoke, I am just writing to say that the moose meat was delicious and the berries were meaningful and my spirit is happy. This is a ceremony.

It feels like I don't have anything. I don't have a skirt. I don't have sage or wiingashk. The only asemaa I have are the cigarettes I'm addicted to in my pocket. But, I do have these neechis. The younger one who makes political hip hop because that's how he communicates his complicated identity. The older one who would never acknowledge she's pretty much ready to be an elder. The two-spirited one who really hates the cold but came out anyway. And that one who helped me learn about friendship. So, I figure, that must be enough. Probably the revolution is cool with that. Or, at least I hope so enough that I make it be true.

"YOU CAN'T HAVE A FIRE HERE," he yells as he storms as quickly as he can through the new snow. He and the other fluorescent-vested city official are obviously worked up. I walk as calmly as I can towards them—as calmly as a kwe without the "official" medicines can walk. And, I say, "Actually, yes, I can. This is my land. I am a treaty Indian."

There are an equal number of mooniyash and Anishinaabeg and Nehayowag gathered around shkode behind me. See, there's a revolution (I may have mentioned), and in times like these, having a fire in the middle of a city constitutes revolution. Just being (and certainly becoming) is revolutionary. And a beautiful minidmooye just arrived with her drum, so, I'm feeling pretty sure about truth in this moment (but, not sure enough to keep my phone with me. I left that with my neechis. With instructions on who to contact if those men took me away).

Anyway, those fluorescent-vested men were yelling real loud and didn't really let me talk and they called the police and I was okay with that, because even the police might be better than these men who felt like not-men because they didn't have guns, only fluorescent vests. And I was used to police at ceremony.

In between and before they got there, we were just gathered around that shkode, exercising our right to be close to daabik giizis. I made some new friends that night. It's easy to make friends while you're laughing around a fire. Even in the middle of winter. Even with the authorities idling a marked van a few feet away.

The fire department showed up before the police. Those fluorescent men made sure they talked to the firemen first. And they talked loudly. "WHAT ARE YOU GOING TO DO ABOUT THE DAMAGE TO THE GROUNDS?" So, I laughed and reminded them we'd been having fires forever and the ground liked shkode anyway. I didn't tell them I was more worried about how those non-Indigenous plants in the park were damaging the grounds, but that's what I was thinking. I asked, who of these inini-who-understood-shkode should I talk to. Ken was the man I should talk to. So, I did.

"Geez. You really can't have open fires in the city," Ken said.

"But, I can, Ken," I said. "It's Crown land. I have a treaty. And, I'm in ceremony."

"Yeah, well, I know," Ken said. "But, it'd be easier if you got a permit."

"Well," I said. "Ken, that's kind of the point. We don't need a permit."

"Yeah, I guess so. I know. You're just putting me in a really hard place," he said.

And, I knew what he meant. I know what it's like to be in a hard place. He told me he called the provincial conservation authorities. And he called the regional fire chief. And, he said he'd come get me when he heard back.

So, I went back to that fire. And, that mindimooye pulled out her drum and sang. And, I sang. We all did. And we talked about strategy. And we talked about the future. We talked about allies and quitting smoking and fasting and ceremony and some people stayed and some people left and we knew we were winning because all those official people with official vehicles couldn't do anything about our humble fire in a park in the middle of Winnipeg in the middle of winter.

Later, when Ken came towards me to tell me what he knew, I was nervous. Debwewin? I was nervous that whole time. But, especially nervous then. Pretty much he said he couldn't do anything. But, then he surprised me with a gift. He made sure that I knew he supported us. That he thought it was wrong that those Catholics came in and took our children and our religion. And, he's just a middleman. And, he wished I hadn't made it difficult for him. But, there was a part of him that understood. So, just make sure you put out the fire all the way. And make sure there's no booze. And make sure next time you get a permit. So, I shook his hand. Because that was his gift and I know what it's like to do something or give something when you feel like you have nothing. Since I shook Ken's hand, I had to make sure I was real respectful when those provincial legislature police showed up (probably called by those fluorescent-vested guys who sat in that idling city van by the park the whole time) and asked more questions—even though the provincial park people and city police never showed up and even though the fire department had left. And, we all made sure we cleaned up that fire real good (even though none of us think shkode is dirty and actually those ashes are good for aki). And, I even made sure I told daabik giizis about fireman Ken, because you should always raise a gift up because it's an honour for someone to give a gift—doesn't matter the time, doesn't matter the context, doesn't matter the colour of your skin—gifts and stories are all we have.

Speaking of stories, I don't know what this story is about, really. But, I received some medicine in a gift that I didn't have before I got there that night. It's sometimes surprising where gifts come from. It's sometimes surprising where medicine comes from. In the middle of a revolution and neechis and shkode and daabik giizis, I remember Ken. I am used to being brave. But, he had to reach deep inside himself to show me his courage. And, I know what it's like to be in a hard place and give a gift when you feel like you have nothing. This is a ceremony.

When the elder sang that West Coast-style song honouring and remembering those murdered and missing sisters, I stared at the fire and felt ikwezens lean up against my leg using my body as an anchor and I felt giizis shine down so hotly that it felt like shkode was not just in front of me but all around me and I felt alive.

I came to this fasting camp—the one with that ogichidaakwe who hasn't eaten for 36 days—because an elder asked me to. She heard that I had been there before and when we had a fire together with other neechis in the dead of winter on the full moon in a park in the middle of Winnipeg she asked me "Can you take some of these ashes to that ogichidaakwe's camp?" I wouldn't say I hesitated but I wondered if I honestly could get ashes to that camp and then she said, "We did that for the TRC, you know. We carried ashes from all the fires where all those people told their stories about residential school and we carried them to each gathering and we carried them home with us." And like a wave, history collided with this moment, so I stopped hesitating and said yes and choked up because there is nothing more powerful than the pain and pride of your ancestors coming through the words of elders or children.

Still. I almost sent those ashes with somebody else. When that big day of protest was being planned and we all wondered what that og-ichidaakwe would do and what the police and people with guns would do, I panicked and was worried those ashes and I would run out of time so I asked a friend if he could carry them for me. That I would give him asemaa if he could do this for me and when he said yes I prepared the ashes without even knowing what it meant to prepare them but I found a glass jar for them and made tobacco ties and wrapped that jar in some cloth for safe travels. But I couldn't. Or maybe they couldn't—those ashes. That elder had spoken to me in front of those ashes and I am not a mother but it felt like those ashes were looking at me with big Anishinaabe eyes begging to not be left. So I never ended up offering my friend any asemaa.

Instead this niijiikwe (who I didn't have to tell about the ashes' eyes because she just knew) said she was going to drive to that camp and even changed her plans so I could come along. So these two Anishinaabekweg and these two abinoojiiyag got into that car and stopped for junk food at least twice and another time for supplies for the camp (squash bread water beans snacks because those people who are supporting those fasters will eat twice as much when they're there all the time—appreciating the food their teachers won't taste and keeping strong in case a faster needs to borrow some of their energy). We brought those supplies into the camp. We stood by the fire. We prayed. We listened to that elder sing that song about those women and I asked that elder to help me do this job that other elder had asked me to do and I was going to offer him asemaa and he said, "No, you can do this yourself" and he came over to show me where that bag of cedar was and showed me how to put those ashes right on top of that sacred fire and I think I forgot to introduce myself to Creation in the way I'm supposed to but I think Creation didn't mind this time because when those ashes and asemaa and cedar all caught fire it was like those ashes were closing their eyes and something I'll never quite know for sure was finally at rest. And that elder hugged me and those prayerful people in that circle shook my hand and I felt like a hundred journeys. Like that song that travelled all this way. Like those ashes. Like the geese who hover around the camp. Like the Anishinaabeg in the cars on the highways. Like the train that will have to wait for the blockades to clear. Like the stories that rush over us moving through us or just moving us. Like shame changing to pride.

I felt like an Anishinaabekwe.

This is a ceremony.

TIMELINE

The final night of Chief Spence's fast, Victoria Island, Ottawa, January 22, 2013. (MELODY MCKIVER)

TIMELINE OF MAJOR EVENTS SPANNING *THE WINTER WE DANCED*

Through the fall of 2012 and the winter and spring of 2013, thousands of Idle No More related events took place across Turtle Island and all over the world. Our attempt to record each of these events in this timeline has proven incredibly difficult. We have therefore selected moments in the Movement that have had an important impact or attracted the attention of Canadians and the media, as well as events that reflect the diversity of actions including protests, ceremonies, teach-ins, and creative expressions in urban, rural, and reserve settings.

October 18, 2012:

- First Reading of Bill C-45 called "A second Act to implement certain provisions of the budget tabled in Parliament on March 29, 2012, and other measures"—which includes stipulations that remove protection for waterways and infringe on treaty and Aboriginal rights. This 457-page omnibus budget bill introduces drastic changes to several Canadian laws, including the Indian Act, the *Fisheries Act*, the *Canadian Environmental Assessment Act*, and the *Navigable Water Act*, and includes a host of other bills impacting financial transparency, homes on reserve and matrimonial interests, elections and drinking water. Bill C-45 comes on the back of the first Omnibus bill, Bill C-38, which was passed in June 2012 and restricted environmental protection amongst a long list of other issues.

October 20, 2012:

- The federal government announces that Bill C-45 will include amendments to the Indian Act to make leasing reserve lands easier (this in addition to nearly a dozen pieces of legislation relating to the Indian Act or treaty rights).

November 4, 2012:

- Jessica Gordon posts the first message on Twitter using the hashtag #IdleNoMore—it is:

@**shawnatleo** wuts being done w #billc45 evry1 wasting time talking about Gwen stefani wth!? **#indianact #wheresthedemocracy #IdleNoMore**

November 10, 2012:

- A "teach-in" called "Idle No More" is held at Station 20 in Saskatoon to discuss Bill C-45. It is led by four women (Sylvia McAdams, Nina Wilson, Jessica Gordon, and Sheelah McLean) and features speakers such as Erica Lee.

November 11-17, 2012:

- Teach-ins occur in Regina, Prince Albert and Winnipeg. Social media platforms like Twitter and Facebook are increasingly used to publicize and organize these events.

November 28, 2012:

- A rally in Toronto is held at the provincial legislature in Ontario. The protest targets Bill C-428, *The* Indian Act *Amendment and Replacement Act*. Speakers include Pam Palmater, Isadore Day, and Beth Elson.

November 29, 2012:

- The Idle No More Facebook page is founded.

November 30, 2012:

- Along with her fellow organizers and followers, Tanya Kappo uses the hashtag #IdleNoMore to drum up interest and support for an upcoming December 2 event at Louis Bull Cree Nation. #IdleNoMore trends across Canada.

December 2, 2012:

- The first "teach-in" outside of Saskatchewan is held in Louis Bull Cree Nation in Treaty 6 territory, Alberta (led by Tanya Kappo, with the assistance of Pam Palmater, Janice Makokis, and Sylvia McAdam).

- Shannon Houle launches the Idle No More website.

December 4, 2012:

- Bill c-45 is discussed in the House of Commons in Ottawa. Meanwhile, at a Chiefs Assembly nearby, several leaders (including Pat Madahbee, Derek Nepinak, Wallace Fox, and Isadore Day) leave their meeting and attempt to enter Parliament to discuss the bill with the federal government. They are stopped by security and hold a rally on the front steps.

- Chief Theresa Spence of the Attawapiskat First Nation announces at the Chiefs Assembly that she will go on a hunger strike to protest unfulfilled treaties and the effects of this on her community, among other issues.

December 10, 2012:

- A National Day of Solidarity and Resurgence in the name of "Idle No More" is held, focusing on opposition to recent legislation, attention to life-threatening situations in Indigenous communities, and political solidarity. Rallies and gatherings involving tens of thousands of people are held in over a dozen communities (Vancouver, Whitehorse, Calgary, Edmonton, Winnipeg, Toronto, Halifax, Goose Bay, and more in towns and Native communities).

December 11, 2012:

- Chief Spence begins a hunger strike (including only the consumption of tea, lemon water, and fish broth) to protest the unfulfilled Treaty Nine.

- Ten hours later, Raymond Robinson (Cross Lake First Nation) begins to fast in solidarity. One week later, they are joined by Jean Sock (Elsipogtog First Nation).

- Hundreds of people across Canada join in day- or week-long solidarity fasts over the course of the next six weeks.

The Guswhenta (Two Row Wampum Belt), a powerful symbol of peace, friendship, respect and mutual autonomy, Ottawa, December 21, 2012. (MELODY MCKIVER)

December 13, 2012:

- Chief Theresa Spence requests a meeting with the Prime Minister and either the Queen or her representative, Governor General David Johnston, to discuss treaty violations..
- The AFN calls for a meeting between First Nations and the Crown.

December 14, 2012:

- Bill C-45 passes through the Senate with a vote of 50-27, receiving royal assent and becoming federal law. It is known as the "Jobs and Growth Act, 2012."

December 15, 2012:

- A sacred jingle dress healing dance is held at Victoria Island led by Rhonda White, Jocelyn White, and family members of the late Maggie White from the community of Naotkamegwanning (Whitefish Bay). Elder Alo White gives Chief Spence the Anishinaabe name "Bominosamook"/Rolling Thunder Woman in a naming ceremony.

December 17-18 2012:

- The first flash mob Round Dance is held at Cornwall Centre Shopping Mall in Regina. The following day a similar flash mob is held at the West Edmonton Mall in Edmonton and, shortly after that, in the Rideau Centre in Ottawa, the Polo Park Mall in Winnipeg, Driftpile Cree Nation, Sandy Bay First Nation, the Mall of America in Minneapolis, Minnesota and in malls, intersections, and reserves across Canada and the United States.
- Over the next few days, hundreds of similar events are held in malls, highways, and streets in towns, cities, and Indigenous communities across Canada and into the United States.

December 19, 2012:

- Over 1,000 people, primarily from Chippewa and Onieda nations on the Thames, shut down Highway 401 outside of London, Ontario.
- On the national CBC radio show *Q*, host Jian Ghomeshi opens with an essay on Idle No More.

December 21, 2012:

- Thousands travel from across the continent for a gathering on Victoria Island in Ottawa, followed by a march to Parliament Hill. Attendees and speakers include Indigenous peoples, Canadians, activists, elders, singers, dancers, students, children, politicians, union leaders, media, and many more.
- Members of Aamjiwnaang First Nation, led by Ron Plain and others, begin rail blockade near Sarnia, Ontario to protest chemical pollution on their territory. It lasts two weeks.
- Activists from the community of Kahnawake shut down an on-ramp to the Mercier Bridge in Montreal for one hour.
- An Idle No More round dance temporarily shuts down Canada's busiest intersection at Yonge and Dundas Square in Toronto. This is followed by Toronto's first teach-in featuring Tantoo Cardinal, Hayden King, and Rebekah Tabobondung. Teach-ins would follow every week for the next eight weeks.
- Over 2,000 academics sign a Statement of Solidarity with Idle No More and Chief Theresa Spence, calling for respectful dialogue on treaties and rights.
- Thousands attend a ceremony at the Oodena Celebration Circle at the Forks in Winnipeg and then walk to a rally at the Manitoba Legislature, culminating in a round dance around the entire building.
- *Decolonization, Indigeneity & Education* journal launches a blog dedicated to publishing Idle No More writings.
- Prince Albert municipal officials warn Idle No More organizers not to attempt a round dance in the city's main intersection.

- Rice University researcher Rachael Peterson reports that the hashtag #IdleNoMore has over 36,000 mentions from sites across North America.[18]

December 23, 2012:

- Lillian Howard (Mowachacht) begins her solidarity fast with Chief Spence in Vancouver, B.C..
- 76-year-old Clyde Bellecourt, co-founder of the American Indian Movement, is arrested in Minneapolis at an Idle No More event. Charges would later be dropped.

December 23-29, 2012:

- Reports of Idle No More rallies of solidarity come from communities across the world, from New Zealand to Bulgaria to India to Mexico. Tens of thousands of messages from allies throughout the world are shared via social media.
- *The Globe and Mail* reports that an average of 20,000+ tweets per day use the hashtag #IdleNoMore (total of over 144,000). Regarding postings, gender is virtually the same (47 percent male and 53 percent female) while 94 percent are "favourable."[19]

December 27-31, 2012:

- The Millbrook and Eskasoni First Nations in Nova Scotia hold a traditional fast in honour of Idle No More.

December 27, 2013:

- While out walking in Thunder Bay, Ontario, a citizen of the Nishnawbe-Aski nation, "Angela Smith" (not her real name to protect her identity), is abducted and then physically and sexually assaulted by two men who, during the attack, tell her

18 See: "The natives are angry… and tweeting: the digital subaltern and #idlenomore." *Global Native Networks Blog* 12 December 2012 <globalnativenetworks.com/2012/12/12/the-natives-are-angry-and-tweeting-the-digital-subaltern-and-idlenomore/>.

19 See: "The hashtag uprising: Analyzing #IdleNoMore's social-media footprint." *The Globe and Mail* 31 December 2012.

"You Indians deserve to lose your rights" and make reference to the Idle No More Movement. This hate crime is immediately reported to police and the family of Smith urge all to remain calm and peaceful.

- An Idle No More rally near Sault Ste. Marie temporarily blocks rail lines.

December 28, 2013:

- The "Returning to Our Sacred Spaces" event calls on Indigenous peoples to reoccupy their sacred spaces. Temporary (and in some cases permanent) reoccupations occur across Canada including near or in the communities of Peterborough, Toronto, Barrie, Ottawa, Grassy Narrows, Winnipeg, Tatamagouche, New Credit First Nation, Six Nations, Batchewna First Nation, Thunder Bay, among many others.

December 30, 2012:

- Peaceful protests and flash mob round dances are held in Calgary, Victoria, and Times Square in New York City.
- Thunder Bay police begin to investigate, after pressure from the Indigenous community through Operation Thunderbird, the sexual assault of "Angela Smith." At the same time, the Native Youth Sexual Health Network releases a statement in response to the assault and organizes a national activism and education campaign.
- Mohawk activists from Tyendinaga block a VIA train near Marysville, Ontario, delaying 2,000 passengers.
- Over a dozen politicians visit Theresa Spence on Victoria Island, including former Prime Minister Joe Clark, Liberal leader Justin Trudeau, and NDP MP Charlie Angus.

December 31, 2012:

- Flash mob round dances are held in Toronto's Eaton Centre and in the middle of one of Winnipeg's busiest intersections, Portage and Main.
- A protest/round dance is held in front of the Canadian consulate in Denver, Colorado.

- The hashtag #IdleNoMore trends on Twitter for the first time.

January 2, 2013:

- "Inside Story Americas" on *Al Jazeera* airs a special on Idle No More with guests Pamela Palmater and Clayton Thomas-Muller.
- Idle No More protesters pack Waterfront Station in Vancouver, B.C.

January 4, 2013:

- Through his office, Prime Minister Stephen Harper announces that he will hold a "meeting" with Aboriginal leaders "coordinated by the Assembly of First Nations" that "will focus on treaty relationship and aboriginal rights and economic development" on January 11. The Governor-General will not attend.
- A Hunger Strike Benefit Concert is held for Chief Spence in Peterborough, Ontario with musicians Tara Williamson, Sarah Decarlo, and Sean Conway.

January 5, 2013:

- One thousand Idle No More supporters in Akwesasne demonstrate along international border.
- Protesters in Sarnia block the Blue Water Bridge to the US for one hour.
- Idle No More activists block the Dehcho Bridge for 40 minutes in Denendeh, near Fort Providence, Northwest Territories.
- A benefit concert featuring artists like Derek Miller, Melody McKiver, and others is held to support Chief Spence and Idle No More in Ottawa.

January 7, 2013:

- Activists across the country begin organizing campaigns under the banner #J11.
- An audit of Attawapiskat First Nation's financial records is leaked to the media, revealing a lack of documentation for some of the community's financial transactions. Many suspect the leak is intended to discredit the still-fasting Spence.

January 8, 2013:

- #Idlenomore Internet Townhall is hosted by Ryan McMahon and broadcast on webcast. Speakers include Khelsilem Rivers, Russ Diabo, Chelsea Vowel, Leanne Betasamosake Simpson, and Jarrett Martineau.

- CBC's *The Current with Anna Maria Tremonti* features a debate between Senator Patrick Brazeau, Niigaanwewidam James Sinclair, and Phyllis Sutherland on financial accountability on First Nations and the Idle No More movement.

- Mikisew and Frog Lake Cree Nations launch a legal challenge of Bill C-45 based on a lack of consultation with First Nations.

January 9, 2013:

- Chief Spence announces she will not attend the meeting between Stephen Harper and First Nations leaders because a representative of the Crown won't be attending.

- Flash mob round dances continue and are held in Canada's capital, at Carleton University and the University of Ottawa.

- The University of Ottawa Indigenous and Canadian Studies Students' Association drafts a document for the decolonization of the campus, including teaching Algonquin and Mohawk languages, increasing indigenous scholarships, and the use of Indigenous names for buildings and public commemorations of history.

- Organized by John K. Samson and Christine Fellows, hundreds of Canadian musicians and artists, including members of The Weakerthans, Broken Social Scene, Feist, Tragically Hip, and Blue Rodeo, amongst others, release a Statement of Solidarity with Idle No More, calling on the federal government to take action on treaty violations.

- Christi Belcourt launches the *Divided No More* website, providing another venue for Indigenous writers to express thoughts on Idle No More.

January 10, 2013:

- Hundreds of Indigenous leaders and people converge on Ottawa, holding assemblies to discuss the upcoming meeting with Prime Minister Stephen Harper. Many chiefs debate boycotting the meeting due to its lack of transparency, exclusivity, and narrow agenda (Bill C-45, for instance, is not up for discussion).

January 11, 2013:

- Stephen Harper meets with Shawn Atleo of the Assembly of First Nations and and 16 other First Nations leaders. Following the meeting, Aboriginal Affairs minister John Duncan reports that the Prime Minister agrees to a "high-level" talks on treaty relationships and comprehensive land claims, "enhanced oversight" on Aboriginal issues and further meetings with the leader of the AFN.

- Boycotting the meeting with Harper, many leaders from Ontario, Manitoba, Saskatchewan, and other communities join over 3,000 activists in rallies and protests outside the meeting and on Parliament Hill.

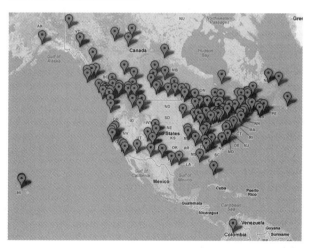

- There are 265 simultaneous rallies held across North America (see map) and as far away as Australia, New Zealand,

Sri Lanka, Finland, Germany, England, and the United States
on this International Day of Action.

- Governor General David Johnston announces he will hold a
"ceremonial meeting" in his residence with First Nations leaders following the meeting with Prime Minister Harper. Several
attend, including Chief Spence.

- In Toronto, an Idle No More Fundraiser is organized by Wanda
Nanibush, Crystal Sinclair, Tannis Neilson, and Charm Logan
and features Digging Roots, Derek Miller, Bear Witness (of a
Tribe Called Red), Cris Derksen, Arthur Renwick, Sean Conway,
Sarah Decarlo, and Mama D.

- Twitter registers the highest level of activity using the
#IdleNoMore hashtag with 56,924 tweets.[20]

January 14, 2013:

- Citing stress and exhaustion, Assembly of First Nations
National Chief Shawn Atleo announces that he will take a
doctor-ordered medical leave. Regional chief Roger Augustine
will chair national executive meetings while Atleo is away.

- *Idle No More: Songs for Life Vol. 1*—the first of an ongo-
ing series of free downloadable compilations of songs by
Indigenous and ally artists who support the vision of Idle No
More—is released on rpm.fm including artists Derek Miller,
Holly McNarland, Digging Roots, Jenn Grant, John K. Samson,
Christine Fellows, George Leach, Plex, Wab Kinew, Sarah
Podemski, Whitehorse, Inez, Lee Harvey Osmond, The Johnnys,
Kevin Kane, and A Tribe Called Red.

January 16, 2013:

- Six youth (and two guides) depart Whapmagoostui on the
James Bay coast on a 1,600 kilmetre walk to Ottawa to promote unity among Indigenous nations. The walk becomes
known as the Journey of the Nishiyuu.

20 See Mark Blevis's study of social media traffic involving #IdleNoMore called
"Idle No More at Six Months" available at: markblevis.com/tag/idle-no-more/

- "#Idlenomore, Where do we go from here?" Teach-in and Public Forum is hosted at First Peoples House, University of Victoria, and features Wab Kinew, Taiaiake Alfred, Janet Rogers, and Mandee McDonald.

January 17, 2013:

- Members of Alderville First Nation hand out coffee and Idle No More information during a traffic slowdown in Northumberland County.
- An Idle No More Benefit Concert is held in Truro, Nova Scotia.

January 18, 2013:

- Canadian Prime Minister Stephen Harper makes his first public comments regarding Idle No More in response to a question at a press conference in Oakville, Ontario. He states: "People have the right in our country to demonstrate and express their points of view peacefully as long as they obey the law, but I think the Canadian population expects everyone will obey the law in holding such protests."

January 12—25, 2013:

- Naomi Klein, Sarah Slean, Maude Barlow, Gurpeet Singh, and Ellen Gabriel refuse to accept Queen's Diamond Jubilee medals as a protest against the Crown in solidarity with Theresa Spence.

January 22, 2013:

- "Idle? Know More!" A Public Panel on Indigenous Issues is held in Vancouver, B.C. with Glen Coulthard, Art Manual, Khelsilem Rivers, Darla Goodwin, Jerilynn Webster, and Cease Wyss. Four hundred people attend, 600 people watch online.
- After an editorial describing Indigenous peoples as "lazy" and "acting like terrorists" is published in the newspaper *The Morris Mirror*, Niigaanwewidam James Sinclair writes a response published in the *Winnipeg Free Press* and journeys to Morris, Manitoba, in an attempt to dialogue with the editor.

January 23, 2013:

- After a brief hospital stay, Theresa Spence ends her fast.
- Second Internet Townhall on Spreecast is hosted by Ryan McMahon and Khelsilem Rivers, with Christi Belcourt.

January 24, 2013:

- *Idle No More: Songs for Life Vol. 2* is released on rpm.fm including artists Blue Rodeo, Indian Handicrafts, Nick Sherman, Kate Rogers Band, Hannah Georgas, Oh My Darling, NRG Rising, Sandy Scofield, Del Barber, Oh Susanna, David St. Germain, Tracy Bone, Amelia Curran, Royal Wood, and Melody McKiver.

January 25, 2013:

- Artists in Winnipeg join together for concert in support of Idle No More including Wab Kinew, John K. Samson, Scott Nolan, William Prince, Lorenzo, and Eagle & Hawk.

January 26, 2013:

- To date, The Canadian Nurses Association, CUPE, Greenpeace, The National Farmers Union, The Council of Canadians, David Suzuki, among others have expressed support of Idle No More.
- Water Walk & Ceremony in Toronto is led by Elder Pauline Shirt.
- Idle No More Women's Townhall webcast is hosted by Chelsea Vowel with Christi Belcourt, Tania Cameron, Koren Lightning-Earle, Leanne Betasamosake Simpson, and Gabrielle V. Fayant.

January 27, 2013:

- First Nations in Northwest Territories and Alberta sign the Fraser River Valley Declaration opposing the proposed Enbridge pipeline.
- Over 100 people travel from Shubenacadie to Indian Brook at one of two "Trail of Fire" walks (the other in Halifax) in honour of Idle No More and residential school survivors.

- Wrecking Ball #14, Idle No More takes place in Toronto with playwrights writing and performing plays on the theme of Idle No More including Waawaate Fobister, Falen Johnson, Andrew Moodie, Yvette Nolan, and Jordan Tannahill.

January 28, 2013:

- Idle No More Day of Action World Day of Action, #J28
- Protests held worldwide including UK, France, Sweden, Greenland, US (Alaska, Michigan, Colorado, Connecticut, Florida, Massachusetts, Minnesota, Montana, North Carolina, Nebraska, New Mexico, Nevada, Oklahoma, New York, Texas, Washington state, Oregon), and all across Canada.
- Idle No More Teach-In at Yale University and Columbia University featuring speakers Niigaanwewidam James Sinclair, Audra Simpson, Theo Van Alst, Alyssa Mt. Pleasant, Ned Blackhawk, and Adam Gaudry.
- Mathias Colomb Chief Arlen Dumas and many community members protest on their traditional territory against HudBay mine.
- Idle No More organizers Alex Wilson and Melody McKiver reach out to the queer community for support and solidarity.

January 29, 2013:

- Plex releases "No More" feat. Lase—an anthem and video featuring Idle No More protests and issues (www.youtube.com/watch?v=u9FXdVnweok).
- Stopping for gas while it is -40C, Cree poet Althea Guiboche meets two homeless men who ask her for help in the north end of Winnipeg, Manitoba. Inspired by the Idle No More Day of Action, she feeds the two men and begins "Got Bannock?"—a community project that feeds and clothes inner city people weekly. By October 2013, over 10,000 people have benefited.

January 30, 2013:

- An Idle No More video conference hosted by Wab Kinew with Eskasoni chief Leroy Denny, Tanya Kappo, Taiaiake Alfred, Chief Isadore Day, Shelley Young, and Molly Peters is watched by people in 41 countries.

February 1, 2013:

- Idle No More Teach-in is held at the University of British Columbia, First Nations House of Learning, with Glen Coulthard, Dory Nason, Linc Kesler, Gordon Christie, and Shelly Johnson.

February 4, 2013:

- The magazine *Rolling Stone* publishes a feature article on Idle No More.

- Lesley Belleau, an Idle No More activist, reports a death threat she received as a result of her organizing in Sault Ste Marie which says: "You are a dead piece of sh-t. A good Indian is a Dead Indian. Stay away from the Soo Lesley Belleau."

- The online hacker group Anonymous releases a map from police reports and online public input that documents cases of missing and murdered Aboriginal women across Turtle Island for the past 10 years.

February 14, 2013:

- Idle No More organizers invite people to join in creating an inclusive Valentine's and organize community events to coincide with The Women's Memorial March, One Billion Rising, and Have a Heart Day.

February 24, 2013:

- Sylvia McAdams, Nina Wilson, Jessica Gordon and Sheelah McLean receive the Carole Geller Award for founding Idle No More and their commitment to the struggle for human rights.

February 25, 2013:

- "Idle? Know More! Take Action" Forum held in Vancouver, B.C. with Ta'Kaiya Blaney, Art Manual, Leena Minifi, Khelsilem Rivers, Carrielynn Xwementelot Victor, and Jerilynn Webster aka JB the First Lady.

March 1, 2013:

- Shelley Young (Eskasoni First Nation) and Jean Sock (Elsipogtog First Nation) begin water-only fast in Millbrook First Nation demanding Indian Act Chiefs pull out of the "Made in Nova Scotia" treaty process.

March 5, 2013:

- Mathias Colomb Chief Arlen Dumas and many community members protest the HudBay Lalor mining project in their traditional territory.

March 9, 2013:

- A teach-in entitled "Niigaan In Conversation: Recreating Indigenous Settler Relations in Canada" is held at the National Arts Centre, Ottawa, Ontario. Speakers include Niigaanwewidam James Sinclair (host), Andrea Landry, Thomas King, Leanne Betasamosake Simpson, Victoria Freeman, Craig Benjamin, and Chief Gilbert Whiteduck. Over 350 people buy tickets and attend.
- Idle No More Benefit Concert takes place in Vernon, B.C.

March 18, 2013:

- Idle No More forms an alliance with Defenders of the Land, an established network of activists formed in 2008 and committed to Indigenous land rights and environmental issues. They jointly release a call to action for "Sovereignty Spring" and later, "Sovereignty Summer."

March 19, 2013:

- HudBay sues Mathias Colomb Cree First Nation over protests impacting work at their mining project in Manitoba. HudBay is granted a court injunction against Pam Palmater and Chief Dumas from holding any more protest at the Lalor mine site.

March 20, 2013:

- Idle No More calls for "Honouring our Sacred Fires" and "Nationhood Global Day of Ceremony and Resurgence."

March 21, 2013:

- International Day for The Elimination of Racial Discrimination—Idle No More and Defenders of the Land call for actions across the country under the "Solidarity Spring" banner.

March 23, 2013:

- A teach-in entitled "Nation to Nation Now: The Conversations" is held in Toronto. Speakers include Naomi Klein, Russ Diabo, Ellen Gabriel, Leanne Betasamosake Simpson, Robert Houle, Art Manual, and Sheelah McLean, and many others.

March 30, 2013:

- Idle No More and Defenders of the Land call for a Day of Solidarity with the Unist'ot'en to support their call for actions against the development and financing of Pacific Trail Pipelines.

March 25, 2013:

- After walking for six weeks in sub-zero temperatures, gathering more than 300 travellers, and covering over 1600 kilometre, the Nishiyuu walkers arrive in Ottawa.

March 31, 2013:

- Spreecast for National Aboriginal Languages Day is hosted by Christi Belcourt with Ellen Gabriel, Leanne Betasamosake

Simpson, Khelsilem Rivers, Susan Blight, Chelsea Vowel, and Maya Chacaby.

April 22, 2013:

- Idle No More/Defenders of the Land make a call to action on Earth Day. There are protests and events in Listuguj, Ottawa, Montreal, Kingston, Toronto, Thompson, Stoney Lake/Treaty 6, Kelowna, Vancouver, Prince George, San Francisco, and Salt Lake City.

April 24, 2013:

- Idle No More Direct Action Training Spreecast hosted by Heather Milton Lightening, with Elle-Máijá Tailfeathers and Satsi Naziel.

May 22, 2013:

- WEC'KINEM (Eric Pelkey), a hereditary chief of the Tsawout First Nation, with support from the Songhees and local WSÁNEĆ nations and 600 Indigenous and non-Indigenous peoples, restores the original name of PKOLS to Mount Douglas in Victoria, B.C..

June 7, 2013:

- Assembly of Manitoba Chiefs Grand Chief Derek Nepinak leads the Treaty Freedom Caravan/Ride, a 10-day trek visiting 43 Prairie communities in a quest to ignite interest in the treaties.

June 11, 2013:

- Internet researcher Mark Blevis releases a study called "Idle No More at Six Months," which states that by the end of May 2013 there were 1,215,569 Twitter mentions by 143,172 different individuals.[21]

June 15, 2013:

- On behalf of Idle No More, Alex Wilson, Sylvia McAdams, Nina Wilson, Jessica Gordon, and Sheelah McLean present to

21 For the report, see: markblevis.com/tag/idle-no-more/

hundreds of international Indigenous scholars and knowledge-keepers at the Native American and Indigenous Studies Annual Meeting at the University of Saskatchewan in Saskatoon.

June 21, 2013:

- Anti-fracking protests continue in Elsipogtog First Nation, New Brunswick, with several arrests occurring throughout the summer and fall

July 25, 2013:

- An Ontario judge orders Ron Plain to pay CN Rail $16,000 in compensation.

- A coalition of Indigenous, Islamic, Jewish, Christian, and many other faiths and cultural communities hold over a dozen events across Canada, calling on the federal government to release millions of documents to the Truth and Reconciliation Commission of Canada and honour the apology to residential school survivors in June 2008. Most of the organizers met during the events of Idle No More and use similar strategies—including holding a Spreecast and using the hashtag #HonourtheApology.

July 31, 2013:

- Idle No More founders release a statement clarifying that the name Idle No More has not (yet) been trademarked, but that an application was made in January to protect the name because they were concerned about the possibility of corporations using the name for profit.

August 11, 2013:

- Under an Access to Information request, Postmedia reports that Aboriginal Affairs and the Canadian Security Intelligence Service accumulated over 1,200 pages of records on Idle No More, including information on over 439 rallies and protests during the winter of 2012-2013.[22]

22 See "Canada's spy agency kept close watch on rapidly growing First Nations protest movement: documents." *National Post.* 11 August 2013. <news.nationalpost.com/2013/08/11/canadas-spy-agency-kept-close-watch-on-rapidly-growing-first-nations-protest-movement-documents/>.

Fall 2013 (and beyond)

- Idle No More organizer Alex Wilson tells CBC that there are approximately 400 regional ally groups formed since Idle No More started and a database of 125,000 people.[23]
- The Idle No More Facebook page has gained 116,000 "likes" with 48,000 members.
- Events, protests, rallies, and reoccupations continue across the country. While less intense and with less media coverage, Indigenous peoples continue to be inspired and motivated by Idle No More. At the time of writing, nearly a year after Idle No More began, the Movement goes on, in one shape or another.

23 See "Idle No More Prepares for Day of Action." CBC News. 7 October 2013.
    < www.cbc.ca/news/canada/idle-no-more-prepares-for-day-of-action-1.1913429>.

Note on the proceeds from *The Winter We Danced*

The royalties from the sale of *The Winter We Danced* will be donated to the **Native Youth Sexual Health Network** (NYSHN)—an organization by and for Indigenous youth that works across issues of sexual and reproductive health, rights, and justice throughout the United States and Canada. NYSHN are resisters of violence from the state, violence on the land, and violence on bodies. Restoration of knowledge, justice, and ways to be safer in communities is critical to their work. And yes, resistance is sexy! For more information, see www.nativeyouthsexualhealth.com.

On December 30, 2012, the Native Youth Sexual Health Network released the following press release in response to the assault of "Angela Smith." Their courage and call to action in response to this horrific event remains pertinent and is a resource for all. It is republished here:

NATIVE YOUTH SEXUAL HEALTH NETWORK STATEMENT & RESOURCES
On Recent Sexual Assault in Thunder Bay in Support of Indigenous Women in Idle No More and All Survivors of Violence

The Native Youth Sexual Health Network (NYSHN) would first like to acknowledge the courage and strength of Angela Smith, an Indigenous woman in Thunder Bay who was sexually assaulted on December 27 to speak out about the violence she experienced. With prayers, tobacco, and in our many Indigenous languages we send you love and community in this difficult time.

We support the requests that have been shared by the family for community members to travel in groups, stay together, take care of each other's needs, protect and love each other while not responding with violence. They want people to feel safe participating in the Idle No More movement and anywhere our peoples may be.

Violence against Indigenous women and girls has been, and continues to be used as a weapon of colonialism and a way to undermine the strength of our leadership. For this reason, NYSHN sees raising our voices together against sexual violence and making change for violence against women to stop as an integral part of ANY movement. This is especially relevant given the fact that Idle No More was started by Indigenous women. The health and well-being of our communities depends on the health and well-being of our mothers—including Mother Earth.

However, this is not only about "protecting women"—it is also about protecting our men, Two-Spirit, Trans and gender non-conforming brothers and sisters and all our communities from the everyday violence of colonialism. Gender-based violence, rape, and sexual assault are not "social issues" that can be dealt with after the fact, they are real and happening NOW.

Resisting all forms of violence, whether it is legislative assaults like Bill C-45 or sexual assault, is everyone's responsibility because gender-based violence affects us all. Laws not only affect our lands but also our bodies: there is a direct connection between the violence in these two areas. We affirm the right survivors or victims of violence have to be believed and supported unconditionally when they say they have been assaulted regardless of whether they report to police or media. Trust that survivors and victims know what is best for them, and support their decisions about what they would like to happen after an assault.

Whether you are #IdleNoMore or #neverbeenidle, here's **what you can do:**

1. Letters of love and support were sent to our sister "Angela Smith" in Thunder Bay (name has been changed for confidentiality).

2. Have specific discussions leading up to/during/after Idle No More events about how to protect each other from various forms of violence and have a list of local resources readily available to share. In the planning, think about creating a "safety

team": people who are designated to respond to incidents of assault or violence should they occur and who could also organize safe transportation to and from events. Ask Elders/ Grandparents that you trust and/or other helpers to attend so they can support and also be available to talk and listen.

3. Different things can potentially be "triggering" for people: meaning they can bring up past or current experiences of violence or trauma. Keep this in mind when people may express difficulty participating in a certain way or come to a place where they might be ready to share about what's happened, happening, or what may happen to them. Having supports in place, as mentioned above in point 2 and resources below is also important for this. When in doubt, ask what type of supports would be appreciated.

4. Consider having teach-ins, which can be workshops, talking circles, panels, or just open forums regarding the many ways in which sexual/gender-based/family violence appear and what we can collectively do to prevent them from happening. Invite local community members who are already working in these areas or contact us at NYSHN for support to make this happen.

In addition to local community resources, here is a list of resources for sexual/domestic/family violence:

In Canada:

- **Talk4Healing** is a free, 24/7 confidential and culturally safe telephone help line for Aboriginal women living in Northern Ontario providing service in English, Ojibwe, Oji-Cree, and Cree. They provide culturally sensitive crisis counselling, advice and support, personalized information and referrals, and acceptance of Aboriginal women's issues in a non-judgemental way. Contact 1-855-554-HEAL(4325) or see www.talk4healing.com
- **National Aboriginal Circle Against Family Violence** has a mandate to reduce family violence in Aboriginal communities, and provides supports and resource development and a list of all Aboriginal shelters in Canada. Contact 450-638-2968 or see www.nacafv.ca

- **Families of Sisters in Spirit** is a volunteer, grassroots, non-profit organization led by families of missing and murdered Aboriginal women and girls. Contact familiesofsistersinspirit@gmail.com or find them on Facebook.
- **Native Women's Association of Canada** contains various toolkits and other resources on violence against Indigenous women and girls. See www.nwac.ca
- **Canadians for Choice** runs an information, access, and referral line for sexual and reproductive health services across Canada: Contact 1-888-642-2725 English available 24/7, service in French 9-5 pm Monday-Friday or see www.canadiansforchoice.ca

In the United States:

- **National Indigenous Women's Resource Center** seeks to enhance the capacity of American Indian and Alaska Native (Native) tribes, Native Hawaiians, and Tribal and Native Hawaiian organizations to respond to domestic violence and safety for Indian women. Contact **1-855-649-7299** or see www.niwrc.org
- **Mending the Sacred Hoop** works from a social change perspective to end violence against Native women and children while restoring the safety, sovereignty, and sacredness of Native women. Contact **1-888-305-1650** or see www.mshoop.org
- **Save Wiyabi Project** Wiyabi is Assiniboine for "Women." In addition to promoting awareness to the pandemic of interpersonal violence, the Save Wiyabi Project highlights legislation that is beneficial to reservations and empowers Native women. Contact save.wiyabi.project@gmail.com or find them on Facebook and Twitter.
- **The National Domestic Violence Hotline** creates access by providing 24-hour support through advocacy, safety planning, resources and hope to everyone affected by domestic violence. Contact 1-800-799-SAFE (7233) or see www.thehotline.org

NYSHN MEDIA CONTACT:
Erin Konsmo, Media Arts and Projects Coordinator
ekonsmo@nativeyouthsexualhealth.com
www.nativeyouthsexualhealth.com

BIOGRAPHIES OF CONTRIBUTORS

Taiaiake Alfred is a Professor and the founding Director of the Indigenous Governance Program at the University of Victoria. He specializes in traditions of governance, decolonization strategies, and land-based cultural restoration. Taiaiake has been awarded a Canada Research Chair in the studies of Indigenous Peoples, a Canadian National Aboriginal Achievement Award in the field of education, and the United States' Native American Journalists Association award for best column writing. He has served as a researcher and advisor for his own and many other Indigenous governments and organizations for 25 years and is the author of *Wasáse* (University of Toronto Press, 2005), named one of the decade's most influential books by the Native American and Indigenous Studies Association in 2010; *Peace, Power, Righteousness* (Oxford University Press, 1999); and *Heeding the Voices of Our Ancestors* (Oxford University Press, 1995). Born in Montréal in 1964, Taiaiake is Kanien'kehaka from Kahnawake. He now divides his time between Kahnawake and the territory of the Wsanec Nation, where he lives with his wife and three sons, who are all Laksilyu Clan of the Wet'suwet'en Nation.

Siku Allooloo is a Haitian/Inuit woman from Somba K'e, Denendeh and is part of a strong lineage of leaders and activists. She has a BA in Anthropology and Indigenous Studies from the University of Victoria, primarily concerning Denendeh's political history and forms of Indigenous resistance across the country. Her work continues to support the resurgence of Indigenous nationhood and autonomy, with particular focus on the strength, resilience, and power of Indigenous women in the healing and emancipation of our communities.

Through museum interventions, large-scale installations, sculpture, photography, printmaking, and paintings, **Sonny Assu** merges the aesthetics of Indigenous iconography with a pop art sensibility in an effort to address contemporary, political, and ideological issues. His work often focuses on Indigenous issues and rights, consumerism, branding and new technologies, and the ways in which the past has come to inform contemporary ideas and identities. Assu infuses his work with wry humour to open the dialogue towards the use of consumerism, branding, and technology as totemic representation. Within this, his work deals with the loss of language, loss of cultural resources, and the effects of colonization upon the Indigenous people of North America. His work has been accepted into the National Gallery of Canada, the Seattle Art Museum, the Vancouver Art Gallery, the Museum of Anthropology at UBC and in other public and private collections across Canada and the US. Sonny is Ligwilda'xw of the We Wai Kai First Nation (Cape Mudge). He graduated from the Emily Carr University in 2002 and is currently enrolled in the MFA program at Concordia University. He received the B.C. Creative Achievement Award in First Nations art in 2011 and was long-listed for the Sobey Art Award in 2012 and 2013. He lives and works in Montreal.

Christi Belcourt (Pitawehaanikwatok) is an Otipemisiwak (Michif) visual artist and author whose ancestry originates from the historic community of *Manitou Sakahigan*, Alberta. Like generations of Indigenous artists before her, Belcourt celebrates the beauty of the natural world within her paintings while exploring nature's symbolic properties. She is author of three books: *Medicines To Help Us* (2008), *Beadwork* (2011), and co-author of *Jeremy and the Magic Ball* (2008). Belcourt cocoordinated the Willisville Mountain Project, an activist art project that resulted in Inco/Vale reversing a decision to begin quarrying the Willisville Mountain within the LaCloche mountain range in Ontario. Currently, she is the lead organizer of the Walking With Our Sisters project. Involving over 1,200 artists in an eight-year international exhibit tour, the project honours the lives of missing and murdered Indigenous Women in Canada and the United States.

Lesley Belleau is an Anishnaabekwe writer, mother of four, educator, and activist from the Ojibwe nation of Ketegaunseebee Garden River First Nation, located outside of Bawating/Sault Ste. Marie, Ontario. She is a PhD student in the Indigenous Studies Department at Trent University in Nogojiwanong (Peterborough, Ontario), and is studying Indigenous feminine literature and narratives. She has taught Indigenous Literature, Creative Writing, and Theatre at Algoma University in Sault Ste. Marie, and is currently a PhD Teaching Assistant at Trent University in the Indigenous Studies Department focusing on Oral History. Lesley enjoys writing fiction, essays, and poetry and is the author of *The Colour of Dried Bones*, a collection of short fiction published by Kegedonce Press, as well as other poetic, fictional, academic, and blog publications both nationally and internationally. Lesley's second novel, *Sweat*, is due to be launched in spring 2014 She has co-edited a dossier of Idle No More writing for Matrix Magazine, and is collaborating on two upcoming academic projects surrounding ideas of Anishinaabe Literature, poetics, and ethics. Lesley also performs her poetry, fictions, and performance art nationally.

Nathalie Bertin hails from Toronto, Ontario. After working as a graphic designer for several years, Bertin began showing her art publicly in 2009. Bertin's work is often described as luminescent, energetic, bold, and colourful. She is also fond of strong shapes and textures. She incorporates elements of her French and Algonquin heritage into her work, including beadwork and furs, in concepts that blend her two cultures. Her most recent works are inspired from traditional storytelling and folk tales. Past projects explored the Canadian fur trade culture and her role within it as a modern subsistence hunter. In 2013, Bertin's artwork was minted on a silver collector coin by the Royal Canadian Mint. In June 2010, Bertin was selected as an artist ambassador for the G20 Summit in Toronto, a volunteer position that garnered global media attention for Canadian artists from Muskoka. Her work can be found in government, corporate, and private collections across Canada, the US, Europe, and Africa. She works from her home studio in Newmarket, ON, and home-away-from-home in Muskoka, ON.

Eugene Boulanger is the Director of Strategic Partnerships and Planning at Dechinta Centre for Research and Learning. He is a Shutagotine Dene artist, hunter, community organizer, and crossmedia producer originally from Tulita, Denendeh. Eugene has worked as a web and social media consultant in content management, branding, digital strategy, public outreach, and audience engagement. He is a founding director of the Vancouver Indigenous Media Arts Festival, an advisor on a training and mentorship pilot program engaging urban Aboriginal and First Nations youth in careers in digital technology sectors, and a contributing editor of RPM.fm. Eugene has worked as program manager on the Vancouver Dialogues Project, a City of Vancouver initiative aimed at discerning challenges faced by First Nations, urban Aboriginal and non-Aboriginal Canadians seeking to build cross-cultural dialogue and collaboration. Eugene is a former communications officer for the W2 Community Media Arts Society, working on projects ranging from social and environmental justice issues to Indigenous media arts showcasing and large-scale event production.

Michael Redhead Champagne is a community organizer who was born and raised in the North End of Winnipeg. Originally from Shamattawa Cree Nation, Michael is the founder/organizer of AYO! Aboriginal Youth Opportunities and is working towards a university degree in education at the University of Winnipeg. Michael is a community youth advocate, a helper and public speaker addressing issues such as youth engagement, suicide prevention and advocating for healthy relationships. Michael is committed to breaking stereotypes, creating opportunities for young people, and leading by example.

Glen Coulthard is a member of the Yellowknives Dene First Nation and an assistant professor in the First Nations Studies Program and the Department of Political Science at the University of British Columbia. Glen has written and published articles and chapters in the areas of Indigenous thought and politics, contemporary political theory, and radical social and political thought. Glen's book, *Red Skin, White Masks: Rejecting the Colonial Politics of Recognition*, is forthcoming from the University of Minnesota Press in 2014. He lives in Vancouver, unceded Coast Salish Territories.

Ethan Cox is Quebec Bureau Chief for rabble.ca and a regular commentator on television and radio in Montreal.

Isadore Day, Wiindawtegowinini is the elected Chief of Serpent River First Nation, which is located on the North Channel of Lake Huron in Northern Ontario. Serpent River First Nation is signatory to the 1836 Bond Head Treaty and the Robinson Huron Treaty of 1850. Under Chief Day's leadership, Serpent River First Nation has undergone a paradigm shift in the areas of fiscal stability, economic investment, health and social policy framework development. As a part of the community's economic direction, the First Nation has taken a strong stand on eradicating poverty and empowering change through economic prosperity. Chief Day believes that Community Development and transformative change can only be achieved when an individual achieves self-efficacy in a communal setting. To achieve this goal the community leadership is working diligently to bring a strong micro-loans program to the forefront of change.

Chief Isadore Day resides in Serpent River with his partner Angela and two daughters Manook and Waasayaa. They enjoy participating in traditional Aboriginal festivals and living in harmony with the natural resources offered throughout their traditional territory.

Russell Diabo is Policy Advisor to the Algonquin Nation Secretariat, a Tribal Council and Senior Policy Advisor to the Algonquin Wolf Lake First Nation. He is also Editor and Publisher of an online newsletter on First Nations political and legal issues, the *First Nations Strategic Bulletin*. He is a member of the Mohawk Nation at Kahnawake, Quebec. He holds a BA in Native Studies from Laurentian University. In 1981, Diabo worked with the National Indian Brotherhood in Parliamentary Liaison. In the 1990s, as an alternative to the federal Comprehensive Land Claims Policy Mr. Diabo helped to negotiate a pioneering Trilateral Agreement (Canada-Quebec-Algonquins of Barriere Lake) to develop an integrated resource management plan for forests and wildlife over 10,000 sq km of the Barriere Lake Algonquin's traditional territory based upon Algonquin traditional knowledge and way of life. From 1990-94, Diabo was vice-president of Policy for the federal Liberal Aboriginal People's Commission and helped develop the 1993 Liberal Aboriginal Electoral Platform. From 1996-97, He helped to defeat a regressive Indian Act amendment package as the Assembly of First Nations-Indian Act Amendments Coordinator under then National Chief Ovide Mercredi. Diabo is part of the Defenders of the Land Network and works closely with Idle No More under a joint agreement between these two groups to work together on Sovereignty Summer.

Rosanna Deerchild is Cree from O-Pipon-na-piwin Cree Nation in northern Manitoba. Her first book of poetry *this is a small northern town* was nominated for several awards and won the Aqua Books Lansdowne Prize for Poetry/Le Prix Lansdowne de Poesie in 2009. These poems are about what it means to be from the north, a town divided along colour lines, and a family dealing with its history of secrets.

She's had her work published in a number of literary magazines and anthologies most recently in *Manitowapow: Aboriginal Writings from the Land of Water.* As a member of the Indigenous Writers Collective of Manitoba her work appears in *urban kool* (2000), *Bone Memory* (2004), *Red City: a spoken word* CD and the anthology *xxx ndn: love & lust in ndn country* (2011).

Jeff Denis is an Assistant Professor of Sociology at McMaster University. Born and raised in Toronto, he is an ally and scholar whose research investigates the barriers to overcoming racism and colonialism and the strategies, alliances, policies, and practices that can bring about more just and sustainable societies.

Ryan Duplassie is a French/Anishinaabe PhD candidate in Native Studies at the University of Manitoba. Through his research, he interprets Treaty 3 through the lens of water, guided by the experiences of the Grassy Narrows FN resistance community as they contend with ongoing mercury poisoning, and unrelenting state-industry collusion in the "development" of their territories.

Ellen Gabriel was chosen by the People of the Longhouse and her community of Kanehsatà:ke to be their spokesperson during the 1990 "Oka" Crisis. For the past 23 years she has been a human rights advocate for the collective and individual rights of Indigenous peoples and has worked to sensitize the public, academics, policing authorities and politicians on the history, culture, and identity of Indigenous peoples. She has been active at the international level participating at the United Nations Permanent Forum on Indigenous issues, negotiations on the Nagoya Protocol of the Convention on Biodiversity and most recently, at the UN Expert Mechanism on the Rights of Indigenous Peoples. She has travelled across Canada, to the Hague in Holland, Strasbourg, France to address the European parliament, and to Japan to educate people about the events in her community. Ms. Gabriel has a Bachelor of Fine Arts degree from Concordia University. She worked as an illustrator/curriculum developer, as an art teacher, and has worked on videos illustrating legends of the Iroquois people and local community stories. She is presently an active board member of Kontinón:sta'ts—Mohawk Language Custodians and First Peoples Human Rights Coalition.

David Garneau is Associate Professor of Visual Arts at the University of Regina. He was born and raised in Edmonton, received most of his post-secondary education (BFA Painting and Drawing, MA American Literature) at the University of Calgary and taught at the Alberta College of Art and Design for five years before moving to Regina in 1999. Garneau's practice includes painting, drawing, curation and critical writing. His solo exhibition, *Cowboys and Indians (and Métis?)*, toured Canada (2003–7) and *Road Kill* toured twenty one centers throughout Saskatchewan (2009–11). His work often engages issues of nature, history, masculinity and postcolonial Indigenous identities. His paintings are in many public and private collections. Garneau has written numerous catalogue essays and reviews and was a co-founder and co-editor of *Artichoke* and *Cameo* magazines. He has given talks and keynote lectures in Australia Canada, and the US. Garneau is currently working on curatorial and writing projects featuring contemporary Indigenous art and curatorial exchanges between Canada and Australia.

Leah Gazan is a member of Wood Mountain Lakota Nation in Saskatchewan and is currently teaching in the Faculty of Education at the University of Winnipeg. Leah has 18 years experience in the area of community capacity building and development, dedicating the majority of her efforts to supporting the advancement of First Nations across Canada. Leah is currently the president of the Social Planning Council of Winnipeg, a non-profit organization committed to providing leadership and support in the area of social planning and socially responsible policy development.. Leah has been a very active participant in social movements, most recently as a participant in Idle No More. Her dedication towards the advancement of community self-sufficiency and self-determination has been the driving force that has guided her career in Winnipeg and Indigenous nations in Canada.

Jessica Gordon is a co-founder of Idle No More, a movement that represents opposition to government and industries' disregard to Indigenous rights and environmental protection. She is a Cree/Saulteaux from Pasqua First Nation in Treaty Four territory and is a mother of five. She is most proud of the work she does empowering people to take control of the issues that affect them the most or those which they feel a passion for. She is committed to working for the people relentlessly until the day she leaves this earth and hopes to leave her children as well as future generations a legacy of tools to help them attain independence.

LauraLee K. Harris is a First Nations artist, born in Toronto in 1956. Her roots of Sioux, Cree, Chipewyan, Montagnais, Ojibwe, and Assiniboine First Nations are mixed with French, Irish. Harris began to seek her Anishinabe roots in 1994. This inspired her to create a unique art practice that melded cultural teachings and identity, through Indigenous Knowledge systems within a framework of the natural world's flow, the direct connection to earth's Creation, and the subconscious into self knowledge and poetry. Her work has been exhibited in solo and group shows across Canada and the US and published in periodicals, journals, and books. She is a self-published author and poet of four books. Her work has been studied at Universities nationally and internationally along varying lines of study Harris's work and life as an indigenous woman artist, innovator, and writer/poet was honoured in the documentary "From the Spirit III" produced by Earth Magic Media, a Dene-owned production company based in Edmonton.

Stephen Hui is the web editor and technology editor at the Georgia Straight. He lives in Vancouver.

Sarah Hunt is Kwagiulth (Kwakwaka'wakw Nation) and is also of Ukrainian and English ancestry. Since she was a teenager, Sarah has worked passionately to address issues of violence and justice as a community-based researcher, educator, writer, and advocate. Sarah is currently a PhD candidate in Geography at Simon Fraser University where she is examining how Canadian law serves to normalize violence in "Indian space" and is seeking to change these norms by engaging the principles and practices of Indigenous law at a community level.

Stephanie Irlbacher-Fox was raised in Inuvik, NT, and currently lives with her husband and two sons in Yellowknife, where she has worked as an advisor to Dene, Metis, and Inuvialuit organizations for the past two decades. She earned her PhD at Cambridge University, England. She is the author of *Finding Dahshaa: Self Government, Social Suffering and Aboriginal Policy in Canada* (2009, UBC Press).

Dru Oja Jay is a writer, community organizer, and web developer. He is a co-founder and current board member of the Media Co-op, and a founding editor of the Dominion. Dru is co-author (with Nikolas Barry-Shaw) of the book *Paved with Good Intentions: Canada's development NGOs from idealism to imperialism*, and the report *Offsetting Resistance: The effects of foundation funding from the Great Bear Rainforest to the Athabasca River*. His organizing has focused on solidarity with Indigenous struggles, reversing Canada's participation in imperialism, war and occupation, and building a solidarity economy. He lives in Montreal.

Tanya Kappo is from the Sturgeon Lake Cree Nation, Treaty 8 Territory. She graduated from the Faculty of Law at the University of Manitoba. Tanya is the mother of three children.

Wab Kinew is a one-of-a-kind talent, named by Postmedia News as one of "Nine Aboriginal movers and shakers you should know." He is a correspondent with Al Jazeera's Fault Lines documentary program and the Director of Indigenous Inclusion at the University of Winnipeg. In 2012, he hosted the acclaimed CBC Television series "8th Fire." His hip hop has won an Aboriginal People's Choice Music Award. His journalism has won an Adrienne Clarkson RTNDA Award and a Gabriel Award, and been nominated for a Gemini Award. He has a BA in Economics, is a Sundancer, and is a member of the Midewin.

Hayden King is Pottawatomi and Ojibwe from Beausoleil First Nation on Gchimnissing (Christian Island) in Huronia, Ontario. He is an Assistant Professor of Politics and Indigenous Governance at Ryerson University in Toronto, Ontario.

Naomi Klein is an award-winning journalist, syndicated columnist and author of the international bestsellers, *The Shock Doctrine: The Rise of Disaster Capitalism* (2007) and *No Logo* (2000). She writes a regular column for *The Nation* magazine and the Guardian newspaper and is a contributing editor at *Harper's* magazine. She is a Puffin Foundation Writing Fellow at The Nation Institute and a former Miliband Fellow at the London School of Economics. Naomi serves on the board of directors for 350.org, a global grassroots movement to solve the climate crisis. Her forthcoming book and film are about the (r)evolutionary power of climate change.

Erin Marie Konsmo is the Media Arts and Projects Coordinator for the Native Youth Sexual Health Network. She is Métis/Cree from Onoway/ Lac St. Anne, Alberta. She is a self-taught community-engaged visual and multimedia Indigenous artist, supporting community to create their own art and expressions about sexual and reproductive health, rights and justice. Her art practice is based in community spaces, culture and Indigenous-led media and arts initiatives and has been referred to as agitprop. Erin is currently serving as one of the North American focal points for the Global Indigenous Youth Caucus at the United Nations Permanent Forum on Indigenous Issues. She is also on the Walking With Our Sisters National Collective as the Youth Coordinator and Media Contact. She holds a Bachelor of Arts in Sociology and a Master of Environmental Studies.

Nadya Kwandibens is Ojibwe (Anishinaabe) and French from the Northwest Angle #37 First Nation in Ontario. She is a self-taught photographer specializing in artistic natural light portraiture, event and concert photography. Since 2006 shee has travelled extensively, photographing people and events throughout Canada and the United States. Nadya has worked for numerous groups and organizations including the National Aboriginal Achievement Foundation, Association for Native Development in the Performing Arts, imagineNATIVE Film + Media Arts Festival, and the Winnipeg Aboriginal Film Festival. In 2008, she founded Red Works Studio and began photographing a series entitled Concrete Indians, "a portraiture series and exploration of collective Indigenous identity." Her photographic work was featured on the cover of SPIRIT Magazine and in other magazines: FACE, THIS, SAY Magazine, and Red Ink. Nadya was also the invited artist-in-residence for the Native American Indigenous Cinema and Arts online exhibition, and has exhibited in group and solo shows in Canada and the US.

Winona LaDuke is an Ojibwe (Anishinaabe) activist, environmentalist, and economist. She is the executive director of Honour the Earth. LaDuke became an activist in Anishinaabe issues, helping found the Indigenous Women's Network in 1985 and becoming involved in continuing struggles to regain reservation land lost since allotments to individual households in the 19th century. In 1996 and 2000, she ran for vice president as the nominee of the Green Party of the United States, on a ticket headed by Ralph Nader. She is also the author of a number of books and publications including *Recovering the Sacred*, and *The Militarization of Indian Country*.

Mary Ellen Turpel-Lafond is president of the Canadian Council of Child and Youth Advocates, an alliance of provincial advocates from across the country who champion the voice and rights of children. She was appointed B.C.'s first Representative for Children and Youth in 2006 and has worked as a criminal law judge in youth and adult courts. Turpel-Lafond has also taught law at Dalhousie University Faculty of Law, and at other Canadian universities and holds a doctorate of law from Harvard Law School. She is active in her Muskeg Lake Cree Nation community and has published a book on the history of the Nation that was short-listed for a Saskatchewan Book Award.

Andrea Landry is working toward her Masters in Communications and Social Justice at the University of Windsor. She has been involved in advocacy roles within the indigenous community on a local, provincial, national, and international level. Andrea sits on the United Nations Global Indigenous Youth Caucus. She has been key in developing local, provincial, national, and international rallies for the Idle No More movement. Andrea hopes to accomplish a lot more in her life in advocacy, social justice, and the role of providing advancement for the Aboriginal community in Canada.

Lori M. Mainville is Anishinaabe member of Treaty 3 and a proud mother and grandmother. She has lived and worked in Winnipeg, Manitoba since the mid-1980s and is actively engaged in grassroots movements. Most her work in activism has focused on lobbying support for murdered and missing women and non-violence in families and communities but she has also supported actions to ensure the spirit and intent of the treaties are honoured in Canada. Lori received her BA from the University of Winnipeg in 2002, majoring in Psychology.

Lee Maracle is the author of a number of critically acclaimed literary works of fiction, short stories, non-fiction, and poetry. She has been widely published in anthologies and scholarly journals worldwide. Lee was born in North Vancouver and is a member of the

Sto: Loh nation. The mother of four and grandmother of four, she is currently the Distinguished Visiting Professor of Canadian Culture at Western Washington University. She has also spent much of her time doing healing and cultural reclamation work in Aboriginal communities in Canada. Maracle is currently an instructor in the Aboriginal Studies Program teaching the Oral Tradition of Ojibway, Salish and Longhouse people. She is also the Traditional Teacher for First Nation's House and instructor with the Centre for Indigenous Theatre. In 2009, Maracle received an Honorary Doctor of Letters for the healing work she has done over the past 40 years. Maracle recently received the Queen's Diamond Jubilee Medal for her work promoting writing among Aboriginal youth.

Jarrett Martineau is a Cree/Dene digital media producer, hip hop artist, and academic from Frog Lake First Nation in Alberta. He is a PhD candidate in Indigenous Governance at the University of Victoria. Jarrett has worked at the intersection of art, media, and activism for many years, and his research examines the role of art and creativity in advancing Indigenous nationhood and decolonization. He is the co-founder and Creative Producer of *Revolutions Per Minute* (RPM.fm), a new music platform to promote Indigenous music culture; an organizer with the *Indigenous Nationhood Movement*; and a founding director of the *New Forms Festival*, an annual festival focusing on contemporary art, culture, and electronic music held in Vancouver. Through the dissemination of decolonizing media and practices, Jarrett's work seeks to articulate strategies for community renewal, based on a commitment to Indigenous teachings and lifeways. He is currently based in Victoria, B.C. on WSANEC and Lekwungen territories.

Sylvia McAdam (Saysewahum) is a mother and grandmother from the Treaty 6 territory of the Nehiyawak (Cree) people on Turtle Island (Canada). Sylvia has her Juris Doctorate from the University of Saskatchewan and Bachelor's in Human Justice from the University of Regina. She is a strong advocate and voice in the struggle for liberation and freedom for her people by way of self-determination and honouring of Treaty 6. Sylvia is co-founder of a global grass-roots movement called "Idle No More" which stands against the genocide and unrelenting legislative attacks from the conservative government. Sylvia is a recipient of the Carol Geller Human Rights Award, Activist of the Year Award, and Social Courage Award. Her greatest joy and solace is enjoying her time on the lands and waters of her people's territory.

Melody McKiver is an Anishinaabe musician, interdisciplinary media artist, and writer based in Ottawa. Melody is Anishinaabe of mixed heritage, with ancestry in Obishikokaang Wemitigoozhiiwitigwaaning Lac Seul First Nation. Melody is presently completing an MA in Ethnomusicology at the Memorial University of Newfoundland and is a graduate of York University (2010), with an Honours BFA in Music, Minor in Race, Ethnicity, and Indigeneity. Melody's musical practice spans across viola/violin, drums and percussion, and guitar, drawing upon a broad set of influences that includes hip hop, electronic, contemporary classical, jazz, and blues. Melody works with digital video and photography to capture images of Indigenous resurgence, and uses this footage editorially and within video and sound art. Melody writes for RPM.fm, is affiliated with Tribal Spirit Music, and plays drums with Toronto's Indigenous hip-hop fusion band Red Slam Collective.

Sheelah McLean is a PhD candidate in integrated anti-racist anti-colonial education at the University of Saskatchewan. Her goal is to bridge scholarship, policies, and praxis in order to address oppressions faced by marginalized groups, particularly focusing on the historical legacy of colonialism experienced by Indigenous peoples in a white-settler society. Her 2007 Master's thesis is called *Beyond the Pale: whiteness as innocence in education*, and her 2012 essay "The whiteness of green: Racialization and environmental education" (which appeared in *Canadian Geographer: The Critical Geographies of Education*) address white supremacy within the Canadian colonial context.

Ryan McMahon is an Anishinaabe/Metis standup comedian, writer, and independent media producer based out of Winnipeg, MB. He's the creator/producer/host of The Red Man Laughing Podcast and his podcast work has been featured on the BBC (Europe), CBC (Canada), and NPR (US). Ryan's standup comedy is irreverent and boundary-pushing as he focuses his attention on the good, the bad, and the ugly of the collision between Indian Country and the mainstream. In the summer of 2012 Ryan McMahon became the first Native comedian to record a one-hour mainstream comedy special, "Ryan McMahon—UnReserved," for CBC Television.

Miskwaasining Nagamojig (Swamp Singers) is a women's hand drum group that sings in Anishinaabemowin. Information about participants and songs can be heard at their website ojibwe.net.

Waneek Horn-Miller is a Mohawk from Kahnawake Mohawk Territory and member of the Bear Clan. She was co-captain 2000 Olympic women's waterpolo team and a North American games participant. At 14 years old Waneek was involved in the Oka Crisis standoff between her Mohawk people and the Canadian armed forces. The crisis changed the face of native and non-native relations in Canada and Waneek's life after she was stabbed by a solder at the end of the crisis. She took this traumatic experience and used it to motivate her towards her goal of the Olympics. Through her work as a sports commentator for CBC and APTN, Waneek has become a community advocate for sport, fitness, and wellness. She also has travelled extensively throughout North America as a motivational speaker. As one of Canada's few Aboriginal Olympians, Waneek has used her passion and experiences in sport to influence Aboriginal and non-aboriginal leadership.

SkyBlue Morin is a creative writer of short stories and poetry. Her work has been published in several different anthology collections that vary from the *Anthology of Canadian Native Writers* (1989-2001) to *Medicine Wheel Writing* (2007). Morin's unique spoken word presentations combine traditional singing with contemporary poetry. These creative works have been celebrated by the Calgary Aboriginal Awareness Society, Amnesty International Art Exhibits, and the International Women's Day in Ottawa, Ontario.

Cara Mumford is a Métis filmmaker and screenwriter from Alberta, currently living in Peterborough, whose short films have screened regularly at the imagineNATIVE Film + Media Arts Festival in Toronto, and toured throughout Australia and internationally with the World of Women Film Festival. Her short screenplay, "Ask Alice," won Best Short Script at the Los Angeles Women's International Film Festival and her poetry dance film, "December 6," is screened every year at

Montreal Massacre memorials across Canada. In 2012, Cara was commissioned by imagineNATIVE to create "When It Rains," a one-minute film for their Stolen Sisters Digital Initiative. She is currently developing two projects: a TV series "Animal Instincts," and a feature film "Endangered Hero," in addition to working on a new short film of Leanne Betasamosake Simpson's spoken-word piece "Leaks."

Wanda Nanibush is the 2013 Dame Nita Barrow visitor at the University of Toronto and curator in residence at the Justina M. Barnicke Gallery. Wanda is an Anishinabe-kwe image and word warrior, curator, community animator, arts consultant and Idle No More organizer. She has co-organized Toronto's major round dances, teach-ins, candle light marches, concerts, water ceremonies, and vigils. She co-organized the "Nation to Nation Now" symposia and "Building Unity To Action" meeting. She has published in *This is an Honour Song* by Arbeiter Ring, *DAG Vol 1*, *FUSE*, *Literary Magazine of Canada*, *C Magazine*, and a number of art catalogues.

Dory Nason (Anishinaabe/Chicana) is an assistant professor of English and First Nations Studies at the University of British Columbia in Vancouver, Coast Salish territory. Her areas of research include contemporary Indigenous feminisms and related Native women's activism, intellectual history, and literature. At UBC she teaches students about theory and methods in Critical Indigenous Studies and the activist foundations of Native literature. She is the recipient of the 2013 Killam Teaching Prize for excellence in teaching.

Derek Nepinak is Grand Chief of the Assembly of Manitoba Chiefs. His Anishinaabe name is Niibin Makwa (Summer Bear) and he was born in Winnipeg. He spent his first few years living in the home of his grandparents on the Pine Creek First Nation. During this time, Derek observed his great-grandparents living the ways of his people: hunting, fishing, gardening, smoking fish, tanning moose hides and other traditional activities. Derek completed a First Class Honours Bachelor of Arts degree in Native studies at the University of Alberta and travelled to the North to work with two Dene communities near Fort Smith, NWT. There, Derek assisted in the development and revision of the Band's Constitution, bylaw development, community planning, and economic development initiatives. He then completed a law degree from the University of Saskatchewan. Continuing his education, Derek received the Duff Roblin Fellowship and enrolled in the Aboriginal Governance Master's Program at the University of Winnipeg. Prior to completing his Master's degree, Derek was called home to become the Chief of the Pine Creek First Nation. During his tenure, he took his community from third party management into a self-sustaining position. As Grand Chief of the Assembly of Manitoba Chiefs, Derek seeks to make Manitoba First Nations sustainable entities while fighting for treaty rights and recognitions.

Tannis Nielsen is a Metis of Cree and Danish descent. As a practising professional Indigenous artist and academic, Tannis has focused her research interests upon the examinations of an anti-colonial, Fourth World Indigenous paradigm, as well as the Western Eurocentric paradigm. Tannis has exhibited her works at such galleries as the Glenbow Museum in Calgary and has co-curated exhibitions such as the Enacting Emancipation show at A-Space Gallery, with Vicky Moufawad Paul. Tannis has written a number of articles on arts and culture, including "Re-materializing the Matriarchy" for *Spirit Magazine*.

Pamela D. Palmater is a Mi'kmaw citizen and member of the Eel River Bar First Nation in northern New Brunswick. She has been a practising lawyer for 15 years and she is an Associate Professor in the Department of Politics and Public Administration and holds the Chair in Indigenous Governance at Ryerson University. She has four university degrees, including a Doctorate in Law from Dalhousie University Law School. Pam has been working and volunteering on First Nation issues for over 25 years on a wide range of social and legal issues, like poverty, housing, child and family services, treaty rights, education, and legislation impacting First Nations. She came in second place in the Assembly of First Nations election for National Chief in 2012 and was one of the spokespeople for Idle No More in 2012-13. She has numerous publications including her book, *Beyond Blood: Rethinking Indigenous Identity* and most recently, the report *Our Children, Our Future, Our Vision: First Nation Jurisdiction over First Nation Education* for the Chiefs of Ontario in response to the National Panel on Education.

Shiri Pasternak is a SSHRC Postdoctoral Fellow in the Department of Middle Eastern, South Asian and African Studies at Columbia University in New York. She holds a PhD from the Department of Geography at the University of Toronto, where she wrote a dissertation on the Algonquins of Barriere Lake and the land claims process in Canada from the perspective of Indigenous law and jurisdiction. She is a founding member of Barriere Lake Solidarity, a member of the Indigenous Sovereignty and Solidarity Network in Toronto, and an ally in the Defenders of the Land network. Her work is published in a number of academic journals and online magazines.

Plex (D. Bedard) is an award-winning hip hop artist based in Toronto. With over 15 years experience Plex has raised the bar amongst his Aboriginal peers while building a strong and relevant presence in mainstream Canadian hip hop. Since releasing his debut solo album in 2009, *Plex* has toured across North America and has also appeared on several televised events including *Arbor Live, The National Aboriginal Achievement Awards, APTN Aboriginal Day Live, Cineplex's Front Row Concert Series* and *The Aboriginal People's Choice Music Awards*.

Judy Rebick is an author, activist, teacher, and journalist. Her latest book is *Occupy This!*—a Penguin special eBook.

Shane Rhodes is the author of five books of poetry including his most recent *X* (2013), and *Err* (2011 and a finalist for the City of Ottawa book award) both with Nightwood Editions. Shane's poetry has won an Alberta Book Award, the Lampman-Scott Award (which made national news when he refused to accept prize money from the Duncan Campbell Scott foundation), the P. K. Page Founder's Award for Poetry and a National Magazine Gold Award. Shane is the poetry editor for *Arc*, Canada's national poetry magazine, and was the 2013 Queensland Poet in Residence in Brisbane, Australia.

Waubgeshig Rice is an author and journalist originally from Wasauksing, Ontario. He developed a strong passion for storytelling as a child while learning about being Anishinaabe. The stories his elders shared and his unique experiences growing up on a First Nation inspired him to write creatively. Some of the stories he wrote as a teenager eventually became *Midnight Sweatlodge*, his first collection of fiction published by Theytus Books in 2011. His journalism career began when he was a 17-year-old exchange student in northern Germany, writing about being Anishinaabe in Europe for newspapers back in Canada. He graduated from Ryerson University's journalism program in 2002, and has worked in a variety of media across Canada since. He started working for CBC in Winnipeg in 2006, and has produced television and radio documentaries and features for the public broadcaster, along with reporting on the news. He currently works as a video journalist for CBC News Ottawa.

Chickadee Richard is a mother, grandmother, and clan mother from Treaty 1 territory. As a member of the bear clan, Chickadee has spent most of her adult life fighting for the protection of women, children, families, lands, waters, and Indigenous rights. This has included her involvement in national and international environmental groups such as the Indigenous Environmental Network and First Nation Environmental Network. Chickadee has sat on several boards including the Elizabeth Fry Societies of Canada and the Thunder Eagle Society which co-founded Children of the Earth High School and Niiji Mukwa School in Winnipeg. Chickadee is well respected for the essential role she has played mobilizing local Indigenous women. She is the co-founder Mother of Red Nations, an advocacy group designed to support Indigenous women within the city of Winnipeg.

Eric Ritskes is a PhD student in Sociology and Equity Studies at the University of Toronto, working at the intersections of decolonization, Indigenous knowledge, and technologies of knowing. He is the founder and editor of the Open Access journal, *Decolonization: Indigeneity, Education and Society*.

Janet Marie Rogers is a Mohawk/Tuscarora writer from the Six Nations territory. She lives on the the unceeded territories of the Coast Salish people. Janet completed a three year term as Victoria's Poet Laureate in 2015. She is known for her performance, spoken word and video poetry. You can hear Janet on the airwaves hosting Native Waves Radio on CFUV FM and Tribal Clefs Music Column on CBC Radio One in British Columbia. She is embarking on a new phase of creativity as a video documentary producer with 2Ro Media.

Toby Rollo is a PhD candidate in the department of Political Science at the University of Toronto where he specializes in the history of political thought, democratic theory, and Canadian politics. During the Idle No More demonstrations of 2012–13, Toby wrote a series of editorial pieces intended to provide Canadians with a context for understanding Indigenous rights and claims. He is also author of "Mandates of the State: Sovereignty and the Internal Exclusion of Indigenous Peoples" published in the *Canadian Journal of Law and Jurisprudence*.

Paul Seesequasis is editor-in-chief at Theytus Books LTD. He is the author of *Tobacco Wars* (Quattro Books).

Leanne Betasamosake Simpson is a Mississauga Nishnaabeg writer, academic and organizer. She is the editor of *Lighting the Eighth Fire* (ARP Books) and *This is an Honour Song* (with Kiera Lander, ARP Books). She is the author of *Dancing on Our Turtle's Back* (ARP Books) *The Gift Is in the Making*, (Highwater Press), and a collection of short stories with an accompanying full-length spoken word album, *Islands of Decolonial Love* (ARP Books).

Niigaanwewidam James Sinclair is Anishinaabe and originally from St. Peter's (Little Peguis) Indian Settlement near Selkirk, Manitoba. He is a regular commentator on Indigenous issues for CTV, CBC, and APTN and his critical and creative work can be found in books such as *The Exile Edition of Native Canadian Fiction and Drama*, newspapers like *The Guardian*, and online with CBC *Books: Canada Writes*. He is also the co-editor of the award-winning *Manitowapow: Aboriginal Writings from the Land of Water* (Highwater Press, 2011) and *Centering Anishinaabeg Studies: Understanding the World Through Stories* (Michigan State University Press, 2013). Currently at the University of Manitoba, Niigaan teaches courses in Indigenous literatures, cultures, histories, and politics and is proud to be a part of the Kino-nda-niimi Collective, who edited, assembled, and—along with hundreds of other activists, artists, and writers—created *The Winter We Danced*.

Theresa Spence is chief of the Attawapiskat First Nation and has spent a lifetime working in the interests of her people and her community. In addition to her work as chief she has held positions as deputy chief, councillor, a member of the local development corporation, and manager of a daycare.

Clayton Thomas-Muller is a member of the Mathias Colomb Cree Nation also known as Pukatawagan in Northern Manitoba. Based out of Ottawa, Clayton is a campaigner for the Defenders of the Land/Idle No More, joint national campaign and is also the co-director of the Indigenous Tar Sands (ITS) Campaign of the Polaris Institute. He is an organizer, facilitator, public speaker and writer on environmental and economic justice who has been published in books, newspapers, and magazines and appeared on local, regional, national, and international television and radio as an expert advocate on Indigenous rights, and environmental and economic justice. For the last 11 years he has campaigned across North America, organizing in hundreds of First Nations, Alaska Native and Native American communities in support of grassroots Indigenous Peoples to defend against the encroachment of the fossil fuel industry.

Daniel Tseghay is a Vancouver writer. His work has appeared in the *Georgia Straight*, *The Toronto Star*, and *Truthout*, among others. He's an editor for Vancouver's progressive online publication, *The Mainlander*, and he also co-hosts a radio show by that name for Vancouver Co-operative Radio.

Dale Turner is a citizen of the Temagami First Nation and teaches political philosophy in the Native American Studies Program at Dartmouth College in Hanover, New Hampshire. His recent work focuses on the relationship between Indigenous knowledge and the Western European philosophical tradition. He is also interested in how photography has been, and remains, a powerful tool of colonialism. He is married to Stephanie Carson, and they live in Sharon, Vermont, with their two teenaged sons.

Richard Van Camp is a proud member of the Dogrib (Tlicho) Nation from Fort Smith, Northwest Territories. He is the author of two children's books with the Cree artist George Littlechild: *A Man Called Raven* and *What's the Most Beautiful Thing You Know About Horses?* He has published a novel, *The Lesser Blessed*, which is now a feature film with First Generation Films; his collections of short fiction include *Angel Wing Splash Pattern*, *The Moon of Letting Go and Other Stories*, and *Godless but Loyal to Heaven*. He is the author of three baby books and has two comicbooks out with the Healthy Aboriginal Network.

Chelsea Vowel is Métis from the Plains Cree and Michif-speaking community of Lac Ste. Anne, Alberta. She and her partner have four girls. Chelsea has a BEd and an LLB and moved to Montreal in 2009. She has taught in the Northwest Territories, Alberta, and Quebec. She also writes articles as âpihtawikosisân (ah-pih-du-wi-GO-si-sahn), which are cross-published on HuffPo Canada and rabble.ca. Passionate about law, culture, and language, she tries to deconstruct harmful myths with the hope that there can be a restructuring and renewal of the relationship between Canadians and indigenous peoples.

Harsha Walia is a South Asian writer and activist based in Vancouver, unceded Musqueam, Skwxwú7mesh, and Tsleil Waututh territories. She is involved in anti-racist, migrant justice, feminist, anti-capitalist, and anti-colonial movements and has been active in Indigenous solidarity efforts for over a decade. She is a co-founder of *No One Is Illegal* and *Radical Desis*, is an organizer in the annual February 14 Women's Memorial March Committee and a number of DTES housing justice coalitions. She is honoured to be collaborating with others for the past eight years to bring together diverse directly affected communities for three powerful annual events: the Annual Community March Against Racism, the Annual Women's Housing March, and the Annual Women's Memorial March for Missing and Murdered Women. Harsha's first book, *Undoing Border Imperialism*, with a preface by Andrea Smith, was released by AK Press in 2013.

Michael Wesley is a registered band member of Constance Lake First Nation in northern Ontario. Constance Lake First Nation has members of Ojibway and Cree ancestry living on and off reserve. Michael's medium is acrylics on stretched canvas. His artistic credits include a group exhibit at the Fall Down Gallery in Ottawa, Ontario sponsored by Sakahàn—National Gallery of Canada; Community Art Wall exhibit at the Elephant Room Gallery in Chicago, IL; solo and group exhibits at the Trickster Gallery in Schaumburg, IL; and two group exhibits in Toronto with the Association for the Native Development in the Performing and Visual Arts (ANDPVA). He also does photography based on his interaction and connection with the environment around him. Michael lives and works in Chicago, Illinois.

Alo White (Gaagaagiibit/Mide Kiwenzie/Bizhew Dodem /Nanaan Mide) is respected for the knowledge he carries of Anishinaabe language, culture, songs, and spiritual ceremonies from his community of Naotkamegwanning First Nation (Treaty 3) in Northwestern Ontario. He is currently working on a series of recordings under his label *Alo White Recording Studios*, recording Elders from the Treaty 3 area under the project titled "Preserving Anishinaabe Music." He is a regular contributor to the blog dividednomore.ca.

Tara Williamson is an Anishinaabekwe/Nehayowak who was raised in Gaabishkigamaag, Swan Lake, Manitoba and is a member of the Opaskwayak Cree Nation. She has degrees in social work, law, and Indigenous governance and is currently a Professor at Fleming College in Nogojiwanong (Peterborough, Ontario). She is a musician, aunty, sister, daughter, and poet.

Alex Wilson is Neynoway Inniniw from the Opaskwayak Cree Nation. She is an Associate Professor of Education and Director of the Aboriginal Education Research Centre and at the University of Saskatchewan. Her academic and community work and passion focus on Indigenous land-based education and social ecological justice. As an organizer, Alex uses education and Cree philosophy to intervene in ongoing practices of colonialism, oppression, and the destruction of land and water.

Nina Wilson is from the Crooked Lake Agency, Kahkewistahaw First Nation in Southeastern Saskatchewan. She is of the Three Pole People, the Nakota, Dakota, Lakota, and the Nehiyo and is a direct descendant of Chief White Bear and of the Cut Mouth and Red Blanket Societies. She is also a mother of five, a grandmother of five, and very respectful of the children all over the world. Nina is currently a Master's student at the University of Manitoba in the Native Studies Department. She has also worked with Indigenous inmates, children, family, and community in child protective services, First Nation administration, and in education and addictions services.

Jenna Wirch is a young community activist and youth worker from the North End of Winnipeg, an area often stigmatized for high crime and poverty rates. Jenna received her Child and Youth certificate from Red

River College in 2013 and has spent most of her recent professional life working and programs and services designed to improve the quality of life for North End Winnipeggers, focusing most of her attention on youth empowerment and engagement. Jenna works closely with the North End Community Renewal Corporation and is currently a Youth Engagement Coordinator for Aboriginal Youth Opportunities (AYO) and a trainer for ARROWS Youth Engagement, a youth leadership program facilitated by AYO. Jenna has become known as the "girl with the megaphone" at rallies in Winnipeg where she is often heard sharing educational messages promoting hope and change.

Rita Wong has written three books of poetry: *monkeypuzzle* (Press Gang, 1998), *forage* (which won Canada Reads Poetry 2011 and the Dorothy Livesay Prize) and *sybil unrest* (co-authored with Larissa Lai, New Star Books). Her work has also appeared in anthologies like *Prismatic Publics: Innovative Canadian Women's Poetry and Poetics*, *Regreen: New Canadian Ecological Poetry*, and *Making a Difference: Canadian Multicultural Literature*. A water lover, she teaches at the Emily Carr University of Art and Design, where she has developed a humanities course on water, for which she received a fellowship from the Center for Contemplative Mind in Society.

Jana-Rae Yerxa is Anishinaabe from Little Eagle and Couchiching First Nation and belongs to the Sturgeon clan. She is an activist, writer, social worker, former professor, and current student. She is committed to furthering her understanding of Anishinaabe identity and resurgence as well as deconstructing Indigenous-settler relations in the contexts of colonization and decolonization. Jana-Rae is enrolled in the Indigenous Governance Program at University of Victoria.

Laura Zahody is a writer, public relations professional, and blogger with a passion for social affairs and food. During Idle No More, she was living and working in Ottawa, but has since moved to Toronto.

About the Kino-nda-niimi Collective

The Kino-nda-niimi Collective is a group of Indigenous writers, artists, editors, curators, and allies who came together to document and disseminate the work that emerged and culminated in the winter of 2012-2013. Taking a variety of forms—whether called *Idle No More, The Indigenous Nationhood Movement, Sovereignty Summer,* or *Honour the Apology* (to name a few)—these intertwined political, social, and cultural movements did not start (nor will end) with us but are part of the ongoing resistance Indigenous peoples have been engaged with for centuries. We felt that the written and artistic works that were generated alongside the movement were unprecedented, and that these collective voices deserved to be brought together into a volume. What is striking is that never before have Indigenous writers and artists had the capacity to write the movement, alongside the movement taking place, and the result is a diverse collection of voices and perspectives that represent our experience of our movement. Lead editors for *The Winter We Danced* include Niigaanwewidam James Sinclair, Leanne Betasamosake Simpson, Tanya Kappo, Wanda Nanibush, and Hayden King who—along with many colleagues, relatives, friends, and organizations—assembled this collection together over the summer and fall of 2013.

At noon on July 25, 2013, tens of thousands of Canadians, newcomers, First Nations, Métis, and Inuit peoples from all walks of life and religious denominations across Canada—most of whom had met during the events of Idle No More—joined together to demand that the federal government live up to the responsibilities offered during the 2008 apology for residential schools and change long-standing cycles of abusive relationships in this country. At the end of the event, such as this one at the Forks in Winnipeg, Manitoba, participants danced, sang, and asked for change, growth in our relationships, and more than what this country has been so far. They showed that through the round dance, a complicated movement filled with the task of finding unity, we can continue to shake up the idleness of our past and struggle to create something more for our future, our children. Like in the winter we danced—and for centuries both past and to come—this is how beauty can be created in our home. This is what life looks like here. (ALYSSA BIRD)